ARCHAEOLOGICAL
THEORY TODAY

ARCHAEOLOGICAL THEORY TODAY

Second Edition

Edited by Ian Hodder

polity

Copyright © this collection Polity Press 2012. Chapter 6 © Colin Renfrew

First published in 2012 by Polity Press

Reprinted 2013, 2014 (twice)

Polity Press
65 Bridge Street
Cambridge CB2 1UR, UK

Polity Press
350 Main Street
Malden, MA 02148, USA

ISBN-13: 978-0-7456-5306-8
ISBN-13: 978-0-7456-5307-5(pb)

A catalogue record for this book is available from the British Library.

Typeset in 10.5 on 12 pt Sabon
by Toppan Best-set Premedia Limited
Printed and bound in Great Britain by T.J. International, Padstow, Cornwall

The publisher has used its best endeavours to ensure that the URLs for external websites referred to in this book are correct and active at the time of going to press. However, the publisher has no responsibility for the websites and can make no guarantee that a site will remain live or that the content is or will remain appropriate.

Every effort has been made to trace all copyright holders, but if any have been inadvertently overlooked the publisher will be pleased to include any necessary credits in any subsequent reprint or edition.

For further information on Polity, visit our website: www.politybooks.com

CONTENTS

LIST OF FIGURES
AND TABLES

Figures

Tables

LIST OF CONTRIBUTORS

John C. Barrett is Professor of Archaeology at the University of Sheffield.

Douglas W. Bird is Senior Research Scientist in the Bill Lane Center for the American West and the Department of Anthropology at Stanford University.

Chip Colwell-Chanthaphonh is Curator of Anthropology at the Denver Museum of Nature and Science.

Chris Gosden is Chair of European Archaeology at the University of Oxford.

Ian Hodder is Dunlevie Family Professor of Anthropology at Stanford University.

Carl Knappett is Associate Professor of Aegean Prehistory at the University of Toronto.

Timothy A. Kohler is Regents Professor of Archaeology at the Washington State University, External Professor at the Santa Fe Institute, and a Research Associate at Crow Canyon Archaeological Center.

Vincent M. LaMotta is Assistant Professor in the Department of Anthropology at the University of Illinois at Chicago.

Lynn Meskell is Professor of Anthropology at Stanford University.

Stephanie Moser is Professor of Archaeology at the University of Southampton.

James F. O'Connell is Distinguished Professor in the Department of Anthropology at the University of Utah.

Bjørnar Olsen is Professor in the Department of Archaeology and Social Anthropology at the University of Tromsø.

Colin Renfrew is Senior Fellow of the McDonald Institute for Archaeological Research.

Stephen Shennan is Professor of Theoretical Archaeology at University College London (UCL) and Director of the UCL Institute of Archaeology.

Julian Thomas is Professor of Archaeology at the University of Manchester.

1

INTRODUCTION

Contemporary Theoretical Debate in Archaeology

Ian Hodder

Any archaeology student is today faced with a large number of volumes dealing with archaeological theory, whether these be introductory texts (e.g. Johnson 2010), historical surveys (Trigger 2006), readers (Preucel and Mrozowski 2010; Whitley 1998), edited global surveys (Hodder 1991; Meskell and Preucel 2004; Ucko 1995), or innovative volumes pushing in new directions (e.g. Schiffer 1995; Shanks and Tilley 1987; Skibo et al. 1995; Tilley 1994; Thomas 1996, etc.). It has become possible to exist in archaeology largely as a theory specialist, and many advertised lecturing jobs now refer to theory teaching and research. Regular conferences are devoted entirely to theory as in the British or USA or Nordic TAGs (Theoretical Archaeology Group). This rise to prominence of self-conscious archaeological theory can probably be traced back to the New Archaeology of the 1960s and 1970s.

The reasons for the proliferation of theory texts are numerous, and we can probably distinguish reasons internal and external to the discipline, although in practice the two sets of reasons are interconnected. As for the internal reasons, the development of archaeological theory is certainly very much linked to the emphasis in the New Archaeology on a critical approach to method and theory. This self-conscious awareness of the need for theoretical discussion is perhaps most clearly seen in Clarke's (1973) description of a loss of archaeological innocence, and in Binford's (1977) call "for theory building." Postprocessual archaeology took this reflexivity and theorizing still further. Much of the critique of processual archaeology was about theory rather than method, and the main emphasis was on opening archaeology to a broader range of theoretical positions, particularly those in the historical and social sciences. In fact, anthropology in the United States had already taken its historical and linguistic "turns," but it was only a view of anthropology as evolution and cultural ecology that the New Archaeologists had embraced. When the same "turns" were taken in archaeology to produce postprocessual archaeology, the theorizing became very abstract and specialized, although such abstraction was also found in other developments, such as the application of catastrophe theory (Renfrew and Cooke 1979). In fact all the competing theories have developed their own specialized jargons and have a tendency to be difficult to penetrate.

One of the internal moves was towards a search for external ideas, and external legitimation for theoretical moves within archaeology. There has been a catching up with other disciplines and an integration of debate. Similar moves towards an opening and integration of debate are seen across the humanities and social sciences. There are numerous examples of close external relations between archaeology and other disciplines in this book. Shennan (chapter 2) describes the productive results of interactions between biology, population demography and archaeology. Human behavioral ecology (Bird and O'Connell, chapter 3) is closely tied to ecology and evolutionary ecology. Discussion of complex systems in archaeology is part of wider debates in cybernetics and systems theory (Kohler, chapter 5). Renfrew (chapter 6) describes debates with cognitive science and evolutionary psychology. Barrett (chapter 7) shows how the agency debate in archaeology owes much to sociology. Thomas (chapter 8) demonstrates that archaeological work on landscapes has been greatly influenced by geography, especially by the recent cultural geographers, and by art history and philosophy. Socio-cultural anthropology is a key partner in the debates described in chapters 7 to 13, and science and technology studies have greatly influenced archaeological discussions of symmetry (Olsen, chapter 10) and materiality (Knappett, chapter 9). History and the history of art are central to many of the chapters in the latter part of this book, especially the work on visualization (Moser, chapter 14). But it should be pointed out that these interactions with other disciplines are not seen as borrowing from a position of inferiority. Increasingly the particular nature of archaeological data, especially their materiality and long-term character, is recognized as having something to offer other disciplines in return.

Gosden (chapter 12) points out the need for archaeologists to engage with post-colonial theory. The critique from other voices and from multiple non-western interests has often forced theoretical debate (Colwell-Chanthaphonh, chapter 13). For example, Norwegian archaeology saw a long theoretical debate about the abilities of archaeologists to identify past ethnic groups as a result of Sami–Norwegian conflicts over origins. Reburial issues have forced some to rethink the use of oral traditions in North American archaeology (Anyon et al. 1996). Indigenous groups in their claims for rights question the value of "objective science" (Langford 1983). A similar point can be made about the impact of feminism. This has questioned how we do research (Gero 1996) and has sought alternative ways of writing about the past (Spector 1994), opening up debate about fundamentals. The same can also be said of debates about representation in cultural heritage and museums (see Moser in chapter 14; Merriman 1991). These debates force a critique of interpretation. They challenge us to evaluate in whose interests interpretation lies, and to be sensitive to the relationship between audience and message.

The community of discourses model

It can be argued that archaeology has a new maturity in that, as claimed above, it has caught up with disciplines in related fields in terms of the theories and issues being discussed. Many now, as we will see in this book, wish to contribute back from archaeology to other disciplines – this emphasis on contributing rather than borrowing suggests a maturity and confidence which I will examine again below. This maturity also seems to involve accepting diversity and difference of perspective within the discipline.

There are always those who will claim that archaeology should speak with a unified voice, or who feel that disagreement within the ranks undermines the abilities of archaeologists to contribute to other disciplines or be taken seriously. A tendency towards identifying some overarching unity in the discipline can be seen in some of the chapters in this volume. Renfrew (1994) has talked of reaching an accommodation between processual and postprocessual archaeology in cognitive processual archaeology. Kohler (chapter 5) suggests that current approaches to complex systems incorporate critiques of a simple positivism, and he refers to Bintliff's (2008) argument that complexity theory integrates culture historical, processual, and postprocessual perspectives. Several authors over the past two decades have argued for some blending of processual and postprocessual approaches (e.g. Hegmon 2003; Pauketat 2001; Wylie 1989) though not without critique (Moss 2005).

There is often an implicit assumption in discussions about the need for unity in the discipline that real maturity, as glimpsed in the natural sciences, means unity. But in fact, Galison (1997) has argued that physics, for example, is far from a unified whole. Rather he sees it as a trading zone between competing perspectives, instrumental methods, and experiments. In archaeology, too, there is a massive fragmentation of the discipline, with those working on, say, Bronze Age studies in Europe often having little in common with Palaeolithic lithic specialists. New Archaeological theories were introduced at about the same time as, but separate from, computers and statistics, as the early work of Clarke (1970) and Doran and Hodson (1975) shows. Single-context recording (Barker 1982) was introduced to deal with large-scale urban excavation, and was not immediately linked to any particular theoretical position. And so on. In these examples we see that theory, method, and practice are not linked in unified wholes. While the links between domains certainly exist, the history of the discipline is one of interactions between separate domains, often with their own specialist languages, own conferences and journals, and own personnel. As Galison (1997) argues for physics, it is this diversity and the linkages within the dispersion which ensure the vitality of the discipline.

We should not then bemoan theoretical diversity in the discipline. Diversity at the current scale may be fairly new in theoretical domains, but it is not new in the discipline as a whole. These productive tensions are important for the discipline as a whole. We should perhaps expect periods of to and fro as regards diversity and unity. Marxist, critical, and feminist archaeologists (Conkey 2003; Leone and Potter 1988; McGuire 1992; Patterson 1994) provide examples of the ways in which important movements in archaeology get incorporated over time into the mainstream. Each of these approaches, fundamental struts of contemporary debate in archaeology, have for many archaeologists now become integrated into all aspects of their work, forming part of the currency of intellectual exchange. And yet at the same time, new tensions and divisions emerge (e.g. Shennan 2002 or Watkins 2003) to create new forms of diversity.

From "theory" to "theory of"

The partial disjunction between theoretical and other domains identified above, as well as the specialization and diversification of theoretical positions, has reinforced the view that there can be something abstract called "archaeological theory," however diverse that might be. For many, archaeological theory has become rarified and removed. In this abstract world, apparently divorced from any site of production of archaeological knowledge, theoretical debate becomes focused on terms, principles, basic ideas, universals. Theoretical debate becomes by nature confrontational because terms are defined and fought over in the abstract. The boundaries around definitions are policed. Abstract theory for theory's sake becomes engaged in battles over opposing abstract assertions. Theoretical issues very quickly become a matter of who can "shout the loudest," of "who sets the agenda?" (Yoffee and Sherratt 1993).

But in practice we see that the abstract theories are not divorced from particular domains at all. Rather, particular theories seem to be favored by certain sets of interests and seem to be related to questions of different types and scales. Thus evolutionary perspectives have been most common in hunter-gatherer or Palaeolithic studies; gender studies have had less impact on the Palaeolithic than on later periods; human behavioral ecology tends to be applied to hunter-gatherers or societies with simple systems; power and ideology theories come into their own mainly in complex societies; and phenomenology seems to be particularly applied to prehistoric monuments and landscapes.

When archaeologists talk of a behavioral or a cognitive archaeology, they tend to have specific questions and problems in mind. For Merleau-Ponty (1962), thought is always "of something." In this book, Thomas (chapter 8) describes how for Heidegger place is always "of something." So too, archaeological theory is always "of something." Theory is, like digging, a "doing." It is a practice or praxis (Hodder 1992). Post-colonial and Indigenous archaeologies (Gosden, chapter 12, and Colwell-Chanthaphonh, 13) have come about as part of a critical and socio-political movement. Much contemporary social archaeology and heritage theory deals with issues such as reconciliation and healing (Meskell, chapter 11). This practical engagement undermines claims for a universality and unity of archaeological theory.

Of course, it can be argued that archaeology as a whole is engaged in a unified praxis, a unified doing, so that we should expect unified theories. But even at the most general theoretical levels, archaeologists are involved in quite different projects. Some archaeologists wish to make contributions to scientific knowledge, or they might wish to provide knowledge so that people can better understand the world around them. Other archaeologists see themselves in a post-colonial context of multiple stakeholders where a negotiated past seems more relevant. This negotiation may involve accommodation of the idea that past monuments may have a living presence in the world today

– that they are "alive" in some sense (Mamani Condori 1989). In the latter context, abstract theory deals less with abstract scientific knowledge and more with specific social values and local frameworks of meaning (see Colwell-Chanthaphonh in chapter 13).

It is in the interests of the academy and of elite universities to promulgate the idea of abstract theory. The specialization of archaeological intellectual debate is thus legitimized. But critique from outside the academy has shown that these abstract theories, too, are embedded in interests – they, too, are "theories of something." Within the academy, archaeologists vie with each other to come up with yet more theories, especially if they can be claimed to be meta-theories that purport to "explain everything." In fact, however, this diversity comes from asking different questions – from the diversity of the contexts of production of archaeological knowledge.

Variation in perspective

As a result of such processes, there are radical divergences in the way different authors in this book construe theory. In summary, these differences stem partly from the process of vying for difference, with innovation often influenced by developments in neighboring disciplines. The variation in perspective also derives from the fact that radically different questions are being asked from within quite different sites of production of knowledge.

Many of the differences of perspective remain those that have dogged the discipline since the 1980s or earlier. Although there are convergent moments (see below), many of the authors in this volume ally themselves to either processual or postprocessual archaeology. Bird and O'Connell (chapter 3) and LaMotta (chapter 4) argue that human behavioral ecology and behavioral approaches derive from processual archaeology. Both Kohler (chapter 5) and Renfrew (chapter 6) recognize links to postprocessual approaches but draw their main heritage from processual archaeology. Post-colonial archaeology is seen by Gosden (chapter 12) as blending with the postprocessual critique, and Colwell-Chanthaphonh (chapter 13) links Indigenous archaeology partly to the same source. Indeed it is possible to argue that the genealogies of current approaches can be traced to three general perspectives: culture history, processual, and postprocessual as shown in Figure 1.1. Despite some blending and slippage to be discussed below, in origin each theoretical position seems to see itself as largely in one or other of these camps. By culture history I mean approaches in archaeology that are concerned with

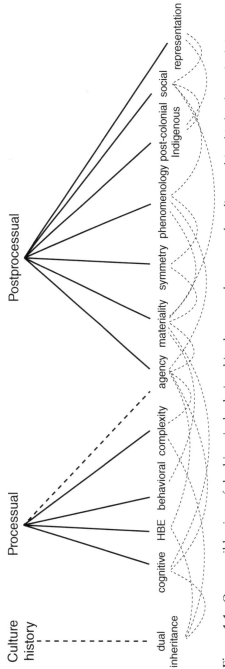

Figure 1.1. One possible view of the historical relationships between the approaches discussed in this book, and of the contemporary relationships claimed by authors between them

Note: HBE = human behavioral ecology

the descent and affiliation of ceramic and other types through time. The differences between processual and postprocessual archaeology have increasingly become aligned with the wider divisions within contemporary intellectual life between universal rationalism and positivism, on the one hand, and contextual, critical reflexivity, on the other.

The opposition between the two main theoretical camps in archaeology is clearly seen in Schiffer's account of behavioral archaeology. "Readers may be nonplussed at the absence in the new theory of much vocabulary...such as meaning, sign, symbol, intention, motivation, purpose, goal, attitude, value, belief, norm, function, mind, and culture. Despite herculean efforts in the social sciences to define these often ethnocentric or metaphysical notions, they remain behaviorally problematic and so are superfluous in the present project" (Schiffer 1999: 9). Many approaches in archaeology are less clearly assignable to one approach or the other. For example, while feminist, Marxist, and Indigenous archaeologies can be claimed to be part of postprocessual archaeology (Hodder and Hutson 2003), others argue for independent positions for these perspectives (Moss 2005). However one cuts the cake, most archaeologists are aware of deep differences between approaches in which actors act rationally according to universal principles (optimizing or minimizing) and those in which activity is meaningfully and socially produced in complex historical and cultural contexts; and they equate the former with positivism and hypothesis testing and the latter with some form of critical reflexive science. It is this broad distinction, so common throughout the humanities and social sciences, that is discussed in terms of the processual–postprocessual debate in archaeology.

These different perspectives and their multiple subdivisions shown in Figure 1.1 are linked to different sites of the production of archaeological knowledge. There are clear underlying differences between the types of interests and questions of those using general evolutionary approaches and those concerned with history and agency. Within this array, individual authors take their own positions. Discourses specific to each approach emerge, and schools are defined. Distinct literatures emerge and separate conferences and circles of citation. It is remarkable how many authors in this volume refer to the burgeoning literature within their own particular approach. With this separation into different communities, communication is difficult as people talk across each other. The differences become exacerbated and entrenched. Today, however, there seems to be increasing evidence of various forms of convergence.

Convergences

In putting together this new edition of *Archaeological Theory Today* I was very struck by the increased evidence for reference across chapters; this was not true of all the revised chapters but it was true of the vast majority. I have tried to map these cross-references and intellectual links in Figure 1.1. What these links show is that any claim for a neat distinction between processual and post-processual archaeology, or between any of the various approaches within these groupings, is unsustainable. In practice each approach borrows from or reacts to developments within other approaches. Kohler (chapter 5) recognizes links between complex systems and agent-based modeling and the contingencies and agencies of many forms of postprocessual archaeology. Barrett (chapter 7) responds to evolutionary approaches within processual archaeology. Cognitive and phenomenological approaches (Renfrew, chapter 6, Thomas, chapter 8, and Knappett, chapter 9) seem equally engaged in problems of mind, perception, and materiality. Agency is a clear linking domain, as central to materiality and post-colonial and Indigenous archaeology as it is to complex systems and evolutionary archaeology.

In the chapters in this volume, several areas of convergence stand out. Many authors are concerned with one of the key issues of our time – the relationships between culture and biology, and their relative importance. Most try to find some integration, arguing that culture and biology are both central to the project of being human (e.g. the dual inheritance approach discussed by Shennan in chapter 2, and see Barrett's revisionist account of agency in chapter 7). Other dichotomies that the authors in this volume seek to break down are between matter and materiality (object and subject), as seen in chapters 8, 9, and 10 (Thomas, Knappett, and Olsen), between individual and group (chapters 2 and 7: Shennan and Barrett), and between us and them, dominant and subordinate, colonial power and subordinate margin (chapters 11–14: Meskell, Gosden, Colwell-Chanthaphonh, and Moser). In all these areas, different ends of the spectrum of intellectual debate seek to explore the interstices and produce integration, hybridity, and resolution.

Other areas of convergence that can be identified in the chapters in this volume are the long term and material culture. As regards the long-term perspective offered by archaeology, there is a general recognition of the importance of multi-scalar approaches in addressing a wide range of issues. As already noted, the scale at which questions

are asked has wider implications in the contexts of production of
archaeological knowledge. Gosden (chapter 12) suggests making a
distinction between general information of wider relevance, and local
knowledge of relevance to local communities. All the authors in this
volume recognize the need to distinguish short-term and long-term
influences on human behavior. LaMotta (chapter 4) argues that
behavioral archaeology seeks to explain behavioral variability and
change at various scales, in both generalizing and particularistic
frames of reference. Shennan (chapter 2) deals with longer-term phenomena, and this involves dealing with the issue of whether selection
operates at group or individual levels. Renfrew (chapter 6) stresses
the need to work at the micro level of the individual and at the macro
level of society. Barrett (chapter 7) emphasizes how long-term processes need to be understood in relation to the working out of micro-
processes. Meskell (chapter 11) explores the differences between
memory and history in terms of the individual and the collective. In
chapter 9, Knappett discusses how materials and materiality do not
occupy the same spatial or temporal scales. Disagreement may occur
about the relative importance of the different scales, about the nature
of the interactions between scales, and about the degree to which the
different scales can be accessed with archaeological data. But there
seems to be a general recognition that a multi-scalar approach is
needed and that archaeology can contribute to a study of the interactions between scales.

Another frequently occurring general theme in this volume is that
material culture has a central role to play in what it means to be
human. Most authors here seem to be suggesting some version of a
dialectical view in which humans and things are dependent on each
other. This is a reformulation of the Childean Marxist view that "man
makes himself" (Childe 1936) or the Geertzian view that it is human
nature to be cultural (Geertz 1973), but with a new emphasis on
the "material cultural." LaMotta (chapter 4) argues that behavior
includes both people and objects. Shennan (chapter 2) describes a
dual cultural-biological process of evolution. Many chapters deal
with theories of materiality, material memory, materialization, material practice, social technologies, and embodiment. In contemporary
politics of heritage, material histories are sites of contestation and
reconciliation (Meskell, chapter 11). In all these ways, then, it is being
argued that an understanding of human behavior, agency, and culture
needs to include a close study of the ways in which human beings
depend on the material world. Disagreement may exist amongst the
authors about how humans and material culture interact. Some may
argue that humans depend on material culture generally just as they

depend on tools specifically. Others assert that the relationship with material culture has to be understood in terms of the very construction of self and being. Thus the "I" or the "we" are always already partly material, as are the most abstract of concepts and theories. This emphasis on situatedness foregrounds an archaeological perspective – on the past and on the present.

Conclusion

So the conclusion, based on this small sample of essays, is positive. Despite the enormous gaps and disagreements about fundamentals, and despite the evidence that archaeological theorists are trapped in separate non-communicating discourses, there is at least some indication of moves forward. There is increasing evidence of dialogue and convergence between perspectives. While there are few signs of grand synthesis (though see above), there is increasing evidence of interaction and common problems, especially in relation to agency, materiality, and temporality.

In addition there is increasing engagement with other disciplines, and the entry of archaeology into wider debates. This more extensive engagement has occurred at a time when archaeologists sense a greater confidence about the particular character of their evidence. In particular, there is a wide recognition that archaeologists have a particular expertise regarding both the long term and the materiality of human life. There is thus emerging evidence of archaeologists contributing to wider debates, not just borrowing. These contributions involve archaeologists speaking in their own right, not as anthropologists or historians.

Perhaps adding to this maturity and confidence is a new phase of reflexivity and critique as archaeological theorists try to respond to the challenges of working within a global and plural environment. The opening of debate to a wider range of voices from feminism to Indigenous interests and minority groups has led to questioning about first principles and taken-for-granteds within the discipline. The chapters in this volume indicate some directions which respond to this situation and focus on issues of representation and power (e.g. Moser and Colwell-Chanthaphonh in chapters 13 and 14). The processes of post-colonialism and global heritage (Meskell and Gosden in chapters 11 and 12) create a new context in which archaeology will work. But it is a fluid and complex context in which theory and practice are in a continual state of challenge and renegotiation. This volume may help that process forward, but it cannot hope to define it or structure it.

Note

I apologize to the authors if I have misrepresented their views but thank them for entrusting their work to my editorial hand. The views expressed in this introduction are my own.

References

Anyon, R., T. J. Ferguson, L. Jackson, and L. Lane 1996. Native American oral traditions and archaeology. *Society for American Archaeology Bulletin* 14(2): 14–16.

Barker, P. 1982. *Techniques of Archaeological Excavation.* London: Batsford.

Binford, L. 1977. *For Theory Building in Archaeology.* New York: Academic Press.

Bintliff, J. 2008. History and continental approaches. In R. A. Bentley, H. D. G. Maschner, and C. Chippindale (eds), *Handbook of Archaeological Theories*, 147–64. Lanham, MD: AltaMira.

Childe, V. G. 1936. *Man Makes Himself.* London: Collins.

Clarke, D. 1970. *Beaker Pottery of Great Britain and Ireland.* Cambridge: Cambridge University Press.

Clarke, D. 1973. Archaeology: the loss of innocence. *Antiquity* 47: 6–18.

Conkey, M. 2003. Has feminism changed archaeology? *Signs* 28: 867–80.

Doran, J. and F. Hodson 1975. *Mathematics and Computers in Archaeology.* Edinburgh: Edinburgh University Press.

Galison, P. 1997. *Image and Logic: A Material Culture of Microphysics.* Chicago: University of Chicago Press.

Geertz, C. 1973. *The Interpretation of Cultures.* New York: Basic Books.

Gero, J. 1996. Archaeological practice and gendered encounters with field data. In R. P. Wright (ed.), *Gender and Archaeology*, 251–80. Philadelphia: University of Pennsylvania Press.

Hegmon, M. 2003. Setting theoretical egos aside: issues and theory in North American archaeology. *American Antiquity* 68: 213–43.

Hodder, I. 1991. *Archaeological Theory in Europe: The Last Three Decades.* London: Routledge.

Hodder, I. 1992. *Theory and Practice in Archaeology.* London: Routledge.

Hodder, I. and S. Hutson 2003. *Reading the Past.* Cambridge: Cambridge University Press.

Johnson, M. 2010. *Archaeological Theory: An Introduction*, 2nd edition. Oxford: Blackwell.

Langford, R. 1983. Our heritage – your playground. *Australian Archaeology* 16: 1–6.

Leone, M.P. and P. Potter 1988. *The Recovery of Meaning: Historical Archaeology in the Eastern United States*. Washington, DC: Smithsonian.

McGuire, R.H. 1992. *A Marxist Archaeology*. San Diego: Academic Press.

Mamani Condori, C. 1989. History and prehistory in Bolivia: what about the Indians? In R. Layton (ed.), *Conflict in the Archaeology of Living Traditions*, 46–59. London: Unwin Hyman.

Merleau-Ponty, M. 1962. *Phenomenology of Perception*. Atlantic Highlands, NJ: Humanities Press.

Meskell, L. and R. Preucel 2004. *A Companion to Social Archaeology*. Oxford: Blackwell.

Merriman, N. 1991. *Beyond the Glass Case*. Leicester: Leicester University Press.

Moss, M.L. 2005. Rifts in the theoretical landscape of archaeology in the United States: a comment on Hegmon and Watkins. *American Antiquity* 70: 581–7.

Patterson, T.C. 1994. Social archaeology in Latin America: an appreciation. *American Antiquity* 59: 531–7.

Pauketat, T. 2001. Practice and history in archaeology: an emerging paradigm. *Anthropological Theory* 1: 73–98.

Preucel, R. and S. Mrozowski (eds) 2010. *Contemporary Archaeology in Theory: The New Pragmatism*, 2nd edition. Oxford: Wiley-Blackwell.

Renfrew, C. 1994. Towards a cognitive archaeology. In C. Renfrew and E.B.W. Zubrow (eds), *The Ancient Mind: Elements of Cognitive Archaeology*, 3–12. Cambridge: Cambridge University Press.

Renfrew, C. and K.L. Cooke 1979. *Transformations: Mathematical Approaches to Culture Change*. New York: Academic Press.

Schiffer, M.B. 1995. *Behavioral Archaeology: First Principles*. Salt Lake City: University of Utah Press.

Schiffer, M.B. 1999. *The Material Life of Human Beings*. London: Routledge.

Shanks, M. and C. Tilley 1987. *Reconstructing Archaeology*. Cambridge: Cambridge University Press.

Shennan, S.J. 2002. *Genes, Memes and Human History*. London: Duckworth.

Skibo, J., W. Walker, and A. Nielsen (eds) 1995. *Expanding Archaeology*. Salt Lake City: University of Utah Press.

Spector, J.D. 1994. *What this Awl Means: Feminist Archaeology at a Wahpeton Dakota Village*. St. Paul: Minnesota Historical Society Press.

Thomas, J. 1996. *Time, Culture and Identity*. Cambridge: Cambridge University Press.

Tilley, C. 1994. *The Phenomenology of Landscape*. Oxford: Berg.

Trigger, B.G. 2006. *A History of Archaeological Thought*, 2nd edition. Cambridge: Cambridge University Press.

Ucko, P. 1995. *Theory in Archaeology: A World Perspective.* London: Routledge.

Watkins, J. 2003. Beyond the margin: American Indians, First Nations, and archaeology in North America. *American Antiquity* 68: 273–85.

Whitley, D. S. 1998. *Reader in Archaeological Theory: Post-Processual and Cognitive Approaches.* London: Routledge.

Wylie, A. 1989. Archaeological cables and tacking. *Philosophy of the Social Sciences* 19: 1–18.

Yoffee, N. and A. Sherratt 1993. *Archaeological Theory: Who Sets the Agenda?* Cambridge: Cambridge University Press.

2

DARWINIAN CULTURAL EVOLUTION

Stephen Shennan

The use of ideas based on Darwinian evolutionary theory to explain patterns in the archaeological record has become increasingly popular in recent years. One can speculate about the reasons for this but they certainly include the view on the part of those who have taken this path that evolutionary theory provides a highly productive framework for archaeology, in the sense that it has the potential to generate open-ended programs of empirical research that produce rigorous and convincing results. By theory here I mean something more specific than what is often meant in archaeology: a set of well-founded principles which provide a basis for explaining patterns of variation in the world. In the case of the biological world the edifice of Darwinian evolutionary theory that has been built up over the last 150 years provides the principles and has produced a variety of remarkably productive research programs at all levels from the micro-scale genetic to macro-scale palaeontological history covering millions of years. The development of the idea that explaining patterns of stability and change in the material record of human existence can be encompassed within the same framework is much more recent, although it has early precursors. The fact that the intensive development of evolutionary research in general, and evolutionary theory in particular, has a much longer history in biology means that it has been a sensible strategy for archaeologists to start with ideas and methods from biology and explore the ways in which they need to be modified to accurately represent cultural processes. Indeed, archaeologists are not alone in this but are part of a broader movement towards the creation of an evolutionary social science that includes psychology, sociology, economics, and anthropology as well as archaeology.

In fact, the adoption of Darwinian approaches to understanding the archaeological record has been based on two distinct foundations, to some degree competitive, to some degree complementary, one based on the ideas of human behavioral ecology (HBE) and the other on some version of cultural evolution or dual inheritance theory (DIT). In the former, hypotheses to account for patterns of stability or change are based on models of the costs and benefits of different courses of action in a given context. Humans, like other animals, are assumed to have evolved cognitive propensities to maximize the ratio of benefits to costs; natural selection operates to favor those with the inherited ability to make the best judgments. On this basis, models of the optimal course of action can be developed: for example, in the making of hunting decisions. It is not assumed that these models account for the patterns observed; the object of the exercise is to assess whether they do or not. The argument is that evolutionary theory provides a strong basis for taking such cost–benefit models as a productive starting point for many archaeological questions. They are not considered in any detail here, not because I consider them unhelpful or invalid but because they are dealt with in another chapter in this volume. However, I will have occasion below to compare them with DIT models.

The key feature of the other category of work is the role it attaches to culture, and thus to cultural transmission and the processes that affect it. Culture does not feature in HBE models except insofar as they consider the role of technology in affecting costs and benefits, but even here the existence or availability of relevant technologies is taken for granted and analysis is limited to the question of how one technology or another affects the relation between costs and benefits in a given situation (e.g. Bettinger et al. 2006; Ugan et al. 2003). In cultural evolution or dual inheritance models a major role in generating patterns in human action and its outcomes is attached to the process of cultural transmission, and the forces that act on it, and not simply to cost–benefit distributions. Culture, generally defined as some version of the formulation "information capable of affecting individuals' behavior which they acquire from other members of their species through teaching, imitation and other forms of social transmission" (Richerson and Boyd 2005: 5), is itself taken as a domain in which evolutionary processes operate, at least semi-independently from the domain of natural selection operating on propensities with some sort of genetic foundation.

In this chapter I will first review the key features of what may be called the "cultural evolutionary program" in archaeology and the social sciences more generally, before going on to look at the problems posed by trying to make use of it to understand the archaeological record, some of the methods that have been developed to do this, and the results they have produced. Finally, I will look at the potential for future developments in the field of gene–culture co-evolution and niche construction theory, where aspects of an extended human behavioral ecology and the cultural evolutionary program come together.

The cultural evolutionary program

The main evolutionary processes operating in the cultural domain have been extensively discussed in the literature since the early work of Cavalli-Sforza and Feldman (1981) and Boyd and Richerson (1985) and there is no need to go into them again in detail here (for recent summaries, see, e.g., Richerson and Boyd 2005; Shennan 2008), but it is important to be clear about the fundamentals. Evolutionary processes require mechanisms that generate variation, that pass it on, and that act on what is passed on to increase the prevalence of some things at the expense of others. Without a transmission process there can be no evolutionary theory of culture, because there is no transmitted variation on which selection and other processes can act. What people do at any particular time simply depends on the goal-dependent choices they make in relation to aspects of their cultural, social, and physical environments; in other words, it is simply an aspect of people's phenotypic plasticity.

Evolutionary processes involving the generation of variation followed by selective retention are fundamental in culture as well as in nature because they provide a foundation for making difficult decisions under uncertainty. (The distinction between nature and culture in this very abstract form is not very helpful, however – to be cultural is part of human biology; it is better seen as a contrast in the specifics of transmission mechanisms; see below.) Information which has led to successful decisions in the past becomes encoded and available to future generations, but because individuals are different and variation is constantly being generated, the possibility exists that novel forms of action will be favored by selection in the future, at the expense of existing cultural practices: for example, if social conditions change. However, because the processes of cultural transmission are much more varied than, and generally different from, the symmetrical transmission of genes from each of two parents, cultural transmission also has the potential to produce outcomes that are maladaptive in biological natural selection terms. This is the case even though it is that same variation in transmission routes and processes which gives cultural evolution the advantages it has over genetic evolution of speedier access to a much wider information pool.

The differing starting points of HBE and DIT approaches, relating to the importance or otherwise of cultural transmission in affecting what people do, have major consequences for the direction of research programs in a variety of disciplines and not just archaeology. Are people's actions mainly affected by some version of a rational evaluation of a given situation, albeit based on incomplete information and simple heuristics (Gigerenzer et al. 1999); or simply by the relative popularity of what those around them are doing? So-called viral marketing is predicated on the latter. Moreover, as Bentley et al. (2011) point out, models of agents with zero intelligence based on particle models from physics have had considerable success in explaining variation in financial asset prices. Such models lie at one end of a spectrum that gives varying amounts of influence to copying others as a basis for decision making. It seems likely that from case to case the importance of some version of rational decision making underpinned by natural selection on psychological propensities, as opposed to cultural transmission processes, will vary, so it is necessary to generate test implications for the alternative hypotheses. Thus, for example, Henrich and Henrich's (2010) study of food taboos for pregnant and lactating women in Fiji showed not only that the taboos were adaptive, in the sense of significantly decreasing women's risk of fish poisoning, but also that they depended on a combination of familial learning and learning from a small number of prestigious individuals. The patterns were not compatible with individual learning alone, parental transmission alone, or a combination of parental transmission and individual learning. A research program that excludes from consideration the possibility that processes operating in the course of cultural transmission, and not simply cost–benefit considerations, affect what people do does not seem satisfactory.

The use of cultural evolutionary ideas as a framework for understanding stability and change in the archaeological record is part of a broader interdisciplinary research programme made up of three interrelated strands (cf. Mesoudi et al. 2006). The first involves characterizing the evolutionary processes, including cognitive biases, that produce variation in human cultures, societies, and economies in space and time. This characterization is understandably far less developed than in evolutionary biology. It involves, for example, carrying out psychological experiments to identify the specific factors affecting social learning and the cultural transmission process (e.g. McElreath et al. 2005); ethnoarchaeological studies of patterns of social learning and their consequences with respect to different aspects of material culture (e.g. Roux 2007); and experimental and ethnographic studies of how people evaluate costs and benefits (e.g. Bird et al. 2009). In Henrich and Henrich's food taboo example the adaptive taboos result not simply from rational decision making based on naturally selected psychological propensities but from a specific transmission process involving learning from family and prestigious individuals. Furthermore, it seems likely that in many cases successful adaptations are achieved by selection acting to favor innovations that accumulate over successive episodes of cultural transmission.

The second strand involves identifying the consequences of the operation of those processes in different conditions by means of modeling (see, e.g., McElreath and Boyd 2007). This is of central importance because the consequences of the operation of specific processes cannot simply be intuited or derived from thinking through the consequences of verbal descriptions. Such modeling has been the core of the cultural evolution research program since its beginning (Boyd and Richerson 1985; Cavalli-Sforza and Feldman 1981) because of the power of the mathematical population genetics tools on which it is based.

The final strand is specifically archaeological and historical, and involves using an understanding of the processes and their consequences to explain patterns of stability and change at particular times and places in a number of interrelated domains. One such domain concerns the histories of culturally transmitted practices and norms. The identification of such culture historical patterns in different parts of the world has been one of archaeology's greatest achievements (e.g. Buchvaldek et al. 2007), but traditional culture history had very weak descriptive methods and explanatory mechanisms at its disposal. The developments in cultural evolutionary theory that have taken place in recent years provide the basis for recognizing that different factors affect the differential inheritance and thus prevalence of different cultural practices.

A second domain concerns the history of human populations. Paradoxically perhaps, cultural evolutionary theory and its fore-grounding of the process of social learning as the foundation of cultural transmission also give new life to that explanatory mainstay of traditional culture history, the idea that cultural change can be a result of population change. The best-known recent example of this argument is the Renfrew–Bellwood farming and language dispersal hypothesis (see, e.g., Diamond and Bellwood 2003). Whether this particular hypothesis is valid or not, behind it lies the recognition that human populations, like those of any other living creature, are subject to natural selection: they expand when new reproductive opportunities arise, are subject to density-dependent checks but can overshoot local carrying capacities and then decline, or can be negatively affected by adverse environmental conditions or competition from other populations. It has also become apparent that some cultural attributes are strongly subject to vertical parent–child inheritance, or within-community inheritance, as a result of such processes as conformist bias, a tendency not simply to copy actions in proportion to their frequency in the local population but to favor only the most common ones. Thus there really may be an association between specific cultural attributes and specific populations, as traditional archaeologists claimed, even if such attributes do not have a specific ethnic signaling function. In this case, such attributes may simply "hitchhike" as the cultural baggage that happens to be associated with a particular expanding, stable, or declining population and will share its fate. Analyses of DNA are beginning to provide independent evidence of such culture–population links (e.g. Bramanti et al. 2009; Linderholm 2008). However, even if cultural attributes are neutral and change simply as a result of drift, effectively random variation in what is copied, the fact that innovation and drift are dependent on the size of populations and the extent of their interaction means that demographic history remains central to any evolutionary perspective (Shennan 2000; Shennan and Bentley 2008).

The third set of histories is concerned with social institutions and is, in a sense, the familiar agenda of social evolution, but viewed from the perspective of evolutionary game theory (Bowles 2004, chapter 11; Skyrms 1996; and the extensive literature on altruism, e.g. Fehr and Gächter 2002), which examines the payoffs of different competing interaction strategies. At its core are social agents, individuals with norms, dispositions, knowledge, and resources, who make decisions in their own interests in the light of constraints and opportunities, who sometimes innovate and at other times follow existing practices. Those social and economic strategies that produce beneficial outcomes for the agents will spread through the members of the groups concerned, potentially changing the distribution of social norms, and may themselves be replaced if circumstances change. Moreover, when outcomes are aggregated they can have consequences unintended by any individual social actor, including the emergence of qualitatively new forms of social and economic patterns.

There are three reasons why these local actions can produce broadscale social evolutionary patterns. First, successful patterns of action may spread because they are perceived to be successful by others in similar situations. Second, selection on social, cultural, and economic strategies will often result in similar outcomes in the face of similar situations. Third, processes of self-organization operate in social interactions, leading to convergence on various kinds of "attractors": thus, for example, in Turchin's warfare model (Turchin 2003, cited in Kohler et al. 2009), where the prevalence of warfare is dependent on population size and the latter in turn is affected by the incidence of warfare, high levels of warfare will decrease population density, which eventually results in a diminution of warfare, leading again to higher rates of population growth. If there is no change in the local carrying capacity, then over time warfare prevalence and population density will fluctuate but will eventually converge on a stable equilibrium. This equilibrium represents an "attractor" to which the system will converge (Kohler et al. 2009). Accordingly, in order to understand specific large-scale transformations, we do not need to indulge in broad abstractions of the type prevalent in 1960s and 1970s neo-evolution, but need to carry out theoretically informed analyses of particular situations.

A last set of histories concerns "constructed niches" that change selection pressures and produce gene–culture interactions. In an archaeological context the altered physical environments produced by human action are the most obvious constructed niches and would have changed selection processes across the whole range of human activities, from the optimal subsistence strategy to be pursued, to the best of various competing social strategies to pursue in terms of their payoffs, to the prevalent form of prestige goods. I will return to niche construction below because it raises interesting and novel issues concerning the relationship between HBE and DIT approaches, and about the relations between culture and genes.

Relating cultural evolution theory to the archaeological record

The vast majority of the theory that has been developed over the last thirty years has looked at the processes of cultural transmission and evolution from the point of view of the agents involved in the processes, and the factors that affect their decision making. This is obviously an extremely important perspective but it is not the only one. For archaeologists at least it is also important to look at the processes from what might be called "the meme's-eye view," the perspective of the cultural attributes themselves, since these are the only data accessible; indeed, they are the only direct data about past cultural traditions and the forces affecting them that we have available. The question then becomes, to what extent is it possible to identify the action of the various cultural evolutionary processes that have been proposed over the last thirty years on the basis of distributions of through-time variation in the past, especially given the often poor temporal resolution of the archaeological record and the enormous range of complex processes that have affected it? This is a classic "inverse problem" of a type very familiar to archaeologists: inferring the micro-scale processes producing a pattern from the pattern itself, as opposed to carrying out designed experiments or making natural-istic observations of processes in the field and examining their consequences.

In fact, even to demonstrate that a pattern of continuity or change through time results from the operation of a cultural inheritance process, as opposed to being a contingent response to local environ-mental conditions, is not straightforward. Going on to make infer-ences about the processes acting on the cultural lineages identified is even more difficult, and they look different from the "meme's" per-spective than from the agent's. Thus, in their recent paper on the evolution of Polynesian canoes, Rogers and Ehrlich (2008) use the term "natural selection" to refer to the process acting on those canoe traits that have a functional significance, and so it is from the perspec-tive of the traits themselves, in that particular traits survive and are copied preferentially as a result of their greater functional effective-ness (cf. Dunnell 1978) – something that could in principle be tested experimentally. What their results do not do is distinguish between *natural selection operating on human agents via cultural traits, and thus on the future frequency of those traits*, and *results bias*, where people compare the success of what they're currently doing with that of others and switch if the latter appears more effective. In other words, the process could have operated as a result of the makers and users of ineffective canoes drowning more frequently, thus leading to the demise of those designs, while groups with better-designed canoes, perhaps different communities, survived and colonized new islands. Alternatively, it could have worked through people observing the performance of different canoe designs and preferentially copying those they perceived as more effective. The latter would potentially be far faster and the implied time-scale difference could provide a basis for distinguishing between the two processes. Making this sort of distinction is actually at the root of some of the most long-standing debates in archaeology: for example, whether the spread of farming into Europe was a process of indigenous adoption (involving results bias) or demographic expansion and extinction (natural selection acting on the bearers of cultural traditions). Note that in both the above scenarios whether or not people reproduce particular traits depends on the specific characteristics of the traits themselves which are under selection; in other words, the characteristics of practices and objects influence the probability that people will replicate them. In the spread of agriculture case, the characteristics are technically functional ones, but that does not have to be the case. They may, for example, be features that appeal to aspects of the human mind, as Gell (1998) suggests in his study of the "enchantment" associated with certain decorative patterns.

An archaeology that attaches importance to cultural transmission and the various selection and bias factors affecting it as playing an important role in accounting for variation in the archaeological record needs to do two things: reconstruct patterns of cultural descent and propose and test explanations for the forces that have shaped such patterns. Reconstruction has been mainly based on seriation studies, and to a lesser extent on the application of phylogenetic methods, though neither is a *sine qua non* (Lyman and O'Brien 2006; O'Brien and Lyman 2000).

Seriation involves putting phenomena in a sequential order on the basis of some measure of their similarity to one another. If we have independent evidence of the chronological order, for example, of a series of ceramic assemblages, we can test whether the phenomena that are most similar to one another are indeed closest to one another in time. To the extent that they are, continuity is implied. Ultimately, however, our conviction that continuity of cultural transmission is behind the pattern in this case is also based on other knowledge: for example, that the making of pottery is an activity acquired by social learning.

Although seriation has a long history as a means of constructing chronologies, attempts to analyze the forces affecting sequences of assemblages linked by descent whose ordering is independently confirmed are much more recent. The key development here was Neiman's (1995) demonstration of the way the mathematics of the neutral theory of evolution could be used to generate quantitative expectations of what a distribution of artifact attribute frequencies should look like if cultural drift – the combined effect of innovation and chance variation in what is copied in a finite population – was the only factor affecting it. Neiman's original case study indicated that patterning in the rim attributes of eastern North American Woodland period pottery was indeed a result of drift, and on this basis he went on to argue that the Woodland period was one of large-scale human interaction, a view that had been held by earlier scholars but had subsequently been rejected. In contrast, my work with Wilkinson (Shennan and Wilkinson 2001) showed that patterning in the frequency through time of decorative attributes of early Neolithic pottery from a small region of Germany indicated a more even distribution of variants than expected under drift in the later phases of the sequence studied: that is, there was an "anti-conformity" bias, with many different types being relatively frequent. Conversely, Kohler et al. (2004) in a case study of decorative designs on pottery from the US Southwest were able to show a departure in the direction of conformity. However, it has become increasingly apparent that non-rejection of the drift model must be treated with caution; it cannot be assumed that drift is the only process operating in these circumstances, since a variety of selection and bias forces may produce outcomes indistinguishable from drift alone (Mesoudi and Lycett 2009; Steele et al. 2010).

Eerkens and Lipo (2005) developed a similar approach to the characterization of neutral variation in continuous measurements and the measurement of departures from it. Psychological studies have shown that below a certain threshold (the so-called Weber fraction), people are incapable of distinguishing differences in physical dimensions; the threshold is relative to the scale of the dimension. Thus, lines that are within 3% of each other in terms of their length cannot be distinguished. Over multiple transmission episodes, and assuming that no other processes are operating, the errors generated by this sub-perceptual copying error will accumulate, although the accumulation rate will gradually slow down. On the other hand, if individuals tend to conform to the mean of the population at any given transmission episode, then the variation in the measurement concerned will reach an equilibrium level, with a range dependent on the strength of the conformity. The authors applied the theory to explaining variation in projectile point dimensions in the western US Owens Valley and in Illinois Woodland ceramic vessel diameters. They showed that drift was sufficient to explain the variation in projectile point thickness, but base width showed less variation than expected, so some biasing process leading to a reduction in variation over time must have been operating, while in the case of the pottery vessel diameters variation-increasing mechanisms were at work. Of course, in the absence of a framework that takes into account cultural transmission, such issues could not even be addressed.

However, the process of cultural transmission still needs embedding in a systemic context; it is not autonomous. Roux's (2008) account of the apparently strange history of the production of wheel-fashioned pottery in the ancient Levant provides an excellent example to illustrate this as the situation at first sight seems rather puzzling: the production of wheel-fashioned pottery comes and goes twice before finally becoming permanently established. It is present in the late Chalcolithic period, disappears in the subsequent initial Early Bronze (EB) Age, appears again in EB III, disappears in EB IV, and finally takes off in the Middle Bronze Age. Roux locates the explanation in the context of the practice and transmission of the craft. For the Chalcolithic period a study of the petrology of the pottery and the techniques used to make it, as well as the contexts in which it was found, indicated that only a few individuals made the pottery, that they moved around, and that they were attached to elites. This restricted group of potters within which wheel coiling was transmitted was distinct from those much more numerous potters throughout the region who made the utilitarian pottery. The same is true of the EB III period in that wheel coiling was restricted to a small number of specialists whose potters' turntables are found in palace contexts. The result in both periods was a technical system that Roux characterizes as fragile and closed.

Fragility refers to the size of the network concerned. Any practice that is restricted to a small number of individuals is vulnerable to loss as a result of external circumstances, regardless of its benefits. The fact that the late Chalcolithic and EB III potters using wheel coiling were few in number meant that the practice disappeared in the face of the socio-economic collapses that ended the Chalcolithic and Early Bronze Age periods, because the transmission network was broken. In contrast, robust transmission networks are sufficiently large that they are not vulnerable to the effects of external historical events, because even if part of the network is destroyed in one place, it will survive elsewhere, and this is what happened in the Middle Bronze Age with the expansion of the wheel-coiling transmission network.

However, the size of the network in itself is only one element in the fragility or robustness of a given technical transmission system. One way in which it can expand is by the transfer of the technique to other areas of production than that in which it originally emerged. Again this did not happen in the Chalcolithic or Early Bronze Age. Wheel coiling remained restricted to a small circle of specialist potters who used it only to produce specific elite items. This changed in the Middle Bronze Age of the southern Levant with the application of this innovative practice to a wide range of different items in widespread use, in the context of the expansion of cities and the probable development of a market economy. Workshops using the wheel-coiling technique and producing a wide range of vessels gradu-ally expanded, leading to the decline of domestic pottery production, which became restricted to the making of cooking vessels.

Broadly similar explanations have been offered for the coming and going of "Upper Palaeolithic" cultural traits in Middle Stone Age Africa (Powell et al. 2009; Shennan 2001) and for the loss of a range of cultural attributes in Tasmania after the end of the last Ice Age (Henrich 2004); in both cases the effective population size and its impact on the probability of innovation and on the maintenance of successful innovations are argued to have the key role in accounting for patterns that are otherwise difficult to explain. The argument that larger populations will tend to have more diverse toolkits than small ones has recently been supported by an analysis showing that in Oceania the populations of larger islands had more complex marine foraging toolkits than those of smaller ones (Kline and Boyd 2010), but the discussion of the general implications of this finding remains open. The above arguments all attach importance to processes depen-dent on cultural transmission. The alternative argument is based on the HBE perspective: that toolkit complexity depends essentially on cost–benefit considerations, and in particular the means of dealing with various kinds of risk (Collard et al. 2011).

Evolutionary phylogenies

The adoption of an evolutionary approach has also made possible the introduction of analytical methods from evolutionary biology that can provide a new perspective on long-standing archaeological questions concerning cultural relationships. Phylogenetic techniques provide a basis for reconstructing relationships among a set of *taxa* (species, genera, families etc.), on the basis that they are linked by a specific version of "descent with modification" involving successive branching. New taxa emerge through the splitting of existing ones and the new taxa are reproductively isolated from one another. When new character states – for example, the ability to breathe on land among amphibians – appear in a particular taxon, they will be inher-ited only by descendants of that taxon and no other. It is the pattern of distribution of the resulting *shared derived* character states that provides the basis for reconstructing the tree of relationships.

In the case of the origin and spread into Europe of crop production systems based on domestic cereals and pulses – i.e. the "founder crops" of Neolithic agriculture – there are several reasons to think that a branching model of descent with modification is an appropriate way of conceptualizing the relationships among the different regional packages of crops and associated weeds found at the earliest farming sites. Most obviously, the spread of domesticated crops involved the transmission of the crops themselves, genetic descendants of the ancestral species of the Near East. Second, the cereal and pulse founder crops that spread into Europe had essentially a single regional origin. Third, the spread of agricultural systems based on those crops, whether or not it involved demic as opposed to cultural diffusion, was a dispersal/expansion process. Expansion processes are inherently likely to produce branching patterns of change as successively modified sets of features spread from one place to another. Finally, ethnographic work on traditional agricultural systems indicates that farming practices are usually both relatively conservative and transmitted vertically between generations (e.g. Netting 1993). It is thus highly probable that Early Neolithic farming practices were characterized by the same features (Bogaard 2004).

In order to explore this idea, the plant assemblage data from 250 Early Neolithic sites (Figure 2.1) were aggregated into a number of regional groups and a phylogenetic analysis was carried out (Coward et al. 2008); the resulting evolutionary tree is shown in Figure 2.2. By and large the branching pattern corresponds to a combination of geographical proximity and ecological/climatic similarity, so that archaeobotanical assemblages from areas closer/similar to the Near Eastern source are less derived – have undergone less evolutionary change – than those from further away. However, the method also revealed interesting anomalies which had not previously been appreciated. Cyprus is remarkably derived for a region which is so close to the founder areas: that is to say, its archaeobotanical assemblages have undergone many changes compared with those of the nearby regions that were ancestral to them. This may well reflect the maritime transmission that led to the introduction of agriculture to Cyprus. It is more derived than Central Anatolia, which, unlike Cyprus, is on a branch of the tree distinct from that immediately ancestral to the European plant assemblages. The indication that there was a route for the spread of farming that went from Cyprus via the southern Anatolian coast to Greece and was distinct from that through central Anatolia is increasingly supported by other evidence (Çilingiroğlu 2010; Perlès 2005). Similarly, another anomaly is represented by Bulgaria, the first stop on the route of a continental spread of cereal agriculture via central and northwest Anatolia, which turns out to be the most derived region in Europe, in the sense that it has undergone more changes from the ancestral state than any other. Given its

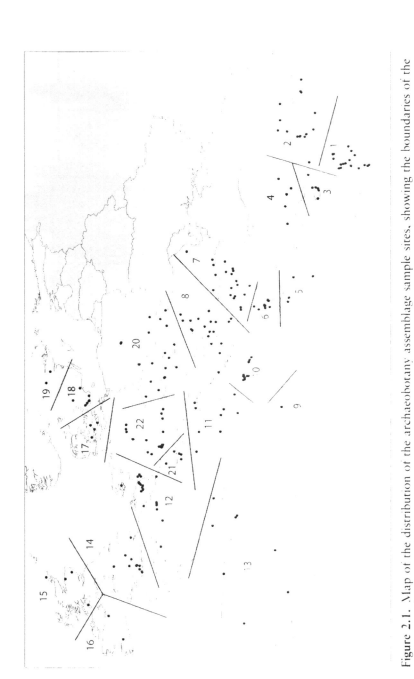

Figure 2.1. Map of the distribution of the archaeobotany assemblage sample sites, showing the boundaries of the regions used in the analysis

Source: Coward et al. 2008, Fig. 1. *Journal of Archaeological Science* by Elsevier. Reproduced with permission of Elsevier.

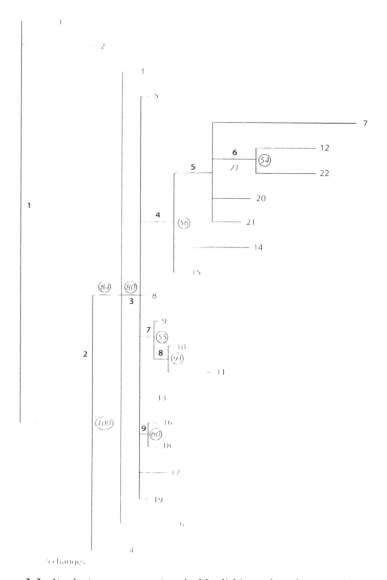

Figure 2.2. Evolutionary tree of early Neolithic archaeobotanical assemblages from southwestern Asia and Europe

Note: The numbers in bold are the branch numbers of the tree. The italic numbers in circles are the probabilities associated with the corresponding nodes off the tree.

location, it should be one of the least derived and might be expected
to be similar to central Anatolia (region 4). Moreover, the highly
derived Bulgarian plant spectrum cannot be considered ancestral
to the assemblages of region 8, the former Yugoslavia, which
look much more like descendants of the Greek/east Mediterranean
line as well as possessing the relatively unchanged features which
make them the plausible ancestors to the Central European early
farming complex that would be expected on other grounds. In short,
taking an evolutionary perspective on the spread of farming and
using appropriate tools enables us to produce a history with
interesting novel elements that can be related to other archaeological
patterns (Coward et al. 2008). Inasmuch as the plant exploitation
patterns differ depending on their transmission history, the question
also arises of the extent to which the differing patterns arise solely
because of that history, or because of different selection or bias forces
produced by different environmental conditions on the different
routes.

However, it should not be thought that the only process operating
in the case of cultural descent with modification is one of branching differentiation from a single origin, or that the cladistic methods
that assume this are the only valid ones. Cochrane and Lipo's (2010)
study of decoration on the Lapita pottery associated with the first
colonization of Oceania uses a variety of methods, including those
of cladistics, to show that a branching process could not account
for the patterns observed, which were better understood as the result
of continuing interaction after initial colonization of the islands
concerned. As Gray et al. point out, "The challenge for empirical
research is to determine how tree-like and how tightly coupled
the evolution of particular aspects of culture are. Both critics and
proponents of cultural phylogenetics need to become "evidence-
based" in their claims about cultural evolution' (Gray et al. 2010:
3931).

Niche construction

What neither HBE nor DIT fully addressed in its initial formulations
was the impact of human action on the environments, meant in the
broadest sense, in which people act and thus the potential feedbacks
created between the changed environment and the payoffs to different
courses of action and their prevalence. As indicated above, HBE was
mainly concerned with developing models to account for the effects
of particular distributions of resources on the costs and benefits of

different choices regarding allocation of effort, in a relatively static kind of way. For DIT the feedback consisted solely of the effects of various kinds of bias and selection processes on the cultural information being transmitted, which in turn would affect the frequency of different realized courses of action in the future. The HBE perspective still ignores cultural information, seeing people's decisions as based on their capacity for learning from experience, but increasingly recognizes that as people change their environment, optimal courses of action will change. Thus Broughton et al. (2010), in a study of the archaeology of resource exploitation by California hunter-gatherers and Mimbres-Mogollon farmers, show how resource depression has a range of consequences, not just for intensified use of low-return resources but for health, violence, and many other areas, such as degrees of inequality. For the DIT perspective the realization has grown that the feedbacks affect not just the cultural information transmitted but the environments created as well, which then have an impact on what is transmitted (see, e.g., Kendal et al. 2011 for recent examples). Indeed, the distinction between the two can be slight: do people decide to decorate pottery vessels in a different style because they see them being made (cultural transmission) or because they see the vessels themselves (a new part of their local environment)?

Moreover, human niche construction involves not just modifications to the physical environment but the creation of new social institutions, which produce novel ecologies for human action and exist at the boundary of cultural and ecological inheritance. For example, the increasing importance of fixed and/or defensible resources in many societies after the end of the last Ice Age led to a shift in the nature of the inter-generational wealth transfers that increase reproductive success, from relatively intangible to material property resources that provided opportunities for massively increased inequality. This also meant that strategies focused on the maintenance and increase of wealth could be even more successful in reproductive terms than strategies directed at maximizing reproductive success in the short term (Shennan 2011)

Gene–culture co-evolution

Although DIT and its alternative formulation as gene–culture co-evolution theory clearly emphasize that the processes of descent with modification in genes and culture are linked, relatively little attention has been paid to those links until recently. HBE ignores genes altogether by assuming the "phenotypic gambit," an approach which postulates that people have the capacity to act in fitness-maximizing ways and to vary what they do to achieve this according to the ecological context. A major reason for this lack of attention has been a lack of information about genetic variation; virtually the only example available for people to cite has been the relation between animal herding and adult lactose tolerance (Feldman and Cavalli-Sforza 1989; Holden and Mace 1997; Itan et al. 2009). This is now changing, as recent analyses of human genome data indicate that many genes have been under recent positive selection and that a key selective factor is likely to have been human cultural practices (Laland et al. 2010), especially those prevalent in the 10,000 years since the origins of agriculture. Just as interest in the evolution of lactose tolerance has led to new archaeological research to identify prehistoric evidence for milk consumption, so it is certain that the new information coming out of human genome studies will lead both to models of gene–culture co-evolution and niche construction in new domains and to new archaeological research to develop and test them (e.g. Barnes et al. 2011)

References

Barnes, I., A. Duda, O. Pybus, and M.G. Thomas 2011. Ancient urbanization predicts genetic resistance to tuberculosis. *Evolution* 65: 842–8.

Bentley, R.A., P. Ormerod, and S.J. Shennan 2011. Population-level neutral model already explains linguistic patterns. *Proceedings of the Royal Society B* 278: 1770–2.

Bettinger, R.L., B. Winterhalder, and R. McElreath 2006. A simple model of technological intensification. *Journal of Archaeological Science* 33: 538–45.

Bird, D.W., R. Bliege Bird, and B.F. Codding 2009. In pursuit of mobile prey: Martu hunting strategies and archaeofaunal interpretation. *American Antiquity* 74: 3–29.

Bogaard, A. 2004. *Neolithic Farming in Central Europe: An Archaeobotanical Study of Crop Husbandry Practices.* London: Routledge.

Bowles, S. 2004. *Microeconomics: Behavior, Institutions and Evolution.* Princeton: Princeton University Press.

Boyd, R. and P.J. Richerson 1985. *Culture and the Evolutionary Process.* Chicago: University of Chicago Press.

Bramanti, B., M.G. Thomas, W. Haak, M. Unterlaender, P. Jores, K. Tambets, I. Antanaitis-Jacobs, M.N. Haidle, R. Jankauskas, C.-J. Kind, F. Lueth, T. Terberger, J. Hiller, S. Matsumura, P. Forster, and J. Burger 2009.

Genetic discontinuity between local hunter-gatherers and Central Europe's first farmers. *Science* 326: 137–40.

Broughton, J. M., M. D. Cannon, and E. J. Bartelink 2010. Evolutionary ecology, resource depression, and niche construction theory: applications to central California hunter-gatherers and Mimbres-Mogollon agriculturalists. *Journal of Archaeological Method and Theory* 17: 371–421.

Buchvaldek, M., A. Lippert, and L. Košnar 2007. *Archaeological Atlas of Prehistoric Europe*. Prague: Karolinum Press, Charles University.

Cavalli-Sforza, L. L. and M. W. Feldman 1981. *Cultural Transmission and Evolution: A Quantitative Approach*. Princeton: Princeton University Press.

Çilingiroğlu, Ç. 2010. The appearance of impressed pottery in the Neolithic Aegean and its implications for maritime networks in the eastern Mediterranean. *TÜBA-AR* 13: 9–22.

Cochrane, E. E. and C. P. Lipo 2010. Phylogenetic analyses of Lapita decoration do not support branching evolution or regional population structure during colonization of Remote Oceania. *Philosophical Transactions of the Royal Society B* 365: 3889–902.

Collard, M., B. Buchanan, J. Morin, and A. Costopoulos 2011. What drives the evolution of hunter-gatherer subsistence technology? A reanalysis of the risk hypothesis with data from the Pacific Northwest. *Philosophical Transactions of the Royal Society B* 366: 1129–38.

Coward, F., S. Shennan, S. Colledge, J. Conolly, and M. Collard 2008. The spread of Neolithic plant economies from the Near East to Northwest Europe: a phylogenetic analysis. *Journal of Archaeological Science* 35: 42–56.

Diamond, J. and P. Bellwood 2003. Farmers and their languages: the first expansions. *Science* 300: 597–602.

Dunnell, R. 1978. Style and function: a fundamental dichotomy. *American Antiquity* 43: 192–202.

Eerkens, J. W. and C. P. Lipo 2005. Cultural transmission, copying errors, and the generation of variation in material culture in the archaeological record. *Journal of Anthropological Archaeology* 24: 316–34.

Fehr, E. and S. Gächter 2002. Altruistic punishment in humans. *Nature* 415: 137–40.

Feldman, M. W. and L. L. Cavalli-Sforza 1989. On the theory of evolution under genetic and cultural transmission with application to the lactose absorption problem. In M. W. Feldman (ed.), *Mathematical Evolutionary Theory*, 145–73. Princeton: Princeton University Press.

Gell, A. 1998. *Art and Agency: An Anthropological Theory*. Oxford: Oxford University Press.

Gigerenzer, G., P. M. Todd, and the ABC Research Group 1999. *Simple Heuristics That Make Us Smart*. New York: Oxford University Press.

Gray, R. D., D. Bryant, and S. J. Greenhill 2010. On the shape and fabric of human history. *Philosophical Transactions of the Royal Society B* 365: 3923–33.

Henrich, J. 2004. Demography and cultural evolution: why adaptive cultural processes produced maladaptive losses in Tasmania. *American Antiquity* 69: 197–214.

Henrich, J. and N. Henrich 2010. The evolution of cultural adaptations: Fijian food taboos protect against dangerous marine toxins. *Proceedings of the Royal Society B* 277: 3715–24.

Holden, C. and R. Mace 1997. Phylogenetic analysis of the evolution of lactose digestion in adults. *Human Biology* 69: 605–28.

Itan, Y., A. Powell, M. A. Beaumont, J. Burger, and M. G. Thomas 2009. The origins of lactase persistence in Europe. *PLoS Computational Biology* 5: e1000491.

Kendal, J. R., J. J. Tehrani, and J. Odling-Smee (eds) 2011. Human niche construction. *Philosophical Transactions of the Royal Society B* 366: 785–92.

Kline, M. A. and R. Boyd 2010. Population size predicts technological complexity in Oceania. *Proceedings of the Royal Society B* 277: 2559–64.

Kohler, T. A., S. VanBuskirk, and S. Ruscavage-Barz 2004. Vessels and villages: evidence for conformist transmission in early village aggregations on the Pajarito Plateau, New Mexico. *Journal of Anthropological Archaeology* 23: 100–18.

Kohler, T. A., S. Cole, and S. M. Ciupe 2009. Population and warfare: a test of the Turchin model in Pueblo societies. In S. J. Shennan (ed.), *Pattern and Process in Cultural Evolution*, 277–95. Berkeley: University of California Press.

Laland, K. N., J. Odling-Smee, and S. Myles 2010. How culture shaped the human genome: bringing genetics and the human sciences together. *Nature Reviews Genetics* 11: 137–48.

Linderholm, A. 2008. *Migration in Prehistory: DNA and Stable Isotope Analyses of Swedish Skeletal Material*. Stockholm: Institutionen för arkeologi och antikens kultur.

Lyman, R. L. and M. J. O'Brien 2006. Seriation and cladistics: the difference between anagenetic and cladogenetic evolution. In C. P. Lipo, M. J. O'Brien, M. Collard, and S. J. Shennan (eds), *Mapping Our Ancestors: Phylogenetic Approaches in Anthropology and Prehistory*, 65–88. New Brunswick, NJ: Aldine Transaction.

McElreath, R. and R. Boyd 2007. *Mathematical Models of Social Evolution: A Guide for the Perplexed*. Chicago: University of Chicago Press.

McElreath, R., M. Lubell, P. J. Richerson, T. M. Waring, W. Baum, E. Edsten, C. Efferson, and B. Paciotti 2005. Applying evolutionary models to the laboratory study of social learning. *Evolution and Human Behavior* 26: 483–508.

Mesoudi, A. and S. J. Lycett 2009. Random copying, frequency-dependent copying and culture change. *Evolution and Human Behavior* 30: 41–8.

Mesoudi, A., A. Whiten, and K. N. Laland 2006. Towards a unified science of cultural evolution. *Behavioral and Brain Sciences* 29: 329–83.

Neiman, F. D. 1995. Stylistic variation in evolutionary perspective: inferences from decorative diversity and inter-assemblage distance in Illinois Woodland ceramic assemblages. *American Antiquity* 60: 7–36.

Netting, R. McC., 1993. *Smallholders, Householders: Farm Families and the Ecology of Intensive, Sustainable Agriculture.* Stanford: Stanford University Press.

O'Brien M. J. and R. L. Lyman 2000. *Applying Evolutionary Archaeology: A Systematic Approach.* New York: Kluwer Academic/Plenum Press.

Perlès, C., 2005. From the Near East to Greece: let's reverse the focus: cultural elements that didn't transfer. In C. Lichter (ed.), *How Did Farming Reach Europe?* (BYZAS 2), 275–90. Istanbul: German Archaeological Institute.

Powell, A., S. J. Shennan, and M. G. Thomas 2009. Late Pleistocene demography and the appearance of modern human behavior. *Science* 324: 1298–301.

Richerson, P. J. and R. Boyd. 2005. *Not By Genes Alone: How Culture Transformed Human Evolution.* Chicago: University of Chicago Press.

Rogers, D. S. and P. R. Ehrlich 2008. Natural selection and cultural rates of change. *Proceedings of the National Academy of Sciences USA* 105: 3416–20.

Roux, V. 2007. Ethnoarchaeology: a non-historical science of reference necessary for interpreting the past. *Journal of Archaeological Method and Theory* 14: 153–78.

Roux, V. 2008. Evolutionary trajectories of technological traits and cultural transmission: a qualitative approach to the emergence and disappearance of the ceramic wheel-fashioning technique in the southern Levant during the fifth to third millennia BC. In M. Stark, B. Bowser, and L. Horne (eds), *Breaking Down Boundaries: Anthropological Approaches to Cultural Transmission and Material Culture in Memory of Carol Kramer,* 82–104. Tucson: University of Arizona Press.

Shennan, S. J. 2000. Population, culture history and the dynamics of culture change. *Current Anthropology* 41: 811–35.

Shennan, S. J. 2001. Demography and cultural innovation: a model and some implications for the emergence of modern human culture. *Cambridge Archaeological Journal* 11: 5–16.

Shennan, S. J. 2008. Canoes and cultural evolution. *Proceedings of the National Academy of Sciences USA* 105: 3175–6.

Shennan, S. J. 2011. Property and wealth inequality as cultural niche construction. *Philosophical Transactions of the Royal Society B* 366: 918–26.

Shennan, S.J. and R.A. Bentley 2008. Style, interaction, and demography among the earliest farmers of Central Europe. In M.J. O'Brien (ed.), *Cultural Transmission and Archaeology: Issues and Case Studies*, 164–77. Washington, DC: SAA Press.

Shennan, S.J. and J.R. Wilkinson 2001. Ceramic style change and neutral evolution: a case study from Neolithic Europe. *American Antiquity* 66: 577–93.

Skyrms, B. 1996. *Evolution of the Social Contract*. Cambridge: Cambridge University Press.

Steele, J., C. Glatz, and A. Kandler 2010. Ceramic diversity, random copying, and tests for selectivity in ceramic production. *Journal of Archaeological Science* 37: 1348–58.

Turchin, P. 2003. *Historical Dynamics: Why States Rise and Fall*. Princeton: Princeton University Press.

Ugan, J., A. Bright, and A. Rogers 2003. When is technology worth the trouble? *Journal of Archaeological Science* 30: 1315–29.

3

HUMAN BEHAVIORAL ECOLOGY

Douglas W. Bird and James F. O'Connell

Many contributions to this volume demonstrate a healthy pluralism in current evolutionary approaches to describing and interpreting the material consequences of human cognition and action. These approaches are sometimes seen to be operating under a unified Darwinian umbrella (Kristiansen 2004), but that appearance is to some degree illusory, particularly with respect to so-called evolutionary (or selectionist) archaeology and human behavioral ecology (HBE) (Boone and Smith 1998). The strict selectionist view originally promoted by Dunnell (1980) – that evolutionary processes can account for variability in artifact form and frequency independent of the processes that shape the behavior that produced those artifacts – is now broadly rejected. Still, Shennan (2008) argues that integrating certain aspects of this and other evolutionary approaches can inform on a wide range of theoretical and empirical problems in archaeology. We maintain that HBE is nevertheless distinct among them owing to its focus on adaptive function. We also stress that while there are important differences between non-evolutionary, agency-based positions and HBE, these very different analytic gambits share common interests in a growing set of questions about the dynamics of individual behaviors, the social, historical, and ecological contexts in which they are embedded, and the material patterns they produce. Several recent reviews provide more comprehensive treatment of HBE in archaeology than we can undertake here (Bird and O'Connell 2006; Broughton and Cannon 2010; Kelly 2000; Kennett and Winterhalder 2006; Lupo 2007). Instead, we focus on HBE's basic theoretical propositions and show how they can be operationalized. We stress the importance of actualistic data for evaluating the potential utility of HBE models in archaeology by reference to two ethnographic examples: Meriam intertidal foragers in the Torres Strait Islands and Martu hunters in Australia's Western Desert. These studies not only show how the models work, but also highlight new questions especially important to archaeologists, and help identify promising means of addressing them.

HBE versus evolutionary archaeology: levels of explanation

Shennan (this volume) and others concerned with integrating elements of evolutionary archaeology (*sensu* Lyman and O'Brien 1998) and dual inheritance theory aim to identify culturally determined patterns in artifact form, reconstruct lineages defined by diachronic variation in those patterns, and account for their shape and trajectory by reference to the processes of cultural information transmission outlined by Boyd and Richerson (1985). Their goal is phylogenetic: they revisit the culture histories of preprocessual archaeology and reposition them within a formal evolutionary framework, analogous to that of palaeobiology (Mesoudi and O'Brien 2009). Important as that exercise may be, interpretations of archaeological patterning require attention to more than one level of explanation (Bird and O'Connell 2006; Codding and Jones 2010): the differences between the descriptive-historical emphasis of this reformulated evolutionary archaeology and the functional explanations that human behavioral ecologists usually seek are important and often under-appreciated.

HBE asks questions about the *function* of behavioral patterns in terms of their immediate, contextually contingent adaptive value to individuals (Tinbergen 1963; see also Cuthill 2005). In emphasizing the utility and dynamism of behavior rather than its phylogeny or ontogeny, HBE retains a sense of the everyday use of the term "function" – its practitioners ask "What is the current, adaptive, fitness-related role of behavior x in a subject's life?" Potential answers focus on the ecological constraints that shape behavior and its material residues. At issue is *not* how behavior is learned or transmitted between individuals, but how behavior functions in ways that promote locally specific adaptive goals of individuals.

Questions about function

The term "function" is used in many different ways in the biological and social sciences, and for good reason "functionalism" in anthropology has largely fallen out of favor. In fact, in many respects HBE's focus on a functional level of explanation grew out of its rejection of the classic functionalism in anthropology and biology: the term is used in behavioral ecology to refer to characteristics that persist because of the advantages they confer to *individuals*, not groups, populations, societies, or institutional structures. The analytical primacy placed on the adaptive value of individual behavior emerges from a fundamental assumption in HBE: that natural selection, at the level of individual differential reproductive success, is the primary process underlying the design features of decision-making capacity (Krebs and Davies 1997; Williams 1966). While specific cultural processes may provide conditions for group-level adaptations (Henrich 2004), the focus on individual trade-offs in HBE forces attention to conflicts of interest among individuals and between individuals and groups, and to the implications of such conflicts for collective action, emergent social arrangements, and their archaeological expressions.

This assumption – that natural selection has shaped us all and that we all face individual fitness-related trade-offs – does not engage any kind of specific determinism, genetic or otherwise, for explaining behavioral variability. HBE assumes that whatever the mechanisms of inheritance, and however history and socialization enfold those mechanisms, people everywhere have, and will always face, problems of life that matter in terms of individual fitness. The nature of the costs and benefits associated with solving those problems is highly contextual, and we expect large differences in adjustments to locally varying opportunities and constraints completely independent of genetic differences. That, in fact, is the (evolutionary) point of behavior, and natural selection is the only general theory we currently have to account for why it evolved.

HBE thus proposes that a full account of behavior – whatever the proximate motivation, intention, ontogeny, cognitive mechanisms, historical paths, or means of transmission – requires attention to its value in terms of the trade-offs that individual agents face in attempting to make a living, provide for dependents, and maintain the social bonds that such arrangements demand. And as much as they are historically contingent, the values of those costs and benefits are also fundamentally ecological: they vary as a function of the nature of experienced relationships in local social and environmental contexts. In many ways, understanding those contexts defines most efforts in contemporary HBE, including those applied to archaeological problems.

HBE versus agency theory: formal modeling

In its focus on contextually embedded individuals and conflicts of interest, HBE shares much in common with archaeological approaches focused on agency (Shennan 2004). As used in archaeology, agency theory is especially concerned with subjective contexts – both past and present (Hodder 1982). By rejecting structuralism, agency theorists focus on how, despite potentially oppressive social structures, individuals in the past facilitated stability or change through daily practice (Bourdieu 1977; cf. Pauketat 2007). They have also been concerned with the historical conditions that give rise to such agency, and how archaeological patterning and structure emerge from and feed back on relations between individuals and their social and material surrounds (Giddens 1984; cf. Barrett 2001). Further, some explore the recursive nature of archaeological practice itself and how contemporary agents (archaeologists) construct meaning out of "the past" they encounter (Dobres and Robb 2000).

Of these approaches, HBE shares most with those drawn from Giddens'. The differences arise especially in how HBE sets aside the problem of *how* subjects acquire, evaluate, and give meaning to the contexts that emerge from and constrain social action. Instead, HBE in archaeology proposes that whatever the processes are that affect how subjects come to experience their worlds, we can assume that they have the capacity to evaluate trade-offs that matter relative to adaptive function. This assumption allows us to get on with the task of asking questions about the design of behavior and what maintains it – a research strategy often referred to as the "phenotypic gambit" (Grafen 1984).

HBE thus attempts to characterize behavioral variability relative to the ecologically embedded values of individual agents. These values emerge from and structure decision-making strategies, which for heuristic purposes can be thought of as contingency rules for achieving hypothetical "fitness-related" goals relative to the set of options available to an agent (Smith and Winterhalder 1992). To operationalize this proposition, HBE utilizes formal models to (a) frame a specific problem faced by an agent, (b) identify assumptions about the goal of behavior, (c) specify the currency in which the trade-offs are measured, and (d) define the constraints that determine the strategy set and its payoffs (Stephens and Krebs 1986: 9). The real utility of such models lies in the specific way that their predictions are at risk of failure relative to observed behavior and its material correlates. Such failures then point towards new questions. If agents do not behave as modeled, it's not their fault (i.e. it doesn't necessarily mean their behavior is maladaptive), nor is it the fault of the theory, for that matter. Rather it suggests the existence of one or more problems with the specific hypotheses at risk in the analysis. The theory itself will fail, or simply fade away, only when it ceases to generate productive hypotheses.

With its assumption that individuals should act as if they care about fitness-related consequences, some may charge HBE with being too narrow to tackle many of the complexities of human sociality, some of which may be determined by considerations other than fitness (Bamforth 2002). We respond with two critical points. First, this assumption is derived from the theoretical proposition that natural selection has "designed" our capacity to respond flexibly to varying contexts in ways that should be understandable relative to the costs and benefits of using resources and securing relationships. This proposition is far too broad to be tested in any direct sense, which is why HBE relies heavily on "middle-range" models (*sensu* Raab and Goodyear 1984) like those discussed below to bridge the broad theoretical statements with potentially observable outcomes. Second, "fitness" itself is theoretical: it cannot be measured in any absolute, universal, or immediate sense – it is the differential reproductive success of specific individuals bearing certain traits and the context-dependent propensity of those individuals to differentially contribute traits to future generations. HBE models do not measure fitness per se, but hypothesize about factors likely to determine it. The theory (natural selection) provides justification for the hypotheses, but does not identify in any direct sense which specific variables matter. Analyses in HBE are thus focused on evaluating the degree to which observable behavior matches the hypothesized variables and their predictive relationships. The real power of the approach lies in its ability to identify and capitalize analytically on the mismatches (Bettinger 2006).

A reliance on formal models and hypothesis testing can impose an analytical inflexibility that many find incompatible with more holistic approaches, such as agency-based analyses that situate individuals and practice in the dynamics of subjectively defined social worlds (Barrett, this volume). Indeed, the use of simple models as a source for hypothesis testing makes HBE reductionist in practice rather than holistic: it entails an attempt to break down complex socio-ecological phenomena to capture key features of a given problem. But the reliance on formal modeling is a heuristic, not a descriptive endeavor: it is used to clear the lens of inquiry, forcing the analyst to hold in focus the question at hand and the assumptions that underlie "*why*" questions about behavior. Most models in HBE thus stipulate a fairly narrow range of variables whose relationships generate precise predictions about potentially observable outcomes. As we discuss below, the more successful of these have emphasized generality (presumably at some cost to descriptive reality) and incorporated variables whose values are fairly easy to measure (Bettinger 2009; O'Connell 1995).

Analytical differences such as a reliance on formal modeling will likely continue to separate HBE and agency theory, but attuning each approach to the other "offers a promising framework for identifying the strategies and responses of individual agents to other actors, as well as to institutional structures over time" (Galle 2010: 20). Below we illustrate this with a discussion of two sets of HBE models now commonly used in archaeology – foraging theory and signaling theory – but other frameworks within HBE also have important links to agent-based approaches, especially those dealing with life-history evolution, colonization, technological change, resource inequalities, and political hierarchies (Bird and O'Connell 2006).

Foraging theory

Though it shares concerns with some postprocessual approaches, HBE in archaeology remains unabashedly processual: it seeks to connect theoretical propositions with predictions about empirical phenomena, and to understand the processes that shape the relationship between behavior and its material consequences (Binford 1977). Many of the questions with which HBE deals have their origins in cultural ecology's focus on subsistence strategies and social integration among foragers (Steward 1955). As such, especially under the rubric of foraging theory, ethnoarchaeological and experimental studies play an important role in the approach, particularly for questions about variability in subsistence strategies and their archaeological signatures (Lupo 2007).

Foraging theory is a set of models designed to address questions about variability in resource acquisition, time allocation, and the spatial organization of foraging strategies (Stephens and Krebs 1986; for review of technical details of commonly used foraging models in archaeology, see Bettinger 2009). Unlike classic decision models that focus on binary, mutually exclusive choices, foraging theory sees the exercise as an interrelated hierarchy of decisions (Stephens 2008). At the most general level, and against the background of other activities that matter, an individual must choose whether or not to forage, and if so where. Traveling to search for resources in one patch precludes the pursuit of opportunities available in others. Patches are thus defined by sets of resources that can be searched for simultaneously. Within a patch, experienced foragers can anticipate how often different types of resources are likely to be encountered, how that encounter rate changes with patch residence time, and the expected yield for time spent *handling* (pursuing, capturing, harvesting, and processing) different prey. Given that background, a forager must make a series of decisions about whether to enter and how long to stay in a particular patch, whether to pursue an encountered resource within that patch, how long to stay in pursuit, how much to process a captured resource at the point of acquisition, and which parts to transport from the procurement locale. Foraging models help one deconstruct and so understand these decisions.

Foraging models require a series of explicit assumptions (more accurately, *hypotheses*) whose relationships provide a solution to a specified decision variable. Imagine a hunter in a homogeneously structured patch where search time can be shared across a number of potential prey types. By foraging in the patch, the hunter allocates time that could be spent elsewhere, and is therefore concerned about how efficiently resources can be acquired relative to those in other patches. If a prey item is encountered during search, the hunter must decide whether to pursue the item or bypass it and continue to search for other resources. The decision to pursue precludes (for a time) the opportunity to continue searching for other prey.

This "decision tree" is formalized in the *prey choice (or diet breadth) model* (Stephens and Krebs 1986). Analysts employing the model assume that foragers will act efficiently in capturing nutrients (usually energy), and that once foraging begins, time spent searching is shared across a range of resources, each of which yields a different return rate if handled. Under conditions of declining overall efficiency, the model predicts that foragers should broaden the range of resources exploited in rank order of their post-encounter return rate (energy gained per unit of handling time). The highest ranked resources should always be pursued on encounter, but as encounters while searching for them decrease, lower-ranked resources will be pursued when their own individual post-encounter return rates exceed the overall patch return rate (energy for time spent searching *and* handling).

Where resources are heterogeneously distributed (searching for one prey set precludes attention to others), foragers face decisions about whether to enter a patch and how long to stay. Increasing patch residence time often leads to diminishing returns. The *marginal value theorem* (Charnov 1976) predicts the point along a diminishing returns curve at which foragers should leave one patch in favor of another. Foragers should spend more time in and extract more resources from patches in poorer habitats, or when travel times between patches are long. Again, opportunity costs underwrite this prediction. If the returns while foraging within a given patch fall below the average available from traveling between all other exploitable patches, the forager should leave that patch and move to another. If average returns from the habitat as a whole decline, the opportunity costs of continuing to exploit a current patch also decline, leading to longer in-patch residence times, less travel between patches, and use of a broader range of resources within any given patch. These developments also increase incentives for improving processing and travel technology (O'Connell et al. 2010).

The archaeological consequences of foraging are determined not only by prey choice but also by decisions foragers make about processing and transporting prey. *Central place foraging models* capture key determinants of those decisions. Regardless of their degree of residential mobility, all humans are central place foragers: they generally transport resources from the point of procurement to a residential base. If a forager takes prey types comprised of parts with different utilities (e.g. meat and bone), has limited transport capability, and is concerned about how efficiently parts of high utility can be delivered home, he or she will face a decision about whether to cull parts of lower utility at the procurement site or transport packages of mixed utility in bulk. Field processing increases the utility of each load, but costs time that could instead be spent acquiring and transporting more resources. The solution to this trade-off – defined by the threshold at which field processing as opposed to bulk transport will increase the home delivery rate of high-utility parts (Metcalfe and Barlow 1992) – provides precise predictions about how transport and depositional behavior should vary relative to changes in load utility with investments in processing. At equal transport distances, those resources characterized by processing that can quickly increase the ratio of high- to low-utility parts are less likely to be transported in bulk, and less likely to leave durable archaeological residues near residential locales.

Framed this way, foraging analyses entail built-in assumptions about the goal, currency, and constraints that underwrite the relevant trade-offs. The models assume that foragers have goals related to solving trade-offs where resources are finite, use the stipulated currency to evaluate the costs and benefits associated with the goal, and operate under constraints relative to the distribution of resources and foragers' knowledge about them. We may be wrong about any or all of these assumptions; the models provide a means to see where we are wrong relative to observed behavior. Moreover, the way that we are wrong can be informative for archaeological issues, especially by highlighting common but questionable assumptions implicit in standard interpretations of archaeological variability.

In the sections that follow we evaluate the utility of foraging models in explaining subsistence transitions, and show how actualistic work supplies information crucial for operationalizing model parameters. The actualistic data we discuss are drawn from our own ethnographic work on foraging and food sharing, though since the mid-1980s such data have become increasingly available (Bird and O'Connell 2006). We use these examples to illustrate how actualistic tests of the assumptions and predictions of models in HBE can generate results that pose new questions with previously unanticipated links to archaeological phenomena. The emergent questions (especially those related to risk and gender) and the theoretical propositions that frame them (especially signaling theory) are taken up in the final sections.

An archaeological problem: broad-spectrum transitions

Today, most human populations are densely entangled in highly intensified, globally interconnected agricultural economies. The processes that created this pattern lie in a series of "broad-spectrum revolutions": trends in ancestral foraging economies towards the use of broader arrays of wild foods, including increasingly diversified strategies for resource acquisition, processing, distribution, and storage (Stiner 2001). Archaeologists have identified a number of factors that may have influenced such transitions, including increasing familiarity with resource quality, increased demand for food in the context of intensifying social relations, technological innovations that affect resource utility, and shifts in the availability of resources as a result of climate change and/or human population growth. Though all of these hypotheses are plausible, and some combinations of them are probable, few have generated clear predictions or well-defined tests regarding the nature of the newly adopted resources involved, the timing and order of their adoption, or the case-to-case variation in the adoption process evident on a global scale.

Early archaeological applications of foraging theory addressed this problem by reference to the prey choice and patch models discussed above, evaluating their predictions about how selectivity should change with fluctuations in expected overall foraging efficiency (e.g. Bayham 1979; Botkin 1980; Jochim 1976; O'Connell and Hawkes 1981). In general, they proposed that archaeological remains of variable subsistence strategies indicating the step-wise inclusion of lower-ranked resources would support the hypothesis that density-dependent high-ranked resource depression lies at the heart of phenomena commonly characterized as broad-spectrum transitions.

Subsequent applications of these models have further clarified key characteristics of broad-spectrum transitions, the resources involved, and the timing and order of their adoption. Such transitions are typically marked by the inclusion of previously unimportant resources characterized by relatively high post-encounter pursuit costs or by nutrient extraction techniques that entail multi-stage handling or specialized processing gear (e.g. Broughton 2002; Edwards and O'Connell 1995; Henshilwood and Marean 2003; Jones et al. 2008; Stiner et al. 2000). Some of these practices are reported from sub-Saharan Africa by 60 kya BP, but they were increasingly common from 50 kya BP onwards, beginning with the Upper Palaeolithic and spread of *Homo sapiens* into Eurasia. Resources added to Palaeolithic diets and those involved in subsequent Mesolithic and Neolithic transitions have relatively high handling costs, despite the fact that they are often situationally abundant and have potentially high energetic yields. Their adoption came only with localized declines in the availability of options with higher post-encounter return rates, at least in part because of climate-mediated human population growth (Richerson et al. 2001).

For resources with predictable differences in pursuit costs, there are broadly consistent patterns between expected and observed results: small, fast prey – low ranked because of their ability to elude capture and their low yields – become important in human diets only with increased human population densities and reductions in the availability of larger, slower-moving items (Stiner 2001). While evidence for the use of resources with high handling costs have been found in some pre-Last Glacial maximum (LGM) deposits (e.g. grass seeds, Henry et al. 2011), complex processing technology indicating far more intensive reliance on such resources only occurs in association with denser human populations, especially with post-LGM shifts marking the onset of Mesolithic and Neolithic economies (e.g. Kennett and Winterhalder 2006). Archaeological evidence for increasing diet breadth since 50 kya BP is particularly clear in coastal zones, with depression of slow-moving/immobile but large package resources (e.g. large molluscs, tortoises), and dramatic shifts towards previously unexploited fish (whose pursuit required unprecedented technological investment) and smaller molluscs with lower yields relative to handling costs (e.g. Klein 2004). Likewise in terrestrial circumstances, the kinds of nuts and seeds whose energy requires considerable work and equipment to extract become a major component of Palaeolithic diets only on the heels of spreading modern human populations, or with rapid increases in population density thereafter (e.g. Barker et al. 2007). A number of behavioral ecologists have argued that a reliance on such resources – and the social and technological complexities that underwrite them – can account for many instances of modern human colonization and displacement (e.g. Bettinger and Baumhoff 1982; O'Connell et al. 2010).

We argue that if HBE has successfully informed questions related to broad-spectrum transitions, it has done so in part because of the constraints the models impose on analysis. Working within those constraints requires: (1) a clear statement of the question, (2) selection of an appropriate model, and (3) actualistic work that supplies information about how to measure the model's variables. While early archaeological applications of foraging models showed the importance of the first two, the actualistic work required to apply the models was initially missing. Until the mid-1980s, for example, analysts had few data on which to base ordinal (let alone interval) rankings of prey types. Something as seemingly straightforward as the possible effects of pursuit costs on the post-encounter return rates for different kinds of prey was often resolved by guesswork. Actualistic studies conducted over the last three decades have not only begun to supply such information, but have also helped identify contexts in which the models "work" and don't – that is, they have helped make sense of ethnographic observations and led to new questions about ethnographic and prehistoric contexts in which we might expect consistent violations of the model predictions.

Actualistic tests: some ethnographic examples

Shellfishing, prey choice, and transport

Shellfish provide some of the most durable archaeological remains, and evidence of changes in mollusc size and assemblage composition plays an influential role in arguments about the processes involved in broad-spectrum transitions. But until recently, precise quantitative data on the costs and benefits of shellfishing were extremely limited (cf. Meehan 1982). Ethnographic and experimental studies have improved this situation (e.g. Bettinger et al. 1997; de Boer 2000; Hildebrandt et al. 2009; Jones and Richman 1995; F.R. Thomas 2007; D.H. Thomas 2008). The Meriam of eastern Torres Strait provide a case in point (Bird and Bliege Bird 1997, 2000, 2002; Bird et al. 2002, 2004).

When the intertidal reefs that surround the Meriam Islands are exposed, foragers can collect shellfish along the rocky intertidal shoreline, or on the middle and outer reef flat, or they can spearfish in the latter area. On average, adults earn about 1500 kcal/hr – searching + handling on the reef flat, but gain only 300 kcal/hr and 575 kcal/hr, respectively, from spearfishing or by collecting along the rocky shore. Women spend most of their intertidal foraging time on reef flat collecting, where post-encounter return rates for different shellfish range from 500 to >13,000 kcal/hr. As predicted by the prey choice model, women focus on prey yielding post-encounter returns significantly higher than the overall return rate from the patch: harvesting tridacnid clams, Lambis conch, and large Trochus (all with post-encounter returns >2000 kcal/hr), but almost always passing over small Strombus conch, small Trochus, and small bivalves (all yielding <1,000 kcal/hr – handling). They are also attentive to changes in patch return rates and, consistent with marginal value expectations, switch from reef flat collecting to rocky shore harvesting when incoming tides force return rates in the mid-littoral below those available from harvesting closer to shore.

While prey choice and marginal value work well at predicting women's time allocation and selectivity in the intertidal, *they do not predict the frequency of different types of shellfish in either contemporary or prehistoric shell middens*. The most important shellfish for modern-day collectors (tridacnids, Lambis) are rare in archaeological deposits, which are dominated instead by the remains of small gastropods (nerites, strombids, Trochus). The differences between ethnographic and archaeological observations result from field processing and forager age-linked differences in foraging returns. While reef flat collecting, children walk more slowly and encounter high-ranked resources at lower rates than do adults, giving them lower overall average return rates and encouraging a broader collecting strategy that includes smaller gastropods. While both adults and children take high-ranked shellfish whenever possible, only children regularly collect the strombids and small Trochus that dominate the shell middens.

What about the rarity of large clams and conch in those deposits? Differences in field-processing costs and their implications for load utility provide an answer. The central-place foraging model antici- pates the observation that Meriam foragers usually cull the shells of large tridacnids and Lambis while on the reef. Women and children commonly forage well beyond the threshold at which transporting these resources in bulk would increase the home delivery rate of edible tissue. Conversely, the smaller shellfish that children often collect in the high intertidal are always moved in bulk. Foragers rarely cross predicted field-processing thresholds while collecting these prey (Bird and Bliege Bird 1997; Bird et al. 2002).

Hunting, sharing, and risk

Meriam intertidal foraging also highlights clear violations of predic- tions that assume a goal of energetic return rate maximization. Meriam men regularly forgo the opportunity to collect shellfish in order to engage in spearfishing, and in so doing greatly reduce their efficiency in capturing energy or other macro-nutrients for themselves and their families. The costs of spearfishing are not offset by benefits gained from cooperative gender specialization in macronutrient har- vesting, or by reciprocal sharing (Bliege Bird et al. 2001). Spearfishing is also risky: owing to the evasiveness of targeted prey, nearly half of all spearfishing episodes fail to produce food (Bliege Bird and Bird 2002). Similar differences in return rates and reliability associated with gender-related differences in prey choice are common among foragers world-wide (Hawkes and Bliege Bird 2002), and have been at the center of debates over prey rankings, foraging goals, and their implications for explaining variability in faunal assemblages (e.g. Broughton and Bayham 2003; Hildebrandt and McGuire 2003). Key issues are further illustrated by the results of recent ethnoarchaeologi- cal work among the Martu.

Martu occupy a large (136,000 km²) Native Title holding in Australia's Western Desert. Much of their foraging involves traveling by motor vehicle from permanent settlements to temporary camps closer to resource-rich patches. Prey taken in the latter are often processed, cooked, distributed, and consumed at those camps. Several foraging options are available at any given camp, each involving mutually exclusive search for different suites of resources (Bird et al. 2009). Two options include *sand monitor* (lizard) and *hill kangaroo* hunting, respectively. Sand monitors are taken in dune fields, where dense, old growth spinifex grass is fired to facilitate search for small- to medium-sized herpetofauna – varanid lizards, skinks, and snakes (Bliege Bird et al. 2008). Foragers working the sand monitor patch forgo opportunities to hunt kangaroo in adjacent rocky ranges.

Two observations important to archaeologists emerge from studies of this activity. First, zooarchaeologists have commonly used prey body size as a proxy measure for post-encounter return rates. Where that holds, decreasing ratios of large- to small-bodied game are read to indicate density-dependent, high-ranked resource depression, leading to increased reliance on smaller game (e.g. Bayham 1979; Broughton et al. 2008). However, for Martu resources, there is no relationship between prey size and rank: for many types of small game, a hunter can expect post-encounter return rates significantly higher than those for larger game. The reason is simple: in Martu country, small game are far less likely to escape when a hunter begins to pursue them. Time invested in pursuing sand monitor or skink is associated with a failure rate of <10% per hunt; that spent going after hill kangaroo has a failure rate of 70%. A failed hill kangaroo pursuit is also more costly, given that encounters in this patch are rare. Hill kangaroo hunts fail outright, through both lack of encounters and failed pursuits, 80% of the time. Failed pursuits while sand monitor hunting are far less costly: multiple encounters in the course of a single hunt are common, and a hunter rarely finishes the day empty-handed (Bird et al. 2009: Tables 1–2). Based on these and similar results from other studies (Hawkes et al. 1982: 391, 1991; O'Connell et al. 1988; Smith 1991: 230–1; Winterhalder 1981: 95–6), we have argued that archaeologists need better-justified parameters of variability in prey behavior to predict prey rank and the outcome of changing prey–predator relationships (cf. Jones et al. 2008; Lyman 2003; Stutz et al. 2009).

This brings us to the second set of results important to archaeologists. Like Meriam spearfishing, Martu kangaroo hunting is a risky way to get food. But it also yields occasional bonanzas that make for high overall average returns. If a forager's goal is to maximize mean overall energetic return rate, sand monitor hunting is a poor choice: hunters achieve only half the average efficiency they could expect from hill kangaroo hunting. But even when both options are available from a dinnertime camp, many Martu choose to hunt for smaller game. Perhaps not surprisingly, there are differences in *who* chooses which activity. Over 70% of women's total foraging time is spent sand monitor hunting; <2% is devoted to hill kangaroo. In contrast, only 25% of men's foraging time is devoted to sand monitor hunting while 20% is spent on hill kangaroo.

Bliege Bird and associates (Bliege Bird and Bird 2008; Bliege Bird et al. 2009; Codding et al. 2011) propose that two interrelated factors determine this contrast: risks of acquisition and risks of non-reciprocity in distribution. While hill kangaroo hunting offers greater overall average efficiency, its coefficient of variation is four times that of sand monitor hunting. The high rate of average efficiency in kangaroo hunting is driven by the rare successful bonanzas, and in seeking those bonanzas a forager trades off the opportunity to search for smaller but far more reliable prey. Kangaroo hunting risks are not reduced by reciprocal sharing. Kangaroo shares flow from those who have made kills to those who have not, regardless of long-term differences in labor investment, nor are successful hunters who share paid back with other foods. Given the amounts kangaroo hunters keep for themselves and dependents *after sharing*, they would almost always increase their foraging efficiency by sand monitor hunting, where they can control the harvest size relative to labor invested (Bird and Bliege Bird 2010).

Codding et al. (2010) recently explored the implications of these observations for arguments about variability in ancient faunal assemblages. Underlying many classic interpretations of archaeofaunal patterns is the assumption that the proportion of large versus small prey is a function of differences in time allocated to acquiring different prey, and that increasing proportions of larger prey (higher "abundance" indices) are evidence of greater overall foraging efficiency and gendered division of labor (e.g. Broughton et al. 2008). Codding et al. show that no matter how much time foragers spend hunting for high-variance prey (large game in general), only that allocated to more predictable items (small game in general) predicts variation in the abundance index. This is again a function of differences in risk associated with different types of subsistence activities: among Martu, successful kangaroo hunts result in a high abundance index, but investing more labor in this activity does not, simply because success is too stochastic. Why, then, would foragers sometimes choose such risky activities? Understanding circumstances in which some individuals are more or less sensitive to such risk has relevance not only for how we approach changing subsistence patterns, but also for broader arguments about the symbolic value of behavior in general.

Signaling theory

Signaling theory is concerned with information exchange, and in particular with how costly "displays" transmit information critical for maintaining relationships between actors with potential conflicts of interest (Grafen 1990; Johnstone 1997; Zahavi and Zahavi 1997). It has been employed in the study of a broad suite of behaviors and their material correlates, ranging from questions about monumental architecture, craft traditions and warfare, to issues of gendered social strategies and inequality, prestige hunting, conspicuous consumption, ritual behavior, and religious commitment (e.g. Alcorta and Sosis 2005; Bliege Bird et al. 2001; Boone 2000; Galle 2010; Hawkes and Bliege Bird 2002; McGuire and Hildebrandt 2005; Neiman 1997; Roscoe 2009; Sosis and Alcorta 2003; see Bliege Bird and Smith 2005 for review). Take the problem identified above: why would some Martu hunters consistently choose activities that put the results of their labor at risk? The group may eat well if some hunt kangaroo and share it out evenly, but each individual would do better by controlling the products of his or her own labor through sand monitor hunting. Risks of non-reciprocation following successful kangaroo hunts are especially high, increasing the opportunities for others to free-ride on a hunter's labor, making their work a public good and exacerbating conflicts between group and individual interests (Hawkes 1993).

Theoretically, all forms of exchange involve some risk, but the amount and kind of risk vary with the flow of resources. The risk of non-reciprocity is especially salient when exchange benefits flow unilaterally, from those who produce to those who are unlikely to. When actors jointly negotiate agreements with binding terms, the risk of non-reciprocity is reduced. But what about where reciprocity is "generalized" as opposed to "direct" (Sahlins 1965)? Why risk giving when it is difficult to control distribution towards those who are likely to reciprocate and away from those who are not? Such questions point towards the symbolic value of strategic interaction and remain at the core of a range of age-old problems attacked by social exchange theorists (e.g. Lévi-Strauss 1969; Mauss 1924; Veblen 1899).

Signaling theory directs our attention to the fact that risks of non-reciprocation are often necessary conditions for individuals to demonstrate their trustworthiness – when trust is ensured, collective action can be realized. In fact, acts of trust and evaluations of trust-worthiness can be made only in risky situations – that is, reputations of trustworthiness can be built only under those conditions where individuals have the opportunity to defect from interactions that might be mutually beneficial (Cook and Rice 2006). Where there are risks of non-reciprocation, what matters is not merely the material benefit of the interaction, but what the interaction itself says about the agents. This is what is meant by the *expressive value of reciprocity* – these are the ways that the act of sharing itself communicates infor-mation about the agents (Molm et al. 2007). When reciprocity is uncertain, the act of giving can convey expressive value by commu-nicating regard for the exchange partner and one's willingness to invest in continuing the relationship.

The persistence of such risky behavior might seem counter-intui-tive relative to the giver's success, especially in terms of fitness. Signaling theory helps frame such questions relative to how the very costs embedded in risky acts ensure the reliability of the information conveyed. Costly signaling explains – in terms of evolutionary stable strategies – how "honest" signaling can be maintained between actors who have potential conflicts of interest, say through sharing without conditions of direct reciprocation.

Returning to the issue of social exchange: increasing the risk of non-reciprocity increases the expressive value of the act of giving – that is, the risks increase the broadcast fidelity of the act. These acts are costly signals: those who can bear the costs of putting their energy on the line demonstrate their underlying qualities, motivation, and commitment. The costs ensure the honesty of the signal. Standardizing them allows for fine-grained judgment of the quality of the signal. And ritualized signals – especially when wrapped in fitness-related currencies such as energy acquisition and distribution – have an enduring impact (Alcorta and Sosis 2005).

Problems in applying signaling theory to archaeological phenom-ena remain, mostly because middle-range models like those described above in foraging theory have proven more difficult to develop when dealing with strategic interaction. Galle (2010) provides an illustra-tion for how we might proceed in her analysis of variation in signal levels among men and women in eighteenth-century slave communi-ties in the Chesapeake region of Virginia. She generates a series of predictions drawn from a model linking signaler quality to the costs and benefits of the signal, anticipating the timing of changing levels of costly display. In the model, signaling strategies specific to indi-viduals in different circumstances (e.g. gender, status, and household composition) should vary in amounts (discard rates) and types of costly display (fashionable buttons versus refined ceramics) with changes in audience composition (peaks in plantation market diversification) and social position within a given plantation. The results give fine-grained insight into the contexts that structured consumption strategies that served to maintain social relationships of exchange in spite of the precarious environment.

Conclusion

Human behavioral ecology is concerned with exploring the socio-ecology of individual agents and the dynamic contexts that define the cost and benefits that they encounter. While it shares a common Darwinian heritage with other evolutionary schools of thought in archaeology, it differs from them in its attention to the material correlates of individual decision making and a defining interest in functional questions about behavior. With its focus on the individual as the fundamental nexus of human relations, and a concern with complex behavioral strategies that underlie artifact patterns, it has much in common with agency-based approaches in archaeology. It differs from these especially in its use of formal models to generate theoretically situated hypotheses about potentially observable phenomena. While constraining in some ways, the use of such models provides clarity of tests and a catalyst for new types of questions and theorizing. But operationalizing these models requires actualistic data – experimental and/or ethnographic work designed to supply values for the models' parameters and contextualize their utility. To the extent that it does this, HBE stands to contribute significantly to both social and evolutionary theory by identifying new directions for testing and refining theoretically based explanations of complex behaviors and their archaeological correlates.

References

Alcorta, C.S. and R. Sosis 2005. Ritual, emotion, and sacred symbols. *Human Nature* 16: 323–59.

Bamforth, D.B. 2002. Evidence and metaphor in evolutionary archaeology. *American Antiquity* 67: 435–52.

Barker, G., H. Barton, M. Bird, P. Daly, D. Ipoi, A. Dykes, et al. 2007. The "human revolution" in lowland tropical Southeast Asia: the antiquity and behavior of anatomically modern humans at Niah Cave (Sarawak, Borneo). *Journal of Human Evolution* 52: 243–61.

Barrett, J. C. 2001. Agency, the duality of structure, and the problem of the archaeological record. In I. Hodder (ed.), *Archaeological Theory Today*, 1st edition, 141–64. Cambridge: Polity.

Bayham, F. E. 1979. Factors influencing the Archaic pattern of animal exploitation. *Kiva* 44: 219–35.

Bettinger, R. L. 2006. Agriculture, archaeology, and human behavioral ecology. In D. J. Kennett and B. Winterhalder (eds), *Behavioral Ecology and the Transition to Agriculture*, 304–22. Berkeley: University of California Press.

Bettinger, R. L. 2009. *Hunter-Gatherer Foraging: Five Simple Models*. New York: Elliot Werner Publishing.

Bettinger, R. L. and M. A. Baumhoff 1982. The Numic spread: Great Basin cultures in competition. *American Antiquity* 47: 485–503.

Bettinger, R. L., R. Mahli and H. McCarthy 1997. Central place models of acorn and mussel processing. *Journal of Archaeological Science* 24: 887–99.

Binford, L. R. 1977. Forty-seven trips: a case study in the character of archaeological formation processes. In R. V. S. Wright (ed.), *Stone Tools as Cultural Markers*, 24–36. Canberra: Australian Institute of Aboriginal Studies.

Bird, D. W. and R. Bliege Bird 1997. Contemporary shellfish gathering strategies among the Meriam of the Torres Strait Islands, Australia: testing predictions of a central place foraging model. *Journal of Archaeological Science* 24: 39–63.

Bird, D. W. and R. Bliege Bird 2000. The ethnoarchaeology of juvenile foraging: shellfishing strategies among Meriam children. *Journal of Anthropological Archaeology* 19: 461–76.

Bird, D. W. and R. Bliege Bird 2002. Children on the reef: slow learning or strategic foraging? *Human Nature* 13: 269–98.

Bird, D. W. and R. Bliege Bird 2010. Competing to be leaderless: food sharing and magnanimity among Martu Aborigines. In J. Kanter, K. Vahn, and J. Earkins (eds), *The Evolution of Leadership: Transitions in Decision Making from Small-Scale to Middle-Range Societies*, 21–49. Santa Fe, NM: SAR Press.

Bird, D. W. and J. F. O'Connell 2006. Behavioral ecology and archaeology. *Journal of Archaeological Research* 14: 143–88.

Bird, D. W., J. L. Richardson, P. M. Veth, and A. J. Barham 2002. Explaining shellfish variability in middens on the Meriam Islands, Torres Strait, Australia. *Journal of Archaeological Science* 29: 457–69.

Bird, D. W., R. Bliege Bird, and J. L. Richardson 2004. Meriam ethnoarchaeology: shellfishing and shellmiddens. *Memoirs of the Queensland Museum, Cultural Heritage Series* 3: 183–97.

Bird, D.W., R. Bliege Bird, and B.F. Codding 2009. In pursuit of mobile prey: Martu hunting strategies and archaeofaunal interpretation. *American Antiquity* 74: 3–29.

Bliege Bird, R. and D.W. Bird 2002. Constraints of knowing or constraints on growing? Fishing and collecting among the children of Mer. *Human Nature* 13: 239–68.

Bliege Bird, R. and D.W. Bird 2008. Why women hunt: risk and contemporary foraging in a Western Desert Aboriginal community. *Current Anthropology* 49: 655–93.

Bliege Bird, R. and E.A. Smith 2005. Signaling theory, strategic interaction, and symbolic capital. *Current Anthropology* 46: 221–48.

Bliege Bird, R., E.A. Smith, and D.W. Bird 2001. The hunting handicap: costly signaling in male foraging strategies. *Behavioral Ecology and Sociobiology* 50: 9–19.

Bliege Bird, R., D.W. Bird, B.F. Codding, C. Parker, and J.H. Jones 2008. The "fire stick farming" hypothesis: Australian Aboriginal foraging strategies, biodiversity and anthropogenic fire mosaics. *Proceedings of the National Academy of Sciences* 105: 14796–801.

Bliege Bird, R., B.F. Codding, and D.W. Bird 2009. What explains differences in men's and women's production? Determinants of gendered foraging inequalities among Martu. *Human Nature* 20: 105–29.

Boone, J.L. 2000. Status signaling, social power, and lineage survival. In M.W. Diehl (ed.), *Hierarchies in Action: Cui Bono?* Occasional Papers 27, Center for Archaeological Investigations, 267–90. Carbondale: Southern Illinois University Press.

Boone, J.L., and E.A. Smith 1998. Is it evolution yet? A critique of evolutionary archaeology. *Current Anthropology* 39: 141–73.

Botkin, S. (1980). Effects of human exploitation on shellfish populations at Malibu Creek, California. In T. Earle and A.L. Christenson (eds), *Modeling Change in Prehistoric Subsistence Economies*, 121–39. New York: Academic Press.

Bourdieu, P. 1977. *Outline of a Theory of Practice.* Cambridge: Cambridge University Press.

Boyd, R. and P.J. Richerson 1985. *Culture and the Evolutionary Process.* Chicago: University of Chicago Press.

Broughton, J.M. 2002. Prey spatial structure and behavior affect archaeological tests of optimal foraging models: Examples from the Emeryville Shellmound vertebrate fauna. *World Archaeology* 34: 60–83.

Broughton, J.M. and F.E. Bayham 2003. Showing off, foraging models and the ascendance of large game hunting in the California Middle Archaic. *American Antiquity* 68: 783–9.

Broughton, J.M. and M.D. Cannon (eds) 2010. *Evolutionary Ecology and Archaeology: Applications to Problems in Human Evolution and Prehistory.* Salt Lake City: University of Utah Press.

Broughton, J.M., D.A. Byers, R.A. Bryson, W. Eckerle, and D.B. Madsen 2008. Did climatic seasonality control late Quaternary artiodactyl densities in western North America? *Quaternary Science Reviews* 27: 1916–37.

Charnov, E.L. (1976). Optimal foraging, the marginal value theorem. *Theoretical Population Biology* 9: 367–90.

Codding, B.F. and T.L. Jones 2010. Levels of explanation in behavioral ecology: understanding seeming paradoxical behavior along the Central California Coast. *California Archaeology* 2: 77–91.

Codding, B.F., D.W. Bird, and R. Bliege Bird 2010. Interpreting abundance indices: some zooarchaeological implications of Martu foraging. *Journal of Archaeological Science* 37: 3200–10.

Codding, B.F., R. Bliege Bird, and D.W. Bird 2011. Provisioning offspring and others: risk–energy trade-offs and gender differences in hunter-gatherer foraging strategies. *Proceedings of the Royal Society B* 278: 2502–9.

Cook, K. and E. Rice 2006. Social exchange theory. In J. DeLamater (ed.), *Handbook of Social Psychology*, 53–76. New York: Springer.

Cuthill, I.C. 2005. The study of function in behavioural ecology. *Animal Biology* 55: 399–417.

de Boer, W.F. 2000. *Between the Tides: The Impact of Human Exploitation on an Intertidal Ecosystem, Mozambique*. Veenendaal, The Netherlands: Universal Press.

Dobres, M.A. and J. Robb (eds) 2000. *Agency in Archaeology*. London: Routledge.

Dunnell, R.C. 1980. Evolutionary theory and archaeology. *Advances in Archaeological Method and Theory* 3: 35–99.

Edwards, D.A. and J.F. O'Connell 1995. Broad spectrum diets in arid Australia. *Antiquity* 69: 769–83.

Galle, J.E. 2010. Costly signaling and gendered social strategies among slaves in the eighteenth-century Chesapeake: an archaeological perspective. *American Antiquity* 75: 19–43.

Giddens, A. 1984. *The Constitution of Society*. Cambridge: Polity.

Grafen, A. 1984. Natural selection, kin selection and group selection. In J.H. Krebs and E.B. Davies (eds), *Behavioral Ecology: An Evolutionary Approach*, 2nd edition, 62–84. Oxford: Blackwell Scientific.

Grafen, A. 1990. Biological signals as handicaps. *Journal of Theoretical Biology* 144: 517–46.

Hawkes, K. 1993. Why hunter-gatherers work: an ancient version of the problem of public goods. *Current Anthropology* 34: 341–61.

Hawkes, K. and R. Bliege Bird 2002. Showing off, handicap signaling, and the evolution of men's work. *Evolutionary Anthropology* 11: 58–67.

Hawkes, K., K. Hill, and J.F. O'Connell 1982. Why hunters gather: optimal foraging and the Ache of eastern Paraguay. *American Ethnologist* 9: 379–98.

Hawkes, K., J. F O'Connell, and N. G. Blurton Jones 1991. Hunting income patterns among the Hadza: big game, common goods, foraging goals, and the evolution of the human diet. *Philosophical Transactions of the Royal Society, London, series B* 334: 243–51.

Henrich, J. 2004. Cultural group selection, coevolutionary processes and large-scale cooperation. *Journal of Economic Behavior and Organization* 53: 3–35.

Henry, A. G., A. Brooks, and D. R. Piperno 2011. Microfossils in calculus demonstrate consumption of plants and cooked foods in Neanderthal diets (Shanidar III, Iraq; Spy I and II, Belgium). *Proceedings of the National Academy of the Sciences* 108: 5209–14.

Henshilwood, C. S. and C. W. Marean 2003. The origin of modern human behavior: critique of the models and their test implications. *Current Anthropology* 44: 625–52.

Hildebrandt, W. R. and K. R. McGuire 2003. Large game hunting, gender-differentiated work organization and the role of evolutionary ecology in California and Great Basin prehistory. *American Antiquity* 68: 790–2.

Hildebrandt, W. R., J. Rosenthal, and G. Gmoser 2009. Shellfish transport, caloric return rates, and prehistoric feasting on the Laguna De Santa Rosa, Alta California. *California Archaeology* 1: 55–78.

Hodder, I. 1982. *Symbols in Action*. Cambridge: Cambridge University Press.

Jochim, M. A. 1976. *Hunter-Gatherer Subsistence and Settlement: A Predictive Model*. New York: Academic Press.

Johnstone, R. A. 1997. The evolution of animal signals. In J. R. Krebs and N. B. Davies (eds), *Behavioural Ecology: An Evolutionary Approach*, 155–78. Oxford: Blackwell.

Jones, T. L. and J. R. Richman 1995. On mussels: *Mytilus californicus* as a prehistoric resource. *North American Archaeologist* 16: 33–58.

Jones, T. L., J. F. Porcasi, J. M. Erlandson, H. Dallas, Jr., T. A. Wake, and R. Schwaderer 2008. The protracted Holocene extinction of California's flightless sea duck (*Chendytes lawi*) and its implications for the Pleistocene overkill hypothesis. *Proceedings of the National Academy of Sciences* 105: 4105–8.

Kelly, R. L. 2000. Elements of a behavioral ecological paradigm for the study of prehistoric hunter-gatherers. In M. B. Schiffer (ed.), *Social Theory in Archaeology*, 63–78. Salt Lake City: University of Utah Press.

Kennett, D. J. and B. Winterhalder (eds) 2006. *Human Behavioral Ecology and the Origins of Food Production*. Berkeley: University of California Press.

Klein, R. G. 2004. The Ysterfontein 1 Middle Stone Age site, South Africa, and early human exploitation of coastal resources. *Proceedings of the National Academy of Sciences* 101: 5708–15.

Krebs, J. R. and N. B. Davies (eds) 1997. *Behavioral Ecology: An Evolutionary Approach*, 4th edition. Oxford: Blackwell Scientific.

Kristiansen, K. 2004. Genes versus agents: a discussion of the widening theoretical gap in archaeology. *Archaeological Dialogues* 11: 77–9.

Lévi-Strauss, C. 1969. *The Elementary Structures of Kinship*. Boston: Beacon Press.

Lupo, K. D. 2007. Evolutionary foraging models in zooarchaeological analysis: recent applications and future challenges. *Journal of Archaeological Research* 15: 143–89.

Lyman, R. L. 2003. Pinneped behavior, foraging theory and the depression of metapopulations and nondepression of a local population on the southern Northwest Coast of North America. *Journal of Anthropological Archaeology* 22: 376–88.

Lyman, R. L. and M. J. O'Brien 1998. The goals of evolutionary anthropology: history and explanation. *Current Anthropology* 39: 615–52.

McGuire, K. R. and W. R. Hildebrandt 2005. Re-thinking Great Basin foragers: prestige hunting and costly signaling during the Middle Archaic Period. *American Antiquity* 70: 695–712.

Mauss, M. 1924. *The Gift*. New York: Free Press.

Meehan, B. 1982. *Shell Bed to Shell Midden*. Canberra: Australian Institute of Aboriginal Studies

Mesoudi, A. and M. J. O'Brien 2009. Placing archaeology within a unified science of cultural evolution. In S. J. Shennan (ed.), *Pattern and Process in Cultural Evolution*, 21–32. Berkeley: University of California Press.

Metcalfe, D. and K. R. Barlow 1992. A model for exploring the optimal tradeoff between field processing and transport. *American Anthropologist* 94: 340–56.

Molm, L. D., J. L. Collett, and D. R. Schaefer 2007. Building solidarity through generalized exchange: a theory of reciprocity. *The American Journal of Sociology* 113: 205–42.

Neiman, F. 1997. Conspicuous consumption as wasteful advertising: a Darwinian perspective on spatial patterns in Classic Maya terminal monument dates. In C. M. Barton and G. A. Clark (eds), *Rediscovering Darwin: Evolutionary Theory in Archaeological Explanation*, 267–90. Archaeological Papers of the American Anthropological Association, No. 7, Washington, DC.

O'Connell, J. F. 1995. Ethnoarchaeology needs a general theory of behavior. *Journal of Archaeological Research* 3: 205–55.

O'Connell, J. F. and K. Hawkes 1981. Alyawara plant use and optimal foraging theory. In B. Winterhalder and E. A. Smith (eds), *Hunter-Gatherer Foraging Strategies: Ethnographic and Archaeological Analyses*, 99–125. Chicago: University of Chicago Press.

O'Connell, J. F., K. Hawkes and N. G. Blurton Jones 1988. Hadza scavenging: implications for Plio/Pleistocene hominid subsistence. *Current Anthropology* 29: 356–63.

O'Connell, J. F., J. Allen, and K. Hawkes 2010. Pleistocene Sahul and the orgins of seafaring. In A. Anderson, J. Barrett, and K. Boyle (eds), *The Global Origins and Development of Seafaring*, 57–68. Cambridge: McDonald Institute for Archaeological Research.

Pauketat, T. 2007. *Chiefdoms and Other Archaeological Delusions*. Plymouth, UK: AltaMira Press.

Raab, L. M. and A. C. Goodyear 1984. Middle-range theory in archaeology: a critical review of origins and applications. *American Antiquity* 49: 255–68.

Richerson, P. J., R. Boyd, and B. Bettinger 2001. Was agriculture impossible during the Pleistocene but mandatory during the Holocene? A climate change hypothesis. *American Antiquity* 66: 387–411.

Roscoe, P. 2009. Social signaling and the organization of small-scale society: the case of contact-era New Guinea. *Journal of Archaeological Method and Theory* 6: 69–116.

Sahlins, M. 1965. On the sociology of primitive exchange. In M. Banton (ed.), *The Relevance of Models for Social Anthropology*, 139–236. ASA Monographs 1. London: Tavistock.

Shennan, S. 2004. An evolutionary perspective on agency in archaeology. In A. Gardener (ed.), *Agency Uncovered: Archaeological Perspectives on Social Agency, Power, and Being Human*, 19–32. London: University College London.

Shennan, S. 2008. Evolution in archaeology. *Annual Review of Anthropology* 37: 75–91.

Smith, E. A. 1991. *Inujjuamiut Foraging Strategies: Evolutionary Ecology of an Arctic Hunting Economy*, Hawthorne, NY: Aldine de Gruyter.

Smith, E. A. and B. Winterhalder 1992. Natural selection and decision-making: some fundamental principles. In E. A. Smith and B. Winterhalder (eds), *Evolutionary Ecology and Human Behavior*, 25–60. Hawthorne, NY: Aldine de Gruyter.

Sosis R. and C. Alcorta 2003. Signaling, solidarity, and the sacred: the evolution of religious behavior. *Evolutionary Anthropology* 12: 264–74.

Stephens, D. W. 2008. Decision ecology: foraging and the ecology of animal decision making. *Cognitive, Affective, and Behavioral Neuroscience* 8: 475–84.

Stephens, D. W. and J. R. Krebs 1986. *Foraging Theory*. Princeton: Princeton University Press.

Steward, J. H. (1955) The Great Basin Soshonean Indians: an example of a family level of sociocultural integration. *Theory of Culture Change: The*

Methodology of Multilinear Evolution, 101–21. Urbana: University of Illinois Press.

Stiner, M.C. 2001. Thirty years on the "broad spectrum revolution" and paleolithic demography. *Proceedings of the National Academy of Sciences* 98: 6993–6.

Stiner, M.C., N.D. Munro, and T.A. Survoell 2000. The tortoise and the hare: small-game use, the broad-spectrum revolution, and paleolithic demography. *Current Anthropology* 41: 39–73.

Stutz, A.J., N.D. Munro, and G. Bar-Oz 2009. Increasing the resolution of the broad spectrum revolution in the Southern Levantine Epipaleolithic (19–12 ka). *Journal of Human Evolution* 56: 294–306.

Thomas, D.H. 2008. *Native American Landscapes of St Catherine's Island, Georgia: I. The Theoretical Framework*. Anthropological Papers, No. 88. American Museum of Natural History, New York.

Thomas, F.R., 2007. The behavioral ecology of shellfish gathering in Western Kiribati, Micronesia 1: prey choice. *Human Ecology* 35: 179–94.

Tinbergen, N. 1963. On aims and methods of ethology. *Zeitschrift für Tierpsychologie* 20: 404–33.

Veblen, T. 1899. *The Theory of the Leisure Class*, 1992 edition, C.W. Mills (ed.). New Brunswick, NJ: Transaction Publishers.

Williams, G.C. 1966. *Adaptation and Natural Selection: A Critique of Some Current Evolutionary Thought*. Princeton: Princeton University Press.

Winterhalder, B. 1981. Foraging strategies in the boreal forest: an analysis of Cree hunting and gathering. In B. Winterhalder and E.A. Smith (eds), *Hunter-Gatherer Foraging Strategies: Ethnographic and Archaeological Analyses*, 66–98. Chicago: University of Chicago Press.

Zahavi, A. and A. Zahavi 1997. *The Handicap Principle: A Missing Piece of Darwin's Puzzle*. Oxford: Oxford University Press.

4

BEHAVIORAL ARCHAEOLOGY

Vincent M. LaMotta

The goal of this chapter is to present a synthesis of the various strands of archaeological method and theory that make up the core of behavioral archaeology. I write from the perspective of a "dirt archaeologist" who struggles to make sense of the archaeological record in order to say something meaningful about the human past, and this chapter is geared especially towards those who do the same. This is not to say that behavioral archaeology, as a social science, is concerned solely with the past, or with the archaeological record, as such. However, where behavioral archaeology *is* concerned with such matters, it provides archaeologists with a powerful vehicle for constructing and evaluating knowledge about the human past from material remains. In this capacity, behavioral archaeology offers the potential to unify a discipline that has become increasingly fragmented, in terms of its goals and theoretical perspectives on the past, over the last half-century.

What is *behavioral archaeology*? Behavioral archaeology is a particular way of viewing the world – it is a way of conceptualizing relationships among people, places, and things, and it is a set of tools for exploring those relationships. It furnishes a lens for viewing the archaeological record, and a means for understanding the processes that created that record, as a way to know the human past.

The behavioral program originally developed as an outgrowth of Americanist processual archaeology of the 1960s and early 1970s (Reid and Whittlesey 2005; Reid et al. 1974, 1975; Schiffer 1972, 1975a, 1975b, 1976). In the four decades or so since behavioral archaeology's initial formulation, core method and theory have undergone continuous expansion and refinement (e.g. Hollenback and Schiffer 2010; LaMotta 2001; LaMotta and Schiffer 1999, 2001; Rathje and Schiffer 1982; Schiffer 1987, 1992, 1995, 2010, 2011; Schiffer and LaMotta 2007; Schiffer and Miller 1999; Skibo and Schiffer 2008; Skibo et al. 1995; Walker 1999, 2001, 2002; Walker and Schiffer 2006; Zedeño 2000). The version of behavioral archaeology presented in this chapter represents yet another step in this process. I have attempted to produce a synthesis that, while expanding upon and revising certain elements of the behavioral toolkit, emphasizes the essential theoretical and methodological frameworks that have been developed within behavioral archaeology for understanding the archaeological record and the human past.

At the same time, I have also attempted to call attention to the need for a shift in our conceptions of the archaeological record and of its formation processes, if we are to better understand archaeological variability and what it signifies about the human past. In particular, I suggest that archaeologists should embrace the notion that the archaeological record is created instrumentally through depositional behaviors and other cultural formation processes, and that the field would benefit from the development of appropriate method and theory for understanding such processes, and their material manifestations, within a broadly anthropological frame of reference: that is, a frame of reference that situates these processes within their social and cultural contexts, and explicitly theorizes the social, political, economic, and ideological entailments of variability in their constituent behaviors. In doing so, I contend that archaeologists should engage in a conscious evaluation of the information potential of the archaeological record in specific research contexts, and retool questions about the past, where necessary, to better fit the realities of that record.

Goals of behavioral archaeology

In the seminal publications that established behavioral archaeology as a field of inquiry, Reid and colleagues (Reid et al. 1974, 1975) defined archaeology's subject matter as "the relationships between human behavior and material culture in all times and places" (Schiffer 1976: 4). The goals of behavioral archaeology, as laid out in these early publications, and as elaborated in more recent works, all stem from this basic definition.

Behavioral archaeologists today define behavior, as an analytical category, as *the interaction of people and objects* (Walker et al. 1995: 5; see also LaMotta and Schiffer 2001: 20; Schiffer 2010: 13–15; Schiffer and Miller 1999: chapter 2). This conception of behavior distinguishes behavioral archaeology from other social and behavioral sciences, and operationalizes behavior in a way that is conducive to archaeological analysis. The term *object*, in this context, refers to any portable or non-portable elements of the material world, including artifacts, ecofacts, sediments, features, and places. In defining behavior in terms of people–object interactions, we emphasize that behavior is not to be envisioned simply as the organism in action (Walker et al. 1995: 5–8). Rather, we conceive of behavior as including three components – *people*, *objects*, and *interaction*. The analytical choice to include objects as well as people in the definition of behavior serves a dual purpose. On the one hand, it highlights the fact that material objects are of central importance in human behavior and social life, and thus it opens up diverse aspects of the human experience to archaeological analysis. On the other hand, in focusing on the interaction *between* people and objects, this perspective frees the researcher from simplistic notions which alternately locate the impetus for behavior entirely within the human actor (behavior arising from mental states), or as coming entirely from outside (behavior as response to environmental stimuli) (LaMotta and Schiffer 2001: 20; Walker et al. 1995: 5–8).

The practice of behavioral archaeology can be divided into three major research domains (after Reid 1995: 15): understanding the formation processes of the archaeological record (e.g. Schiffer 1976: chapter 3, 1983, 1987); reconstructing behavior through inference, in contexts where behavior is not directly observable (i.e. in the archaeological record) (e.g. Schiffer 1976: chapter 2, 2010: chapter 3); and explaining behavior and behavioral change (e.g. LaMotta and Schiffer 2001; Schiffer 1979). These research domains are discussed below, beginning with the last.

Behavioral archaeology seeks to explain behavioral variability and change at various scales, and in both generalizing and particularistic frames of reference (LaMotta and Schiffer 2001; Reid et al. 1975; Schiffer 1975a). Importantly, explanation focuses on people–object interactions at the core of a behavioral process, rather than reducing behavior's status to that of a dependent variable, or treating behavior as a function of some superordinate phenomenon or process. Given the complex nature of social phenomena, and the incremental process of archaeological analysis, not to mention the multiplicity of possible perspectives on a given issue, explanation is best considered as a long-term goal. What behavioral archaeologists strive to do, in the interim, is to build ever-more sophisticated understandings of how particular behavioral processes work, and why they change (e.g. Schiffer 2005, 2010, 2011).

Behavioral archaeology encompasses generalizing *and* particularistic approaches to the study of human behavior, and the program strives to cultivate both. In the generalizing mode, behavioral archaeologists develop what may be referred to as *behavioral generalizations* – principles that describe "how behavior works," given certain antecedent and boundary conditions. Behavioral generalizations include *nomothetic principles* and *historical principles* (cf. Reid 1985: 13): nomothetic principles have no temporal or spatial parameters, whereas historical principles (also called empirical generalizations) are circumscribed within specific spatio-temporal parameters. Any such principles of behavior are best considered as provisional and hypothetical, open to continuous testing and refinement. To date, much research in behavioral archaeology has focused on the development of nomothetic principles. Generally speaking, these are not *universal* principles of behavior, but principles that operate wherever and whenever the specified boundary conditions are met (LaMotta and Schiffer 2001; see Schiffer 2010: chapter 2 for discussion).

In the particularistic mode, behavioral archaeologists are committed to understanding specific cases of behavior or behavioral change. Much of the work that is carried out under the umbrella of behavioral archaeology is at least partly directed towards answering particularistic questions – for example, understanding how a particular archaeological context formed, explaining behavioral change during a certain era, reconstructing the histories of particular communities, or explicating the developmental trajectories of specific technologies (e.g. Reid 1973; Reid and Whittlesey 2005; Schiffer 1976, 1991, 2008a, 2008b; Schiffer and Skibo 1987; Schiffer et al. 1994, 2003; Walker et al. 2000; Whittlesey 1978). While behavioral archaeologists may draw upon nomothetic and historical principles to understand behavior in such specific cases, they also recognize that historically contingent factors and circumstances not easily subsumed under existing behavioral generalizations may play a principal role in the unfolding of a particular behavioral process. The complex nature of actual behavioral processes, compounded by their embeddedness within a field of political relations, typically precludes simple explanations.

Generalizing and particularistic approaches in behavioral archaeology are in fact complementary. Research on specific prehistoric or historical cases provides the raw material for developing and testing behavioral generalizations. Such generalizations, in turn, play an important role in the interpretation of behavior and its material consequences in particular cases. That role is something akin to supplying a null hypothesis: a behavioral generalization specifies how we *think* behavior works, within certain boundary conditions. If a particular case conforms to expectations derived from the generalization (i.e. we fail to falsify the null hypothesis), then we have provisionally accounted for some aspect of that case. If expectations are not met, then one or more assumptions about some aspect of the case are incorrect (or the generalization itself is flawed). The latter outcome ostensibly tells us something we didn't know about the case (or about the generalization), and directs our inquiry in a new direction. Thus, the goal is *not* to develop a "laundry list" of behavioral generalizations that purports to explain all human behavior. Rather, it is to formulate generalizations that codify our assumptions and our provisional knowledge about behavior, as tools for determining if, and to what extent, specific instances of past behavior deviate from our expectations (cf. Gould's [1980: 138–41] concept of *argument by anomaly*). Behavioral generalizations, in this sense, can be understood as tools for exploring and understanding specific episodes of human action.

Behavioral archaeology differs from other schools of archaeology in that its research questions and its perspectives on human behavior and human social life are not governed by a single, pre-existing body of high-level theory (LaMotta and Schiffer 2001: 19; Schiffer 2010: 3). Rather, it is a goal of the program to develop its own body of uniquely archaeological and distinctively behavioral theory, written in terms of people–object interactions, and forged over the long term through a continuous dialectic between hypothesis and observation; between provisionally defined behavioral generalizations and specific prehistoric and historical cases. Behavioral archaeologists are simply not willing to assume, a priori, that any particular body of theory developed outside of archaeology is necessarily adequate for making sense of archaeological data, which have a unique character, and which are generally beyond the purview of other social sciences.

It is a goal of behavioral archaeology, instead, to build theory that is attentive to the distinctive character of archaeological data (cf. Shott 1998). Behavioral archaeologists therefore attach great importance to understanding the nature of the archaeological record, as the source of archaeological data. We recognize that the nature of the archaeological record does, in fact, impose certain conditions and constraints on how we go about creating knowledge of the human past, and what we can ultimately say about the past. First, past behavior cannot be observed directly in the archaeological record, but must be inferred or reconstructed from surviving material remains (through *traces*, discussed below). Second, the archaeological record is formed through various processes, and how it is formed determines what we can say about it and about the past. The archaeological record is also not strictly speaking a static entity – it may undergo modification through cultural and non-cultural processes up until the time it is subject to archaeological recovery, and this also affects the information that can be gleaned from it. Finally, since the archaeological record is a product of human behavior (non-cultural processes aside), statements about any and all aspects of the human past based on that record must ultimately be grounded in inferences about people–object interactions. Behavioral archaeologists seek, therefore, to understand and partition variability in the archaeological record, and do so primarily through the study of traces and through the study of archaeological formation processes (e.g. LaMotta and Schiffer 1999; Reid 1985; Schiffer 1972, 1983, 1987, 2010: chapters 3–6; Schiffer and LaMotta 2007; Sullivan 1978).

A trace is material evidence that a particular interaction (e.g. behavior) has occurred – it is an alteration in the form and/or context of objects and object assemblages that transmits information about the past to the present (after Rathje and Schiffer 1982: 64–5; Schiffer 1987: 15; Sullivan 1978: 191–5). When human behavior is defined in terms of people–object interactions, it follows that all behaviors potentially leave a trace. However, a particular behavior may not leave a very specific or diagnostic trace. Likewise, a trace may be ephemeral, disappearing soon after a particular interaction has occurred. In other cases, a trace may endure for a lengthy period. The archaeological record can be conceived as an aggregate of traces of past human behavior that have endured into the present, albeit with possible modification by natural processes (e.g. post-depositional disturbance by animals, decay). If traces in the archaeological record are both adequately preserved and sufficiently diagnostic, and the archaeologist has the tools to properly describe and interpret them, then important insights potentially can be gained into past human behavior and social life, through the process of inference. One of behavioral archaeology's most important goals, therefore, is to develop method and theory for discerning and interpreting traces of human behavior in the archaeological record. This includes determining how traces are related to specific behaviors, understanding how traces are incorporated into the archaeological record, and assessing how traces are potentially modified by post-depositional processes.

Along these lines, behavioral archaeology is perhaps best known as the school of archaeology that has most thoroughly investigated the formation processes of the archaeological record. Beginning with Schiffer's foundational work on formation processes (Schiffer 1972, 1975b, 1976, 1983, 1987), it has been a goal of the behavioral program to develop a detailed understanding of the processes by which cultural materials exit systemic context (i.e. the realm of human activities) and enter the archaeological record, and of the post-depositional processes that can subsequently modify such materials (e.g. LaMotta 2001; LaMotta and Schiffer 1999, 2001: 40–7, 2005; Montgomery 1992, 1993; Montgomery and Reid 1990; Reid 1973, 1985; Schiffer and LaMotta 2007; Seymour and Schiffer 1987; Walker 1995, 2002; Walker et al. 2000). Formation processes are classified as cultural or non-cultural, according to the agent responsible. For present purposes, cultural formation processes can be divided into two broad families: *cultural deposition* and *cultural disturbance*. Cultural deposition refers to human activities that cause cultural materials to enter the archaeological record – for example, through discard, loss, or abandonment. Cultural disturbance refers to post-depositional modification of archaeological materials by human agents, as when people reclaim or redeposit archaeological objects. Non-cultural formation processes, in contrast, include physical, chemical, and biological processes that either cause cultural materials to enter the archaeological record (e.g. volcanic eruption, landslide), or modify deposited materials (e.g. disturbance by animals, decay) (see, e.g., Wood and Johnson 1978). The study of archaeological formation processes is accorded high priority in behavioral archaeology because such processes determine, to a significant extent, the information potential of the archaeological record in specific research contexts.

Formation processes can introduce traces of human behavior into the archaeological record, but they can also modify or obliterate traces, and introduce spurious patterns. Behavioral archaeologists are therefore interested in documenting different types of formation processes, the kinds of contexts in which they occur, and their impacts on the archaeological record. Ethnoarchaeological studies (e.g. Binford 1978; Cameron and Tomka 1993; Hayden and Cannon 1983) and experimental research (e.g. Nielsen 1991) have contributed to our knowledge of such processes, yet much remains to be learned.

One of the principal goals of behavioral archaeology is to account for variation in the archaeological record. Much of that variation is the product of archaeological formation processes. In the past, the negative, pattern-destroying aspect of formation processes has rightly been emphasized, and researchers must certainly take such processes into account when constructing inferences about the past (Reid 1985, 1995; Schiffer 1976, 1983, 1985, 1987; cf. Binford 1981). However, we also emphasize that much can be learned about human societies through the study of cultural formation processes (LaMotta and Schiffer 2001: 40–7; Tani 1995). The various processes by which objects, architectural spaces, and settlements enter an archaeological context, and the processes by which anthropogenic deposits are formed, are anthropologically interesting in their own right, and archaeologists would do well to study their sources of variation (e.g. Hill 1995; Hodder 1987; Inomata and Webb 2003; McAnany and Hodder 2009). How, and to what extent, are such processes embedded in politics, power relations, gender and ethnic identities, religious practices, and economic systems? Archaeologists working in the North American Southwest, for example, have begun to explore the possibility that variation in abandonment and post-abandonment deposition in houses and other architectural spaces in ancient Southwestern villages can provide a window into socially meaningful events and processes: some studies point to evidence for traditional religious practices associated with the abandonment or "closure" of particular kinds of spaces, while some also highlight the impact that specific events, such as the dispatching of an accused witch, might have on the structure of deposits in a particular context (e.g. LaMotta 1996; Montgomery 1992, 1993; Montgomery and Reid 1990; Seymour and Schiffer 1987; Walker 1996, 1998; Walker et al. 2000; Walker and Lucero 2000; Wilshusen 1986, 1988). Further research into patterns of cultural deposition and cultural disturbance – both as traditional cultural practices and as context-specific expressions of agency – will undoubtedly yield new and exciting insights. Since cultural formation processes account for a significant portion of the material patterning encoded in the archaeological record, it only makes sense that archaeologists should attempt to learn as much as possible about past societies through the lens of such processes.

This section has summarized the major goals of behavioral archaeology, with particular emphasis on those aspects of the behavioral program that deal with the study of the human past. In the next section, I describe some of the conceptual frameworks and methodological tools that have been developed for studying the human past through the medium of the archaeological record. Much of this discussion revolves around the related topics of partitioning and accounting for material variation in the archaeological record.

Behavioral frameworks for studying the past through the archaeological record

The archaeological record can be defined as the entirety of past cultural materials – artifacts, ecofacts, sediments, and features (collectively, *objects*) – that have survived into the present day, but which are no longer actively engaged in a living behavioral system. The archaeological record and its constituent objects vary in a number of physical dimensions, and this variability reflects both traces of past human activities and traces of non-cultural processes that have acted upon the record. The principal dimensions of variability are formal (physical) properties of objects; quantities of objects; disposition of objects in space; and co-occurrence (relational association) of objects (after Rathje and Schiffer 1982: 64–5). Behavioral archaeologists have developed a number of tools for partitioning traces in the archaeological record according to the past activities and processes that created them, and for interpreting those traces; these tools include life history models and behavioral chain analysis.

Life history models

Life history models (see Schiffer 1972, 1975b, 1976: chapter 4, 2010: chapter 3, 2011: chapter 3) describe the behavioral lives of objects, from the procurement of their raw materials, through manufacture and use, to the time they finally enter the archaeological record and are no longer directly involved in human activities. Such models serve two major roles: general life history models provide a framework for understanding material variability in the archaeological record, whereas models of specific object life histories or life history segments, reconstructed from the archaeological record, serve as basic units for exploring and understanding the human past. Following some general comments on the nature of activities and life histories, each of these roles is discussed, in turn, below.

Life history models are grounded in a conception of human societies as networks of linked activities. Activities are defined as specific people–object interactions (behaviors) occurring in particular contexts (e.g. Schiffer and Miller 1999: chapter 2). An activity typically does not occur in isolation, but is linked to other activities through flows of matter, energy, and information (Schiffer 1979). Oftentimes, an object participates in a number of different activities before finally entering the archaeological record – that sequence of activities constitutes its life history. Life history models trace the paths that objects follow (literally or, in the case of immovable objects, metaphorically) through the networks of linked activities which comprise human societies. As an object follows a particular path, traces of activities along that path may be inscribed upon the object, through modification of its formal properties and other dimensions of variability (Schiffer 1987: chapter 2). At the same time, traces of those activities may also be inscribed upon the archaeological record, through processes of cultural deposition (Schiffer 1975b, 1987: chapter 4). Life history models may even include post-depositional processes and archaeological recovery processes.

General life history models provide a basis for partitioning and interpreting archaeological traces pertaining to a particular type of object. Such models specify the kinds of activities that might have occurred in the life history of that type of object, as well as the usual sequence of those activities. This information may be derived from ethnographic and historical accounts, or other pertinent sources. A general life history may be a composite drawn from multiple particular cases, some of which may be incomplete or represent variant sequences. Constructing such a model is one of the first steps in a behavioral chain analysis (Schiffer 1975b), which provides a framework for predicting the specific form of traces generated in the course of life history activities (more on this below). For example, the archaeologist might construct a general life history model for ceramic cooking vessels as the first step in the process of unraveling the traces observed in an assemblage of cooking ware and related material culture from a particular site.

General life history models direct the archaeologist's attention to the fact that distinct kinds of trace-producing activities may characterize different phases in a particular object's life history. While each individual life history is unique, there is, nonetheless, a certain overarching logic to the general progression of activities (Schiffer 1972, 1987: 13). Thus, it is useful to recognize eight general processes in the life history of an object, each of which is characterized by certain kinds of activities. The processes are procurement, manufacture, use, maintenance, reuse, cultural deposition, reclamation, and recycling (Figure 4.1). Objects need not go through all eight processes (Schiffer 1972). Some life histories may be very short; others may be long and

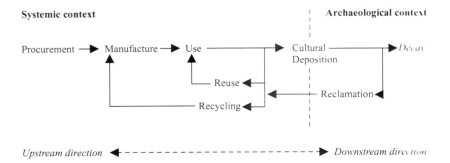

Systemic context   **Archaeological context**

Procurement → Manufacture → Use ────────→ Cultural ──────→ *Decay*
                                           Deposition

                            └── Reuse ◄───
                                          ◄──── Reclamation ◄─
                          Recycling ◄───

Upstream direction ◄ ─────────────────────── ► *Downstream direction*

General Life History Processes
Procurement: acquisition of raw materials necessary to manufacture a particular object
Manufacture: production or assembly of an object from its constituent materials
Use: principal function(s) of an object – the activity or activities for which it was specifically designed or obtained, and in which it was actually used
Maintenance: periodic modification or repair of an object to allow its continued use
Reuse: repurposing of an object, especially after it has become broken or worn
Cultural deposition: processes through which objects leave systemic context and enter the archaeological record, including loss, discard, and abandonment
Loss: accidental deposition of objects
Discard: purposeful disposal of objects, for example in a trash midden
Abandonment: leaving behind of objects and architectural spaces, for example during a residence move
Reclamation: retrieval of objects from the archaeological record, for purposes of using, reusing, or recycling those objects
Recycling: returning of objects to the manufacture stage, breaking them down into raw materials which may be used to manufacture new objects

Figure 4.1. A generalized object life history
Source: Adapted from Schiffer 1976: Figure 4.1.

complicated, involving multiple cycles of reuse, reclamation, and recycling.

The second major role of life history models involves the study of life histories of specific archaeological objects (Walker and LaMotta 1995). Here, the starting point is a specific life history model – a reconstruction or partial reconstruction of the life history of an actual object or group of objects from a particular archaeological context. Such models are based primarily on analysis of material traces inscribed upon the object and its context, although in historical periods written records and other sources may also supply important information. The study of reconstructed object life histories can potentially furnish a unique perspective on the organization, operation, and history of past societies. For example, in the Pueblo Southwest, researchers have been able to distinguish several classes of architectural spaces in ancestral Hopi sites on the basis of patterned differences in their construction, use, and abandonment, as inferred from form, features, and abandonment-related deposits (LaMotta 1996; Walker 1996; Walker and Lucero 2000; Walker et al. 2000). These differences suggest, minimally, a functional distinction between ceremonial and non-ceremonial spaces – a distinction that is reflected in the divergent life histories that these spaces experienced, from construction to abandonment.

One of the enduring difficulties involved in reconstructing specific object life histories is that typically not all activities will be reflected in traces inscribed upon the object and its immediate archaeological context. This may be a matter of non-preservation of traces, or simply failure on the part of the archaeologist to recognize traces of particular activities. In any event, given the limits of reconstruction, the analyst may often have to work with partial life histories. Moreover, some preserved activity traces may appear in sharper focus than others.

Typically, an object's archaeological context most directly reflects the depositional process or processes that caused that object to enter the archaeological record (post-depositional processes notwithstanding). Thus, for portable objects at least, the object's spatial location and association with certain quantities of other objects in its immediate depositional environment most directly reflects the final activity in the object's life history – often a discard or abandonment event, or loss. Under most circumstances, these dimensions of variability do not directly inform on the use of the object or on any other activities located upstream from its point of entry into an archaeological context (Figure 4.1), unless the object and others associated with it happened to enter the archaeological record at the exact location where an activity was performed. For portable objects, archaeologists must often rely on formal properties for evidence of earlier stages in the life history, such as manufacture and use. Researchers have already developed a number of sophisticated techniques for partitioning and interpreting traces manifest as formal properties of objects – for example, use alteration analysis (Keeley 1974, 1980; Skibo 1992) and experimental research on the performance characteristics of objects introduced through choices at the design and manufacture stages (Schiffer 2010: 89–92, 2011; Schiffer and Skibo

1987; Skibo and Schiffer 2008). Nonetheless, our knowledge of upstream activities based on traces inscribed upon the object itself is partial, at best. However, another analytical tool developed by behavioral archaeologists – called behavioral chain analysis – provides a different method for inferring such activities, by modeling their potential depositional signatures, formed through the output of wastes and other residues to an archaeological context. Behavioral chain analysis can complement the study of object life histories by fleshing out certain aspects of an object's life history that are not directly accessible from the object itself and its immediate archaeological context.

Behavioral chain analysis

Whereas the focus of life history models is the object and its pathway through a network of linked activities, in behavioral chain analysis focus shifts to the sequences of functionally linked activities, or behavioral chains, that make up those pathways. Here, the archaeologist is particularly concerned with modeling the material traces that are produced during any and all activities of behavioral chains – especially those activities that act as agents of cultural deposition, and contribute directly to the formation of archaeological deposits (Schiffer 1975b, 1976: chapter 4). In focusing on such activities, behavioral chain analysis provides a means for identifying articulations between sociocultural processes of interest, on the one hand, and processes that directly inscribe material variability upon the archaeological record, on the other.

Behavioral chain analysis is typically initiated to investigate variation in a specific component of the archaeological record, from a particular site or region (e.g. Magers 1975) – for instance, an assemblage of ceramic cooking ware, to continue the example from the previous section. The investigator begins by constructing one or more general life history models for ceramic cooking vessels, using sources of information that are relevant to the particular region and culture, including ethnographic or ethnohistoric accounts, cross-cultural studies, experimental archaeology or ethnoarchaeological research, and previous archaeological research in the region. In the current example, the goal would be to create a specific model of all the linked activities involved in production, use, and disposal of cooking vessels. Obviously, any such model is hypothetical, and in the early stages of research may be rather incomplete – but this is the point. The model behavioral chains constructed by the archaeologist are best considered as elaborate hypotheses. The researcher must evaluate how well these hypotheses explain observed variation in the archaeological record. Where the fit is poor, the model is revised. Ultimately, through repeated cycles of testing, it should be possible for the archaeologist to develop a model that better explains the archaeological record, and which therefore more closely approximates the past behavioral chain(s) that created that record.

A key component of behavioral chain analysis involves modeling various material and behavioral parameters for each activity. This information is arranged in a table (e.g. Table 4.1). For each activity, the relevant parameters include (1) human social units participating in the activity; (2) non-human energy sources; (3) objects brought together for the activity (*conjoined elements*); (4) duration, frequency, and location of activity performance; (5) specific interactions, and modifications to people or objects resulting from interactions; (6) objects or materials leaving the behavioral chain and directly entering the archaeological record (*outputs*), and where exactly those objects or materials are deposited; and (7) objects or materials leaving the behavioral chain and entering a different one (note that this is a somewhat expanded reformulation of Schiffer's [1975b] original model, illustrated in Table 4.1; see also Schiffer 2011: 31). In combination, these parameters serve to operationally define the activity in question, and to offer a set of expectations regarding material traces produced by the activity under various conditions.

There are four basic ways that traces of a particular activity can become inscribed upon the archaeological record. First, the conjoined elements of a particular activity could all be abandoned at the location of activity performance, and remain there until discovered by the archaeologist. In such a scenario, the assemblage of conjoined elements would retain something close to the formal, spatial, relational, and quantitative properties that it exhibited during activity performance. This might happen, for instance, if a site were catastrophically buried in a mudslide or volcanic eruption. Under more typical circumstances, however, behavioral processes such as curation and scavenging tend to militate against objects remaining indefinitely at any particular use location, so the hypothetical scenario described above is rare. Second, conjoined elements could be removed from the location of activity performance and, as a group, enter an archaeological context somewhere else. This would preserve the formal, relational, and quantitative properties of the activity assemblage, but not its location. For example, a particular toolkit might be ritually buried, as in a grave, or placed in a storage context that is subsequently abandoned or forgotten. Third, an activity may generate

Table 4.1 A behavioral chain segment for maize in Hopi subsistence activities (*ca.* AD 1900)

Activity	Energy Sources		Conjoined elements	Time and frequency	Location	Outputs	Intersections	
	Social units	*Non-human*					*Additions*	*Deletions*
Harvest	Able villagers of both sexes[3,4]		Baskets[4]	Several days in September[4]	Fields of h.h.[3,4]	Stalks, wasted or unharvested maize		
Transport	Able villagers of both sexes[3,4]		Baskets, blankets[3,4]	Once in September	From fields to roof of h.h. area	Pollen		
Husk	Women of h.h. and other females[3,4]		Wooden or bone peg[9]	One or several days in September	On roof of h.h. area[3,4]	Pollen		Husks
Dry		Sunlight[4]	Roof of h.h. area[4]	Several days in September	On roof of h.h. area[3,4]	Pollen		
Transport	Women of h.h.		Baskets	Once in September	From h.h. area to storeroom	Occasional kernels, pollen		
Storage			Storeroom[3,4,9]	1 to 100 weeks[?]	Storeroom[3,4,9]	Occasional kernels, pollen		
Transport	Women of h.h.		Baskets	Several mornings weekly	From storeroom to habitation room			

Remove kernels	Women of h.h.[3]	Short stick, yucca basket	Several mornings weekly	Habitation room	Occasional kernels, pollen
Coarse grind	Women of h.h.[1]	Mealing bin, stick, coarse mano and metate, yucca basket[1,2]	Several mornings weekly	Habitation room[1]	Wasted kernels and meal, pollen
Remove chaff	Women of h.h.[1] _(Wind)_	Yucca basket[3]	Several mornings weekly	Outside of structure	Chaff
Medium grind	Women of h.h.[1]	Mealing bin, stick, medium mano and metate, bowl[1,2]	Several mornings weekly	Habitation room[1]	Wasted meal
Fine grind	Women of h.h.[1]	Mealing bin, fine mano and metate, stick, bowl[1,2]	Several mornings weekly	Habitation room[1]	Wasted meal
Transport	Women of h.h.	Bowls[2]	Several mornings weekly	Habitation room to storeroom	Wasted meal
Storage		Bowls[2]	Several days to a week	Storeroom	Wasted meal
Transport	Women of h.h.	Bowls[2]	Twice daily	Storeroom to habitation room	Wasted meal

Cobs

(Continued)

Table 4.1 (Continued)

Activity	Energy Sources — Social units	Non-human	Conjoined elements	Time and frequency	Location	Outputs	Intersections — Additions	Deletions
Make dumplings	Women of h.h.		Cooking jar, bowl	Twice daily	Habitation room	Wasted meal	Water, other ingredients	
Cook		Fire	Juniper twigs, cooking jar, fire pit[6]	Twice daily[3]	Habitation room	Spillage-waste		
Serve	Women of h.h.		Serving bowls, cooking jars, ladles[5]	Twice daily[3]	Habitation room	Spillage-waste		
Eat	Entire h.h.		Bowls[5]	Twice daily[3]	Habitation room	Waste		
Digest/ transport	Entire h.h.			Almost continuously	Location of h.h. members		Other foods	
Defecate/ discard	Entire h.h.		A broad leaf	Once daily	Away from occupied rooms	A broad leaf, residues		

Key: [1] Bartlett 1933   [3] Beaglehole 1937   [5] Turner and Lofgren 1966   h.h. = household
[2] Bartlett 1936   [4] Stephen 1936   [6] Whiting 1939
Source: Adapted from Schiffer 1975b: Figure 2. Used with kind permission of Michael B. Schiffer.

characteristic waste products or residues – material outputs – as a byproduct of its operation. Additionally, there is a certain probability that conjoined elements of an activity will break, wear out, or become lost during activity performance, and join the output stream. Depending on the mode of deposition, such outputs may or may not remain in the location of activity performance, or retain their mutual association (e.g. if waste is segregated), but their formal properties alone may constitute a diagnostic trace of the activity. Fourth, and finally, an activity may cause the formal properties of objects to be modified in a characteristic fashion. This could involve various additive and reductive processes, and range in severity from minor physical alteration to a fundamental physico-chemical transformation. Of course, people participating in an activity may be physically modified in ways that also leave a trace.

Drawing on the provisional material and behavioral parameters specified in a particular behavioral chain model, the archaeologist can proceed to generate a series of expected material traces for various activities along the behavioral chain, under various conditions. Some activities might not be expected to produce any recognizable traces, except under unusual circumstances (e.g. catastrophic burial). At the other extreme, some activities might leave highly diagnostic traces, including formal modifications to objects and characteristic residues output to an archaeological context. The archaeologist would then need to evaluate the fit between predictions of the model and the specific archaeological contexts under examination. If the model does not adequately account for observed variation in the archaeological record, the archaeologist should explore the possibility that one or more parameters of the model are incorrect; that there were additional behavioral processes at work, which the model does not take into account; or that non-cultural processes have influenced patterning in the record.

Behavioral chains provide a model for how a certain sector of a past society worked – how activities were linked together, and how materials flowed through that network. Once a particular behavioral chain model has become reasonably well established, archaeologists can use the model as a guide in designing future research into specific socio-cultural processes of interest. Such a model would provide a useful set of guidelines for where to search for traces related to the phenomenon of interest, as well as expectations regarding what form(s) those traces might take. It would also provide a reasonable assessment of whether or not the process of interest is likely to generate recognizable material traces. If it is not, the model might be able to guide the researcher to potentially linked activity contexts that would be more likely to produce recoverable traces. It then becomes a matter of determining how the process of interest is linked to other activities that actually generate archaeological traces, and what can be said about the former based on the linked activities. This is determined on a case-by-case basis.

Understanding variation in the archaeological record is a major component of behavioral archaeology, but life histories and behavioral chains do not comprise the entire program. In fact, the interpretation of variation in the archaeological record using the tools described above is predicated, in part, on knowledge generated in other sectors of behavioral archaeology. In the final section of this chapter, I outline the various integrated research strategies of behavioral archaeology, with particular emphasis on their utility for exploring and understanding material patterning in the archaeological record.

Frameworks for studying human behavior in the past and in the present

In a pair of brief articles that introduced behavioral archaeology in the early 1970s, Reid and colleagues (Reid et al. 1974, 1975) outlined a research program consisting of four interrelated strategies whose stated aim was "the study of material objects regardless of time or space in order to describe and explain human behavior" (Reid et al. 1975: 864). Through the four strategies of behavioral archaeology (Table 4.2), they sought to highlight an underlying unity in the increasingly diversified activities of archaeologists, which had come

Table 4.2. The four strategies of behavioral archaeology

		Material Objects	
		Past	Present
Human Behavior	Past	1. Prehistoric, historical, and classical archaeologies (idiographic)	2. Ethnoarchaeology and experimental archaeology (nomothetic)
	Present	3. Study of long-term behavioral change (nomothetic)	4. Modern material culture studies (idiographic)

Source: Adapted from Reid et al. 1975: Figure 1; Reid 1995: Figure 2.1.

to include pursuits such as ethnoarchaeology, experimental archaeology, and modern material culture studies, alongside more traditional archaeological research on the past. Reid and colleagues (1975; see also Schiffer 1975a) also sought to dispel the notion that archaeology is necessarily at the mercy of outside disciplines, such as ethnology, for the development of what they called *behavioral laws*. Such laws, they argued, could be developed through archaeological research designed to answer general questions about human behavior and material culture: that is, research operating in a nomothetic mode. Strategies 2 and 3 were conceived as nomothetic strategies, or law producers. Strategy 2, which encompasses ethnoarchaeology and experimental archaeology, crafts general principles through the study of present-day behavior and material culture. Strategy 3, on the other hand, seeks general principles through study of past behavior, as reconstructed from the archaeological record. These were viewed as functionally linked to Strategies 1 and 4, the idiographic strategies, or law consumers, which require generalizations to infer and explain behavior in specific contexts. Strategies 1 and 4, concerned with understanding particular contexts in the human past and in present-day societies, respectively, were also seen as potential sources of general questions to stimulate research in the nomothetic mode. Thus, behavioral archaeology was founded upon a research model that emphasized the mutual interpenetration of generalizing and particularistic research.

The McKellar Principle (Schiffer 1976: 188–9, 1987: 62–3) provides an early example of a behavioral generalization concerning cultural deposition. The principle was originally developed through an undergraduate student's observations of trash on the University of Arizona campus. In general form, it suggests that in regularly maintained activity areas, only smaller items of refuse will be permitted to remain on surfaces where they are dropped during activity performance or as a result of casual discard or loss. Larger items of refuse, on the other hand, will tend to be collected and redeposited elsewhere. The McKellar Principle is especially useful for archaeologists interested in inferring activity-area use from artifacts – all else being equal, it suggests that one is more likely to find evidence for the use of a particular activity surface in small items found on, or embedded within, that surface, rather than in larger objects, which are more likely to have been deposited elsewhere. The McKellar Principle is generally supported by data from ethnoarchaeological research, although as Schiffer (1976: 189, 1987: 63–4) notes, the principle could be further refined through research on factors that condition the size threshold of objects that escape clean-up activities (the original study placed the threshold at four inches in overall dimensions).

Early publications in behavioral archaeology emphasized the potential for an expanded archaeology to develop its own behavioral generalizations, through Strategy 2- and 3-type research, in part to affirm the discipline's independent status among the behavioral sciences. The McKellar Principle is an example of a behavioral generalization that was developed in such a fashion, within a broadly conceived ethnoarchaeological framework (Strategy 2). In practice, however, such generalizations can and do come from various quarters – from outside scholarship, creative speculation, or sudden inspiration. What is more important is that behavioral generalizations, regardless of source, are formulated in terms of people–object interactions, and that they are tested widely against specific cases to establish their general validity and to ascertain their boundary conditions (after Gould 1980: 140–1). Similarly, although early publications emphasized the development of nomothetic principles of behavior, which are not bound to specific time-space contexts, this does not mean that generalizations that apply only in certain times and places are not useful for understanding variability in human behavior or the archaeological record within those limited contexts. Thus, while behavioral archaeologists are committed to developing nomothetic principles, they are also interested in developing historical principles, which describe behavioral processes that operate within a specific spatio-temporal frame of reference (see Reid 1985: 13; Schiffer 1987: 22–3, 292–3).

As a framework for explicitly defining the scope of behavioral generalizations, behavioral archaeologists advocate the development of what they refer to as *behavioral contexts* (LaMotta and Schiffer 2001: 24–7; Schiffer 1996, 2010: 11; Walker et al. 1995: 4). A behavioral context is the locus of a behavioral process. Operationally, a behavioral context specifies the conditions under which a behavioral generalization is valid: that is, its boundary conditions. A behavioral context is defined in terms of a number of material, behavioral, and other *critical variables* that are relevant to the occurrence of the process. For example, if one were to define a behavioral context for the McKellar Principle, some of the critical variables might include location of refuse-generating activity, intensity of use, type of substrate, size and nature of refuse generated, and type and intensity of maintenance activity (see, e.g., Schiffer 1987: 63–4). Critical variables have associated values: that is, specific attributes or states. Together, critical variables and their associated values define the behavioral principle's boundary conditions.

The construction of behavioral contexts promotes analytical rigor by insisting that researchers specify the variables that are relevant to a particular behavioral process, and by requiring that the behavioral generalization in question be tested in specific settings to establish values, or ranges of values, for the critical variables. This should be envisioned as an open-ended, dialectical process, in which both a behavioral generalization and its associated behavioral context will undoubtedly evolve through repeated, long-term testing. Likewise, by foregrounding boundary conditions, behavioral contexts allow for great flexibility in defining principles of behavior that apply along a continuum from general to specific. Furthermore, there is no par-ticular reason why boundary conditions cannot include temporal, spatial, or even cultural variables. It may be useful and instructive, for instance, to develop behavioral generalizations and behavioral contexts for specific cultural settings. For example, the observation that Diné (Navajo) of the North American Southwest traditionally abandoned and dismantled or burned a dwelling in which a death occurred (e.g. Brugge 1978; Frisbie 1978; Kent 1984: 140; Ward 1980: 31–4) might serve as a useful starting point for defining a historical principle of behavior and its associated behavioral context. While it might also be possible to understand the behavior(s) in ques-tion within a broader frame of reference, the point is that the frame-work expounded here is potentially useful at a variety of scales, and can effectively deal with behavioral variability associated with cul-tural traditions and other historical entities. One can even imagine developing behavioral generalizations and behavioral contexts tailored to specific historical social entities nested within a broader cultural tradition – for example, sodalities, genders, or ethnic groups. Again, such behavioral generalizations are intended not to be ends in themselves, but rather to serve as heuristics or null hypotheses against which to evaluate specific instances of human action in the archaeological or historical record.

The development of behavioral generalizations that operate within more localized frames of reference (i.e. historical principles of behav-ior) may also be instrumental in helping archaeologists to better understand material variability in the archaeological record. Behavioral archaeologists have long been committed to developing principles of cultural deposition, describing regularities in the behav-ioral processes through which objects leave the systemic context of human activities and enter the archaeological record. The concern with processes of cultural deposition, and formation processes in general, emerged in part as a response to early case studies of the Americanist processual archaeology of the 1960s and early 1970s, in which researchers often failed to consider the transformative effects of such processes on archaeological materials, and tacitly assumed that archaeological patterns faithfully reflected systemic-context activities and organization (Schiffer 1972, 1976). Behavioral archaeologists argued that if one were to reconstruct aspects of the systemic context from archaeological materials, it was necessary to understand how cultural deposition, among other processes, transformed the formal, spatial, relational, and quantitative dimensions of objects and assemblages, as those materials passed from systemic-context activities into the archaeological record. They therefore sought to develop general principles of cultural deposition, which could be implemented in specific contexts to reconstruct cultural processes that had contributed to the formation of the archaeological record, and to estimate what impact those processes might have had on any preserved material patterns. Early approaches focused on developing nomothetic principles of cultural deposition, which could be applied across a broad range of contexts.

The Americanist tradition of processual archaeology that emerged in the 1960s cultivated a boldly optimistic view of the archaeological record and of the totality of information it contains about the organization and operation of past societies (e.g. Binford 1962, 1964, 1968: 23). Binford (1964: 425), for instance, argued that "[t]he archaeological structure of a culture should, and in my opinion does, reflect all other structures, for example, kinship, economic, and political. All are abstracted from the events which occur as part of the normal functioning of a cultural system. The archaeological structure results from these same events." Statements such as this greatly influenced the way subsequent generations of archaeologists envisioned the archaeological record and the possibilities it presented for illuminating diverse aspects of past societies. From the perspective of behavioral archaeology, however, it must be pointed out that material patterning in the archaeological record (post-depositional processes notwithstanding) is first and foremost a product of cultural deposition – including abandonment, discard, and loss behaviors. Thus, we emphasize that kinship, economic and political structures, and all of the systemic-context activities and processes that archaeologists might be interested in reconstructing are reflected in the archaeological structure *only* to the extent that such phenomena are linked to processes of cultural deposition, and *only* to the extent that they create traces as observed on the formal, spatial, relational, and quantitative dimensions of objects and object assemblages that enter an archaeological context. In principle, such phenomena could also be linked to processes of cultural disturbance, such as post-depositional movement or manipulation of deposits, which also affect the archaeological record. It is up to archaeologists to establish these linkages, and to explicitly evaluate the information potential of the archaeological record on a case-by-case basis.

Behavioral chain analysis and nomothetic principles of cultural deposition are potentially useful analytical tools for establishing such linkages between cultural deposition and other activities and processes of interest. However, since it seems highly unlikely that cultural deposition should be linked in the same fashion to different systemic-context structures, activities, and processes across all human societies, or even across all societies of a given "type" (e.g. hunter-gatherers), archaeologists should look to develop principles of cultural deposition that operate within more localized frames of reference – that is, historical principles. In different cultures and time periods, certain aspects of the systemic context may be more closely and more directly linked to cultural deposition than they were in other cultures and time periods. Archaeologists need to make these determinations in order to correctly evaluate the information potential of the archaeological record in different research contexts. For example, in some quarters of the ancient North American Southwest, researchers contend that ritual abandonment processes significantly affected the artifact assemblages and sediment matrix found on the floors and in the post-occupational fill of certain kinds of architectural contexts (LaMotta 1996; Montgomery 1992, 1993; Montgomery and Reid 1990; Seymour and Schiffer 1987; Walker 1996, 1998; Walker and Lucero 2000; Walker et al. 2000; Wilshusen 1986, 1988). If this is indeed the case, then the archaeological structure of these deposits provides information most directly on ancient religion and ritual. In other contexts, ritual processes may play no role in the abandonment and post-abandonment filling of architectural spaces, in which case the archaeological structure of those contexts reflects something else. Principles of cultural deposition based on atemporal and aspatial regularities in depositional processes will only go so far towards elucidating such critical differences in information potential among archaeological contexts. Rather, principles of cultural deposition tailored to specific historical contexts are needed to establish the relevant linkages in different localities. The foregoing arguments could also be applied in the context of behavioral generalizations concerning relevant processes of cultural disturbance.

What this all suggests is that archaeologists need to take up the study of processes of cultural deposition and cultural disturbance in a serious and concerted fashion, both in archaeological contexts and in living societies where linkages between such processes and other realms of the systemic context can be established directly. Archaeologists need to understand the local, historical, and cultural determinants of variability in depositional behaviors, in addition to the atemporal and aspatial factors that condition such processes in human societies generally. Behavioral archaeologists should act as the vanguard in developing a new anthropological science of discard, abandonment, and other deposit-forming and deposit-transforming processes. In doing so, they are likely to discover that variability in such behaviors has significance, and is nuanced, in ways that Western scholars may never have imagined, and undoubtedly a new analytical lexicon will need to be created to reflect such variability. Such discoveries should allow archaeologists to more effectively interpret the material traces in the archaeological record.

Conclusions

In this chapter I have attempted to summarize and update certain core aspects of behavioral archaeology that scholars who are faced with the challenge of making sense of variability in the archaeological record will find most useful. Thus, I have purposefully omitted entire realms of research where behavioral archaeologists have made significant advances in recent years (for recent summaries, see, e.g., Hollenback and Schiffer 2010; Schiffer 2010, 2011; Skibo and Schiffer 2008). Nevertheless, behavioral archaeology was developed in the first place as a body of method and theory for understanding the archaeological record and the patterning encoded in that record, and this will remain one of its enduring contributions – a contribution that is still evolving. In this chapter, for instance, I have argued for a shift in perspective to further refine our tools for understanding variability in the behavioral processes that actually form the archaeological record. I have suggested that cultural deposition, as the set of cultural processes most directly responsible for material patterning in the archaeological record, should play a more central role in general archaeological thought. This is a realm of behavior that is under-theorized, particularly on a local historical scale, as are cultural formation processes in general (Shott 1998). Behavioral archaeologists seek to achieve an anthropologically informed understanding of variability in such processes, and of the resultant variability in the archaeological record. In this sense, behavioral archaeology can potentially serve as a theoretical and methodological nexus for archaeologists with diverse research interests who strive to understand the archaeological record as a means to understanding the human past, regardless of their commitments to particular theoretical frameworks.

Acknowledgments

I am especially grateful to J. Jefferson Reid, Michael Schiffer, Rebecca Seifried, James Skibo, and William Walker for providing copies of their publications and/or for reading and commenting on drafts of this chapter.

References

Bartlett, K. 1933. Pueblo milling stones of the Flagstaff region and their relation to others in the Southwest. *Museum of Northern Arizona, Bulletin* no. 3. Flagstaff: Museum of Northern Arizona Press.

Bartlett, K. 1936. The utilization of maize among the ancient Pueblos. *University of New Mexico, Bulletin* no. 269. Albuquerque: University of New Mexico Press.

Beaglehole, E. 1937. Notes on Hopi economic life. *Yale University, Publications in Anthropology* no. 15. New Haven: Yale University Press.

Binford, L.R. 1962. Archaeology as anthropology. *American Antiquity* 28: 217–25.

Binford, L.R. 1964. A consideration of archaeological research design. *American Antiquity* 29: 425–41.

Binford, L.R. 1968. Archeological perspectives. In S.R. Binford and L.R. Binford (eds), *New Perspectives in Archeology*, 5–32. Chicago: Aldine.

Binford, L.R. 1978. Dimensional analysis of behavior and site structure: learning from an Eskimo hunting stand. *American Antiquity* 43: 330–61.

Binford, L.R. 1981. Behavioral archaeology and the "Pompeii premise." *Journal of Anthropological Research* 37: 195–208.

Brugge, D.M. 1978. A comparative study of Navajo mortuary practices. *American Indian Quarterly* 4: 309–28.

Cameron, C.M. and S.A. Tomka (eds) 1993. *Abandonment of Settlements and Regions: Ethnoarchaeological and Archaeological Approaches.* Cambridge: Cambridge University Press.

Frisbie, C.J. 1978. Introduction. *American Indian Quarterly* 4: 303–8.

Gould, R.A. 1980. *Living Archaeology.* Cambridge: Cambridge University Press.

Hayden, B. and A. Cannon 1983. Where the garbage goes: refuse disposal in the Maya Highlands. *Journal of Anthropological Archaeology* 2: 117–63.

Hill, J.D. 1995. *Ritual and Rubbish in the Iron Age of Wessex: A Study on the Formation of a Specific Archaeological Record*. Oxford: British Archaeological Reports, British Series, 242.

Hodder, I. 1987. The meaning of discard: ash and domestic space in Baringo. In S. Kent (ed.), *Method and Theory for Activity Area Research: An Ethnoarchaeological Approach*, 424–48. New York: Columbia University Press.

Hollenback, K.L. and M.B. Schiffer 2010. Technology and material life. In D. Hicks and M. Beaudry (eds), *The Oxford Handbook of Material Culture Studies*, 313–32. Oxford: Oxford University Press.

Inomata, T. and R.W. Webb 2003. Archaeological studies of abandonment in Middle America. In T. Inomata and R.W. Webb (eds), *The Archaeology of Settlement Abandonment in Middle America*, 1–10. Salt Lake City: University of Utah Press.

Keeley, L.H. 1974. Technique and methodology in microwear studies. *World Archaeology* 5: 323–36.

Keeley, L.H. 1980. *Experimental Determination of Stone Tool Uses: A Microwear Analysis*. Chicago: University of Chicago Press.

Kent, S. 1984. *Analyzing Activity Areas: An Ethnoarchaeological Study of the Use of Space*. Albuquerque: University of New Mexico Press.

LaMotta, V.M. 1996. The use of disarticulated human remains in abandonment ritual at Homol'ovi. M.A. report, Department of Anthropology, University of Arizona, Tucson.

LaMotta, V.M. 2001. Behavioral variability in mortuary deposition: a modern material culture study. *Arizona Anthropologist* 14: 53–80.

LaMotta, V.M. and M.B. Schiffer 1999. Formation processes of house floor assemblages. In P. Allison (ed.), *The Archaeology of Household Activities*, 19–29. London: Routledge.

LaMotta, V.M. and M.B. Schiffer 2001. Behavioral archaeology: toward a new synthesis. In I. Hodder (ed.), *Archaeological Theory Today*, 1st edition, 14–64. Cambridge: Polity.

LaMotta, V.M. and M.B. Schiffer 2005. Archaeological formation processes. In C. Renfrew and P. Bahn (eds), *Archaeology: The Key Concepts*, 121–7. London: Routledge.

McAnany, P.A. and I. Hodder 2009. Thinking about stratigraphic sequence in social terms. *Archaeological Dialogues* 16: 1–22.

Magers, P.C. 1975. The cotton industry at Antelope House. *The Kiva* 41: 39–47.

Montgomery, B.K. 1992. Understanding the Formation of the Archaeological Record: Ceramic Variability at Chodistaas Pueblo, Arizona. Ph.D. dissertation, Department of Anthropology, University of Arizona. Ann Arbor: University Microfilms.

Montgomery, B. K. 1993. Ceramic analysis as a tool for discovering processes of pueblo abandonment. In C. M. Cameron and S. A. Tomka (eds), *Abandonment of Settlements and Regions: Ethnoarchaeological and Archaeological Approaches*, 157–64. Cambridge: Cambridge University Press.

Montgomery, B. K. and J. J. Reid 1990. An instance of rapid ceramic change in the American Southwest. *American Antiquity* 55: 88–97.

Nielsen, A. E. 1991. Trampling the archaeological record: an experimental study. *American Antiquity* 56: 483–503.

Rathje, W. L. and M. B. Schiffer 1982. *Archaeology*. New York: Harcourt Brace Jovanovich.

Reid, J. J. 1973. Growth and Response to Stress at Grasshopper Pueblo, Arizona. Ph.D. dissertation, Department of Anthropology, University of Arizona. Ann Arbor: University Microfilms.

Reid, J. J. 1985. Formation processes for the practical prehistorian. In R. S. Dickens, Jr. and H. T. Ward (eds), *Structure and Process in Southeastern Archaeology*, 11–33. Tuscaloosa: University of Alabama Press.

Reid, J. J. 1995. Four strategies after twenty years: a return to basics. In J. M. Skibo, W. H. Walker, and A. E. Nielsen (eds), *Expanding Archaeology*, 15–21. Salt Lake City: University of Utah Press.

Reid, J. J. and S. M. Whittlesey 2005. *Thirty Years into Yesterday: A History of Archaeology at Grasshopper Pueblo*. Tucson: University of Arizona Press.

Reid, J. J., W. L. Rathje, and M. B. Schiffer 1974. Expanding archaeology. *American Antiquity* 39: 125–6.

Reid, J. J., M. B. Schiffer, and W. L. Rathje 1975. Behavioral archaeology: four strategies. *American Anthropologist* 77: 836–48.

Schiffer, M. B. 1972. Archaeological context and systemic context. *American Antiquity* 37: 156–65.

Schiffer, M. B. 1975a. Archaeology as behavioral science. *American Anthropologist* 77: 836–48.

Schiffer, M. B. 1975b. Behavioral chain analysis: activities, organization, and the use of space. Chapters in the prehistory of Eastern Arizona, IV. *Fieldiana: Anthropology* 65: 103–19.

Schiffer, M. B. 1976. *Behavioral Archeology*. New York: Academic Press.

Schiffer, M. B. 1979. A preliminary consideration of behavioral change. In C. Renfrew and K. Cooke (eds), *Transformations: Mathematical Approaches to Culture Change*, 353–68. New York: Academic Press.

Schiffer, M. B. 1983. Toward the identification of formation processes. *American Antiquity* 48: 675–706.

Schiffer, M.B. 1985. Is there a "Pompeii premise" in archaeology? *Journal of Anthropological Research* 41: 18–41.

Schiffer, M.B. 1987. *Formation Processes of the Archaeological Record*. Albuquerque: University of New Mexico Press.

Schiffer, M.B. 1991. *The Portable Radio in American Life*. Tucson: University of Arizona Press.

Schiffer, M.B. 1992. *Technological Perspectives on Behavioral Change*. Tucson: University of Arizona Press.

Schiffer, M.B. 1995. *Behavioral Archaeology: First Principles*. Salt Lake City: University of Utah Press.

Schiffer, M.B. 1996. Some relationships between behavioral and evolutionary archaeologies. *American Antiquity* 61: 643–62.

Schiffer, M.B. 2005. The devil is in the details: the cascade model of invention processes. *American Antiquity* 70: 485–502.

Schiffer, M.B. 2008a. *Power Struggles: Scientific Authority and the Creation of Practical Electricity before Edison*. Cambridge, MA: MIT Press.

Schiffer, M.B. 2008b. A cognitive analysis of component-stimulated invention: electromagnet, telegraph, and the Capitol dome's electric gas-lighter. *Technology and Culture* 49: 376–98.

Schiffer, M.B. 2010. *Behavioral Archaeology: Principles and Practice*. London: Equinox.

Schiffer, M.B. 2011. *Studying Technological Change: A Behavioral Approach*. Salt Lake City: University of Utah Press.

Schiffer, M.B. and V.M. LaMotta 2007. Behavioral archaeology and formation processes. In K. Paddayya, R. Jhaldiyal, and S.G. Deo (eds), *Formation Processes and Indian Archaeology*, 3–14. Pune, India: Deccan College Post-Graduate and Research Institute.

Schiffer, M.B. and A.R. Miller 1999. *The Material Life of Human Beings: Artifacts, Behavior, and Communication*. London: Routledge.

Schiffer, M.B. and J.M. Skibo 1987. Theory and experiment in the study of technological change. *Current Anthropology* 28: 595–622.

Schiffer, M.B., T.C. Butts, and K.K. Grimm 1994. *Taking Charge: The Electric Automobile in America*. Washington, DC: Smithsonian Institution Press.

Schiffer, M.B., K.L. Hollenback, and C.L. Bell 2003. *Draw the Lightning Down: Benjamin Franklin and Electrical Technology in the Age of Enlightenment*. Berkeley: University of California Press.

Seymour, D.J. and M.B. Schiffer 1987. A preliminary analysis of pithouse assemblages from Snaketown, Arizona. In S. Kent (ed.), *Method and Theory for Activity Area Research: An Ethnoarchaeological Approach*, 549–603. New York: Columbia University Press.

Shott, M.J. 1998. Status and role of formation theory in contemporary archaeological practice. *Journal of Archaeological Research* 6: 299–329.

Skibo, J.M. 1992. *Pottery Function: A Use-Alteration Perspective*. New York: Plenum.

Skibo, J.M. and M.B. Schiffer 2008. *People and Things: A Behavioral Approach to Material Culture*. New York: Springer.

Skibo, J.M., W.H. Walker, and A.E. Nielsen (eds) 1995. *Expanding Archaeology*. Salt Lake City: University of Utah Press.

Stephen, A.M. 1936. *The Hopi Journal of Alexander M. Stephen*, ed. E. C. Parsons, 2 vols. New York: Columbia University Press.

Sullivan, A.P., III 1978. Inference and evidence in archaeology: a discussion of the conceptual problems. *Advances in Archaeological Method and Theory* 1: 183–222.

Tani, M. 1995. Beyond the identification of formation processes: behavioral inference based on traces left by cultural formation processes. *Journal of Archaeological Method and Theory* 2: 231–52.

Turner, C.G., II and L. Lofgren 1966. Household size of prehistoric Western Pueblo Indians. *Southwestern Journal of Anthropology* 22: 117–32.

Walker, W.H. 1995. Ceremonial trash? In J.M. Skibo, W.H. Walker, and A.E. Nielsen (eds), *Expanding Archaeology*, 67–79. Salt Lake City: University of Utah Press.

Walker, W.H. 1996. Ritual deposits: another perspective. In E.C. Adams (ed.), *River of Change: Prehistory of the Middle Little Colorado River Valley, Arizona*, 75–91. Arizona State Museum Archaeological Series 185. Tucson: Arizona State Museum.

Walker, W.H. 1998. Where are the witches of prehistory? *Journal of Archaeological Method and Theory* 5: 246–308.

Walker, W.H. 1999. Ritual life histories and the afterlives of people and things. *Journal of the Southwest* 41: 383–405.

Walker, W.H. 2001. Ritual technology in an extranatural world. In M.B. Schiffer (ed.), *The Anthropology of Technology*, 87–106. Albuquerque: University of New Mexico Press.

Walker, W.H. 2002. Stratigraphy and practical reason. *American Anthropologist* 104: 159–77.

Walker, W.H. and V.M. LaMotta 1995. Life histories as units of analysis. Paper presented at the 62nd Annual Meeting of the Society for American Archaeology, Minneapolis.

Walker, W.H. and L.J. Lucero 2000. The depositional history of ritual and power. In M.-A. Dobres and J. Robb (eds), *Agency in Archaeology*, 130–47. London: Routledge.

Walker, W.H., and M.B. Schiffer 2006. The materiality of social power: the artifact acquisition perspective. *Journal of Archaeological Method and Theory* 13: 67–88.

Walker, W.H., J.M. Skibo, and A.E. Nielsen 1995. Introduction. In J.M. Skibo, W.H. Walker, and A.E. Nielsen (eds), *Expanding Archaeology*, 1–12. Salt Lake City: University of Utah Press.

Walker, W.H., V.M. LaMotta, and E.C. Adams 2000. Katsinas and kiva abandonment at Homol'ovi: a deposit-oriented perspective on religion in Southwest prehistory. In M. Hegmon (ed.), *The Archaeology of Regional Interaction: Religion, Warfare, & Exchange across the American Southwest and Beyond*, 341–60. Boulder: University Press of Colorado.

Ward, A.E. 1980. Navajo graves: an archaeological reflection of ethnographic reality. *Ethnohistorical Report Series* no. 2. Albuquerque: Center for Anthropological Studies.

Whiting, A.E. 1939. Ethnobotany of the Hopi. *Museum of Northern Arizona, Bulletin* no. 15. Flagstaff: Museum of Northern Arizona.

Whittlesey, S.M. 1978. Status and Death at Grasshopper Pueblo: Experiments toward an Archaeological Theory of Correlates. Ph.D. dissertation, Department of Anthropology, University of Arizona. Ann Arbor: University Microfilms.

Wilshusen, R.H. 1986. The relationship between abandonment mode and ritual use in Pueblo I Anasazi Protokivas. *Journal of Field Archaeology* 13: 245–54.

Wilshusen, R.H. 1988. The abandonment of structures. In E. Blinman, C.J. Phagan, and R.H. Wilshusen (eds), *Dolores Archaeological Program Supporting Studies: Additive and Reductive Technologies*, 673–702. Denver: Bureau of Reclamation, Engineering and Research Center.

Wood, W.R. and D.J. Johnson 1978. A survey of disturbance processes in archaeological site formation. *Advances in Archaeological Method and Theory* 1: 315–81.

Zedeño, M.N. 2000. On what people make of places: a behavioral cartography. In M.B. Schiffer (ed.), *Social Theory in Archaeology*, 97–111. Salt Lake City: University of Utah Press.

5

COMPLEX SYSTEMS AND ARCHAEOLOGY

Timothy A. Kohler

A complex system, according to Mitchell (2009: 13), presents "large networks of components with no central control and simple rules of operation giv[ing] rise to complex collective behavior, sophisticated information processing, and adaptation via learning or evolution." Such systems exhibit emergent and self-organizing behaviors. They commonly exhibit "frustration" – a condition in which it is impossible to satisfy all competing interests within the constraints imposed (Sherrington 2010). They frequently exist in far-from-equilibrium conditions. They are not merely complicated – meaning that they have many "moving parts" – but they also exhibit non-linear interactions involving structural contingencies or positive feedbacks. In this chapter I survey the implications for archaeology of the not-fully-formed theories of such systems, and the attempts by archaeologists to employ aspects of complexity theory, and its methods, in the study of prehistory.

Before beginning, though, I need to demarcate the territory. Many archaeologists immediately connect the term "complexity" with the cultural-evolutionary literature of the 1950s and 1960s, and the large literature in archaeology dealing with how "more complex" societies (meaning societies exhibiting inegalitarian social relations and political hierarchies) evolved from more egalitarian, smaller-scale societies. This is an interest of complexity theory – since it involves the emergence of new political actors, levels of organization, and social relations – but the scope of complexity theory is much broader, and encompasses even the smallest-scale human societies (and, for that matter, societies of ants, and networks of neurons inside an ant's brain). Unlike many of the approaches outlined in this book, complexity theory is not first of all for and by archaeologists. It is therefore legitimate to wonder whether it has anything useful to offer us.

As we explore the territory covered by complexity theory, we shall see that its borders are unguarded and its inhabitants diverse. Archaeologists – especially those with an evolutionary orientation – wander freely about, either selecting particular concepts or just drifting. Physicists, biologists, and economists are quite common. While abundant, mathematicians and computer scientists tend to be crepuscular because they are in such demand. Historians, political scientists, and ecologists likewise make important contributions to this community.

The web of interests connecting these diverse actors consists of:

- a real interest in theory seeking commonalities across levels of organization within a system, and across abiotic and biotic systems of various sorts;
- a special attraction to systems composed of many moving parts – dynamic systems – and the patterns that emerge from the interactions of these components through time;
- a quantitative orientation and a commitment to computation;
- dissatisfaction with traditional, reductive practices as embodied by the positivistic, hypothesis-testing, highly analytic approach to science most of us learned in high school – especially since such approaches cope poorly with highly connected complex systems; and
- an attraction to asking big, often transdisciplinary questions that may be shunned by disciplinary approaches, and a willingness to try to take a look at whole systems, even if it is a crude look (Gell-Mann 1994), particularly through the use of computer models.

Several additional characteristics of complexity research are reviewed by McGlade and Garnsey (2006). Here I begin by examining some of the roots of these tendencies in anthropology, archaeology, and elsewhere. Then I'll discuss in more detail some key concepts and methods in the study of complex systems (hereafter "CS"), with special attention to what archaeologists have done, or might do, with these approaches.

Some history

Cybernetics and general systems theory

The important involvement of some of anthropology's leading lights in the mid-twentieth-century development of cybernetics is a little known but fascinating story. Cyberneticians studied mechanisms for control and communication in both machines and living organisms. Cybernetics stood in relation "to the real machine – electronic, mechanical, neural, or economic – much as geometry stands to a real object in our terrestrial space" (Ashby 1956: 2). In other words, cybernetics abstracted from real systems to attempt to study the general properties of all systems, with particular interest in processes such as feedback, stability, amplification, and regulation, accepting as underlying metaphor that a system is a machine of greater or lesser complexity. From the mid-1940s through the early 1950s a core group of about twenty scientists, including anthropologist-psychologist Gregory Bateson and ethnographer Margaret Mead, occasionally joined by Clyde Kluckhohn, met in a series of nine conferences funded by the Josiah Macy, Jr. Foundation to discuss the underpinnings of what came to be known as cybernetics (Heims 1991). Other members of the core group were mathematicians John von Neumann and Norbert Wiener. It is probable that Bateson's unique evolutionary and ecological orientation, his anti-reductionist tendencies, and his extremely wide-ranging interests, were all reinforced by these interactions.[1]

The Macy conferences eventually fell apart; a participant in some of the later, less productive, meetings considered them no more than "bull sessions with a very elite group" (Mitchell 2009: 297). But cybernetics and its ally, general systems theory (von Bertalanffy 1950), made intriguing suggestions about how information and computation are embedded in living systems. Their cross-disciplinary analogies between machines and living organisms, and especially between the marvelous new digital computers and brains, informed a generation of research. Elements of cybernetics and general systems theory were incorporated into systems ecology,[2] systems analysis, artificial intelligence, and eventually the sciences of complexity.

And archaeology. The processualists engaged in a lively back-and-forth on the relative merits of a strict hypothetico-deductive approach versus a "systems" approach. Tuggle et al. (1972: 9), on behalf of the latter, argued that " 'processual analysis' does not center only upon the search for dynamic laws, but also on the attempt to explain cultural phenomena in terms of system interrelationships. The system paradigm does not demand the use of laws and it accommodates the unique as well as the recurrent in the scheme of explanation." North American archaeologists of a certain age probably gained an acquaintance with cybernetics through Kent Flannery's influential "Archeological Systems Theory and Early Mesoamerica" (1968), published the same year as the first edition of David Clarke's *Analytical Archaeology*. Both were major contributors to the stream of research reviewed here.[3]

Kent Flannery and systems theory

Flannery cites Maruyama (1963) as his source for the idea that positive feedback (the "second cybernetics") can amplify small deviations into large differences. In the case of highland southern Mexico, Flannery proposed that very small genetic changes in beans and especially in maize, perhaps brought on by increases in their range, initiated positive feedbacks within the wild-grass procurement system: "The more widespread maize cultivation, the more opportunities for favorable crosses and back-crosses; the more favorable genetic changes, the greater the yield; the greater the yield, the higher the population, and hence the more intensive cultivation" (Flannery 1968: 80). Flannery lauded cybernetics for encouraging archaeologists to think of cultures as systems, and for stimulating "inquiry into the mechanisms that counteract change or amplify it," famously concluding that

> it is vain to hope for the discovery of the first domestic corn cob, the first pottery vessel....Such deviations from the pre-existing pattern almost certainly took place in such a minor and accidental way that their traces are not recoverable. More worthwhile would be an investigation of the mutual causal processes that amplify these tiny deviations into major changes in prehistoric culture. (Flannery 1968: 85)

A few years later Flannery employed a similar perspective but a larger set of concepts to attempt to explain the origins of the state. He identified processes of segregation ("internal differentiation and specialization of subsystems") and centralization ("degree of linkage between...subsystems and the highest-order controls") (Flannery 1972: 409). These, he proposed, may be encouraged by mechanisms such as promotion (as in the case of an institution moving from special to general purpose) or linearization, in which lower-order controls are "repeatedly or permanently bypassed by higher-order controls" (Flannery 1972: 413). He treats the various "prime movers" proposed over the years as drivers for state formation (irrigation, warfare, population growth, etc.) as stresses that in various cases can select for these mechanisms, though systems can also evolve towards pathologies such as "hypercoherence" (e.g. Rappaport 1977) in which disruptions to any part cascade through the entire system.[4]

For Flannery, the ultimate goal of such thinking was to establish the rules by which one could simulate the origin of the state, and he suggests fifteen rules to be implemented in any such attempt. These focused mainly on structural changes to existing institutions, emergence of new institutions, and changing linkages among institutions – a focus on information and control very much in keeping with theory in cybernetics, though implemented by Flannery within an ecological framework.

The participants in the School of American Research's 1970 advanced seminar on prehistoric change (J. N. Hill 1977b) saw three attractive features in systems theory (Plog 1977) – as a source of concepts; as a source of propositions describing the behaviors of systems; but most of all, for the analytic utility of simulation implementing a systems-theoretic approach (Plog 1977). Plog accordingly sketched a sixteen-step pseudo-code on behalf of the group outlining their understanding of the role of redistribution and warfare in the operation of the Hawaiian paramountcy. This did not, so far as I am aware, ever culminate in a simulation, but was intended as a thought exercise.

David Clarke and Analytic Archaeology: rescuing an undisciplined empirical discipline

David Clarke's ambitious *Analytical Archaeology* (1968) attempted not only to integrate systems perspectives into archaeology, but also to thoroughly systematize archaeological theory and put it in step with contemporary developments in geography, numerical taxonomy, and statistics, all of which were in full florescence, stimulated by newly available digital computers (Figure 5.1).

In his exposition for how cultures build up communication through material culture, decomposable into attributes and artifacts, and transmit these to successive generations, Clarke anticipates contemporary interests in building cultural phylogenies. Doran (1970: 293) points out that Clarke's discussion of self-regulating properties of a

Figure 5.1. David Clarke in 1972
Source: Photograph by Tim Frost.

cultural system "depends upon the amount of variety it shows; that is, upon the amount of information it contains or can transmit in some sense" – an extrapolation of a theorem in information theory owing to Shannon and Weaver (1949). Clarke likewise develops a theory of how continuity (equilibrium) in societies can emerge from high levels of agreement or redundancy among "subsystems." Clarke's emphasis on "phase pattern regularities" and "time pattern regularities" as emergent properties at successively more general levels, moving from attribute to artifact, type, assemblage, culture, culture group, and techno-complex, resonates with metaphors used currently in describing complex systems. His repetitive images of networks of relationships and constraints, his attraction to abstraction and to models of all sorts, his fascination with how processes like diffusion could shape patterns seen in the archaeological record – all presage interests of later "complexity archaeologists." Moreover, in edited collections (Clarke 1972) he provided a rallying point for like-minded archaeologists. One wonders what this restless and original mind might have achieved, given more than thirty-eight years. Aspects of this program were, however, kept alive and shaped by other researchers at Cambridge, including Colin Renfrew (e.g. 1973) and Sander van der Leeuw and James McGlade (e.g. 1997).

Not all archaeologists of this era with an interest in systems approaches agreed on how these approaches should be realized. In a prescient article, John J. Wood and R. G. Matson (1973) complained about the assumption or requirement of homeostasis in cybernetics (or general systems theory), its seeming requirement that sources of change always be outside the system, and its implicit functionalism. They suggested pursuing a more open model of system allowing for change coming from within the system (as self-organization or morphogenesis), and one that emphasized relations of conditionality and constraint among the entities in the system. Following Buckley (1967), they called this the "complex adaptive systems" model.

The end of the beginning

These tendencies on both sides of the Atlantic saw their symmetric and logical culmination in the publication of two edited volumes on simulation in archaeology (Hodder 1978; Sabloff 1981). Although both were reviewed in a generally positive fashion (e.g. Lowe 1982), one gets the sense that the accomplishments of the case studies therein were a little underwhelming, given the possibly unrealistic expectations raised by the polemics of Flannery, Clarke, and others.

The same year Hodder's edited volume appeared, Merilee Salmon, a philosopher of science with a special interest in archaeology, asked "What can systems theory do for archaeology?" and concluded, not much. She argued that in archaeological applications the notion of "system" was not adequately defined. Following Rapoport (1972), she saw no general characteristics of various sorts of systems that were not simply consequences of their definition as a system. She found Flannery's 1968 article on domestication interesting, but suggests that the sorts of positive and negative feedbacks he proposed were available as concepts before the development of cybernetics. In general, she saw the "systemic approach" in archaeology as potentially productive, but did not wish any of this credit to go specifically to the successes of general systems theory: "[A]ttention generated by the program of the general systems theorists has been instrumental in expanding our conception of systems and their importance, but we cannot look to [it] for an explicit methodology" (Salmon 1978: 178).[5]

Finally, Salmon drew a strict line of demarcation between general systems theory and what she calls "mathematical systems theory." This she considered to be a "pure mathematical theory" (Salmon 1978: 178) originally intended to help construct digital computers, which were beginning to be used with some success, at the time of her writing, to model biological systems. (She would apparently characterize any formal [mathematical] model of any system as being part of "mathematical systems theory," though of course most would regard this as a method, not a theory.) Her quite legitimate worries with such approaches included the fact that the points of contact between such systems of equations and the world they reference may be few and vague, and the fit between their predictions and the world quite rough.

And suddenly she sounds very contemporary:

> Archaeology, even more than biology, studies extremely complex systems whose boundaries are not well defined. Modeling always ignores some, often fundamental, aspects of a system in order to focus on others. No one model should or does model every feature of a system. Whether a model is good or bad depends partly on our purposes in constructing the model. Unless the components of a system and their systemic relationships are well understood it is difficult to decide which features may be ignored in constructing useful models....Much more must be known about crucial components of biological systems and their important relationships before they can be modeled successfully. And biologists, not systems theorists, are the ones who are equipped to do this sort of work. I believe that archaeology is in a position similar to that of biology in this respect. (Salmon 1978: 179)

In the end she rejects mathematical models as

> too simple to be applied with much success to the complex systems that interest archaeologists. Mathematical Systems Theory is limited by its own lack of mathematical richness to applicability to only rather simple real systems.... It has limitations that make it applicable to few, and only very simple, real systems. It is *not complex enough* to handle the sorts of situations that interest archaeologists. (Salmon 1978: 174, 181; emphasis added)[6]

Trouble was brewing on other fronts as well. Only eight years after editing a volume in which he was cautiously optimistic about its prospects, Hodder (1986) does not even mention simulation in an influential review of current approaches in archaeology – a disinterest Chippindale (1993: 34) attributes to a destructive tendency for archaeologists to consume one theory or technique after another, without being able to make any of them work. But Hodder, and other post-processualists, had become dissatisfied with a failure of processualism generally to be sufficiently contextual and historical, to account for active agency, and to progress beyond a "surface" level and a focus on function in order to approach cultural meanings.[7]

With many archaeologists thus looking the other way, the larger scientific community's interests in complexity rather suddenly galvanized in the early 1990s (Figure 5.2). Articles examining simple computational systems called cellular automata (Wolfram 1984) or defining concepts such as self-organized criticality (Bak et al. 1988) or the edge of chaos (Kauffman and Johnsen 1991) led the way but were soon joined by more empirical studies, including, for example, complexity-inspired analyses of food webs (Pimm et al. 1991) and approaches to simulating the evolution of cities using cellular automata (R. White and Engelen 1993). Computational approaches to the

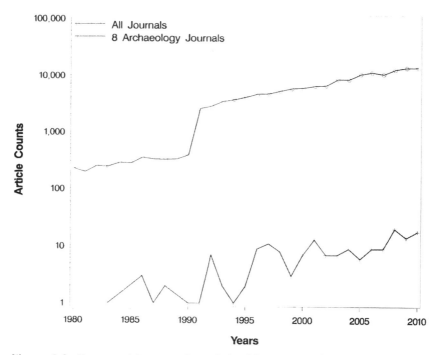

Figure 5.2. Papers with "complexity" in title or topic from 1980 to 2010 in journals indexed by ISI Web of Knowledge (note logarithmic y-axis) © ISI Web of Knowledge Service

problem of emergence of cooperation in human societies (Axelrod 1984), building on earlier uses of game theory to study animal conflicts (Maynard Smith 1974), opened a vast strand of research that to date has had less effect on archaeology than it should. These conceptual developments were enhanced by increasing speed and availability of computers, the development of object-oriented languages, and by the mid-1990s the availability of platforms for agent-based modeling. Before long, archaeologists, too, began to explore these new concepts and tools (e.g. Bentley and Maschner 2003; Kohler and Gumerman 2000).

Central concepts

Most of these new approaches break systems down into their constituent interacting entities. Instead of dealing with abstract variables describing system organization, they instead focus on how these entities interact with each other, and how various characteristics of the systems in which they are embedded arise from these interactions, which are often spatialized and local. Moreover, these entities can be heterogeneous, even within classes. Depending on the problem, entities might be individuals, households, villages, cities, or all of those.

This way of thinking is much more in line with how most of us think about societies than is the earlier systems paradigm. It not only highlights what we usually consider to be the agents of interest; it also provides a natural framework within which to consider questions that are perennial favorites for archaeologists, who for good reasons are drawn to questions of origins. How does a community arise from a collection of independent households? How do norms arise where previously there were none? Or how, as Adam Smith (1761/1985: 201) wondered, can "two savages, who had never been taught to speak, but had been bred up remote from the societies of men ... begin to form that language by which they would endeavour to make their mutual wants intelligible to each other ..."?

Emergence

Emergence as a concept may seem non-problematic to most archaeologists, as we can readily imagine, for example, the emergence of a new technology or a new level of socio-political hierarchy. With a little more difficulty we can visualize the invisible hand guiding the emergence of stable prices and a product distribution possibly beneficial to all from the self-interested interactions of producers and consumers. Emergent properties are also commonly identified in physical systems: convection cells emerge as we heat a pan of water on the stove, and a characteristic slope of a sandpile (its angle of repose, or critical slope) emerges as we add sand to its top. It's not hard to be convinced, following Anderson (1972), that more is often different: classical physics, for example, must arise from the rules of quantum physics, even though it works differently; chemistry in turn doesn't contradict any of those rules, but adds new ones.

Yet although virtually everyone agrees that "emergence relates to phenomena that arise from and depend on some more basic phenomena yet are simultaneously autonomous from that base" (Bedau and Humphreys 2008: 1), there are many open questions about the concept, and neither researchers nor philosophers have converged on a more specific and comprehensive definition. Indeed it seems likely that various classes of emergent phenomena need to be identified and more specifically defined. Do we mean precisely the same thing when we say that phase changes emerge as we cool water from 100° C to 0°; that thoughts and feelings somehow emerge from the biochemical and electrical interaction of neurons in our brain; that segregation can emerge from the local interactions of agents who are quite tolerant of living in integrated neighborhoods (Schelling 1978); or that chiefdoms may emerge from competition among tribes? So while complexity theorists have difficulty avoiding use of the term "emergence" since they are attracted to systems exhibiting it, they treat the concept with some caution. Characterizing a property as emergent is at best a general description and never an explanation.

Self-organization

Let's go back to our sandpile and continue to dribble sand onto the top of the cone. As the slope reaches its critical value, we will find that there are many small avalanches, fewer medium-sized ones, and the occasional really large one. Avalanches reduce the slope, but adding more sand builds it up again, so we can say that the sandpile's slope is "attracted" to the critical value. If we graph the distribution of sizes of avalanches on these piles, moving from small to large on the x-axis, and if both the y-axis (the frequency of avalanches of various sizes) and the x-axis are logarithmic, the distribution follows a straight line with a slope of approximately -1.

Per Bak and his colleagues used this system to define the concept of self-organized criticality – "self-organized" since the slope is attracted to its critical value without any external management. The distribution of avalanche sizes is said to follow a power law. While this may not seem very remarkable or even interesting in this particular case, what is remarkable is how commonly power-law-like distributions emerge in a variety of apparently unrelated contexts. Indeed, they are often said to be a characteristic of complex systems.

With living systems in mind, Stuart Kauffman developed the superficially similar idea of evolution to the "edge of chaos." The governing ideas here were developed using simple computational models (random Boolean networks and NK fitness landscapes) whose behaviors Kauffman analyzed in a long series of articles, many summarized in *The Origins of Order* (Kauffman 1993). Random Boolean networks (RBN) are briefly but lucidly described by Mitchell (2009: 282–4), and elsewhere I have used them as abstract models for reciprocal exchange systems (Kohler et al. 2000b). They consist of N nodes, each having a state of either 0 (inactive) or 1 (active) connected to other nodes (including possibly a self-link). The linkages between nodes are directional, though if node A links to node B, it is possible (but not required) that B also links to A. The number of links coming into each node (i.e. the in-degree) is called K. Each node is governed by one of two rules: OR or AND. For example, a node in a state of 0 governed by OR with an in-connection to two other nodes, one of which is in a state of 1, will, in the next time step, take on a value of 1, since the switch to activity depends on only one of its connections being active in the previous step. If the rule were AND, the switch to activity would require both connected nodes to be active in the previous time step. These networks can be in only a finite number of states (though that number might be very large) and one way to characterize their behavior is to measure how many discrete time steps they require to return to a particular state entered earlier. Once this happens, since these networks are deterministic, they will continue to cycle through that same space of possibilities. This is called the cycle length, and any realized cycle is called an attractor of the system.

Among the many things Kauffman and his colleagues learned about such networks through simulation using various values for N and K, and random wiring and logic, is that their typical long-run behavior is very dependent on the value of the in-degree measure K. In general, these networks exhibit three regimes of behavior: ordered, complex, and chaotic. When N = K, their behavior is maximally disordered, with high sensitivity to initial conditions (the original states of the nodes), and very long state cycles. When K = 1, the networks tend to fall apart into discrete, structurally isolated loops

– the maximally ordered regime. Of special interest is the K = 2 case, in which the networks exhibit what Kauffman (1993: 198–202) calls complex behavior, at the (somewhat metaphorical here) "phase transition" between order and chaotic regimes. He proposes that we take these networks as abstract models for N genes being regulated by K other genes, suggesting that K = 2 epistatic interactions provide the most desirable compromise between stability and limiting damage from errors, and an ability to adapt. Less cautiously he has sometimes proposed that all living systems are driven to an analogously similar "edge of chaos" by processes of either self-organization, adaptation, or both. Objections arise to these broader claims, however, when they refer to levels of organization such as ecosystems that cannot plausibly act as units of selection (Levin 1999: 183–4).

Innovation

These interests in emergence and self-organization are also leading to new approaches to understanding innovation in socio-cultural systems that depart from the variation–selection account received from Darwinian theory. Beginning from a recognition of the importance of *organizations* in socio-cultural systems (versus *populations* in Darwinian theory), Lane et al. (2009) develop a theory of the processes peculiar to socio-cultural systems that seeks to explain the innovation cascades (and, therefore, rapid change) they commonly exhibit. Especially important are innovations to which individuals or organizations can attribute new kinds of functions, even though these innovations may have begun only as a "better–faster–cheaper" means of carrying out an existing function. Gutenberg's press is used as an example. Organizational transformations then promote the proliferation of the innovation (for our example, through the use of traveling representatives to peddle the newly printed books). As the new artifacts are used, novel patterns of human interaction develop around them (as the peddlers make their whereabouts known and people buy their wares). These interactions lead to new "attributions of functionality" describing what participants are or might be getting from the interactions – as when the presses conceived the idea of using the same printing technology that made books possible to produce flyers advertising the whereabouts of the peddlers and their wares. Finally, these new artifacts (the flyers) are in fact produced, and we are back again where we started in the cycle of innovation – though, of course, in this case and many others, these innovations would continue to ramify endlessly. Brian Arthur (2009) points out that new technologies are quite commonly novel combinations of existing technologies, a combinatorial process which would tend to enhance such cascades.

Lane et al. (2009: 37–40) call this entire cycle "exaptive bootstrapping." Their approach can be linked to findings from scaling exercises that show consistent differences between biological and social systems with respect to activities linked to innovation. Van der Leeuw et al. (2009) and D.R. White (2009) explore some implications of this approach for understanding human social evolution. In important ways these suggestions return us to V. Gordon Childe's (1936) conception of the Neolithic and urban revolutions as (in part at least) idea-driven transformations connected to hinge points in the rate of accumulation of knowledge and productivity.

Methodological attractors

To date, archaeologists interested in complex systems have brought three main approaches to their analyses: scaling studies, agent-based modeling, and various network-based methods. These are not necessarily independent: agent-based models, for example, might generate social networks, which in turn could be examined for scaling behavior.

Scaling and the nearly ubiquitous power law

A very wide range of phenomena – from the frequencies of baby names to numbers of sexual contacts to the sizes of cities and frequencies of words in a text – correspond at least approximately to a power law (Bentley and Maschner 2008). In such a distribution (briefly mentioned above), the frequency of any phenomenon (such as the word "it" in a text) is inversely proportional to its rank in the frequency of all words in the text. Indeed, this statistical regularity was first made generally known for words in texts by Harvard philologist George Kingsley Zipf (1949), and later generalized by Benoit Mandelbrot, who also connected this regularity with his fractal geometry (Mandelbrot 1977: 239–45; see also 272–3 for Mandelbrot's reflections on Zipf's career).

As Bentley and Maschner (2008: 247) put it, "[M]any see [the ubiquity of these distributions] as profound...whereas others caution that it could be a mathematical coincidence." One such cautionary note is that many distributions that have been described as conforming to a power law do not, on more rigorous mathematical scrutiny (Clauset et al. 2009). Of course, for some purposes this may not really matter; it may simply be of more importance that a distribution be power-law-like in having a "fat" or "heavy" right tail.

Of more concern is the difficulty of identifying the process(es) giving rise to such distributions. For example, it seems likely that the fact that personal wealth distributions in many societies, or the sizes of firms, follow power-law-like distributions is more attributable to a "rich-get-richer" phenomenon than to the sort of "invisible hand" guiding the process described by Per Bak and his colleagues. A rich-get-richer phenomenon probably also explains why Maschner and Bentley (2003) were able to show that corporate household size on the north Pacific coast of North America is power-law-like, and why Bentley and Shennan (2003) could suggest with similar tools that those with prestige are likely to garner even more prestige. (See Grove [2011] for more discussion of plausible generating processes for such relationships.)

In general it is becoming less exciting to discover that some new phenomenon conforms to a power-law-like distribution than it is to begin to use the scaling parameters of those distributions in a comparative fashion to provide insight into the processes generating the distributions. Recently a new kind of scaling study has arisen with this idea in mind. Instead of graphing a rank (in a frequency distribution) against a measure of size or frequency, as Zipf did for word frequencies and many archaeologists have done for site sizes, the idea here is to generalize this approach for any quantity of interest Y (e.g. the number of patents granted) in relationship to some measure N of size of the system (e.g. city populations):

$$Y = cN^{\beta}$$

where c is a constant and β is the exponent (or power) from which the power law derives its name. When $\beta = 1$, the relationship scales linearly; values for $\beta < 1$ are called sublinear, and values $\beta > 1$, superlinear. Bettencourt et al. (2007) found that the relationship between recent patenting activity and the population sizes of US metropolitan areas scales superlinearly, with a value for β of about 1.29, meaning that as cities grow in size, their patenting activities grow more rapidly than do their populations. This is what economists call increasing returns to scale. Since that time, researchers have found superlinearities for other aspects of cities that have to do with knowledge or money generation and different creative activities (including crime!), even though other aspects of cities often scale sublinearly (gas stations or hospitals) or linearly (doctors or pharmacies) with size (e.g. Helbing et al. 2009). Conversely, various aspects of biological systems (e.g. metabolic rates, life-spans) tend to scale sublinearly with average body mass (e.g. West et al. 1997), though here, too, the mechanisms responsible are still debated (Savage et al. 2010).

A similar willingness to play creatively with such distributions, in conjunction with simulations beginning from recently hypothesized mean sizes of nested groups from R. A. Hill and Dunbar (2003), has allowed Grove (2010) to identify the recurrent group sizes hypothesized as responsible for forming a nested, hierarchical structure in the sizes of Bronze Age stone circles in Ireland (Figure 5.3). These nested levels may appear, in part at least, because of constraints on information processing or communication bandwidths that are general to human societies (Hamilton et al. 2007; Johnson 1982).

Agent-based modeling

Many useful applications of systems-style (equation-based) modeling in archaeology continue to appear and could legitimately be reviewed in this chapter. Space limits require me to focus on a newer style of simulation provided by agent-based models, which is particularly congenial to a CS archaeology. In such simulations, the "system" is broken down into its constituent interacting agents, from whose behaviors and interactions various systems-level properties may emerge. Although the earliest experiments with agent-based models in the social sciences were very abstract and general (like Axelrod's repeated prisoner's dilemma tournaments or Schelling's studies of neighborhood segregation), two more empirical projects in the prehispanic US Southwest helped introduce agent-based modeling to archaeologists. One, in Long House Valley of northeastern Arizona, is described by Dean et al. (2000) and Axtell et al. (2002; see also comment by Janssen 2009). The other, the Village Ecodynamics Project, is set in southwestern Colorado (Kohler et al. 2000a, 2007).

Although different in detail, both projects seek to make various systems-level properties, such as the local population trajectories, or the placement and sizes of residential sites, emerge from the interaction of households with each other and with the dynamic environments they inhabit. Both benefit from the high-resolution chronologies and climate proxies made possible by tree-rings.

Studies such as these value realism with respect to some particular setting at the expense of generality. Since it is difficult to evaluate very general models precisely because they do *not* fit any specific

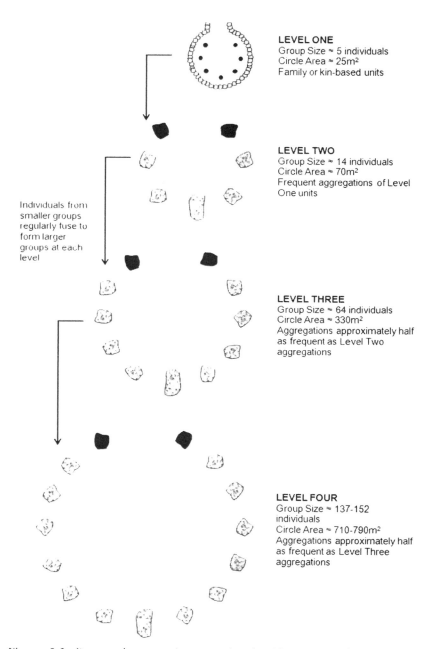

LEVEL ONE
Group Size ≈ 5 individuals
Circle Area ≈ 25m²
Family or kin-based units

LEVEL TWO
Group Size ≈ 14 individuals
Circle Area ≈ 70m²
Frequent aggregations of Level
One units

Individuals from
smaller groups
regularly fuse to
form larger
groups at each
level

LEVEL THREE
Group Size ≈ 64 individuals
Circle Area ≈ 330m²
Aggregations approximately half
as frequent as Level Two
aggregations

LEVEL FOUR
Group Size ≈ 137-152
individuals
Circle Area ≈ 710-790m²
Aggregations approximately half
as frequent as Level Three
aggregations

Figure 5.3. Proposed group sizes associated with stone circles of various sizes in Bronze Age Ireland. Each higher level incorporates lower-level groupings occurring proportionally less frequently

Source: Reprinted from *Journal of Archaeological Science*, 37, M. Grove "Stone circles and the structure of Bronze Age society," p. 2619, 2010, with permission from Elsevier and the author.

setting, a potential advantage to these more empirical approaches is that they may allow us to rigorously evaluate a general model by first "instantiating" it in a local setting, and then assessing how well its predictions fit the data from that archaeological record. For example, my colleagues and I have instantiated an abstract evolutionary public goods game developed by Hooper et al. (2010) in our study area in southwestern Colorado between AD 600 and 1300 (Kohler et al. 2012). We find that this model fits the available data for the rise of leadership in our area during its first 300 years reasonably well, though we identify the need for additional mechanisms to explain the more hierarchical systems that appear there after AD 1070.

Another recent example of an empirically rich agent-based model is Griffin and Stanish's (2007) instantiation of a general fission/fusion model for polity formation in the Lake Titicaca basin. A related model has also been proposed by Gavrilets et al. (2008), and Griffin (2010) has since generalized the Titicaca model and assessed its behavior using scaling tools. All of these focus on the problem of how we can explain the cycling phenomenon often seen in early polities, and also show how it is possible in agent-based models to generate new levels of organization from lower-level entities.

At the same time, applications of agent-based modeling of a more general, conceptual nature by and for archaeologists seem to be increasing rapidly. Here is a small sample displaying the diversity of problems being addressed:

- As a means for evaluating arguments for selection of lithic materials based on quality, optimization, or risk management, Brantingham (2003) developed an agent-based model for stone raw material procurement in which agents simply sampled the materials they encountered in a random walk.
- Premo and Hublin (2009) show how a process of culturally mediated migration in the Pleistocene could result in the low levels of genetic diversity found in modern humans.
- Powell et al. (2009) extend a version of Henrich's (2004) model for the demographic conditions allowing "cumulative adaptive evolution" to suggest how number and size of subpopulations in a metapopulation, and the degree of migration among them, affect cultural complexity. Their results suggest that the transient appearance of increased symbolic and technological complexity in various areas of Eurasia and Africa, prior to their fixation around 45,000 years ago, is plausibly explained by such demographic factors.

- Premo and Kuhn (2010) somewhat similarly show how local group extinctions could explain the very slow rates of cumulative culture change and low total cultural diversity in Lower and Middle Palaeolithic stone tool assemblages.

Note how all these studies – and others that could be cited – use agent-based modeling to explore the consequences for the archaeological record of some specific process, or set of processes, extended over a long period (and often across space). This is a task that is usually too difficult for the human mind to perform accurately unless the proposed processes are extremely simple. Thus agent-based models will often be useful as we attempt to reconstruct the processes responsible for the patterns we perceive in the record.

Most of the models produced so far by archaeologists feature "reactive" agents that receive input, process it, and produce an output according to the rules provided by the programmer. Costopoulos (2008) and Lake (2004) call for use of more "deliberative" agents "characterized by a wide diversity of individual viewpoints, strategic goals, and even belief systems" (Costopoulos 2008: 278). Although this would indeed address some of the critiques that postprocessualists originally levied against systems theory and other aspects of processualism, so far at least most modelers in archaeology have shown a preference for the relative clarity and interpretability provided by simpler agents, preferring to focus on the complexities arising from the interactions among these agents.

Networks

If scaling studies and agent-based modeling have recently emerged as promising methods whereby archaeologists can approach complexity, we might say that the use of networks in archaeology is in the process of emerging. One index of this is that it is easier to find creative quantitative applications of network concepts in recent dissertations (e.g. M. A. Hill 2009; Phillips 2011) than in current publications. Many of the seminal papers on network research are made available in Newman et al.'s *The Structure and Dynamics of Networks* (2006) and the major theoretical developments are briefly reviewed by Newman (2003). As for agent-based modeling, the study of networks was really not possible prior to ready access to high-speed computation. Network studies have been particularly transformed by the huge digital databases formed by and accessed through the web.

Network scientists have developed various ways to characterize any network based on measures such as the distribution of numbers of linkages among the nodes (degree distribution), the extent of clustering (or transitivity) in a network, and the extent to which networks are resilient to the removal of one or more nodes. Examinations of large numbers of social, informational, technological, and biological networks have shown that "small-world effects" – discovered by Stanley Milgram (1967) – are quite common. In such networks, most pairs of nodes can be connected by a relatively short path through the network, even if the network is very large. This property is called high transitivity. Power-law degree distributions ("scale-free" networks) also turn up very regularly in citation networks, the world wide web, metabolic networks, and power grids, for example (Newman 2003: 186–8). Network researchers generally attribute this property to preferential attachment, a variant of the "rich-get-richer" phenomenon mentioned above; researchers are more likely to cite a paper that is already commonly cited than to dig a possibly equally relevant article out of obscurity. According to Newman (2003: 176), this property was in fact first identified in citation networks, by Price (e.g. 1976), who called it the principle of cumulative advantage.

Although a vast number of archaeological studies invoke network concepts verbally, very few attempt to rigorously apply "network thinking." Bentley and Shennan (2003) explored some connections between network models and cultural transmission theory. Evans et al. (2009) develop an approach from statistical physics to graph an "archaeology of relations" in the Middle Bronze Age Cyclades. Their approach allows them to take as input to the model the known locations of archaeological sites (which become the nodes in the network) with important output from the model being the population sizes and most likely linkages among those sites. Essentially, they seek to define a state for the system that minimizes energy expenditure within constraints imposed by the locations of the sites (as given by the archaeological record, generally coarse-grained to the level of the island), the distances between sites, and parameters that control degree of site independence or self-sufficiency. In addition, they penalize (but do not prohibit) long-distance contacts. A graphical product of this work is shown in Figure 5.4.

Trajectories

Some additional promising approaches can be glimpsed on the horizon. In a time when people can point their phones at a mountain

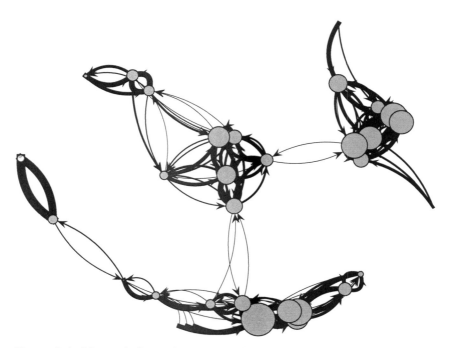

Figure 5.4. Network formed among Middle Bronze Age Cycladic sites by taking the size of the vertices (sites) to be proportional to their strength and to the total weight of the in- and out-going edges
Source: Output from the model described in T. Evans, C. Knappett, and R. Rivers 2009. Using statistical physics to understand relational space: a case study from Mediterranean prehistory. In D. Lane, S. van der Leeuw, D. Pumain, and G. West (eds.), *Complexity Perspectives in Innovation and Social Change*. Dordrecht: Springer. By permission of the author.

and be told that they are viewing Mont Blanc, archaeologists could do a much better job of recognizing patterns in data! DeDeo et al. (2010) develop an approach to extracting the payoffs to and the strategies used by primates from observations of their conflicts over time. This can be contrasted with normal uses of game theory, in which the strategies and payoffs are posited in advance, and then the dynamics of the interactions over time are deduced. DeDeo et al. call their approach "inductive game theory." I mention this not as a method that can be exported directly to archaeology, but as an example of the directions in which a CS archaeology might take us as we attempt to infer behaviors from time-series data on material associations.

As archaeology has accumulated vast quantities of all sorts of data over the last few decades, especially from what we in the US call cultural resource management, it is imperative that we develop more powerful techniques for building linkages among these datasets and analyzing them as a totality. Projects such as Digital Antiquity (*http:// www.digitalantiquity.org/*) and the Archaeological Data Service (*http://ads.ahds.ac.uk/*) are beginning to make these data accessible; to us falls the interesting task of addressing them creatively and with useful result.

Conclusions: relationships of CS with other archaeologies

I have portrayed CS approaches as partially descendant from proces-sualism via their connections with systems theory and simulation. The connections of CS archaeology with evolutionary archaeology (defined broadly) are also obvious. Indeed, complex systems of living agents are often called complex *adaptive* systems. It is difficult (and often pointless) to differentiate these two perspectives. Nevertheless – just as Kauffman's work tries to show how processes of self-orga-nization generate structure on which selection can act – archaeolo-gists beginning from a CS perspective may be more willing than evolutionary archaeologists to study processes constraining selection, or more prone to identify processes not envisioned by the modern synthesis, as I briefly noted for the papers on innovation from Lane et al. (2009).

Bintliff (2008: 160) considers CS to provide an integrative perspec-tive for archaeology:

> I have placed the theory under integrative programs because one of its chief appeals for contemporary archaeology...lies in the centrality of a subtle role for individual agents, unique events, in constant dialectic with constraining and enabling structures of their social and environ-mental context....Significantly, as forms of social life unfold into larger and more elaborate variations, new properties of culture appear which are not observed in simpler versions (emergent complexity). The advantages of the culture historical, processual, and post-processual paradigms are all available within the theoretical umbrella of chaos-complexity.

Whether or not one agrees with Bintliff, what seems obvious is that a CS perspective offers a completely open, rapidly evolving, and nondogmatic set of approaches to the archaeologist eager to embrace computation for clarifying the structure and behavior of the complex systems our ancestors created and inhabited.

Acknowledgments

I thank Henry Wright for discussion of some history; Luke Premo, Jeremy Sabloff, and Sander van der Leeuw for comments on an earlier draft; and Jesse Clark and Claire Kohler for help with aspects of production. Norman Hammond kindly made available the picture of David Clarke (Figure 5.1), taken by Tim Frost during Hammond's wedding at Peterhouse, Cambridge. Thanks to them both. Finally, I thank Tim Evans for providing Figure 5.4, a previously unpublished figure from his research.

Notes

1   Harries-Jones (1995: 103–44) explores Bateson's ambivalent relationship with cybernetics. Bateson was fascinated by the role of feedback – a key principle of cybernetics – in ecological systems, and how cybernetics elevated the role of information, in conjunction with feedback, to allow for self-organization. He also saw a correspondence between feedback and learning. His opposition to the more mechanistic, deterministic, and control-oriented aspects of cybernetics led him, though, to consider noise and error as having creative possibilities for systems, rather than as nuisances to be eradicated.

2   Ecology was of great interest to many students in US graduate schools in the 1960s and 1970s. There these students were exposed to systems approaches through texts such as E.P. Odum's *Fundamentals of Ecology* (1972), and his brother H.T. Odum's "Ecological Potential and Analog Circuits for the Ecosystem" (1960).

3   Space limits force selectivity here. Many other archaeologists, especially in the 1970s, employed aspects of cybernetics or systems theory either in their empirical research or in their theorizing, including J.N. Hill (1977a), Watson et al. (1971), Wright (1977), and Zubrow (1975); see also Plog (1975) and references therein.

4   Those interested in the networks joining people and ideas may find a link with Bateson here as well, since Rappaport, a

colleague of Flannery's at Michigan, was on sabbatical at the East–West Center, where he interacted with Bateson while writing his first pieces employing cybernetics concepts in the late 1960s (Rappaport 1971); perhaps he in turn influenced his younger colleague.

5 Jim Doran comes to a rather similar conclusion about cybernetics, though he is much more hopeful about the potentially constructive role of "the use of the computer to construct and test a 'simulation' of some complex system evolving in time" (Doran 1970: 296).

6 There is an ironic historic twist to Salmon's critique. Her authority on mathematical systems was Arthur Burks (1975), who helped in aspects of the design or implementation of the first important digital computers ENIAC and EDVAC. Eventually he joined the faculty at the University of Michigan, helping found the "BACH group" (Burks, Robert Axelrod, Michael Cohen, and John Holland), an important precursor to both the Santa Fe Institute and Michigan's Center for the Study of Complex Systems.

7 See Wobst (2010) for another view of the reasons for the demise of the first wave of simulation. Some current approaches in complex systems attempt to address many of the post-processual critiques, though the reconstruction of cultural meanings may be beyond any archaeology except in special circumstances.

References

Anderson, P. W. 1972. More is different. *Science* 177: 393–6.

Arthur, W. B. 2009. *The Nature of Technology: What It Is and How It Evolves*. New York: Free Press.

Ashby, W. R. 1956. *An Introduction to Cybernetics*. New York: Wiley.

Axelrod, R. A. 1984. *The Evolution of Cooperation*. New York: Basic Books.

Axtell, R. L., J. M. Epstein, J. S. Dean, G. J. Gumerman, A. C. Swedlund, J. Harburger, S. Chakravarty, R. Hammond, J. Parker, and M. Parker 2002. Population growth and collapse in a multiagent model of the Kayenta Anasazi in Long House Valley. *PNAS* 99: 7275–9.

Bak, P., C. Tang, and K. Wiesenfeld 1988. Self-organized criticality. *Physical Review A* 38: 364–74.

Bedau, M. A. and P. Humphreys 2008. Introduction to philosophical perspectives on emergence. In M. A. Bedau and P. Humphreys (eds), *Emergence: Contemporary Readings in Philosophy and Science*, 1–6. Cambridge, MA: MIT Press.

Bentley, R.A. and H.D.G. Maschner (eds) 2003. *Complex Systems and Archaeology: Empirical and Theoretical Applications*. Salt Lake City: University of Utah Press.

Bentley, R.A. and H.D.G. Maschner 2008. Complexity theory. In R.A. Bentley, H.D.G. Maschner, and C. Chippindale (eds), *Handbook of Archaeological Theories*, 245–70. Lanham, MD: AltaMira Press.

Bentley, R.A. and S.J. Shennan 2003. Cultural transmission and stochastic network growth. *American Antiquity* 68: 459–85.

Bettencourt, L.M.A., J. Lobo, and D. Strumsky 2007. Invention in the city: increasing returns to patenting as a scaling function of metropolitan size. *Research Policy* 36: 107–20.

Bintliff, J. 2008. History and continental approaches. In R.A. Bentley, H.D.G. Maschner, and C. Chippindale (eds), *Handbook of Archaeological Theories*, 147–64. Lanham, MD: AltaMira Press.

Brantingham, P.J. 2003. A neutral model of stone raw material procurement. *American Antiquity* 68: 487–509.

Buckley, W. 1967. *Sociology and Modern Systems Theory*. Englewood Cliffs, NJ: Prentice Hall.

Burks, A.W. 1975. Logic, biology and automata – some historical reflections. *International Journal of Man–Machine Studies* 7: 297–312.

Chippindale, C. 1993. Ambition, deference, discrepancy, consumption: the intellectual background to a post-processual archaeology. In N. Yoffee and A. Sherratt (eds), *Archaeological Theory: Who Sets the Agenda?* 27–36. Cambridge: Cambridge University Press.

Clarke, D.L. 1968. *Analytical Archaeology*. London: Methuen.

Clarke, D.L. (ed.) 1972. *Models in Archaeology*. London: Methuen.

Clauset, A., C.R. Shalizi, and M.E.J. Newman 2009. Power-law distributions in empirical data. *SIAM Review* 51: 661–7093.

Childe, V.G. 1936. *Man Makes Himself*. London: National Council of Labour Colleges.

Costopoulos, A. 2008. Simulating society. In R.A. Bentley, H.D.G. Maschner, and C. Chippindale (eds), *Handbook of Archaeological Theories*, 273–81. Lanham, MD: AltaMira Press.

Dean, J.S., G.J. Gumerman, J.M. Epstein, R.L. Axtell, A.C. Swedlund, M.T. Parker, and S. McCarroll 2000. Understanding Anasazi culture change through agent-based modeling. In T.A. Kohler and G.J. Gumerman (eds), *Dynamics in Human and Primate Societies: Agent-Based Modeling of Social and Spatial Processes*, 179–205. New York: Oxford University Press.

DeDeo, S., D.C. Krakauer, and J.C. Flack 2010. Inductive game theory and the dynamics of animal conflict. *PLoS Computational Biology* 6(5). Available: *http://www.ploscompbiol.org/article/info%3Adoi%2F10.1371%2Fjournal.pcbi.1000782* (accessed August 10, 2011).

Doran, J. 1970. Systems theory, computer simulation, and archaeology. *World Archaeology* 1: 289–98.

Evans, T., C. Knappett, and R. Rivers 2009. Using statistical physics to understand relational space: a case study from Mediterranean prehistory. In D. Lane, S. van der Leeuw, D. Pumain, and G. West (eds), *Complexity Perspectives in Innovation and Social Change*, 451–79. Dordrecht: Springer.

Flannery, K. 1968. Archeological systems theory and early Mesoamerica. In B. J. Meggers (ed.), *Anthropological Archeology in the Americas*, 67–87. Washington, DC: Anthropological Society of Washington.

Flannery, K. 1972. The cultural evolution of civilizations. *Annual Review of Ecology and Systematics* 3: 399–426.

Gavrilets, S., E. A. Duenez-Guzman, and M. D. Vose 2008. Dynamics of alliance formation and the egalitarian revolution. *PLoS ONE* 3(10). Available: *http://www.plosone.org/article/info:doi%2F10.1371%2Fjournal.pone.0003293* (accessed August 10, 2011).

Gell-Mann, M. 1994. *The Quark and the Jaguar: Adventures in the Simple and the Complex*. New York: Freeman.

Griffin, A. F. 2010. Emergence of fusion/fission cycling and self-organized criticality from a simulation model of early complex polities. *Journal of Archaeological Science* 38: 873–83.

Griffin, A. F. and C. Stanish 2007. An agent-based model of prehistoric settlement patterns and political consolidation in the Lake Titicaca basin of Peru and Bolivia. *Structure and Dynamics* 2(2). Available: *http://escholarship.org/uc/item/2zd1t887* (accessed August 10, 2011).

Grove, M. 2010. Stone circles and the structure of Bronze Age society. *Journal of Archaeological Science* 37: 2612–21.

Grove, M. 2011. An archaeological signature of multi-level social systems: The case of the Irish Bronze Age. *Journal of Anthropological Archaeology* 30: 44–61.

Hamilton, M. J., B. T. Milne, R. S. Walker, O. Burger, and J. H. Brown 2007. The complex structure of hunter-gatherer social networks. *Proceedings of the Royal Society Biological Sciences* 274: 2195–203.

Harries-Jones, P. 1995. *A Recursive Vision: Ecological Understanding and Gregory Bateson*. Toronto: University of Toronto Press.

Heims, S. J. 1991. *The Cybernetics Group*. Cambridge, MA: MIT Press.

Helbing, D., C. Kühnert, S. Lämmer, A. Johansson, B. Gehlsen, H. Ammoser, and G. B. West 2009. Power laws in urban supply networks, social systems, and dense pedestrian crowds. In D. Lane, S. van der Leeuw, D. Pumain, and G. West (eds), *Complexity Perspectives in Innovation and Social Change*, 11–41. Dordrecht: Springer.

Henrich, J. 2004. Demography and cultural evolution: how adaptive cultural processes can produce maladaptive losses: the Tasmanian case. *American Antiquity* 69: 197–214.

Hill, J. N. 1977a. Systems theory and the explanation of change. In J. N. Hill (ed.), *Explanation of Prehistoric Change*, 433–50. Albuquerque: University of New Mexico Press.

Hill, J. N. (ed.) 1977b. *Explanation of Prehistoric Change*. Albuquerque: University of New Mexico Press.

Hill, M. A. 2009. The Benefit of the Gift: Exchange and Social Interaction in the Late Archaic Western Great Lakes. Unpublished Ph.D. dissertation, Department of Anthropology, Washington State University, Pullman. Available: *http://www.dissertations.wsu.edu/Dissertations/Spring2009/m_hill_042309.pdf* (accessed August 10, 2011).

Hill, R. A. and R. I. M. Dunbar 2003. Social network size in humans. *Human Nature* 14: 53–72.

Hodder, I. (ed.) 1978. *Simulation Studies in Archaeology*. Cambridge: Cambridge University Press.

Hodder, I. 1986. *Reading the Past: Current Approaches to Interpretation in Archaeology*. Cambridge: Cambridge University Press.

Hooper, P. L., H. S. Kaplan, and J. L. Boone 2010. A theory of leadership in human cooperative groups. *Journal of Theoretical Biology* 265: 633–46.

Janssen, M. A. 2009 Understanding artificial Anasazi. *JASSS* 12: A244–60.

Johnson, G. A. 1982. Organizational structure and scalar stress. In C. Renfrew, M. J. Rowlands, and B. A. Segraves (eds), *Theory and Explanation in Archaeology: The Southampton Conference*, 389–422. New York: Academic Press.

Kauffman, S. A. 1993. *The Origins of Order: Self-Organization and Selection in Evolution*. New York: Oxford University Press.

Kauffman, S. A. and S. Johnsen 1991. Coevolution to the edge of chaos: coupled fitness landscapes, poised states, and coevolutionary avalanches. *Journal of Theoretical Biology* 149: 467–505.

Kohler, T. A. and G. J. Gumerman (eds) 2000. *Dynamics in Human and Primate Societies: Agent-Based Models of Social and Spatial Processes*. New York: Santa Fe Institute and Oxford University Press.

Kohler, T. A., J. Kresl, C. Van West, E. Carr, and R. H. Wilshusen 2000a. Be there then: a modeling approach to settlement determinants and spatial efficiency among late Ancestral Pueblo populations of the Mesa Verde region, US Southwest. In T. A. Kohler and G. J. Gumerman (eds), *Dynamics in Human and Primate Societies: Agent-Based Modeling of Social and Spatial Processes*, 145–78. New York: Oxford University Press.

Kohler, T. A., M. Van Pelt, and L. Y. L. Yap 2000b. Reciprocity and its limits: considerations for a study of the prehispanic Pueblo world. In B. J. Mills (ed.), *Alternative Leadership Strategies in the Prehispanic Southwest*, 180–206. Tucson: University of Arizona Press.

Kohler, T. A., C. D. Johnson, M. Varien, S. Ortman, R. Reynolds, Z. Kobti, J. Cowan, K. Kolm, S. Smith, and L. Yap 2007. Settlement dynamics in the prehispanic Central Mesa Verde region. In T. A. Kohler and S. E. van der Leeuw (eds), *The Model-Based Archaeology of Socionatural Systems*, 61–104. Santa Fe: SAR Press.

Kohler, T. A., D. Cockburn, P. Hooper, R. K. Bocinsky, and Z. Kobti 2012. The coevolution of group size and leadership: an agent-based public goods model for prehispanic Pueblo societies. *Advances in Complex Systems*. DOI No.: 10.1142/S0219525911003256.

Lake, M. W. 2004. Being in a simulacrum: electronic agency. In A. Gardner (ed.), *Agency Uncovered: Archaeological Perspectives on Social Agency, Power, and Being Human*, 191–209. London: UCL Press.

Lane, D., R. Maxfield, D. Read, and S. van der Leeuw 2009. From population thinking to organization thinking. In D. Lane, S. van der Leeuw, D. Pumain, and G. West (eds), *Complexity Perspectives in Innovation and Social Change*, 11–41. Dordrecht: Springer.

Levin, S. 1999. *Fragile Dominion: Complexity and the Commons*. Reading, MA: Perseus Books.

Lowe, J. W. G. 1982. Simulation in archaeology (review). *American Anthropologist* 84: 724–6.

McGlade, J. and E. Garnsey 2006. The nature of complexity. In E. Garnsey and J. McGlade (eds), *Complexity and Co-evolution: Continuity and Change in Socio-economic Systems*, 1–21. Cheltenham, UK: Elgar.

Mandelbrot, B. 1977. *Fractals: Form, Chance, and Dimension*. San Francisco: Freeman.

Maruyama, M. 1963. The second cybernetics: deviation-amplifying mutual causal processes. *American Scientist* 51: 164–79.

Maschner, H. D. G. and R. A. Bentley 2003. The power law of rank and household on the north Pacific. In R. A. Bentley and H. D. G. Maschner (eds), *Complex Systems and Archaeology: Empirical and Theoretical Applications*, 47–60. Salt Lake City: University of Utah Press.

Maynard Smith, J. 1974. The theory of games and the evolution of animal conflicts. *Journal of Theoretical Biology* 47: 209–21.

Milgram, S. 1967. The small world problem. *Psychology Today* 2: 60–7.

Mitchell, M. 2009. *Complexity: A Guided Tour*. Oxford: Oxford University Press.

Newman, M. E. J. 2003. The structure and function of complex networks. *SIAM Review* 45: 167–256.

Newman, M. E. J., A.-L. Barabási, and D. J. Watts 2006. *The Structure and Dynamics of Networks*. Princeton: Princeton University Press.

Odum, E. P. 1971. *Fundamentals of Ecology*, 3rd edition. Philadelphia: Saunders.

Odum, H. T. 1960. Ecological potential and analog circuits for the ecosystem. *American Scientist* 48: 1–8.

Phillips, S. C. 2011. Networked Glass: Lithic Raw Material Consumption and Social Networks in the Kuril Islands, Far Eastern Russia. Unpublished Ph.D. dissertation, Department of Anthropology, University of Washington, Seattle.

Pimm, S. L., J. H. Lawton, and J. E. Cohen 1991. Food web patterns and their consequences. *Nature* 350: 669–74.

Plog, F. T. 1975. Systems theory in archeological research. *Annual Review of Anthropology* 4: 207–24.

Plog, F. T. 1977. Systems theory and simulation: the case of Hawaiian warfare and redistribution. In J. N. Hill (ed.), *Explanation of Prehistoric Change*, 259–70. Albuquerque: University of New Mexico Press.

Powell, A., S. Shennan, and M. G. Thomas 2009. Late Pleistocene demography and the appearance of modern human behavior. *Science* 324: 1298–301.

Premo, L. S. and J.-J. Hublin 2009. Culture, population structure, and low genetic diversity in Pleistocene hominins. *PNAS* 106: 33–7.

Premo, L. S. and S. L. Kuhn 2010. Modeling effects of local extinctions on culture change and diversity in the Paleolithic. *PLoS ONE* 5(12). Available: *http://www.plosone.org/article/info%3Adoi%2F10.1371%2Fjournal. pone.0015582* (accessed August 10, 2011).

Price, D. J. de S. 1976. A general theory of bibliometric and other cumulative advantage processes. *Journal of the American Society of Information Science and Technology* 27: 292–306.

Rapoport, A. 1972. The search for simplicity. In E. László (ed.), *The Relevance of General Systems Theory*, 13–30. New York: Braziller.

Rappaport, R. A. 1971. Ritual, sanctity, and cybernetics. *American Anthropologist* 73: 59–76.

Rappaport, R. A. 1977. Maladaptation in social systems. In J. Friedman and M. Rowlands (eds), *Evolution in Social Systems*, 49–71. London: Duckworth.

Renfrew, C. (ed.) 1973. *The Explanation of Culture Change: Models in Prehistory*. London: Duckworth.

Sabloff, J. A. (ed.) 1981. *Simulations in Archaeology*. Albuquerque: University of New Mexico Press.

Salmon, M. H. 1978. What can systems theory do for archaeology? *American Antiquity* 43: 174–83.

Savage, V. M., L. P. Bentley, B. J. Enquist, J. S. Sperry, D. D. Smith, P. B. Reich, and E. I. von Allmen 2010. Hydraulic trade-offs and space filling enable better predictions of vascular structure and function in plants. *PNAS* 107: 22722–7.

Schelling, T. 1978. *Micromotives and Macrobehavior*. New York: Norton.

Shannon, C.E. and W. Weaver 1949. *The Mathematical Theory of Communication*. Urbana: University of Illinois Press.

Sherrington, D. 2010. Physics and complexity. *Philosophical Transactions of the Royal Society A* 368: 1175–89.

Smith, A. 1761/1985. Considerations concerning the first formation of languages, and the different genius of original and compounded languages. In J.C. Bryce (ed.), *Adam Smith: Lectures on Rhetoric and Belles Lettres*, 201–26. Indianapolis: Liberty Fund.

Tuggle, H.D., A.H. Townsend, and T.J. Riley 1972. Laws, systems, and research designs: a discussion of explanation in archaeology. *American Antiquity* 37: 3–12.

van der Leeuw, S. and J. McGlade (eds) 1997. *Time, Process and Structured Transformation in Archaeology*. London: Routledge.

van der Leeuw, S., D. Lane, and D. Read 2009. The long-term evolution of social organization. In D. Lane, S. van der Leeuw, D. Pumain, and G. West (eds), *Complexity Perspectives in Innovation and Social Change*, 85–116. Dordrecht: Springer.

von Bertalanffy, L. 1950. An outline of general systems theory. *The British Journal for the Philosophy of Science* 1(92): 134–65.

Watson, P.J., S.A. LeBlanc, and C.L. Redman 1971. *Explanation in Archaeology: An Explicitly Scientific Approach*. New York: Columbia University Press.

West, G.B., J.H. Brown, and B.J. Enquist 1997. A general model for the origin of allometric scaling laws in biology. *Science* 276: 122–6.

White, D.R. 2009. Innovation in the context of networks, hierarchies, and cohesion. In D. Lane, S. van der Leeuw, D. Pumain, and G. West (eds) *Complexity Perspectives in Innovation and Social Change*, 153–93. Dordrecht: Springer.

White, R. and G. Engelen 1993. Cellular-automata and fractal urban form – a cellular modeling approach to the evolution of urban land-use patterns. *Environment and Planning A* 25: 1175–99.

Wobst, H.M. 2010. Discussant's comments, Computer Simulation Symposium, Society for American Archaeology. In A. Costopoulos and M.W. Lake (eds), *Simulating Change: Archaeology into the Twenty-First Century*, 9–11. Salt Lake City: University of Utah Press.

Wood, J.J. and R.G. Matson 1973. Two models of sociocultural systems and their implications for the archaeological study of change. In C. Renfrew (ed.), *The Explanation of Culture Change*, 673–83. London: Duckworth.

Wolfram, S. 1984. Universality and complexity in cellular automata. *Physica D* 10: 1–35.

Wright, H. T. 1977. Toward an explanation of the origin of the state. In J. N. Hill (ed.), *Explanation of Prehistoric Change*, 215–30. Albuquerque: University of New Mexico Press.

Zipf, G. K. 1949. *Human Behavior and the Principle of Least Effort: An Introduction to Human Ecology*. Cambridge, Mass.: Addison-Wesley.

Zubrow, E. B. W. 1975. *Prehistoric Carrying Capacity: A Model*. Menlo Park, CA: Cummings Publishing.

6

TOWARDS A COGNITIVE ARCHAEOLOGY

Material Engagement and the Early Development of Society

Colin Renfrew

The development of a cognitive archaeology, within the context of contemporary archaeological theory, has been a relatively slow one. The potential was noted already by Lewis Binford in 1962 in what may be regarded as the inaugural paper of the New Archaeology. There he identified "ideotechnic artefacts" which "have their primary functional context in the ideological component of the social system" (Binford 1962: 221). He set out a clear critique (Binford 1968: 21) of the formal ladder of reliability which had been formulated by Christopher Hawkes (1954: 161–2):

1   To infer from the archaeological phenomena to the techniques producing them I take to be relatively easy.
2   To infer to the subsistence-economies of the human groups concerned is fairly easy.
3   To infer to the socio-political institutions of the groups, however, is considerably harder.
4   To infer to the religious institutions and spiritual life...is the hardest inference of all.

Binford challenged this view and asserted that there was no underlying principle which made the recovery of aspects of one dimension or sub-system of the culture system more difficult than another, or that made the fourth rung of Hawkes's ladder of inference more difficult to attain than the first. Indeed this aspiration of a balance among such dimensions was precisely what I attempted to achieve in analyzing the early Bronze Age Aegean a few years later and in dealing in detail with symbolic and projective systems, following discussion of the subsistence subsystem, and of craft specialization and social systems (Renfrew 1972: 404–39).

In practice, however, the early studies by most exponents of the New Archaeology, or "processual archaeology" as it came to be called, were mainly focused, much as Hawkes had anticipated, upon tool production or upon the subsistence economy, and sometimes on the socio-political system, rarely upon the cognitive dimension (including religion). I discussed the matter in an inaugural lecture a decade later (Renfrew 1982). Indeed much of the traction achieved by "postprocessual archaeology" at that time (Hodder 1982a, 1982b), later termed "interpretive archaeology" (Hodder et al. 1995), may be ascribed to the relative neglect by the early processual archaeology of the symbolic or cognitive dimension.

More recently, however, a clearly defined field of cognitive archaeology has come into being (Renfrew 1994, 2005) and its outlines have become reasonably clear (Renfrew and Bahn 2008: 391–428). It is possible to speak of a cognitive-processual archaeology which can extend and develop the earlier functional-processual archaeology of the 1970s and 1980s. The making of the human mind has become a major focus of study (Renfrew 2007; Renfrew and Morley 2009). A frequent starting point for discussion is the nature of the transitions which occurred with, or were the result of, the emergence of our own species, *Homo sapiens*.

The sapient paradox

In recent works which discuss the origins of "mind," and the crucial evolutionary developments which led to the emergence of human societies as we know them, it is often asserted that there was one decisive moment (or period) in which the "human revolution" took place (Mellars and Gibson 1996), although this view has been criticized by Gamble (2007). It is often asserted, rather than demonstrated, that with the emergence of our own species, *Homo sapiens*, perhaps 150,000 years ago in Africa and certainly by 40,000 years ago in Europe, there emerged not only physically modern humans, but also the formulation of fully developed language as we know it, a more sophisticated material culture, and fully human self-consciousness. It should be stressed, however, that after this momentous conjuncture (if such it was), looking at the question broadly and at a distance, there were few decisive happenings in human existence for another 30,000 years. Hunter-gatherer communities peopled much of the earth – what the biologists term an adaptive radiation. But there were few other profound and long-lasting changes, at any rate when the picture is perceived in very general terms, until the end of the Pleistocene period.

Why was this? Why did subsequent change – the cultural trajectories that in many parts of the world later led to the development of complex societies – come so slowly? The central theme of this chapter is that it was human *engagement* with the material world which turns out to have been the decisive process.

Language may well have been fully developed in all humans by 40,000 years ago. And words are indeed symbols, the most flexible of symbols by which reality can be conceived, represented, and communicated. But language itself does not seem to have made all that much difference. Hunter-gatherer societies, with a few exceptions, seem to have been conservative – adaptive certainly, but not often innovative. Words and narratives there may have been, but until humans became more interactively involved with the material substance of the world, until they began to act upon the world in a range of new ways, using a wider range of materials, not very much changed. And it was when some of these materials themselves took on, or were led to take on, symbolic power that the process of engagement became a powerful driving force for social and economic change.

With the emergence and dispersal of *Homo sapiens* it can be said that the speciation phase in the development of humankind had been achieved. It is likely that the human genome, as documented in human DNA, had by then been broadly established. This, however, can only be further investigated when ancient DNA studies become as effective at sequencing the DNA of early fossil humans of our own species of some 40,000 years ago as they have been in sequencing the Neanderthal genome of our cousins *Homo neandertalensis*. Since that time, the behavioral changes cannot be ascribed primarily to changes in our DNA. Human development had entered a new phase where change in the genome was no longer significant; this we can call the *tectonic* phase (Renfrew 2007: 97: after the Greek *tekton*, carpenter or builder), laying emphasis upon the construction of human culture, recalling the title of V. Gordon Childe's book *Man Makes Himself* (1936). This phase is characterized by new forms of human engagement with the material world, and the name refers to the human construction of the world in which we live. It is of course the case that the first, speciation phase of human development was already marked by such revolutionary new forms of human engagement with the world as the first use of tools and later the systematic production and use of fire. The distinction now, however, is that in the tectonic phase the genotype is broadly fixed. Within the tectonic phase, the evolution that is taking place is essentially cultural evolution.

We may discern at least two crucial episodes in this process, prior to the development of writing, which, as Merlin Donald (1991) has shown, ultimately came to offer the most flexible and significant form of "external symbolic storage." But he and others have overlooked a series of fundamental developments before the inception of writing became possible (see Renfrew 1998a; Renfrew and Zubrow 1994). In the first episode the development of sedentary society allowed a much more varied relationship with the material world to develop. In the second, the emergence of certain materials as embodying wealth and prestige led to fundamental changes in the nature of human culture and society.

In an earlier essay (Renfrew 1996) I sought to show how strange it is, on the conventional view of the "human revolution," as indicated above, that the new genotype producing the new phenotype *Homo sapiens* did not at once produce a whole new range of interesting behavior patterns. What, then, was so novel about this new species? Usually when a new species emerges it develops the new behavior patterns by which we recognize it. Here we may speak of the "praktotype," from the word *praxis*, referring to activity and behavior. In retrospect we may regard this new human animal as a very special one, when we survey its achievements over the forty or so millennia since its appearance in Europe, or the hundred or more since its initial emergence in Africa. But why is it only in the past ten millennia that we see strikingly new behavior patterns – constructions, innovations, inventions – which are changing the world? That is the sapient paradox.

My answer is that the true human revolution came only much later, with the emergence of a way of life which permitted a much greater engagement between the human animal and the world in which we live. Human cultures become more substantive, more material. We came to use the world in new ways, and become involved with it in new ways. I suggest that the key to this new embodiment, this new materialization, may have been sedentism.

A hypostatic view

Hominids learned to make tools way back in the time of *Homo habilis*, and this step has rightly been hailed by anthropologists as a crucial one by which a new kind of engagement with the world could be effected. Clearly many other species use the substance of the world for their own purposes – not just for food, but in many cases for shelter: for example, by the elaborate constructions of the termite ants or the bower birds. But by the time of *Homo erectus*, the deliberate artifact, the hand-ax, has reached a sophistication matched by no other species. Often the raw material had first to be procured from a distance, and the artifact carefully shaped, using techniques which were passed down over the centuries and millennia, no doubt through a process of mimesis. With the emergence of *Homo sapiens* came a greater range and sophistication of toolkits, such as are seen in the Upper Palaeolithic blade industries of Europe.

That this was a sophisticated animal may be inferred from the likelihood that well-developed language abilities had emerged before the dispersals of *ca.* 70,000 years ago. It is documented by the exceptionally sophisticated Franco-Cantabrian cave art which is seen in Europe (but only in Europe) during the late Pleistocene period.

Despite all that, however, hunter-gatherer societies in Palaeolithic times showed only a limited range of behaviors. Indeed if we look at hunter-gatherer societies down to the present day, it is possible to argue much the same point, although in the past 5,000 or 10,000 years some may have developed more elaborate behaviors than were seen in the Pleistocene period. Certainly one can point to impressive village settlements of hunter-gatherer-fisher communities with a complex pattern of behavior (I am thinking notably of the potlatch of the communities of the North American northwest coast). But the most sophisticated of these appear to have been sedentary communities, albeit with a hunter-gatherer-fisher economy.

I would argue that it was the development of a sedentary existence (which, among other things, is of course dependent upon a steady food supply) that opened the way to a more complex way of life, and that it did so through a process of "substantialization." This is where the old "mind" versus "matter" dichotomy breaks down. The mistake made by commentators who focus exclusively upon the "mind" is that they emphasize the potential for rich symbolic behavior without indicating that the ultimate criterion is the praxis in the material world. This supposed potential only reaches fulfillment when mind and matter come together in a new material behavior. To deal with these issues properly requires what one may term a *hypostatic* approach which transcends the mind/matter dichotomy (even if such terminology recalls medieval theological debates about the essence of the Holy Trinity). My approach in this chapter is that in many cases it is not correct to assume that mind precedes practice, or that concept precedes material symbol. As we shall see, symbols are not always

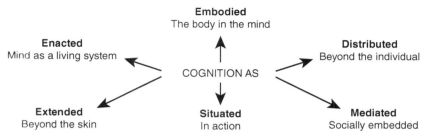

Figure 6.1. Variations of cognition

just the reflection or "materialization" (DeMarrais et al. 1996) of pre-existing concepts. The substantive engagement process brings the two forward together.

The cognitive basis of material engagement

Since the first edition of this volume (Hodder 2001), the bases for a theory of material engagement have been considerably developed. As Lambros Malafouris has indicated (2004: 57, fig. 5.2), it is necessary to redefine the boundaries of the mind, seeing cognition as an embodied process which is socially embedded and which is distributed beyond the individual (Figure 6.1).

Material engagement theory is concerned with the relationships between humans and the material world, and focuses upon the use and the status of material objects (mainly created objects or artifacts) which are employed to mediate in the interactions between human individuals and between humans and their environment (Renfrew 2004: 23). It has been formulated in part as a response to the "sapient paradox" as outlined above. It seeks to overcome the traditional mind/matter duality by stressing the knowledge-based nature of human action. From such experience-based constructs as "weight" and "length" and "sameness" emerge the possibility of measure and of taxonomy (Morley 2010). From a practical knowledge of the properties of matter, such as the flaking of flints or the baking of clay, emerge the possibilities of material production and hence of engineering. From the *praxis* of exchange transactions or of house building arise "the highly-structured temporalities that differentiate agriculturalists from hunter-gatherers" (Boivin 2004: 66). It is from the engagement process between humans and artifacts that new meanings are generated. New "affordances" are created which themselves encourage further innovation (Knappett 2004).

These considerations lead on to further discussion of the capacities of the human mind and so towards neuroscience (Malafouris 2009). Indeed one recent tendency in archaeological theory has been to focus specifically upon the workings of the brain, on what has been described as "the biology of mind" (Changeux 1985; Changeux and Ricoeur 2000), and to seek to relate this approach to the evolution of social behavior patterns (Runciman et al. 1996). Brain scans, for instance by fMRI (functional Magnetic Resonance Imaging), have been used to explore the neurophysiological implications of tool making (Schick and Toth 1993; Stout et al. 2009).

An important emphasis, however, is to look beyond the brain itself, and to emphasize the social and cultural context (Tomasello 1999). Philosophers such as Andy Clark (1997, 2010) have adopted a broadly evolutionary approach in which the human engagement with the material world plays a central role. The role of cultural practices in the emergence of modern human intelligence (Hutchins 2009) is a central theme, and the place of practical procedures and of language in the development of cognition (Roepstorff 2009) is a current topic.

Symbol before concept

It is widely agreed that what distinguishes humankind most obviously from other species is the ability to use symbols. Ernst Cassirer (1944: 26) defined man as *animal symbolicum*, and all that we learn supports the validity of that definition. Words, of course, are symbols and the definition embraces speech and language. But there is also non-verbal communication and symbol can precede language, as the dance of the bees (indicating direction and distance) exemplifies.

Here I want to make the point that material culture can have its own active role, as Hodder (1986) has emphasized, and that there are categories of "symbol" which are not adequately described by the formulation:

$$X \text{ represents } Y \text{ in } C \text{ (where } C \text{ is the context)}$$

which is the usual definition of the symbol X, the signifier representing Y as signified. I want to draw attention to a range of cases where the material *thing* which does indeed work as a symbol – that is to say, has a symbolic role, is not representing something else but is itself active. We might call it a *constitutive symbol*.

The philosopher John Searle, in *The Construction of Social Reality*, has drawn attention to the key role of what he terms "institutional facts," which are realities by which society is governed (Searle 1995: 31ff.). As he puts it:

> Some rules regulate antecedently existing activities.... However, some rules do not merely regulate, they also create the very possibility of certain activities. Thus the rules of chess do not regulate an antecedently existing activity.... Rather the rules of chess create the very possibility of playing chess. The rules are *constitutive* of chess in the sense that playing chess is constituted in part by acting in accord with the rules. (Searle 1995: 27)

The institutional facts to which Searle refers and which are the building blocks of society include such social realities as marriage, kingship, property, value, law, and so forth. Most of these are concepts which are formulated in words and which are best expressed by words – that is how Searle sees it, and philosophers operate with words. Searle draws attention to what he terms the self-referentiality of many social concepts, and he takes "money" as a prime example. But the point I wish to stress today is that in some cases – and money is a very good example – the material reality, the material symbol, takes precedence. The concept is meaningless without the actual substance (or at least in the case of money it was for many centuries, until further systems of rules allowed promissory notes to become formalized as paper money, then as equities and bank cheques, and now as electronic transactions). In an early society you could not have money unless you had valuables to serve as money, and the valuables (the material) preceded the concept (money).

Some material symbols, then, are constitutive in their material reality. They are not disembodied verbal concepts, or not initially. They have an indissoluble reality of substance: they are substantive. The symbol (in its real, actual substance) actually precedes the concept. Or, if that is almost claiming too much, they are self-referential. The symbol cannot exist without the substance, and the material reality of the substance precedes the symbolic role which is ascribed to it when it comes to embody such an institutional fact. If this discussion seems rather abstract, the concept of weight offers a concrete example (Renfrew 1982; Renfrew 2007: 117). In that instance it is the experience of material, heavy things and the further experience of two things which are equally heavy which must have generated the possibility of assessing weight by measurement and so opened the way to metrication. The development of measure by weight was a significant step (Morley and Renfrew 2010), as is discussed further below.

It is my argument here that this process lies at the nub of the development of human societies. Moreover, in non-literate societies it is material symbols which play a central role by allowing the emergence and development of institutional facts. Some classes of institutional fact may well be a feature of all human societies. Affinal kinship relations – including the institution of marriage or something like it – seem to be a feature of all human societies (and indeed one could argue that enduring pair-bonding among many other species hints at something like it more widely). But I shall argue that other kinds of material symbol are not generally a feature of mobile hunter-gatherer societies. It is not until the emergence of sedentary societies (usually in conjunction with food production) that the process of the human engagement with the material world takes on a new form and permits the development of new modes of interaction with the material world permitting the ascription of (symbolic) meaning to material objects.

This, I will argue, is the solution of the sapient paradox – why so little that was truly and radically novel accompanied the emergence of our own species, *Homo sapiens*, despite what we can now recognize as its enormous inherent potential to undergo and initiate radical change.

A crucial nexus: towards inequality and power

In many societies of the Old World, and possibly of the New World, one may seek to identify a crucial nexus of symbolic concepts for which the above remarks are highly relevant. The nexus is less obvious than another more prominent configuration, the power nexus, which is very widely recognized as central to the existence of non-egalitarian societies in which the exercise of power is of paramount significance. Such is the case in those polities which are generally recognized as state societies. There the exercise of power and the institutionalization of power are generally regarded as defining criteria. The institutions of power generally involve elaborate symbolism which accompanies a wide range of institutional facts, including kingship itself, the various offices of state, and the mutual obligations of ruler and ruled. There is a symbolism associated with military force which allows its effective exercise without the frequent outbreak of open conflict. The role of material symbols in all these areas remains to be analyzed with thoroughness.

Here, however, I would like to stress a different nexus: the inter-relationship between at least four crucial concepts, three of which are

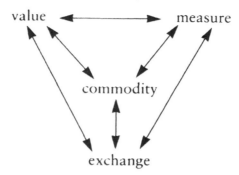

Figure 6.2. The interrelationship between four crucial concepts

undoubtedly symbolic and of the kind described above where the material reality has to accompany or precede the concept. The symbol is not simply a projection of an antecedent concept, but in its substantive reality is constitutive of the concept. The configuration is as in Figure 6.2. Value and measure are both primary concepts of this kind. Commodity perhaps depends upon the pre-existence of both, and also on the prior reality of exchange (since individual objects can be exchanged without any notion of commodity, but the notion of goods as commodities is difficult to conceive without the possibility of their changing hands).

Measure

Using the special case of the Indus Valley stone cubes, it can be shown (Renfrew 1982) that from direct archaeological observation and inference one may establish that in the Indus Valley civilization there was in operation a procedure equivalent to that which we would describe as *weighing*, with a system of counting by *standard units* of weight. The further inference is that the practice of weighing has a utilitarian purpose, which is to establish some sort of equivalence between what is being weighed on the left and what is being weighed on the right, and that (if the enterprise is to be more than vacuous) two different materials are involved. This brings us close to the notion of equivalence between different materials in terms of measured parameters. This allows the notion of quantifying such equivalencies, and does not in itself necessitate exchange. But it is easy to see that the quantification of equivalencies will fit easily with notions of value and with the practice of exchange.

The essential point here, in terms of the earlier discussion, is that "weight" can have no meaning in a disembodied sense. Only material things have weight and the concept has no meaning without experience of these. The substantive reality precedes any notion of quantifying it or of standardizing it by balancing a standard object (the "weight") against other objects.

The same observation applies to any form of measurement. The phenomenon (extension, volume) pre-exists its measure. Any standard of measure, by which X may be compared with Y (which now therefore enters the symbolic domain), is secondary to the substantive realities. Obviously this applies as much to measure of extension as to weight, of time as to volume (whether liquid or dry), of temperature as to field intensity. Each requires a prior notion of computation, of counting (see Morley and Renfrew 2010). (The early development of counting systems in Mesopotamia, involving a different form of material engagement, has been discussed by Schmandt-Besserat [2010], and the development of other mnemonic systems used for computation in the Andes by Urton [2010].)

Value

Value is one of the most elusive of concepts. Ultimately value is clearly ascribed. Nothing is "of value" unless it is "valued." As I have pointed out in relation to the earliest known goldworking and the Copper Age site of Varna in Bulgaria, the notion of intrinsic value amounts to an institutionalized fact (Renfrew 1986). It is indeed the case that in many cultures particular materials are singled out and considered to be of value.

We are familiar in our own society with the notion of the "intrinsic" value of gold and diamonds. In prehispanic Mexico, turquoise and macaw feathers were highly esteemed – and, as in China, jade (J.G.D. Clark 1986). It seems clear, however, that none of these things could be coveted (and thus valued) without their inherent qualities being noticed and admired. The material becomes "valuable" only when it is noticed.

This discussion applies to prestige materials and commodities, and does not directly extend to what Marx described as the "use value" of everyday things and commodities. Here a different argument needs to be developed. Clearly an edible material is useful in that it may be eaten. But that it is valuable must depend on other possibilities, and in particular the potential for exchange. The concept of "value" generally implies some measure of "agreed value" as determined between individuals: it is a social concept. Underlying the ascription is the notion of K amount of X being worth L amount of Y. The equivalence again brings us to the notion of X as equivalent to (in some sense may stand for) Y, and we discover again that the potential exchange interaction implies a symbolic relationship, or what stands close to one.

To return to "valuables," their value may be ascribed, but it is inseparable from their substantive and material existence. (This is not the place for a long disquisition on value. Some individual objects acquire their "value" exclusively from their history, for instance a lock of Napoleon's hair. That is a different case and depends upon other symbolic constructs.)

The development of systems of value is an interesting feature in the emergence of most, or perhaps all, complex societies. What will interest us further below is that such systems may rarely be seen among egalitarian societies, including most hunter-gatherer societies.

Commodity

Commodity is clearly a symbolic concept at one remove from the range of possible specific instances: wheat, maize, olives, wool, linen, perfumed oil, computer chip, refrigerator, television set, or whatever. But in its initial sense it relates to substances (the first six on the above list) rather than to manufactured and assembled products (the last three). It refers to a material whose quantity may be measured, which may have a definite value, and which may be exchanged. Its central position in the nexus is evident.

Exchange

"Exchange" is, like "value" and "measure" but unlike "commodity," a verb as well as a noun. As we have noted, it implies a transaction between two agents, with some notion of balance or equivalence between what is given and what is received. To set up an exchange therefore creates the relationship "X balances Y," which is very close to the defining relationship of a symbol: "X stands for Y." There is something special about this homology, just as there is in the substitution which operates in the metaphor where "X replaces Y."

It may be that, in dealing with this nexus, we should not characterize the various equivalencies as "symbolic" so much as "catallactic" (i.e. pertaining to exchange). For the moment we will continue to proceed as if the latter is subsumed within the former.

These relationships seem to be crucial to the growth and development of most complex societies. I will illustrate in a moment with the prehistoric European case how the development of metallurgy brought forth new kinds of valuables which permitted the development of many social features and roles not previously prominent – the warrior, the craft specialist, the constitution of masculinity as seen in the European Iron Age (and therefore of femininity also), the seafarer, the trader. In a way that is often subtle, the notion of value (and sometimes the related notion of prestige) had a part in most of these developments. In every case we can see how the products of material culture and their evaluation were of central significance.

This is a point which I made some years ago in relation to the emergence of complex society in the prehistoric Aegean:

> The interactions among the subsystems of the society take place chiefly at the level of the human individual since the subsystems of a culture are defined ultimately by the activities of individuals. It is the individual who equates wealth with prestige or social rank, for instance, or who forms for him- or herself a projection of the world where social roles and religious concepts both find a place.... Underlying these expressions of social status, these mechanisms for enhancing reputation and self-satisfaction, is a *symbolic equivalence of social and material values*, an equivalence without which the multiplier effect could scarcely operate. The well-being which comes from the satisfaction of primary animal needs is no longer the chief human goal, but rather the satisfaction accruing from prestige, status and good reputation. These can sometimes be acquired and expressed though material goods. The material world is now the field for a symbolic competition. (Renfrew 1972: 496–8)

The emphasis here upon the individual is in some sense valid – the approach is one of what is often termed "methodological individualism" (Bell 1994) – but we should emphasize Searle's point that these symbolic equivalencies are "institutional facts" which are valid for society as a whole, not just for individuals. The symbols we are speaking of are in that sense social products as well as cognitive ones.

This, then, is the central point of this chapter – that the crucial transitions in prehistory were dependent upon the development of a series of quite sophisticated concepts. Their sophistication is not, however, instantly obvious today because they have by now become obvious to us, and are embedded within our own thinking. Indeed in a capitalist society, where money is the measure of everything, not just of wealth, to question the intrinsic worth of gold may seem close to a heresy. These distinctions are, however, crucial, and their emergence, and the far-reaching consequences of that emergence, can be seen in the archaeological record of prehistoric Europe and beyond.

The European trajectory in the Bronze Age

The trajectory of cultural development in the European Bronze Age well exemplifies some of these points. In Neolithic Britain, the societies of the later Neolithic had some degree of central organization capable of creating large monuments such as Stonehenge (Bradley 1993, 1998). But these were "group-oriented" societies, contrasting with the "individualizing" societies of the early Bronze Age (Renfrew 1974), where the status of the individual came to be expressed in individual burial under a tumulus (burial mound) and with the accompaniment of sometimes rich grave goods.

Although polished stone axes (sometimes of jade) and bracelets and pendants of shell must be regarded already during the Neolithic as prestige goods (shells of the marine mollusc *Spondylus gaederopus* were traded over great distances), it was during the Copper Age of southeast Europe that high-prestige burials are first discerned in the cemetery of Varna (Renfrew 1986). Significantly the materials there include some innovations – the first appearance of gold ornaments on any scale anywhere in the world, and the use of copper as what appears to be a prestige commodity. These are, however, simply the beginnings during the Copper Age.

Two millennia later, at the onset of the early Bronze Age in northwest Europe we see very clearly the use of a significant new artifact, the bronze dagger. It is here that a new nexus develops between bronze, weapons of war, and a masculine ethos which continued to develop over three millennia, leading first to the chiefly societies of the "Celtic" Iron Age, and subsequently to the chivalry of the medieval knights.

Paul Treherne (1995) traced the emergence of masculine self-identity and the notion of the warrior's beauty during the Bronze Age. Here once again the metal weapons and the finery of the warrior are constitutive of these qualities, not merely reflective. The "materialization" of which DeMarrais et al. (1996) speak is not the embodiment in material culture of pre-existing concepts; it is a hypostatic union of idea and material. Without the bronze, without the weapons, there would have been no Bronze Age warrior idea. I have tried to show (Renfrew 1998b) how the horse and chariot, and later the horse supporting the mounted warrior, formed elements of "cognitive constellations" which caught the imagination of the time, and are seen in models, carvings, and other representations during the Bronze Age (for the chariot) and the Iron Age (for the horseman).

We may see here how the sedentism of the European Neolithic permitted the development of group-oriented societies, whose religious and ideological aspirations found expression in and were given shape by monuments. The shift towards individual prestige was accompanied by the nexus of value, commodity, and exchange discussed earlier, and by the specifically European nexus of bronze, weaponry, and masculinity, reinforced later by the chariot and then the cavalry. In these cases the symbolic role of these things is crucial, but the symbol did not reflect so much as constitute the perceived and conceptualized reality.

Symbols, ritual, and religion

The early New Archaeology did not effectively address the archaeology of religion, despite Binford's aspiration to ascend the fourth rung of Hawkes's ladder. A systematic attempt was made in *The Archaeology of Cult* (Renfrew 1985) to develop a system of inference to allow the demonstration and exploration of ritual practice at one particular Aegean Bronze Age site, Phylakopi in Melos. This treatment proved influential in encouraging a more rigorous general approach towards the field of ritual and religion (Insoll 2004, 2011; Kyriakidis 2005). The systematic work by Kent Flannery and Joyce Marcus on the cognitive systems of early Oaxaca in Mesoamerica, including the practice of ritual (Flannery and Marcus 1983; Marcus and Flannery 1996; Marcus 2007), has been similarly cautious and skeptical in its treatment of religion. The same may certainly be said of the recent work by Richard Burger (1995) and by John Rick (Kembel and Rick 2004) at the key Peruvian ritual site of Chavín de Huántar.

The role of the material symbol in the development of ritual and religion, touched upon earlier, is worth emphasizing. Jacques Cauvin (1994) has rightly stressed the use of images – plastered skulls and clay effigies – in the religious life of the earliest sedentary societies of the Near East. The belief system we see there, and which was (with some transformations) carried to southeast Europe by the first farmers, may be described as *iconic*: it involved representations of human and/or divine forms. However, we should note that the power of the symbol in the religious field goes far beyond that.

In northwest Europe it is clear from the distribution of special sites, notably the henge monuments of the British Isles, that religious rituals of considerable intensity were carried out at special places. But the evidence is almost entirely aniconic. An almost puritanical reluctance to represent the human form prevails, and the spirals on the Irish Neolithic monuments are the nearest one comes in the Atlantic zone to the Mediterranean profusion of Neolithic Greece or Malta.

The form of ritual and religious practice seen in Britain was as much shaped by constitutive material symbolism as that in southeast Europe, however. The burial monuments and chapels ("megalithic tombs") and the ritual monuments of Neolithic Britain continue to impress, indeed to awe us, today, although we no longer have the narrative, the myth, to interpret them fully. But they well exemplify the points made by DeMarrais et al. (1996), by Earle (1997), and by Mithen (1998) concerning the importance of the material presence for ritual and its wider appreciation and perpetuation. By their works ye shall know them. Comparable remarks may be made about the great houses and kivas of the American Southwest, notably at Chaco Canyon. Again the belief system which took shape there was an aniconic one, but one whose compelling power was constituted as well as reflected by these great and indeed awe-inspiring structures. Such remarks are obviously pertinent also for the great religious centers of Mesoamerica. These are all testimony to the active and constituent role of material culture in the development of human society.

Some aspects of the content of the belief systems of prehistoric societies are difficult to recover in the absence of written testimony. Visual imagery, however, is often informative, even if its appearance in the Upper Palaeolithic of France and Spain remains enigmatic (Renfrew and Morley 2009). The rich iconography of the ancient Maya was used to very good effect by Schele and Miller in their pioneering survey *The Blood of Kings* (1986), where they were assisted in their interpretation by the decipherment of the Maya script. Visual imagery remains a key approach for the interpretation of prehistoric religious practices (Hodder 2006; Renfrew and Morley 2007). But neither cognitive archaeology nor interpretive archaeology has yet succeeded in developing an entirely convincing methodology for the investigation and analysis of prehistoric ritual.

Converging approaches

The development of cognitive archaeology, as I have described it here, lies very much in the tradition of processual archaeology, now in its cognitive-processual stage of development. The theme of material engagement, as reflected in some recent publications (DeMarrais et al. 2004; Malafouris and Renfrew 2010; Morley and Renfrew 2010), sits well with the pragmatic and even scientific turn of some recent philosophical approaches (A. Clark 1997; Searle 1995). But it should be stressed that very much the same problems have been discussed effectively within the avowedly different "postprocessual" tradition, although this has at times rejected the processual tradition which indeed it purports to succeed. Sometimes, indeed, the rhetorical distinctions between the interpretive and the cognitive-processual traditions can seem more apparent than real. For example, the treatment of "agency" by Robb (2004) or by Barrett (2001) addresses very much the same issues as are discussed by Malafouris (2004) in his discussion of material engagement, although the terminologies may differ somewhat. The themes considered by Miller (1987) or by Thomas (1991) are significant as much to a cognitive-processual archaeology as to the interpretive archaeology in which context they emerged. Indeed some of the issues addressed in the edited volume *Material Symbols* (Robb 1999) would not be out of place in the edited volumes *Rethinking Materiality* (DeMarrais et al. 2004) or *The Cognitive Life of Things* (Malafouris and Renfrew 2010). In some cases the polarities may be more apparent than real.

The central thesis here, sketched out only in outline, attempts to grapple with the dilemma which faces much of today's archaeological theory: that it fails to give much insight into the processes of culture change, or to explain why these took place when and where they did. I argue that the "human revolution" – that is to say, the emergence of our own species – was not in itself followed very rapidly by decisive changes in the archaeological record. Many of these came only with the development of sedentism, which became widespread only in the Holocene period. In particular the new productive capacities made possible the production, on a deliberate basis, of commodities for exchange. New concepts of value developed, and it was indeed these concepts of value which made possible the development of other aspects of human society, including the development of social hierarchies, and the sustained exercise of power.

They made possible also, or at least much easier and richer, the expression of other symbolic aspects of human existence, including more generalized concepts of gender and status. Some of these are indeed found in hunter-gatherer communities today, particularly in sedentary ones, but it was in the developed agricultural societies in the Old World and in the sedentary societies of the New World that they found more complete expression. Prehistoric archaeology has yet to exploit the insights offered by the study of the social lives of things, and by a fuller examination of the process of engagement by which human individuals and societies involve themselves more fully with the material world in constructing their own social realities.

References

Barrett, J.C. 2001. Agency, the duality of structure, and the problem of the archaeological record. In I. Hodder (ed.), *Archaeological Theory Today*, 1st edition, 141–62. Cambridge: Polity.

Bell, J.A. 1994. *Reconstructing Prehistory: Scientific Method in Archaeology*. Philadelphia: Temple University Press.

Binford, L.R. 1962. Archaeology as anthropology. *American Antiquity* 28: 217–25.

Binford, L.R. 1968. Archaeological perspectives. In L.R. Binford and S.R. Binford (eds), *New Perspectives in Archaeology*, 5–32. Chicago: Aldine.

Boivin, N. 2004. Mind over matter? Collapsing the mind–matter dichotomy in material culture studies. In E. DeMarrais, C. Gosden, and C. Renfrew (eds), *Rethinking Materiality: The Engagement of Mind with the Material World*, 63–72. Cambridge: McDonald Institute for Archaeological Research.

Bradley, R. 1993. *Altering the Earth*. Edinburgh: Society of Antiquaries of Scotland.

Bradley, R. 1998. *The Significance of Monuments*. London: Routledge.

Burger, R. 1995. *Chavín and the Origins of Andean Civilization*, 2nd edition. London: Thames and Hudson.

Cassirer, E. 1944. *An Essay on Man*. New Haven: Yale University Press.

Cauvin, J. 1994. *Naissance des divinités, naissance de l'agriculture*. Paris: CNRS.

Changeux, J.-P., 1985. *Neuronal Man: The Biology of Mind*. Oxford: Oxford University Press.

Changeux, J.-P. and P. Ricoeur 2000. *What Makes Us Think?* Princeton: Princeton University Press.

Childe, V.G. 1936. *Man Makes Himself*. London: Watts.

Clark, A. 1997. *Being There: Putting the Brain, Body and World Together*. Cambridge, MA: MIT Press.

Clark, A. 2010. Material surrogacy and the supernatural: reflections on the role of artefacts in "off-line" cognition. In L. Malafouris and C. Renfrew (eds), *The Cognitive Life of Things*, 23–8. Cambridge: McDonald Institute for Archaeological Research.

Clark, J.G.D. 1986. *Symbols of Excellence: Precious Materials as Expressions of Status*. Cambridge: Cambridge University Press.

DeMarrais, E., L.J. Castillo, and T. Earle 1996. Ideology, materialization and power ideologies. *Current Anthropology* 37: 15–31.

DeMarrais, E., C. Gosden, and C. Renfrew (eds) 2004. *Rethinking Materiality: The Engagement of Mind with the Material World.* Cambridge: McDonald Institute for Archaeological Research.

Donald, M. 1991. *Origins of the Modern Mind: Three Stages in the Evolution of Culture and Cognition.* Cambridge, MA: Harvard University Press.

Earle, T. 1997. *How Chiefs Came to Power.* Stanford: Stanford University Press.

Flannery, K.V. and J. Marcus (eds) 1983. *The Cloud People: Divergent Evolution of the Zapotec and Mixtec Civilizations.* London: Thames and Hudson.

Gamble, C. 2007. *Origins and Revolutions: Human Identity in Earliest Prehistory.* Cambridge: Cambridge University Press.

Hawkes, C. 1954. Archaeological theory and method: some suggestions from the the Old World. *American Anthropologist* 56: 155–68.

Hodder, I. 1982a. *The Present Past.* London: Batsford.

Hodder, I. 1982b. Theoretical archaeology: a reactionary view. In I. Hodder (ed.), *Symbolic and Structural Archaeology,* 1–15. Cambridge: Cambridge University Press.

Hodder, I. 1986. *Reading the Past.* Cambridge: Cambridge University Press.

Hodder, I. 2001. *Archaeological Theory Today,* 1st edition. Cambridge: Polity.

Hodder, I. 2006. *Çatalhöyük: The Leopard's Tale.* London: Thames and Hudson.

Hodder, I., M. Shanks, M. Alexandri, V. Buchli, J. Carman, J. Last, and G. Lucas 1995. *Interpreting Archaeology.* London: Routledge.

Hutchins, E. 2009. The role of cultural practices in the emergence of modern human intelligence. In C. Renfrew, C. Frith, and L. Malafouris (eds), *The Sapient Mind: Where Archaeology Meets Neuroscience,* 119–34. Oxford: Oxford University Press.

Insoll, T. 2004. *Archaeology, Ritual, Religion.* London: Routledge.

Insoll, T. (ed.) 2011. *The Oxford Handbook of the Archaeology of Ritual and Religion.* Oxford: Oxford University Press.

Kembel, S.R. and J.W. Rick 2004. Building authority at Chavín de Huántar. In H. Silverman (ed.), *Andean Archaeology,* 51–76. Oxford: Blackwell.

Knappett, C. 2004. The affordances of things: a post-Gibsonian perspective on the rationality of mind and matter. In E. DeMarrais, C. Gosden, and C. Renfrew (eds), *Rethinking Materiality: The Engagement of Mind with the Material World,* 43–52. Cambridge: Cambridge Institute for Archaeological Research.

Kyriakidis, E. 2005. *Ritual in the Aegean: The Minoan Peak Sanctuaries.* London: Duckworth.

Malafouris, L. 2004. The cognitive basis of material engagement: where brain, body and culture conflate. In E. DeMarrais, C. Gosden, and C. Renfrew (eds), *Rethinking Materiality: The Engagement of the Mind with the Material World*, 53–62. Cambridge: McDonald Institute for Archaeological Research.

Malafouris, L. 2009. Between brains, bodies and things: *tectonoetic* awareness and the extended self. In C. Renfrew, C. Frith, and L. Malafouris (eds), *The Sapient Mind: Where Archaeology Meets Neuroscience*, 89–104. Oxford: Oxford University Press.

Malafouris, L. and C. Renfrew (eds) 2010. *The Cognitive Life of Things*. Cambridge: McDonald Institute for Archaeological Research.

Marcus, J. 2007. Rethinking ritual. In E. Kyriakidis (ed.), *The Archaeology of Ritual*, 43–76. Los Angeles: Cotsen Institute of Archaeology, UCLA.

Marcus, J. and K. V. Flannery 1996. *Zapotec Civilization: How Society Evolved in Mexico's Oaxaca Valley*. London: Thames and Hudson.

Mellars, P. A. and K. Gibson (eds) 1996. *Modelling the Early Human Mind*. Cambridge: McDonald Institute for Archaeological Research.

Miller, D. 1987. *Material Culture and Mass Consumption*. Oxford: Blackwell.

Mithen, S. 1998. The supernatural beings of prehistory and the external storage of religious ideas. In C. Renfrew and C. Scarre (eds), *Cognition and Material Culture: The Archaeology of Symbolic Storage*, 97–106. Cambridge: Cambridge University Press.

Morley, I. 2010. Conceptualising quantification before settlement: activities and issues underlying the conception and use of measurement. In I. Morley and C. Renfrew (eds), *The Archaeology of Measurement: Comprehending Heaven, Earth and Time in Ancient Societies*, 7–18. Cambridge: Cambridge University Press.

Morley, I. and C. Renfrew (eds) 2010. *The Archaeology of Measurement: Comprehending Heaven, Earth and Time in Ancient Societies*. Cambridge: Cambridge University Press.

Renfrew, C. 1972. *The Emergence of Civilisation: The Cyclades and the Aegean in the Third Millennium BC*. London: Methuen.

Renfrew, C. 1974. Beyond a subsistence economy: the evolution of social organization in prehistoric Europe. In C. B. Moore (ed.), *Reconstructing Complex Societies: An Archaeological Colloquium*, 69–95. Cambridge, MA: Supplement to the Bulletin of the American Schools of Oriental Research 20.

Renfrew, C. 1982. *Towards an Archaeology of Mind* (Inaugural Lecture). Cambridge: Cambridge University Press.

Renfrew, C. 1985. *The Archaeology of Cult: The Sanctuary at Phylakopi*. London: British School at Athens.

Renfrew, C. 1986. Varna and the emergence of wealth in prehistoric Europe. In A. Appadurai (ed.), *The Social Life of Things*, 141–68. Cambridge: Cambridge University Press.

Renfrew, C. 1994. Towards a cognitive archaeology. In C. Renfrew and E. B. W. Zubrow (eds), *The Ancient Mind: Elements of Cognitive Archaeology*, 3–12. Cambridge: Cambridge University Press.

Renfrew, C. 1996. The sapient behaviour paradox: how to test for potential? In P. A. Mellars and K. Gibson (eds), *Modelling the Early Human Mind*, 11–14. Cambridge: McDonald Institute for Archaeological Research.

Renfrew, C. 1998a. Mind and matter: cognitive archaeology and external symbolic storage. In C. Renfrew and C. Scarre (eds), *Cognition and Material Culture: The Archaeology of Symbolic Storage*, 1–6. Cambridge: Cambridge University Press.

Renfrew, C. 1998b. All the King's horses: assessing cognitive maps in later prehistoric Europe. In S. Mithen (ed.), *Creativity in Human Evolution and Prehistory*, 260–84. London: Routledge.

Renfrew, C. 2004. Towards a theory of material engagement. In E. DeMarrais, C. Gosden, and C. Renfrew (eds), *Rethinking Materiality: The Engagement of Mind with the Material World*, 23–32. Cambridge: McDonald Institute for Archaeological Research.

Renfrew, C. 2005. Cognitive archaeology. In C. Renfrew and P. Bahn (eds), *Archaeology: The Key Concepts*, 41–5. London, Routledge.

Renfrew, C. 2007. *Prehistory: The Making of the Human Mind*. London: Weidenfeld & Nicolson.

Renfrew, C. and P. Bahn 2008. *Archaeology: Theories, Methods and Practice*, 5th edition. London: Thames and Hudson.

Renfrew, C. and I. Morley (eds) 2007. *Image and Imagination*. Cambridge: McDonald Institute for Archaeological Research.

Renfrew, C. and I. Morley (eds) 2009. *Becoming Human: Innovation in Prehistoric Material and Spiritual Culture*. Cambridge: Cambridge University Press.

Renfrew, C. and E. B. W. Zubrow (eds) 1994. *The Ancient Mind: Elements of Cognitive Archaeology*. Cambridge: Cambridge University Press.

Robb, J. (ed.) 1999. *Material Symbols: Culture and Economy in Prehistory*. Carbondale: Southern Illinois University Press.

Robb, J. 2004. The extended artefact and the monumental economy: a methodology for material agency. In E. DeMarrais, C. Gosden and C. Renfrew (eds), *Rethinking Materiality: The Engagement of Mind with the Material World*, 131–40. Cambridge: Cambridge Institute for Archaeological Research.

Roepstorff, A. 2009. Things to think with: words and objects as material symbols. In C. Renfrew, C. Frith, and L. Malafouris (eds), *The Sapient*

Mind: Where Archaeology Meets Neuroscience, 177–86. Oxford: Oxford University Press.

Runciman, W.G., J. Maynard Smith, and R.I.M. Dunbar (eds) 1996. *Evolution of Social Behaviour Patterns in Primates and Man*. London: British Academy.

Schele, L. and M.E. Miller 1986. *The Blood of Kings: Dynasty and Ritual in Early Minoan Art*. New York: George Braziller.

Schick, K.D. and N. Toth 1993. *Making Silent Stones Speak: Human Evolution and the Dawn of Technology*. New York: Simon and Schuster.

Schmandt-Besserat, D. 2010. The token system of the ancient Near East: its role in counting, writing, the economy and cognition. In I. Morley and C. Renfrew (eds), *The Archaeology of Measurement: Comprehending Heaven, Earth and Time in Ancient Societies*, 27–34. Cambridge: Cambridge University Press.

Searle, J.R. 1995. *The Construction of Social Reality*. Harmondsworth: Allen Lane/Penguin Press.

Stout, D., N. Toth, K. Schick, and T. Chaminade 2009. Neural correlates of ESA toolmaking. In C. Renfrew, C. Frith, and L. Malafouris (eds), *The Sapient Mind: Archaeology Meets Neuroscience*, 1–17. Oxford: Oxford University Press.

Thomas, J. 1991. *Rethinking the Neolithic*. Cambridge: Cambridge University Press.

Tomasello, M. 1999. *The Cultural Origins of Human Cognition*. Cambridge, MA: Harvard University Press.

Treherne, P. 1995. The warrior's beauty: the masculine body and self-identity in Bronze Age Europe. *Journal of European Archaeology* 3: 105–44.

Urton, G. 2010. Recording measure(ment)s in the Inka khipu. In I. Morley and C. Renfrew (eds), *The Archaeology of Measurement: Comprehending Heaven, Earth and Time in Ancient Societies*, 54–68. Cambridge: Cambridge University Press.

7

AGENCY

A Revisionist Account

John C. Barrett

Why agency and not empathy?

(Gero 2000: 35)

It is hardly surprising that archaeologists are preoccupied with questions of causation. Unlike the historian, who might be tempted to treat documentary sources as accounts of the ways things once were, archaeologists must give account as to how their evidence was formed before being able to employ its descriptive power. Indeed it is often claimed that the primary purpose of archaeology is to explain the archaeological record, implying that archaeology understands the past in terms of what created that record. If this were indeed the case, it would explain the two kinds of causation that dominate archaeological thinking. The first addresses the mechanical changes wrought upon materials providing us with the residues that are recoverable today. The second kind of causality is of a different quality, as it seeks to explain why people once acted to create different material realities. It confronts the conditions that motivated human behavior, either to maintain traditional patterns of behavior or to bring about change. The concept of agency has been employed at this point in archaeological reasoning to make explicit the problematic need to specify the conditions under which the human subject has operated as a historical agent.

There have been various attempts to define the concept of human agency in a way that is archaeologically useful, although Dobres and Robb detect an overall lack of consensus, and a failure in theoretical sophistication in such attempts. Indeed, they argue that the concept of agency has been imported into archaeology to little practical effect, other than being used as a decoration in academic discourse, resulting in an "ambiguous platitude meaning everything and nothing" (Dobres and Robb 2000: 3). It is a criticism that needs to be taken seriously (cf. Gardner 2004). It is best that we begin with the simple idea: agents do work, with which comes certain implications. Doing work requires: a mechanism, something for that mechanism to work on, information to direct its application, and the transference of energy with resulting material consequences (cf. Fair 1979). From this generalized perspective we might recognize that human agency shares a common ground with the rest of the animal kingdom: its body is the mechanism, but one that does more than work on the material world around it. It also does work to grow, mature, and renew itself biologically, it does work to reproduce, and the work it does on the world secures the transference of the energy necessary for its own sustenance. These features maintain the distinction between biological agencies and the agency of machines that can all too easily be lost when archaeology treats human agency simply as the producer of things (cf. Boivin 2008: 129ff.). How might we further distinguish human agency from those agencies that operate throughout the rest of nature? Is it that the work it does on the material world (the archaeological concern) is of a particular kind (complex in the forms of the cultural constructions produced), that this cultural work includes talking, and that the work that it does on its own biological growth and reproduction creates a particularly developed and developing form of self-awareness? Or is it more simply the way humans orient their work with reference to particular kinds of information? Either way, we can take human agency as having emerged from the larger evolutionary process, resulting in bodies capable of making culture and self-awareness.

It follows from this that the individual bodies of human agents are made and develop as part of the reproduction of populations that act as agencies in their own right: populations do considerable amounts of work, including the work involved in their own reproduction. Indeed we might conclude that the study of human agency must start with the ways human populations are reproduced through the work of biological reproduction and the growth of their individual members. If this is a workable starting point, then it is not one that is clearly enunciated in most of the recent archaeological literature on the topic of agency. The archaeological project has emphasized the human agent as the maker of things, rather than the reproducer of life, and it has placed the intentions expressed in the acts of the production of things at the center of its concerns. Consequently, the definition of agency has become entangled with the desire to recognize the intentional and strategic behavior of individuals manifest in the production of objects. Even when the human body itself has become the focus of archaeological inquiry it has done so as a cultural product: that is, as an existing object upon which culture is written (e.g. Fowler 2004; Hamilakis et al. 2002).

A survey of the issue of agency as it has been drawn into archaeology is therefore likely to trace a lengthy detour away from the biological imperatives of life. I can only assume that one reason for taking this detour is that it avoids the possible taint of biological determinism entering into the narrative explanations for human behavior. However, if humanity is the product of nature, as it surely is, then how might we both accept this and at the same time claim the "cultural" character of human populations as existing beyond the world that we take to constitute nature? Maintaining the dualistic opposition between culture and nature as given simply fails to provide the basis from which to answer this question (Oyama 2000).

The explanatory detour

What are the sources by which archaeology has bastioned the separation of the human project from the forces of nature? Archaeological residues display patterns of human behavior as if it were relatively uniform for long periods of time and extending over relatively large geographical regions. These patterns obviously need explaining, and this was initially attempted by treating them as the expression of behavioral conventions shared by members of particular social solidarities. Although such solidarities were only vaguely defined in any recognizably sociological sense, the case was accepted that archaeologists study "the results of human behaviour, but not so much the instinctive behaviour, specific to *Homo sapiens* – that would be the subject of zoology – but the patterns of behaviours learned from, and distinctive of, human societies" (Childe 1956: 7). Human behavior came to be described relative to two axes: one was conventional behavior, which was represented by the ways things were made; the other was behavior as functionally organized and represented by the patterned arrangement of artifact, settlement, and monument assemblages.

Two closely related questions that attended upon this depiction of human behavior came to the fore in the 1960s and 1970s: what precipitated change in conventional and in organisational behaviors, and was the change in one driven by change in the other (i.e. which, if either, was historically determinate)? The "New Archaeology" of this period seemed to treat the two behaviors as having relative autonomy. It argued that human behavior, whilst adhering to the formal demands of cultural conventions, was organizationally designed to adapt to certain functional requirements, and that it was changes in the latter that were historically determinate and therefore of prime archaeological interest. As a consequence, human behavior was treated as following conventional procedures to sustain the adaptive and operating requirements of systemic organization. Thus Binford (1973: 229) could state: "I have never suggested that culture is not manifest in the archaeological record or that observable difference in the archaeological record might not have cultural significance. What I have suggested, however, is that behaviour is the by-product of the interaction of a cultural repertoire with the environment."

Hopefully, it is unnecessary to labor the point to recognize that human behavior was being treated as a response to both convention and needs (i.e. responding to how things should be done and to the material effects those things were designed to have). In both cases the implication was that behavior was determined by conditions that originated externally to the conscious agent. In the case of the former, the demands were for social conformity acting on individual bodies and expressed as rules to which those bodies responded, whilst in the case of the latter, the stimuli of satisfying needs structured the organization of populations. This posed the obvious problem of deciding how conventions and needs were internalized in the motivations that drove the behavior of the individuals who made up these populations.

Eventually, the explanatory claims made for forces of social convention and adaptive necessity were criticized for reducing the human subject simply to the product of these determinates without any recourse to understanding the motivations that derived from its own subjectivity. Archaeology's encounter with structuralism in the 1980s prompted a change in the treatment of behavior and its material products. Material culture was now seen as both communicating the conceptual order of categories internalized by the human subject and expressing that subject's strategic desires (Hodder 1982a).

Society, agency, and structure

In his treatment of archaeological cultures and the processes of their historical development, Childe was explicit in the intellectual debt he owed to the founding figures of Durkheim and Marx (Childe 1944, 1956). It was from them that he unquestionably granted human society the status of the reality from whence people learned the behaviors that were expected of them. This social reality was certainly complex. It comprised what Childe maintained was the Marxist distinction between real material necessities and the ideological claims of a governing order, which together formed the system of actually existing social conditions. Between the mid-1970s and mid-1980s, Anthony Giddens established a detailed rejection of this kind of dualistic relationship between society and people's behavior (Giddens 1979, 1984). For Giddens, social institutions, and thus societies, gained a reality extending across time and space only by dint of the recursive actions of human subjects. Human subjects could not therefore be determined by "society" because it was the practices of human subjects that brought society into being. Giddens, however, avoided the charge that he had reduced the constitution of society to that of methodological individualism (i.e. regarding societies as no more than collectives of individuals) by arguing that human subjects achieved the status of knowledgeable agents by monitoring their practical deployment of such resources as the knowledge of how to proceed ("rules") and available material conditions. Thus the subject could only bring itself into being (and so contribute to the time-space extension of social patterns) by having access to structural conditions (existing resources) and by having the practical competence to develop the rules required to act effectively with reference to those resources. The reproduction of these structural conditions gives social institutions their reality (Searle 2010). Giddens took rules and resources to be both constraining and enabling of human agency, and they were "both the medium and the outcome" of action (Giddens 1981: 27). Structural conditions and human agency are therefore, Giddens claimed, involved in their joint reproduction, although it is the human subject's agency that is treated as doing most of this reproductive work.

There are three important reasons why the theoretical position developed by Giddens, and which is often compared with the practice theory of Bourdieu (1977, 1990), has appeared challenging to archaeology. First, it displaces society as the determinate for normative behavior and consequently from being the central object of study. Societies can only be brought into existence by people's practical engagement with structural conditions, and it is this relationship that therefore becomes the central issue in social analysis. This means that much of the effort that has been expended in "social archaeology" to match particular patterns of material remains to particular kinds of social organization will not provide the methodological foundation to explain socio-cultural change. Nor can we treat societies as organic entities that adapt themselves to changing environmental conditions without a far more detailed understanding of what we mean by adaptation from the perspective of human practice, a point to which we must return. Sadly, these important methodological implications have received scant attention in an archaeological discipline which continues to dismiss theoretical work as a matter of transient intellectual fashion. Second, Giddens's own definition of structure as comprising rules and resources "remains frustratingly underspecified" (Sewell 1992: 5) and our understanding of how human agency engages with these conditions therefore fares little better. Taken together it becomes remarkably unclear what we might mean when archaeology claims to offer historical explanations from the perspective offered by Giddens: if structure and agency are locked into a recursive relationship, why does anything ever change (other than history ending in maladaptation and therefore extinction)? Thirdly, the question of agency has long been confused with the status of individual motivations. This might be understandable given that agency theory was deployed in archaeology to counter the ways human behavior had been characterized in strongly deterministic terms by processual archaeology. As Dorman (2002: 304) puts it: "[T]he birth of agency theory has reflected a desire to counter deterministic models of human action by acknowledging that people purposefully act and alter the external world through their actions." However, any idea that human agency is simply a matter of free will obviously won't do; nor is it helpful to regard the structure–agency relationship as equivalent to the relationship between individual actors and structural principles, where the question can all too easily be reduced to asking which of these should form the unit of archaeological analysis (cf. Dorman 2002: 315). Attempting to resolve this false conundrum returns us, somewhat perversely, to the Childean duality in which individuals are supposed to "consciously" use (rather than being "unconsciously" determined by) the rules of either social or mental structures to govern their own behavior. It hardly matters in this light which option is chosen (individual or structure) because the individual actor merely becomes the cipher for the application of structural rules (Johnson 2000: 214–16). Indeed it was an escape from the idea that "action is seen as sheer en-actment or execution of rules and norms" (Ortner 1984: 150) that was supposedly provided by a theory of practice.

The problem for Giddens is that he builds the constitution of society from conditions whose own existence requires explanation but which he ignores. These conditions are the growth and making of conscious beings (human subjects) through the reproduction of particular behavioral populations. Giddens's sociology has, in other words, forgotten that it is dealing with a biological phenomenon.

An outline alternative

Step 1: biological realities

In the generalized terms that I have employed, agency is defined as something that does work. The specific character of human agency can therefore be described in terms of the ways that work is executed and the particular nature of its products. All work requires the transference of energy (which includes the processes of metabolism for biological agencies), and the unit that is doing the work can operate at different levels of complexity, ranging from biological individuals to various collectives of such individuals. In the human case, biological individuals are made by the sexual work of parents and are built from the work of various relationships between chemical and biological components that drive the growth and maturation of those individual bodies. The failure in current analysis is that it employs an ill-defined distinction to isolate human agency as a sociological phenomenon from the biological processes that constitute it. Adherents to such a distinction are unlikely to endow the work of cellular division and growth with the qualities of a specifically human agency, even though the developing phylogenetic trajectory of cellular development describes the evolution of hominins, and even though parental agency contributes significantly to the foetus's ontological development from the womb to the child's development in infancy. This means that we lose sight of the fact that those characteristics that we identify with human agency are the evolutionary products of a particular developmental biology and that they are emergent at the organizational level necessary for the reproduction of human populations.

It is obviously important, when making these observations, to be abundantly clear that even though human agency is expressed as a quality of working that emerges at particular levels of biological organization (reproducing populations), its operation cannot be explained via a reduction to a lower level of biological organization: it is not reducible to a genetic cause. Genes may contribute to coding for amino acid sequences in protein production, but they don't "do" much else (Moss 2003). Reductionist arguments that attempt to trace the sources of human behavior to the level of genetic determination can therefore be rejected without abandoning the biological context of that behavior.

Given that the characteristics traditionally associated with human agency (language, cultural complexity, and complex social structures) occur at the level of a population's behavior, and given that Darwinian evolution is a process whereby traits within a population are supposedly selected for (Mayr 1976), then human agency might be identified with the particular kinds of work involved in maintaining populations whose particular characteristics became fixed by the process of evolution. Putting to one side the larger question of whether or not we actually know what we mean by "Darwinian evolution," we are obviously going to have to decide what those characteristics are that are selected for. I will argue that the development of human agency in these terms does not conform to one stricter interpretation of the Darwinian process.

All animal populations display regularities in the behaviors of their members. They are reproduced as relations of cooperation and competition, labor distinctions, reproductive and nurturing arrangements, patterns of dominance and subservience, and they operate by exploiting particular ecological zones, which their behaviors transform and which are set within particular territorial ranges (Dawkins 1999; Olding-Smee et al. 2003). Famously, E.O. Wilson (1975) was so struck by the similarities between invertebrate and vertebrate behaviors in creating ordered populations that he sought to develop the analytical synthesis of sociobiology to explore the common biological basis for these patterns. The inherent reductionism in Wilson's argument (well expressed in E.O. Wilson 1999) seemed to imply that these various behaviors were encoded for by inherited genetic material and had been fixed over time by means of natural selection. Thus, when he came to specify the behavioral characteristics of humanity, ranging from the plasticity of social organization to moral pluralism, he treated these as the products of behavioral genetics that had gained a proven adaptive advantage in the history of human evolution.

Although Wilson hardly addressed material culture as a product of human behavior, a similar evolutionary argument has been extended to treat the history of material culture in terms of the selected advantages in human behavior that were achieved by its ongoing production. Whilst, in Wilson's terms, genetics might endow the human body with the mental facility and embodied dexterity to produce material culture, it would seem very unlikely that the same genetic code could act as an effective replicator for the transmission of the wide-ranging and highly diverse details that these cultural traditions express. Consequently, it has been proposed that human agency is unique in expressing a dual system of inheritance, comprising both the genetic code and the encoded transmission of cultural knowledge. According to this argument, the two mechanisms of Darwinian evolution (inherited variability and natural selection) are applicable to both systems of inheritance, although evolutionary change in cultural coding occurs at a more rapid pace than in biological coding (Boyd and Richerson1985; Dawkins 1978: 203ff.).

There are two problems associated with the idea of dual inheritance. First, it maintains the distinction between biological history and cultural history by asserting that each is secured in the transmission of different kinds of encoded information and that each is guided by different regimes of selection. The second problem is fundamental. The reductionist argument that treats genetics as coding for biological characteristics and treats units of cultural information (sometimes referred to as memes [Blackmore 1999; Dawkins 1978]) as coding for traits of cultural behavior holds that each of these generates the phenotypical characteristics that are operated upon by natural selection. Under this classically Darwinian rubric, the traits that are successfully reproduced across generations are selected for their adaptive efficiency by the environments in which they operate, thus ensuring the successful replication of the particular codes that generated them. However, this is counter to the process operating in cultural histories. These would normally be considered as treating the form of artifacts as being strategically designed to adapt to the conditions at hand and in which the consequences of their use is monitored for its effectiveness (Leonard 2001: 72). As Fodor and Piattelli-Palmarini (2010) have argued, these processes of adaptation do not have the same sense. In the first, the inherited code (normally referred to as the "replicator") is blind to its consequences and is selected for its adaptive effectiveness by nature: natural selection therefore designs history. In the second, it is the strategic intention of the agent seeking to adapt to the conditions in which it finds itself that selects the design of things to be adaptive. In this case it is the monitored intention of the agent desiring to be effective in the world that works in the design of history.

Once this distinction is accepted, the danger is that it will be used once again to distinguish between biological and sociological process, namely between nature and culture. The former might thus be claimed by the classically Darwinian position where it is natural selection that designs the path of biological evolution. But, if this is so, are we to assume that cultural evolution, which arises from intentional designs to adapt, is non-Darwinian (perhaps Lamarckian)? In other words, are we to assume that humanity has somehow detached itself from nature? The full implications of this apparent contradiction cannot be worked through here, but the conclusion would seem to be that we need to understand the evolution of human agency from a position that gets beyond the nature–culture dichotomy.

Step 2: rules

In the dual inheritance systems that Dawkins originally proposed, different kinds of replicators are at work, and in the case of the cultural replicator it is the transmission processes of learning that would seem to be of central importance. What, then, is the basis of this learning process? Rules play a fairly central part in Giddens's theory of social structural reproduction (Giddens 1984: 16ff.) and cultural rules are what Childean archaeology assumed were transmitted across time and space. Indeed, Durkheim's sociology held that it was from the reality of social existence that the subject learned the rules to guide his or her competency as a social agent. The term *rule* does, however, have a number of applications. As Giddens and others define them, rules can be regulative, in proscribing what should be done and constitutive, by stating explicitly how one might go about doing those things. However, the ways any of us become culturally competent hardly depend on either of these applications. Indeed, if action was to be guided by reference to such explicitly stated rules, then we would rapidly exhaust the possibilities of what should be done, or fail to act as others might expect, simply because an explicit set of rules can never be rich enough to cover all eventualities. Nor indeed would any of us have the capacity to rapidly access some memorized rulebook to cope with the subtly changing circumstances in which we found ourselves. Not only would the originality and flexibility of practice be lost, but such rules would hold out the possibility of a multiplicity of conflicting interpretations (Wittgenstein 1963: §§139–242). Therefore, if human agency is to act in a way that can not only cope with rapidly changing and relatively unpredictable circumstances but also act in a way that others would find understandable, it must do so as the expression of a practical understanding of the context in which it operates, and from a perspective in which its effectiveness is monitored. The intuitive understanding of how to behave is experienced as a growing and embodied confidence that is inculcated though a cumulative history of personal experiences gained in the company, and with the approval or disapproval, of others. This emphasis upon practical and socialized experience is distinct from the intellectual and explicit formulation of rules that can undoubtedly be used either to regulate a person's actions or to explain retrospectively what has taken place. The procedure of understanding "how to go on" is to experience a growing comfort and feeling of confidence that derives from the skill of knowing how to move forward in a particular place, at a particular moment, and in particular company. It also demonstrates a degree of intimate awareness, not only of the architecture and timing of the context, but also in the ability to read the bodily dispositions of others. This is what Bourdieu captured as the embodied competence (*hexis*) of a set of generally accepted dispositions (*habitus*); it is an entirely practical reasoning that eludes objective formulation and is exemplified in the strategically deployed tempo of the gift exchange (Bourdieu 1977: 4ff.) and in bodily dispositions:

> The man of honour's pace is steady and determined. His way of walking, that of a man who knows where he is going and knows he will arrive in time whatever the obstacles, expresses strength and resolution, as opposed to the hesitant gait…announcing indecision, halfhearted promises…, the fear of commitments and the incapacity to fulfil them. (Bourdieu 1977: 94)

Step 3: the phenomenological mind

By privileging the practical learning-by-doing, against the intellectualized image of learning the rules designed to govern behavior, we work "against the grain of much modern thought and culture; in particular, of our scientific culture and its associated epistemology, which in turn, have moulded our contemporary sense of self" (Taylor 1993: 48). It challenges the common assumption that the world is known by means of the formulations of mental representations, and that once these representations are established they are then expressed in action. It is this idea of knowledge as mental representation and action as performance of those inner representations that archaeology adopted as the result of its initial encounter with structuralism. In this light the work of agency, as the maker of things, was treated as the expressive performance of internal, mental, representations that had become recognizable archaeologically in virtue of their material products.

This perspective, as Taylor notes, is deeply embedded in the way we see ourselves. It is a perspective that treats agency not simply as a producer of things but as a producer of things that encode mentally formulated knowledge. It is a position that appears to satisfy the identification of human agency with knowledgeable action. This locks us onto a path of reasoning that has considerable implications. First, it tends to equate agency with individual action because individuals are the possessors of their own conceptual knowledge. Secondly, it grounds the methodological challenge upon establishing the meaning of things by reference to the concepts that they supposedly once stood for and which resided "in people's heads." Thirdly, it is employed to equate the origin of "humanity" with a stage in mental development that was capable of externalizing mental representations (Donald 1991) (otherwise expressed in the definition of humanity as the "producer of symbols"). The last point recurs throughout the extensive body of literature that repeatedly reduces the story of human evolution simply to a question of development in the size and structure of the human brain.

Perhaps we may now begin to grasp the ways in which the dichotomies that pervade our thinking, and that divide nature from culture, body from mind, evolution from history, animal behavior from human agency, ensnare us to demand the impossible: to explain how the human mind, as the producer of cultural meanings and the maker of histories, emerges as something distinct from the forces of nature within which it supposedly evolved. Another way of considering this question is by reference to the so-called "hard problem of consciousness" (Chalmers 1995), namely to explain the way that knowing what it is to be ourselves and to be human can arise from experience: that is, to explain subjectivity as a product of physical processes. It is after all

> one thing to be able to establish correlations between consciousness and brain activity; it's another thing to have an account that explains how and why certain physiological processes suffice for consciousness. At present, we not only lack such an account, but we are also unsure about the form it would need to have in order to overcome the conceptual gap between subjective experience and the brain. (Thompson 2004: 383)

Emphasis upon the way brain activity operates in response to the body's physical experiences has resulted in an increasingly refined understanding of the innately modular structure of the brain. We can certainly trace different regions of brain activity associated with different stimuli and the execution of different tasks. This does not, however, help in any way to explain consciousness (Fodor 2000). Consciousness is not contained in that structure (despite imaginative suggestions to the contrary, such as Mithen 1996) but is instead the bodily processes of living and feeling. Agents exist as corporal beings, as the "unitary locus capable of experience" (Weber and Varela 2002: 101), and should be treated as such and not, as is so often the case, as the aggregation of genetic and mental processes. Consciousness is the mind embodied, rather than being some mysterious by-product of brain activity (*contra* Dennett 1993). The living agent moves into the world, a process of brute physical experience rather than detached mental reflection (Barrett and Ko 2009). This agency maintains itself as a bounded identity that sustains its own organization and replenishment by ingesting energy; these strategies constitute the simple practicalities of making sense of the world towards which its actions are directed. Living is thus the creation of an emotional and physical security for the self and a movement towards the world that is as if it had a value for the self. These principles fulfill the biological necessity of self-production through the metabolic processes necessary for life, and they secure the idea that life has a forward direction, that it is purposeful in the direction it takes towards the world. This latter point returns us to the second meaning of adaptation which we identified above: to live is to adapt to the world that can only be discovered through inhabitation.

Everything that is being proposed here can be taken as characteristic of life in general (Thompson 2007). Consequently, human agency must have evolved its own form of life by selecting for ways of "sense making" that were effective and particular to itself. This human sense making might best be understood as finding certain specific values and qualities as immanent to the world. Again I must emphasize the contrast with a structuralist reasoning that holds the human brain to be the source of the meanings that it writes upon the world. A phenomenological analysis, by contrast, concerns the ways humans discover a practical competence and an emotional security simply by means of getting on with life. Through life the world is revelatory because experiences fall into place and life becomes the increasingly assured capability of knowing how to proceed. This does not deny that from such life comes the discursive ability to call to mind and reflect upon the claims of existence, but such self-consciousness is reliant upon first finding ourselves part of an ordered world, rather than it being the product of a detached contemplation of existence.

The work of human agency now emerges not at base as a producer of symbolic representations that a particular evolutionary stage of the brain's development has made possible, but as the discoverer of what the world can reveal. It is the particular nature of that revelation which makes us human. It is the remarkable character of humanity that it finds versions of a common grounding upon which to set the, sometimes conflicting, diversity of things experienced; a common grounding that comes to be widely expressed in terms of how all things originated through the forces of creation. The importance of language in the exploration of these commonalities by means of simile, metaphor, and the possibility of abstraction is fundamentally important: language takes us into the world and towards that which is most easily defined as the sacred. It is this that has given rise to what Miller (2005: 1) identifies as the "underlying principle to be found in most of the religions that dominate recorded history. Wisdom has been accredited to those who claim that materiality represents the merely apparent, behind which lies that which is real." Religion, however, is but an attempt to give objective form to what is already felt to exist, a wisdom simply lived out in terms of "this is how the world is," whose objective form is also expressed in western experience by scientific naturalism. What is significant about religious narratives is their expressions of cause and purpose which can appear to underpin the feeling that life is lived towards the goal of its preservation. But what I seek here is the pre-religious and pre-discursive "feeling of what happens" (Damasio 2000), because "if we were radically feelingless, and if ideas were only things our minds could entertain, we should lose all our likes and dislikes at a stroke, and be unable to point to any one situation or experience in life more valuable or significant than any other" (James 1996: 51). Human life would, in other words, become directionless. What humans express in responding to those feelings include, most remarkably, a commitment towards an underlying unity that extends across the diversity of things as encountered and that can be expressed to reveal a common purpose for life.

If feeling is primary, then it is expressed in the body's performances of movement and displays of emotion. These behaviors can be regarded as an initial form of representation because they signify a recognition of the qualities that are taken to exist in the world as it is encountered. This form of signification is therefore marked by the body's response to the moment and to the place, and it may be read by others as being appropriate (or inappropriate) to that occasion. To become human, therefore, is to be recognized as such in virtue of the body's own responses to the qualities that appear to be manifest in existence. Surely this is the empathy to which Gero directs us in the quotation with which I preface this chapter, and it is an empathy that relocates our definition of humanity not in the agency of symbolic production, but in the responses of recognition and dependencies that each owes to others (cf. Rifkin 2009). However, this is also an empathic humanity that has its limits. In various contexts there may be acts that are particularly appropriate, executed by those who thus display their own authority or virtue and through whose bodies the fundamental qualities of existence appear to shine, just as the outsider might fail to respond, or mistake, or reject the qualities in the things that others perceive. Qualities of humanity, the pure, the marginalized, and the non-human are seen at such moments and help to determine the degrees of care shown or withheld.

The archaeology of agency

And so to the obvious question: what is the significance of any of the above to the procedures of archaeology? I would suggest that a number of conclusions are to be drawn, the first being that humanity could well be much older than the date given by the initial appearance of the stone tools, perforated beads, or whatever other cultural products are traditionally sought to mark the beginning of "symbolic" behavior. Humanity emerged, I have argued, with embodied responses to the world that others accepted as signifying a recognizable coherency to the origin of things of which humanity was a part. Indeed it would seem reasonable to suppose that commitment to such an origin and sacred purpose to existence provided for much of the security necessary to move towards that which was unexpected and exotic. Perhaps this is one behavioral adaptation that eased movements into environments not previously experienced, as is witnessed by the uniquely widespread colonization of hominins beyond Africa. Of course this conclusion has the slightly disconcerting implication that the origins of "modern" humanity, whilst certainly being behavioral, might well lie beyond the archaeological discovery of traditional artifact categories. The second conclusion then follows: throughout their lengthy history, hunter-gatherers have occupied worlds that were revealed through practice to be holistic and meaningful. The division that we erect between nature and culture has become our problem; it is not one with which we should encumber the lives of our hunter-gatherer ancestors (Ingold 2000: 39–60).

Archaeology's continuing commitment to the idea that humanity emerges out of natural reproduction and into a world of cultural production has profound implications. It gives rise to what Renfrew has termed the "sapient paradox": that is, the apparently irresolvable puzzle that humans only began to undertake the widespread production of complex cultural inventories millennia after nature had endowed them with the necessary mental capacity for such work

(Renfrew 2006 and this volume). The problem here is that artifact production is treated as an issue of semiotics, by holding artifacts to be the representations of mental concepts. It follows that cultural artifacts might be expected to appear around the same time that the brain developed the capacity to formulate such concepts. However, artifact production is, at base, little more than the maintenance of an order with which the world is endowed. This order is reaffirmed through practice which maintains life and is therefore empirically demonstrated to work. The momentary veneration of a rock formation as the manifestation of the creative forces at work in the world is as much sense making as is the flaking of stone to recover the artifact form inherent within the material, or the molding of a clay figurine to bring to the fore the logic of human creation. There is no sapient paradox in the history of human development, but there is still something of a puzzle, and this involves the scale of the transformation that accompanies the development of agriculture.

The nature–culture duality has dominated the narratives of agricultural origins. It was employed explicitly by Ian Hodder (1990), who characterized domestication as coming into being when certain resources were associated with, or indeed were "housed" within, the domestic realm and so distinguished in opposition to the world of nature and the wild. Did agriculturalists therefore create the idea of the wild as being beyond that over which they had domain? If, as we suggest, hunter-gatherers belonged in worlds that were soaked though with humanly recognizable qualities, then did agriculturalists begin to work towards the fragmentation of that unity? This would have necessitated making the difference between the two domains explicit, and this in turn has been widely associated with the production of the material elaboration and long-term maintenance of domestic architecture, monument building, and the creation of decorative and representational objects (Cauvin 2000; P. J. Wilson 1988). The argument inevitably draws archaeologists towards an understanding of the origins of agriculture as a purely social construction and, perhaps, as the implementation of a new way of thinking about the world.

Alternatively, the Neolithic evolved as an ecological system describing the particular reproductive relationships between human, plant, and animal populations. Rather than resulting from an explicitly human strategy of dividing the concept of the domestic from that of the wild, a symbiotic dependency with human communities could well have resulted in the isolated reproduction of sub-sets of plant and animal populations from the wider developmental environment in which they had previously lived (Rindos 1984). As with all living populations, this developing form of organization had to build its internal order at the expense of the resources beyond its margins. Internally, entropy decreased as order increased whilst energy was imported across the boundary between one biological structure and external resources. The increase in the scale of organization that marked out the Neolithic system of reproduction was achieved because instead of human populations procuring energy directly from the plants they gathered and animals they killed, they began to store the seasonally available energy that could be derived from the fertility of the land in the growth of crops, the storage of grain, and the isolation of breeding stocks of animals (Barrett 2011). The evolution and spread of these changing biological relationships depended on bringing identifiable portions of land into view as a material quality whose exploitation was bound to the reproduction, and thus the continuation, of human life. The investment of labor in tillage and in the maintenance of pasture and browse, as well as in the storage of food, carried forward the changing relationship to land, as did the constant replenishment of domestic structures (Hodder 2010) or the founding and enhancement of other forms of monument (Barrett 2006).

By defining human agency as the behaviors that treat diverse physical experiences as the manifestation of a coherent causality and purpose to life, I have been concerned to depict material culture as the enhancement of the revelation of how life and world converge within a single scheme. This argument has attempted to move us away from the more common view that the human agent is the owner of various cognitive schemes, and that the things that agency produces gain their meaning by reference to those forms of cognition. The world is, instead, meaningful by the simple virtue of being able to sustain life: it is meaningful because it makes sense through use. And in the making sense by living in the world, this agency comes to recognize others as itself. The constant refurbishment of material culture can now be regarded as primarily the enhancement of the world as experienced (cf. Renfrew 2001), an enhancement of things that maintains an architecture whose inhabitation brings the world more clearly into view.

An archaeology of human agency should explore the historical conditions under which the development of different agencies became possible. Most simply this will consider the ways the material architecture and technology of any period might have contributed to the reproduction of a particular form of life. Whilst the contrast with archaeologies that treat the meaning of things as lodged within the motivations of their producers is deliberate, I do not deny that materials are produced that represent and communicate in traditional semiotic terms. My point, however, is that this kind of communicative production is not the general characteristic of the relationship between human agency and its material conditions but one that operates instead through particular political institutions.

Conclusion

Agency theory enabled archaeologists to move beyond grounding the motivations for people's actions upon the satisfaction of general systemic needs, with the consequent rendering of history as a process operating behind people's backs. Instead it sought the motivation for action in strategic desires that had been formulated with reference to the cultural logics through which "agents" understood their place in history, such that "the cultural framework within which we act, and which we reproduce in our actions is historically derived and ... each culture is a particular historical product. The uniqueness of cultures and historical sequences must be recognised" (Hodder 1982b: 4–5).

The emphasis upon culturally constituted knowledge as a resource upon which agents draw in practice has tended to align agency theory with social theory, regard knowledge as the product of mental representations, and resist reference to biological processes as necessarily returning us to deterministic explanations for human action. The archaeological response to this overall position has been to treat the production of material culture as the representation of cognitively formulated schemes for action.

The challenge that I have attempted to raise is to treat humanity as a way of reproducing life. Consequently, human agency is the particular ways complex and diverse developmental processes are accommodated to undertake that work.

References

Barrett, J. C. 2006. A perspective on the early architecture of Western Europe. In J. Maran, C. Juwig, H. Schwengel, and U. Thaler (eds), *Constructing Power: Architecture, Ideology and Social Practice*, 15–30. Hamburg: LIT Verlag.

Barrett, J. C. 2011. The Neolithic revolution: an ecological perspective. In A. Hadjikoumis, E. Robinson, and S. Viner (eds), *Dynamics of Neolithisation in Europe: Studies in Honour of Andrew Sherratt*, 67–91. Oxford: Oxbow Books.

Barrett, J. C. and I. Ko 2009. A phenomenology of landscape: a crisis in British landscape archaeology? *Journal of Social Archaeology* 9: 275–94.

Binford, L.R. 1973. Interassemblage variability – the Mousterian and the "functional" argument. In C. Renfrew (ed.), *The Explanation of Culture Change: Models in Prehistory*, 227–54. London: Duckworth.

Blackmore, S. 1999. *The Meme Machine*. Oxford: Oxford University Press.

Boivin, N. 2008. *Material Cultures, Material Minds*. Cambridge: Cambridge University Press.

Bourdieu, P. 1977. *Outline of a Theory of Practice*. Cambridge: Cambridge University Press.

Bourdieu, P. 1990. *The Logic of Practice*. Cambridge: Polity.

Boyd, R. and P.J. Richerson 1985. *Culture and the Evolutionary Process*. Chicago: University of Chicago Press.

Cauvin, J. 2000. *The Birth of the Gods and the Origins of Agriculture*. Cambridge: Cambridge University Press.

Chalmers, D.J. 1995. Facing up to the problem of consciousness. *Journal of Consciousness Studies* 2: 200–19.

Childe, V.G. 1944. *Progress and Archaeology*. London: Watts.

Childe, V.G. 1956. *Piecing Together the Past*. London: Routledge and Kegan Paul.

Damasio, A. 2000. *The Feeling of What Happens: Body, Emotion and the Making of Consciousness*. London: Vintage.

Dawkins, R. 1978. *The Selfish Gene*. London: Granada Publishing.

Dawkins, R. 1999. *The Extended Phenotype: The Long Reach of the Gene*, revised edition. Oxford: Oxford University Press.

Dennett, D.C. 1993. *Consciousness Explained*. London: Penguin Books.

Dobres, M.-A. and J. Robb 2000. Agency in archaeology: paradigm or platitude? In M.-A. Dobres and J. Robb (eds), *Agency in Archaeology*, 3–17. London: Routledge.

Donald, M. 1991. *Origins of the Modern Mind: Three Stages in the Evolution of Culture and Cognition*. Cambridge, MA: Harvard University Press.

Dorman, J.L. 2002. Agency and archaeology: past, present and future directions. *Journal of Archaeological Method and Theory* 9: 303–29.

Fair, D. 1979. Causation and the flow of energy. *Erkenntnis* 14: 219–50.

Fodor, J. 2000. *The Mind Doesn't Work That Way: The Scope and Limits of Computational Psychology*. Cambridge, MA: The MIT Press.

Fodor, J. and M. Piattelli-Palmarini 2010. *What Darwin Got Wrong*. New York: Farrar, Straus and Giroux.

Fowler, C. 2004. *The Archaeology of Personhood: An Anthropological Approach*. London: Routledge.

Gardner, A. 2004. Introduction: social agency, power, and being human. In A. Gardner (ed.), *Agency Uncovered: Archaeological Perspectives on Social Agency, Power and Being Human*, 1–15. London: UCL Press.

Gero, J.M. 2000. Troubled travels in agency and feminism. In M.-A. Dobres and J. Robb (eds), *Agency in Archaeology*, 34–9. London: Routledge.

Giddens, A. 1979 *Central Problems in Social Theory: Action, Structure and Contradiction in Social Analysis*. London: Macmillan.

Giddens, A. 1981. *A Contemporary Critique of Historical Materialism: Volume 1. Power, Property and the State*. London: Macmillan.

Giddens, A. 1984. *The Constitution of Society*. Cambridge: Polity.

Hamilakis, Y., M. Pluciennik, and S. Tarlow (eds) 2002. *Thinking through the Body: Archaeologies of Corporeality*. London: Kluwer Academic.

Hodder, I. (ed.) 1982a. *Symbolic and Structural Archaeology*. Cambridge: Cambridge University Press.

Hodder, I. 1982b. Theoretical archaeology: a reactionary view. In I. Hodder (ed.), *Symbolic and Structural Archaeology*, 1–16. Cambridge: Cambridge University Press.

Hodder, I. 1990. *The Domestication of Europe*. Oxford: Blackwell.

Hodder, I. (ed.) 2010. *Religion in the Emergence of Civilisation*. Cambridge: Cambridge University Press.

Ingold, T. 2000. *The Perception of the Environment: Essays in Livelihood, Dwelling and Skill*. London: Routledge.

James, W. 1996. On a certain blindness in human beings. In S. C. Rowe (ed.), *The Vision of James*, 51–76. Rockport, MA: Element Books.

Johnson, M. 2000. Conceptions of agency in archaeological interpretation. In J. Thomas (ed.), *Interpretive Archaeology: A Reader*, 211–27. Leicester: Leicester University Press.

Leonard, R.D. 2001. Evolutionary archaeology. In I. Hodder (ed.), *Archaeological Theory Today*, 1st edition, 64–97. Cambridge: Polity.

Mayr, E. 1976. Typological versus population thinking. In E. Mayr, *Evolution and the Diversity of Life: Selected Essays*, 26–9. Cambridge MA: The Belknap Press of Harvard University Press.

Miller, D, 2005. Materiality: an introduction. In D. Miller (ed.), *Materiality*, 1–50. Durham, NC: Duke University Press.

Mithen, S. 1996. *The Prehistory of the Mind: A Search for the Origins of Art, Religion and Science*. London: Thames and Hudson.

Moss, L. 2003. *What Genes Can't Do*. Cambridge MA: MIT Press.

Olding-Smee, F.J., K.N. Laland, and M.M. Feldman 2003. *Niche Construction: The Neglected Process in Evolution*. Princeton: Princeton University Press.

Ortner S.B. 1984. Theory in anthropology since the sixties. *Comparative Studies in Society and History* 26: 126–66.

Oyama, S. 2000. *The Ontogeny of Information*, 2nd edition. Durham, NC: Duke University Press.

Renfrew, C. 2001. Symbol before concept: material engagement and the early development of society. In I. Hodder (ed.), *Archaeological Theory Today*, 1st edition, 122–40. Cambridge: Polity.

Renfrew, C. 2006. Becoming human: the archaeological challenge. *Proceedings of the British Academy* 139: 217–38.

Rifkin, J. 2009. *The Empathic Civilization: The Race to Global Consciousness in a World in Crisis*. Cambridge: Polity.

Rindos, D. 1984. *The Origins of Agriculture: An Evolutionary Perspective*. London: Academic Press.

Searle, J. R. 2010. *Making the Social World: The Structure of Human Civilization*. Oxford: Oxford University Press.

Sewell, W. H. 1992. A theory of structures: duality, agency, and transformations. *American Journal of Sociology* 93: 1–29.

Taylor, C. 1993. "To follow a rule ..." In C. Calhoun, E. LiPuma, and M. Postone (eds), *Bourdieu: Critical Perspectives*, 45–60. Cambridge: Polity.

Thompson, E. 2004. Life and mind: from autopoiesis to neurophenomenology. A tribute to Francisco Varela. *Phenomenology and the Cognitive Sciences* 3: 381–98.

Thompson, E. 2007. *Mind in Life: Biology, Phenomenology, and the Sciences of Mind*. Cambridge MA: The Belknap Press of the University of Harvard Press.

Weber, A. and F. J. Varela 2002. Life after Kant: natural purposes and the autopoietic foundations of biological individuality. *Phenomenology and the Cognitive Sciences* 1: 97–125.

Wilson, E. O. 1975. *Sociobiology: The New Synthesis*. Cambridge MA: The Belknap Press of Harvard University Press.

Wilson, E. O. 1999. *Consilience: The Unity of Knowledge*. New York: Vintage Books.

Wilson, P. J. 1988. *The Domestication of the Human Species*. New Haven: Yale University Press.

Wittgenstein, L. 1963. *Philosophical Investigations*. Oxford: Blackwell.

8

ARCHAEOLOGIES OF PLACE AND LANDSCAPE

Julian Thomas

Introduction: duplicitous landscapes

Even within Britain, the roots of what has come to be called "landscape archaeology" are complex and tangled. From the seventeenth century onwards, antiquaries such as Stukeley and Colt Hoare developed an awareness of boundaries, enclosures, and burial mounds that clearly predated modern roads and systems of land division (Darvill 2008: 61). By the end of the nineteenth century, General Pitt Rivers was effectively using the landscape as an analytical frame within which to set the results of multiple excavations (Bowden 1991: 118). This employment of the landscape as a spatial unit of analysis was complemented by a concern with chronological depth that arose from Crawford's "field archaeology," and its use of photography, documents, maps, field survey, and place-name evidence, sometimes to the exclusion of excavation (M. Johnson 2007: 55). In the work of the historian W. G. Hoskins, this approach produced a vision of landscape as a palimpsest of material traces, revealed by meticulous work in the field and the archive, an "assemblage of real-word features – natural, semi-natural and wholly artificial" which is available to us in the present (Roberts 1987: 79). Landscape archaeologists have emerged as multi-period investigators, who seek to prise apart the different phases of a landscape's development (Aston and Rowley 1974). The limitation of this perspective is that its products have often amounted to "a history of things that have been done to the land" (Barrett 1999: 26), apparently rather remote from the past human lives that were lived in the places under investigation. Although the practitioners were undeniably informed by rich experiences in the field (Fleming 2006: 271), and perhaps even inspired by a romantic sensibility (M. Johnson 2007: 36), their written outputs were often stolidly descriptive rather than explicitly theoretical.

Since the 1990s, a critique of the concept of landscape has developed within archaeology, influenced by developments in human geography, anthropology, and continental philosophy. The resultant "postprocessual landscape archaeology" (*sensu* Fleming 2006: 268) is actually a rather diverse phenomenon, characterized by dissonant perspectives on human nature, perception, experience, and meaning. Perhaps as a result, the archaeology of landscape has recently been an area of lively debate, and has given rise to some of the most radical and experimental work within the discipline (e.g. Bender 1998; Edmonds 1999). Some practitioners consider this "theoretical landscape archaeology" to be an alternative to its more empirical predecessor; for others, the two may be complementary ways of investigating the same object. But it is also possible to argue that the two traditions are seeking entirely different kinds of knowledge, and addressing "landscapes" of different kinds, even if they can potentially be mutually informative and enriching.

The critical evaluation of the notion of landscape begins with a questioning of the modern outlook. As such, it finds support in forms of human geography that have rejected the "spatial science" of the 1960s, opting instead to concentrate on culture and social relations, power and politics, identity and experience (e.g. Gregory 1978: 49; Gregory and Urry 1985; Peet and Thrift 1989; Seamon and Mugerauer 1985). Within this very diverse set of approaches, a more distinct school of cultural geography can be identified (Cosgrove and Daniels 1988), which has drawn upon the work of theorists who have explicitly addressed the issue of landscape as a cultural phenomenon (Berger 1972; Williams 1973). For these thinkers the vision of landscape as an accumulated record of continuity and tradition, which gives us access to an authentic past, is an ideological one. It serves to conceal inequality and conflict (Bender 1998: 33; Daniels 1989: 196). Seeking harmony and authenticity, we may find only fragmentation and multiple encodings (Daniels and Cosgrove 1988: 8).

One reason for this is that landscape is a singularly complex and difficult concept. The word has multiple meanings, and its precise significance has shifted repeatedly. Landscape can mean the topography and land-forms of a given region, or a terrain within which people dwell, or a fragment of the land that can be overseen from a single vantage point, and represented as such (Ingold 1997: 29; Olwig

1993: 307). Landscape can be an object, an experience, or a representation, and these different meanings frequently merge into one another (Lemaire 1997: 5). For this reason, it can refer simultaneously to a way of seeing the world which is specific to elite social groups, and to the inhabited lifeworld of a broader community (Daniels 1989: 206). Moreover, Hirsch (1995: 3) argues that any landscape which provides the context for human life necessarily incorporates a relationship between a lived reality and a potential for other ways of being, between the everyday and conditions that are metaphysical, imagined, or idealized. Every use of the term "landscape" brings a series of resonances with it, of alienation and liberation, sensuous experience and coercion, aspiration and inequality. The challenge of working with landscape is one of holding these elements in a productive tension rather than hoping to find a resolution (Bender 1998: 38; Daniels 1989: 217).

It is instructive to chart the historical development of these issues. Contemporary western conceptions of landscape are lodged within a broader modern worldview, key elements of which include the distinction between subject and object, and that between culture and nature. In the pre-modern era, there was no great gulf between people and their world, which was understood as animate and imbued with moral qualities (Collingwood 1945: 111; Taylor 1989: 144). While Renaissance thinkers portrayed humanity as struggling to subdue nature, this was a struggle between two comparable beings. But in the work of Galileo and Newton, nature increasingly became a mechanical realm governed by knowable laws, to which both God and humans were external. These laws of nature were expressed in terms of causal relations between definable entities. Mind, value, ethics, and divinity are thus opposed to motion and matter, the objects of science (Collingwood 1945: 100). This had two significant consequences: the growth of an instrumentalist attitude towards the world and its creatures; and, with the eclipse of religion, the Enlightenment project of grounding morality and governance on autonomous human reason (Gray 1995: 147). These developments lay behind the emergence of what Martin Heidegger (1977: 129) referred to as the "age of the world picture," an epoch in which the world comes to be conceived and grasped as an image that can be apprehended by humanity. In a sense, humanity has gradually usurped God in the modern era, assuming a position at the center of creation. But instead of the creator, Man (sic) has become the arbitrator of reality, so that that which exists is that which has been brought before Man (Heidegger 1977: 130). In consequence, vision has become the dominant metaphor for the acquisition of knowledge, and observational science has gained a pre-eminent position in the definition of reality and truth. Object and subject have been split, so that Man becomes the active subject who observes a passive nature. Furthermore, the valorization of human beings as the bearers of reason creates an imperative to construe nature as something that exists *for* them: at once a home and a store of resources (Zimmerman 1985: 250).

Defined as an object of investigation, nature is understood as being composed of a number of discrete entities or events (Ingold 1993: 154). These can be expected to operate in a lawlike and comprehensible fashion because, at a fundamental level, they all possess spatial extent and spatio-temporal motion. Forces, motion, and distance thus compose what Heidegger (1977: 119) identifies as the "ground plan' of the Cartesian worldview, a set of assumptions which render all things amenable to investigation through a certain kind of mechanics, even before any analysis is undertaken. In the modern west, then, human beings and nature have been positioned as separate and opposed entities. Both can be subjected to study, but, as observing intelligences, people appear to be self-evidently possessed of a mind and a soul, which exist outside of space and materiality, disengaged and ahistorical. Nature is no longer an active subject or a source of value (Bauman 1992: x; Gray 1995: 158). Meanings and ideas are now considered to reside in the mind, and accurate knowledge of the world is understood as faithful mental representation (Taylor 1989: 144). The combination of the conception of the world as image and object, and that of human beings as external observers, provides the condition for the emergence of the modern western notion of landscape.

Landscape art and the landscape idea

One of the most tangible manifestations of the modern worldview is landscape painting, which emerged in northern Italy and Flanders during the fifteenth century (Cosgrove 1984: 20). Indeed, the English word "landscape" comes from the Dutch, and originally referred to a particular kind of pictorial representation (Olwig 1993: 318). Cosgrove (1984) has linked the development of landscape painting to that of capitalism, implying that it is a way of seeing which exists under quite specific historical conditions. He argues that the linear perspective that was employed by Brunelleschi and formalized by Alberti depends upon the conception of land as an alienable commodity. The realist representation of the world through perspective places the artist and the viewer outside of the frame, perceiving the land visually without immersion, engagement, or emotional commitment (Cosgrove 1984: 27; Jay 1993: 116). As John Berger (1972: 109) puts it, a landscape painting is "not so much a framed window onto the world as a safe let into the wall, a safe into which the visible has been deposited." Of course, those who commissioned these paintings were not the peasants who lived on the land, but the landowners who increasingly saw it as something to be measured, partitioned, and bought and sold at will. Landscape painting opens the world up to simultaneous perception, allowing visual pleasure to be taken without any form of reciprocation. As a phenomenon, it provides an indication that capitalism is itself a product of a modern sensibility, in which the things of the world are atomized and estranged from human involvement, as objects produced and consumed by subjects. Moreover, by visually appropriating the land in a specific manner, landscape painting had a series of significant effects, particularly in respect of the ways in which places were understood and physically transformed. Notions of the pastoral, of Arcadia, of the sublime, of scenery and of wilderness were promoted through the circulation of painterly imagery. This conditioned the interpretation of unfamiliar landscapes in the colonized world (Mugerauer 1985), and influenced the construction of parks and gardens, which were increasingly laid out around prospects and vistas (Hirsch 1995: 2).

Despite its close ties with landed capital, landscape painting has often been considered to embody ethical and aesthetic values. Although modernity has eventually seen the divine supplanted by Man, humanity firstly assumed the position of the deity's privileged interpreter. We should remember that the scientific revolution initially charged itself with revealing God's design in nature, an orientation that was only finally rooted out of natural science by the Darwinian theory of evolution. In a similar way, Ruskin believed that landscape art was a means by which the divine order which is manifested in nature could be reconstructed in the artwork: a kind of act of aesthetic piety (Daniels and Cosgrove 1988: 5; Fuller 1988: 16). Even as a form of representation, landscape appears to be complex and paradoxical.

The principal determinant of landscape art, though, is the look. Vision has achieved the status of the "master sense" of modernity, signifying the objective and dispassionate gathering of knowledge (Jay 1993: 114). Indeed, ocular instruments such as the telescope, the microscope, and the camera obscura played a crucial role in the scientific revolution (Shapin 1996: 28). Through the naturalistic rendering of objects and organisms as scale drawings in science and natural history, vision is connected to classification and ordering, the intellectual control of nature (Pickstone 2001: 63). Consuming the world visually, processing atomized knowledge with his reason, the observer is active and cultural, while the viewed object takes on the characteristics of passive nature (Bender 1999: 31). In this sense, landscape art and empirical science are linked variations on a modern way of looking, which is also a power relationship. It is a look that is disengaged but controlling, which assumes superiority, and which is embedded in the historically contingent gender relations of the modern era. The look is the prerogative of the *flâneur*, the male metropolitan citizen of high modernity, who is free to stroll the arcades of the modern city, "taking it all in." The *flâneur* glimpses shop windows, events, people, but is not involved with any of them. He "embodies the gaze of modernity which is both covetous and erotic" (Pollock 1988: 67). This gendered gaze is characteristically the way in which we look at landscape. Just as western painting defines men as the active producers and viewers of images, while women are passive objects of visual pleasure, so landscape is feminized (Ford 1991). The female body provides a series of metaphors for landscape and nature, and this promotes the impression that the land is a sutured and integrated entity (Best 1995: 184).

In archaeology, we apply to landscapes a series of visual and spatial technologies (geographical information systems, satellite imagery, air photography, virtual reality) which are often presented as neutral means of acquiring and presenting evidence (Barceló 2000: 21). Potentially, though, these technologies partake of ways of looking that are unequal, disengaged, voyeuristic, and androcentric, and these are perhaps characteristic of our way of addressing past landscapes (Thomas 1993: 25). For instance, Witcher et al. (2010: 121) demonstrate the way in which modern visual sensibilities conspire to maintain an anachronistic understanding of Hadrian's Wall in northern England. An emphasis on surveillance and visual control promotes an implicit belief that Roman military priorities were similar to modern ones, and that the structure was primarily defensive. But conversely, Helen Wickstead (2009: 257) has argued that geographical information systems (GIS) can be employed in ways that delegitimize authoritative ways of looking. She argues both that the gaze should not be linked to essentialized gender identities, and that GIS should not be understood as "distorting" any coherent and definitive grounding reality. These points are well taken, and her arguments for a non-representational use of GIS are suggestive and appealing (Wickstead 2009: 265). Yet they do not entirely address the exclusive

visuality of the medium, and the distancing and disaggregating consequences of electronic visual representation.

Closely related to both perspective art and empirical natural science
is the representation of land through cartography. Even more than
landscape painting, maps can appeal to a status of objectivity, yet
they represent a technology of power and knowledge (Harley 1988:
279; A. Smith 1998). Map-making has traditionally been a preserve
of elite groups, who are literate, numerate, and empowered to carve
the world up on paper. Maps are made and used by landowners, the
military, the nobility, and the bureaucracy, and are as notable for
what they omit as for what they depict (Harley 1988: 287). What
Don DeLillo (1997) describes in his novel *Underworld* as the "white
spaces on the map" are locations that have been removed from view
by hegemonic forces. From the papal line which defined Spanish and
Portuguese spheres of influence in the New World to the Versailles
peace agreement, maps have provided an instrument which renders
the world malleable. Like other manifestations of the western gaze,
cartography presents a distanced view as a dispassionate one, manip-
ulating the world while at the same time de-humanizing it. Injustice
and human suffering are not visible on any map. An important aspect
of this manipulation has been the role of maps in the promotion and
construction of national identity (Herb 1989). And just as maps
depict the land in an orthographic, Cartesian fashion and delimit the
nation-states of the modern era, so, too, is the nation bound up with
the concept of landscape. A landscape may be an area which was
carved out by the national ancestors, but alternatively the archetypal
landscape of a region (the German forest; the English downland; the
American prairie) may be held to have nurtured the national spirit
(Lowenthal 1994; Olwig 1993: 311). These ideas about the relationship between the land and the community, most forcefully expressed
in the work of Friedrich Ratzel, were deeply influential in the formation of culture historic archaeology. Developed into Gustaf Kossinna's
"settlement archaeological method" (Veit 1989), they betray a distinctive modernist preoccupation: the search backward through time
to identify the origin of the nation and its primordial relationship
with the land from which it sprang.

Landscape, perception, and being-in-the-world

If the dominant western perspective on landscape is one that is alienated, objectified, distanced, and de-humanized, one response might
be to follow the "humanist geographers" (e.g. Tuan 1974) into an

investigation of the human awareness and perception of space. By this means, we might hope to "put the people back" into the past (Fleming 2006: 276). It is arguable that the use of phenomenology in archaeology has sometimes amounted to this: a kind of "subjective epistemology" which attempts to recover the experiences of past people (Barrett and Ko 2009: 279; Thomas 2008: 301) (see below). This is problematic not simply because it misrepresents phenomenology, but also because it is an attempt to introduce an intimate and personal element into *the same world* as is addressed by conventional landscape archaeology: a world of measurable distances, velocities, and densities. Such an approach maintains that the world that is revealed to us in maps, diagrams, and aerial photographs is a foundational reality, and that its experience is a secondary matter. Landscapes are in the first instance empty of meaning (Ingold 1992: 39), so that "space" is transformed into "place" through a human intervention. This means that archaeologists are at liberty to investigate past landscapes as aggregates of land-forms, soil types, rainfall zones, and vegetation patterns in the first instance, only later turning to how these phenomena might have been *perceived* by past people. The implication is that through our objective, high-tech methodologies we have access to a stratum of reality that was unavailable to people in the past. Their perceptions of these landscapes would necessarily have been distorted and impoverished versions of a reality that we can more fully grasp.

All of this can only be entertained while we continue to rely upon the modernist divisions of mind and body, and subject and object. The notion of *landscape perception* is founded in the splitting of human beings into an inner and an outer person, so that information gathered in the outside world is internalized, and used to reconstruct a "mental picture" of the environment (Taylor 1993: 317). This implies that sense-impressions are thing-like bits of information which are rendered intelligible by the mind (N. H. Smith 2002: 54). If this is the case, we arrive at a very harsh Cartesianism in which the human body inhabits a geometrical world of mere objects, and all meanings are events that take place in the metaphysical space of the mind. Banishing meaning from the material world, we have to hypothesize that language and symbols are means by which meanings produced inside one mind are transformed into something physical (an object or a sound), and then decoded by another mind using the same apparatus as it uses to perceive the world in general. This is a manifestation of what Tim Ingold (1995: 66) calls the "building perspective," in which culture is imagined as "an arbitrary symbolic framework built on the surface of reality."

In an insightful discussion of these issues, Johnston (1998: 57) seeks to distinguish between "explicit" and "inherent" perceptions of the landscape. In the former, perception intercedes between an outer reality and an internalized mental image, while in the latter, it is embedded in the lived experience of being within the land. This is rather akin to the notion of "direct perception" that Ingold (1998: 39) takes from the environmental psychologist J.J. Gibson. Direct perception is a process in which creatures get to know their surroundings through their complete bodily immersion in the world, finding out what affordances it can provide, rather than simply representing it in their minds. Although these arguments have much to recommend them, there is reason to avoid the term "perception" altogether, on the grounds that it inevitably carries a sense of subsidiarity or supplementarity. Instead, I would choose to talk of "disclosure" or "experience," which do not imply that our understanding of the world is somehow a failed attempt to come to terms with things as they really are.

Clearly, the model of perception as the construction of a mental picture is closely related to landscape as a way of representing the world. However, I would like to argue that while we cannot rid ourselves of this conception of landscape, another, parallel understanding is possible, based upon the relational and embedded way in which people conduct themselves in the world. Such a perspective would follow Ingold in arguing that there are no boundaries between mind and world, or between earth and sky. We are immersed in a world that is continually coming into being around us, and our thinking is an activity that takes place within that world (Ingold 2007: 28). Rather than encountering meaningless objects and rendering them significant, we encounter worldly things in their meaningfulness. We apprehend them *as* meanings, rather than as objective sense data. To put this another way, the world in which we find ourselves is a horizon of intelligibility, a relational background which provides the context that enables anything that we focus upon to be rendered comprehensible. As a result, the condition of being-in-the-world is not simply a matter of being physically contained within a much larger entity; it is a *relational involvement* like being "in business" or "in love." It is "residing, dwelling, and being accustomed to a world" (Heidegger 1962: 79). Being-in-the-world involves an everyday way of "getting on with things" in which we skillfully negotiate and make sense of our surroundings, without having to think about them analytically for much of the time (Relph 1985: 16). But it is not something that we could extract ourselves from: there is no other way to be than in the world. Moreover, our involvement in a world is always presupposed in any comprehension of things: they only make sense because they have a background to stand out from.

Ethnographies of landscape: embedded and multiple worlds

While humanistic geography and phenomenological philosophy have provided inspiration for new approaches to landscape in archaeology, ethnographic accounts of the relationships between people and their immediate environment have also been fundamentally significant. If the conception of landscape as something separate and visually apprehended is a modern western one, it is instructive to attend to the everyday experiences of people who understand themselves to be more embedded in the land. Of course, we westerners do inhabit experiential and relational landscapes, but the significance of this experience is sometimes passed over. Non-western relationships with landscape are not uniform, and cannot simply be imposed on the archaeological past, but an awareness of the range of possibilities can beneficially inform our interpretations. For example, amongst the Australian Yolngu, it is believed that ancestral beings moved across the land in the Dreaming, and that they were eventually incorporated into the landscape, providing the distinctive character of significant places. Gaining a familiarity with the land is at the same time an acquisition of knowledge of the Dreaming, which still exists embodied in the land. People's movements along ancestral tracks and their experiences of places reproduce the Dreaming (Morphy 1995: 187). Similarly, many New Guinea societies consider the land to embody ancestral energies, which are nurtured through human involvement (Tilley 1994: 58). Yet the full meanings of places and the energies that they contain may be socially restricted, and gaining knowledge of the landscape may be a means of achieving authority (Tilley 1994: 59). The Saami of northern Scandinavia understand the sacred sites that they use for sacrifices to be imbued with spiritual forces (Mulk 1994: 125). These places are generally outstanding topographical features like mountain peaks, springs, and rivers. At the risk of oversimplifying this material, each example appears to present the landscape as in some sense animate, and involved in some form of reciprocity with human beings. Similarly, the sea can also be perceived as an animate realm, but one inhabited by terrifying creatures and imbued with dangerous spiritual energy (McNiven 2004: 332).

One particular way in which people's interconnection with the land is often expressed is through the medium of kinship. This can take a number of forms. Land may be connected with ancestry in various ways: ancestors may have formed the land, or emerged out of it, or cleared the wilderness and created fields and gardens (Toren 1995: 178). In each case, the landscape provides a continuous reminder of the relationship between the living and past generations, and consequentially of lines of descent and inheritance. The traces of human activity in the landscape may therefore represent a source of detailed information about kin relations. For instance, in western Amazonia the pattern of houses and gardens gradually falling into decay and decrepitude within the forest is recognized as a physical record of residential history, which can be directly related to genealogical lore (Gow 1995: 48). Over the generations the movements and fissioning of households have produced a complex landscape, and movement through it in the present is a means of recapitulating their histories. As well as physical traces, the names given to places and locations may be a means by which past people and events can be continuously drawn into the present (Basso 1996: 32). In the case of New Ireland, Küchler (1987: 249) has shown how the mapping of the places in the landscape and of kin relations may be more or less congruent. If kinship is a means of expressing relationships among human beings, it is instructive that it is so often embedded in landscape. Land, place, people, and material substances may all be fundamentally linked rather than constituting entirely separate classes of things.

We have suggested that lived landscapes are relational entities constituted by people in their engagement with the world. It follows from this that different people may experience and understand the same landscape in rather different ways (Bender 1998: 87). As a consequence of their gender, class, ethnicity, sexuality, age, cultural tradition, and personal life history, people are differentially located. So each person has a particular set of possibilities when it comes to presenting an account of his or her own landscape. Landscapes might thus be said to be multiple or fragmented. It is not simply that they are perceived differently; the same location may effectively be a different place for two different persons. This is particularly the case when people possess different cultural inheritances. Discussing the Cape York Peninsula in Australia, Veronica Strang (1999) describes the utterly incompatible understandings of the land held by the Aboriginal community and the Euro-Australian cattle herders. The Aborigines believe that every part of the landscape is distinctive and embodies ancestral beings from the Dreamtime. Human lives extend between places of special spiritual potency which bring about birth and death. Personal and group identity, moral order, and social organization are all embedded in human relationships with the land. However, for the inhabitants of the cattle stations the landscape is a hostile and dangerous wilderness. If the Aborigines see themselves as engaged in reciprocity with the land, the cattle herders are its adversaries. From a western capitalist viewpoint, the land has to be overcome, controlled, enclosed, and used to produce wealth. The value of land is its financial worth, and the Aborigines are said to "do nothing" with the country, for they do not use it to accumulate income (Strang 1999: 212). These two communities do not simply have distinct mental images of the same landscape; they are engaged in different sets of lived relationships, even if they find themselves in the same physical space.

Experiencing monuments and landscapes

One of the areas in which a theoretical landscape archaeology has had its most profound impact has been in the study of prehistoric monuments in Britain and Europe. The earliest construction of ceremonial monuments at the start of the Neolithic has been connected with new experiences of place, and a closer identification between people and particular locations (Bradley 1998: 18). The investigation of monuments has proved especially productive, since it offers the opportunity to study the details of architecture, mortuary activity, and depositional practices in the context of the surrounding topography, while overcoming the limitations of approaches based upon typology. This concern with the place of monuments within lived landscapes is also demonstrated by a renewed interest in the implications of mobility (e.g. Whittle 1997). While chambered tombs and stone circles have often been identified as central places, implicitly assumed to have been located close to sedentary habitations, it seems that they may just as often have been constructed on route-ways. Patterns of movement between and around monuments may have been important in the seasonal round practiced by prehistoric communities, and at a smaller scale they may also have been fundamental to the ways in which these sites were used. In her studies of the locations of passage tombs in the cemetery of Loughcrew in Ireland (1998), and of Clyde tombs in western Scotland (2004), Shannon Fraser points to the way that the very particular immediate topographies of these sites would have influenced the ways in which they might have been used, and how people could have gathered and moved in relation to them. In the case of Loughcrew, the growth of the tomb group appears to have gradually elaborated upon the natural features of the hilltops, defining and constraining areas of congregation and setting up particular relationships between monuments and assemblies of people. Fraser's argument is that if these tombs and their use were instrumental in the maintenance of authority and traditions of knowledge, this reproduction could only have been secured in public, rather than exclusively within the secluded spaces of the tomb interiors (Fraser 1998: 209). Both prehistoric monuments and later structures are increasingly being recognized as dependent upon their landscape setting for their meaning and reception, both in the past and in the present (Witcher et al. 2010: 109). On the basis of her extensive investigations of the locations of megalithic tombs in the Irish Sea basin, Vicky Cummings (2009: 186) has argued that places with extensive views of the sea, rivers, loughs, and mountains were judged appropriate for construction, and were intrinsic to the significance of the eventual structure.

Fraser's account of Loughcrew suggests that the place itself was already marked out as sacred before the tombs began to be constructed. More generally, monuments may have been a means of reconfiguring or enhancing landscapes, rather than an imposition which negated the existing identity of a place. This insight has prompted a growing concern with the way that building takes place within an integrated world of materials, conducted by people who weave elements together to draw new possibilities out of familiar surroundings (McFadyen 2008: 309). Monuments such as stone circles and henges sometimes appear to have been conceived as microcosms of their surrounding landscapes (Bradley 1998: 128), and it has been suggested that they were often composed of materials that held a symbolic or cosmological significance, so that their construction and use amounted to a re-engineering of the landscape itself (Bender 1998: 49). Equally, monuments built of wood, and deliberately destroyed by fire, had much shorter use-lives than ones made of stone, and would have engendered collective memories in very different ways (Thomas 2007: 264).

More influential than this work on construction, though, has been an experiential approach to monuments and landscapes, pioneered in Christopher Tilley's *A Phenomenology of Landscape* (1994). While Tilley's approach in this volume was based as much in the ethnography of people's relationship to the land as in phenomenological philosophy, it is nonetheless grounded in the insight that the lived world is a place of meaning rather than inert matter. If our contemporary experiences of prehistoric sites are as symbols on maps or field trip visits, we can enrich our understanding by encountering monuments in the course of walking the landscape. This is not so much an attempt to achieve empathy with past people as a means of placing the architecture within a broader context. This context is still, in appreciable ways, comparable with the past, for although the superficial detail of the land has changed, the broad outlines of the topography are unaltered since the Neolithic (Tilley 1994: 73–4). Tilley's vivid accounts of walking the environs of the long cairns of the Black Mountains, the Dorset Cursus, and the megaliths of southwest Wales have proved inspirational to a generation of archaeologists, but the approach has attracted criticism. Some of this has been empirical in character, focusing on the representativeness of Tilley's observations (Fleming 1999: 124), but a broader critique identifies a tendency amongst a number of "post-processual landscape archaeologists" to present "hyper-interpretive" texts which exceed the capacity of the evidence to substantiate them (Fleming 2006: 276).

Another series of arguments concern the status of any knowledge created through corporeal experience of ancient architecture. Both Meskell (1996: 6) and Hodder (1999: 13) have suggested that while these approaches are preoccupied with an encounter between a human body and a location, the bodies involved are anonymous and universal. These authors argue that a concern with individual lives in the past is the element which is missing. Brück (1998: 28) makes a related point when she asks how a pregnant woman, or a child, or a disabled person might have negotiated the Dorset Cursus five thousand years ago: there was presumably no one universal experience to be had. Arguably, though, I can only encounter the world through the body of a male, twenty-first-century academic, and I cannot occupy anyone else's body. This need not render the project of an experiential archaeology invalid (Thomas 2004: 32). More troubling is the issue of whether such an archaeology commits us to either the notion of a universal human nature, or the attempt to empathize with past people. Barrett and Ko (2009: 279) argue that Tilley's "subjective epistemology" rests on the assumption that our own experiences can be used to inform us about those of people in the past. By implication, we must be the same kind of beings as those past people. As they quite rightly point out, such a view is at odds with the hermeneutic phenomenology of Martin Heidegger, which Tilley cites approvingly. For Heidegger, phenomenology is not simply the study of human experience, but an investigation of the grounds of the possibility of both humanity and experience: how there can be anything at all, instead of just nothing (Frede 1993: 51). This involves a thorough rejection of any unchanging human nature, and an emphasis on the historicity of being. To be fair, however, Tilley may use the term "phenomenology," but his primary commitment is to theories of objectification, which might admit a more stable human subject and human body (Tilley 2006: 61).

Barrett and Ko (2009: 280) contend that Tilley's project (and that of Cummings) is to give meaning to the archaeological record through the presence of a human body in the present, and in the process to encounter a past Being. This is the flip side of Hodder's argument that archaeologies which concern themselves with bodily practice cannot absolve themselves of any need to consider meaning or empathy with the past (Hodder 1999: 133–4). Barrett and Ko maintain that we cannot empathize with people who are likely to have very little in common with ourselves, while Hodder argues that we cannot avoid doing so if we are to make sense of the evidence. In a related argument, Layton and Ucko (1999: 12) proposed that prehistoric landscapes represent sets of "empty signs" which archaeologists attempt at their peril to fill with a "surrogate discourse." Their implication is that specific meanings probably were given to places and features in the past, but that we may be deluding ourselves if we imagine that we can gain access to them in the present. A possible answer to this apparent impasse is that our phenomenology of landscape should be a hermeneutic one, which acknowledges that we can never directly encounter the past, only the traces of the past in the present (H. Johnson and Olsen 1992: 429). Through this encounter we produce a meaning, but it is a contemporary meaning, not the thoughts of a past person. While Layton and Ucko might dismiss this as a "surrogate" for a past meaning, it might be considered instead as an allegory, a present-day understanding which "stands for" the past meaning. Past and present are separate horizons that never entirely meet, and an experiential archaeology of landscape is best understood as contributing to the conversation between these horizons, rather than an end in itself. Our engagement with the material traces of the past does not give us access to past experiences, but it provides a basis for understanding how far they may have been unlike our own. Fraser (1998: 204) puts this rather well when she describes our practice as "inhabiting the archaeological landscape in the present," a phrase which echoes Ingold's description of archaeology as the most recent form of dwelling on an ancient site (Ingold 1993: 152). However, we should be mindful that the "background" against which ancient objects and structures reveal themselves to us is a largely modern one, composed of contemporary skills, understandings, and practices that we may be only partially aware of. Our experience of a place or artifact in its landscape context is of value because the thing itself is more than the product or outcome of an extinct pattern of social life. On the contrary, it represents an integral

and still-extant element of that pattern. But appreciating its significance requires that the part should be placed into as complete as
possible a whole.

Conclusion

I have argued that there are two quite different understandings of the
term "landscape": as a territory that can be apprehended visually,
and as a set of relationships between people and places which provide
the context for everyday conduct. In a more or less explicit way,
archaeologists have recognized that landscape provides a framework
for integrating many different forms of information and different
aspects of human life. However, the landscapes to which they have
been referring have generally been specular and objectified. Identifying
the historical specificity of the landscape idea has opened up the
conceptual space for a new kind of landscape archaeology. A new
approach will still require that we identify and plot the traces of past
activity in the countryside. But the uses to which these traces will be
put will have to go beyond the reconstruction of economic regimes
and speculations as to how the land may have been perceived by past
people. In considering the ways in which the significance of the landscape gradually emerged, through practices of building, maintenance,
tending, harvesting, and dwelling, we are constructing in the present
an analogy for past worlds of meaning.

References

Aston, M. and T. Rowley 1974. *Landscape Archaeology: An Introduction
   to Fieldwork Techniques on Post-Roman Landscapes*. Newton Abbot,
   UK: David and Charles.
Barceló, J. A. 2000. Visualizing what might be: an introduction to virtual
   reality techniques in archaeology. In J. A. Barceló, M. Forte, and D. H.
   Saunders (eds), *Virtual Reality in Archaeology*, 9–35. Oxford: British
   Archaeological Reports S843.
Barrett, J. C. 1999. Chronologies of landscape. In P. Ucko and R. Layton
   (eds), *The Archaeology and Anthropology of Landscape*, 21–30. London:
   Routledge.
Barrett, J. C. and I. Ko 2009. A phenomenology of landscape: a crisis in
   British landscape archaeology? *Journal of Social Archaeology* 9: 275–94.
Basso, K. H. 1996. *Wisdom Sits in Places: Landscape and Language among
   the Western Apache*. Albuquerque: University of New Mexico Press.

Bauman, Z. 1992. *Intimations of Postmodernity.* London: Routledge.

Bender, B. 1998. *Stonehenge: Making Space.* Oxford: Berg.

Bender, B. 1999. Subverting the western gaze: mapping alternative worlds. In P. Ucko and R. Layton (eds), *The Archaeology and Anthropology of Landscape*, 31–45. London: Routledge.

Berger, J. 1972. *Ways of Seeing.* Harmondsworth: Penguin.

Best, S. 1995. Sexualizing space. In E. Grosz and E. Probyn (eds), *Sexy Bodies: The Strange Carnalities of Feminism*, 181–94. London: Routledge.

Bowden, M. 1991. *Pitt Rivers.* Cambridge: Cambridge University Press.

Bradley, R. J. 1998. *The Significance of Monuments.* London: Routledge.

Brück, J. 1998. In the footsteps of the ancestors: a review of Christopher Tilley's *A Phenomenology of Landscape: Places, Paths and Monuments. Archaeological Review from Cambridge* 15: 23–36.

Collingwood, R. G. 1945. *The Idea of Nature.* Oxford: Clarendon.

Cosgrove, D. 1984. *Social Formation and Symbolic Landscape.* London: Croom Helm.

Cosgrove, D. and S. Daniels (eds) 1988. *The Iconography of Landscape.* Cambridge: Cambridge University Press.

Cummings, V. 2009. *A View from the West: The Neolithic of the Irish Sea Zone.* Oxford: Oxbow Books.

Daniels, S. 1989. Marxism, culture, and the duplicity of landscape. In R. Peet and N. Thrift (eds), *New Models in Human Geography, Volume 2*, 196–220. London: Unwin Hyman.

Daniels, S. and D. Cosgrove 1988. Introduction: iconography and landscape. In D. Cosgrove and S. Daniels (eds), *The Iconography of Landscape*, 1–10. Cambridge: Cambridge University Press.

Darvill, T. C. 2008. Pathways to a panoramic past: a brief history of European landscape archaeology. In B. David and J. Thomas (eds), *Handbook of Landscape Archaeology*, 60–76. Walnut Creek, CA: Left Coast Press.

DeLillo, D. 1997. *Underworld.* London: Picador.

Edmonds, M. R. 1999. *Ancestral Geographies of the Neolithic: Landscapes, Monuments and Memory.* London: Routledge.

Fleming, A. 2006. Post-processual landscape archaeology: a critique. *Cambridge Archaeological Journal* 16: 267–80.

Ford, S. 1991. Landscape revisited: a feminist reappraisal. In C. Philo (compiler), *New Words, New Worlds: Reconceptualising Social and Cultural Geography*, 151–5. Lampeter, UK: St. David's University College.

Fraser, S. 1998. The public forum and the space between: the materiality of social strategy in the Irish Neolithic. *Proceedings of the Prehistoric Society* 64: 203–24.

Fraser, S. 2004. Metaphorical journeys: landscape, monuments, and the body in a Scottish Neolithic. *Proceedings of the Prehistoric Society* 70: 129–51.

Frede, D. 1993. The question of Being: Heidegger's project. In C. Guignon (ed.), *The Cambridge Companion to Heidegger*, 42–69. Cambridge: Cambridge University Press.

Fuller, P. 1988. The geography of Mother Nature. In D. Cosgrove and S. Daniels (eds), *The Iconography of Landscape*, 11–31. Cambridge: Cambridge University Press.

Gow, P. 1995. Land, people and paper in western Amazonia. In E. Hirsch and M. O'Hanlon (eds), *The Anthropology of Landscape*, 43–62. Oxford: Oxford University Press.

Gray, J. 1995. *Enlightenment's Wake; Politics and Culture at the Close of the Modern Age*. London: Routledge.

Gregory, D. 1978. *Ideology, Science and Human Geography*. London: Hutchinson.

Gregory, D. and J. Urry 1985. *Social Relations and Spatial Structures*. London: Macmillan.

Harley, J. B. 1988. Maps, knowledge and power. In D. Cosgrove and S. Daniels (eds), *The Iconography of Landscape*, 277–312. Cambridge: Cambridge University Press.

Heidegger, M. 1962. *Being and Time*. Oxford: Blackwell.

Heidegger, M. 1977. The age of the world-picture. In M. Heidegger, *The Question Concerning Technology and Other Essays*, 115–54. New York: Harper and Row.

Herb, H. 1989. Persuasive cartography in *Geopolitik* and National Socialism. *Political Geography Quarterly* 8: 289–303.

Hirsch, E. 1995. Landscape: between place and space. In E. Hirsch and M. O'Hanlon (eds), *The Anthropology of Landscape*, 1–30. Oxford: Oxford University Press.

Hodder, I. R. 1999. *The Archaeological Process: An Introduction*. Oxford: Blackwell.

Ingold, T. 1992. Culture and the perception of the environment. In E. Croll and D. Parkin (eds), *Bush Base, Forest Farm*, 39–56. London: Routledge.

Ingold, T. 1993. The temporality of the landscape. *World Archaeology* 25: 152–74.

Ingold, T. 1995. Building, dwelling, living: how animals and people make themselves at home in the world. In M. Strathern (ed.) *Shifting Contexts: Transformations in Anthropological Knowledge*, 57–80. London: Routledge.

Ingold, T. 1997. The picture is not the terrain: maps, paintings and the dwelt-in world. *Archaeological Dialogues* 4: 29–31.

Ingold, T. 1998. From complementarity to obviation: on dissolving the boundaries between social and biological anthropology, archaeology and psychology. *Zeitschrift für Ethnologie* 123: 21–52.

Ingold, T. 2007. Earth, sky, wind and weather. *Journal of the Royal Anthropological Institute* (N.S.) Special Issue: S19–S38.

Jay, M. 1993. *Downcast Eyes: The Denigration of Vision in Twentieth-Century French Thought*. Berkeley: University of California Press.

Johnson, H. and B. Olsen 1992. Hermeneutics and archaeology: on the philosophy of contextual archaeology. *American Antiquity* 57: 419–36.

Johnson, M. 2007. *Ideas of Landscape*. Oxford: Blackwell.

Johnston, R. 1998. Approaches to the perception of landscape. *Archaeological Dialogues* 5: 54–68.

Küchler, S. 1987. Malangan: art and memory in a Melanesian society. *Man* (N.S.) 22: 238–55.

Layton, R. and P. Ucko 1999. Introduction: gazing at the landscape and encountering the environment. In P. Ucko and R. Layton (eds), *The Archaeology and Anthropology of Landscape*, 1–20. London: Routledge.

Lemaire, T. 1997. Archaeology between the invention and destruction of the landscape. *Archaeological Dialogues* 4: 5–21.

Lowenthal, D. 1994. European and English landscapes as national symbols. In D. Hooson (ed.), *Geography and National Identity*, 15–38. Oxford: Blackwell.

McFadyen, L. 2008. Building and architecture as landscape practice. In B. David and J. Thomas (eds), *Handbook of Landscape Archaeology*, 307–14. Walnut Creek, CA: Left Coast Press.

McNiven, I. 2004. Saltwater people: spiritscapes, maritime rituals and the archaeology of Australian indigenous seascapes. *World Archaeology* 35: 329–49.

Meskell, L. 1996. The somatization of archaeology: institutions, discourses, corporeality. *Norwegian Archaeological Review* 29: 1–16.

Morphy, H. 1995. Landscape and the reproduction of the ancestral past. In E. Hirsch and M. O'Hanlon (eds), *The Anthropology of Landscape*, 184–209. Oxford: Oxford University Press.

Mugerauer, R. 1985. Language and the emergence of the environment. In D. Seamon and R. Mugerauer (eds), *Dwelling, Place and Environment*, 51–70. New York: Columbia University Press.

Mulk, I. M. 1994. Sacrificial places and their meaning in Saami society. In D. L. Carmichael, J. Hubert, B. Reeves, and A. Schanche (eds), *Sacred Sites, Sacred Places*, 121–31. London: Routledge.

Olwig, K. 1993. Sexual cosmology: nation and landscape at the conceptual interstices of nature and culture; or what does landscape really mean? In B. Bender (ed.), *Landscape: Politics and Perspectives*, 307–43. Oxford: Berg.

Peet, R. and N. Thrift (eds) 1989. *New Models in Geography, Volume 2*. London: Unwin Hyman.

Pickstone, J. V. 2001. *Ways of Knowing: A New History of Science, Technology and Medicine*. Manchester: Manchester University Press.

Pollock, G. 1988. *Vision and Difference: Femininity, Feminism and the Histories of Art*. London: Routledge.

Relph, E. 1985. Geographical experiences and being-in-the-world: the phenomenological origins of geography. In D. Seamon and R. Mugerauer (eds), *Dwelling, Place and Environment*, 15–32. New York: Columbia University.

Roberts, B. K. 1987. Landscape archaeology. In M. Wagstaff (ed.), *Landscape and Culture*, 77–95. Oxford: Blackwell.

Seamon, D. and R. Mugerauer 1985. *Dwelling, Place and Environment*. New York: Columbia University Press.

Shapin, S. 1996. *The Scientific Revolution*. Chicago: University of Chicago Press.

Smith, A. 1998. Landscapes of power in nineteenth-century Ireland: archaeology and Ordnance Survey maps. *Archaeological Dialogues* 5: 69–84.

Smith, N. H. 2002. *Charles Taylor: Meaning, Morals and Modernity*. Cambridge: Polity.

Strang, V. 1999. Competing perceptions of landscape in Kowanyama, north Queensland. In P. Ucko and R. Layton (eds), *The Archaeology and Anthropology of Landscape*, 206–18. London: Routledge.

Taylor, C. 1989. *Sources of the Self: The Making of the Modern Identity*. Cambridge: Cambridge University Press.

Taylor, C. 1993. Engaged agency and background in Heidegger. In C. Guignon (ed.), *The Cambridge Companion to Heidegger*, 317–36. Cambridge: Cambridge University Press.

Thomas, J. S. 1993. The politics of vision and the archaeologies of landscape. In B. Bender (ed.), *Landscape: Politics and Perspectives*, 19–48. Oxford: Berg.

Thomas, J. S. 2004. The great dark book: archaeology, experience and interpretation. In J. L. Bintliff (ed.), *The Blackwell Companion to Archaeology*, 21–36. Oxford: Blackwell.

Thomas, J. S. 2007. *Place and Memory: Excavations at the Pict's Knowe, Holywood and Holm Farm, Dumfries and Galloway*. Oxford: Oxbow Books.

Thomas, J. S. 2008. Archaeology, landscape and dwelling. In B. David and J. Thomas (eds), *Handbook of Landscape Archaeology*, 300–6. Walnut Creek, CA: Left Coast Press.

Tilley, C. Y. 1994. *A Phenomenology of Landscape: Places, Paths and Monuments*. Oxford: Berg.

Tilley, C. Y. 2006. Objectification. In C. Y. Tilley, W. Keane, S. Küchler, M. Rowlands, and P. Spyer (eds), *Handbook of Material Culture*, 60–73. London: Sage.

Toren, C. 1995. Seeing the ancestral sites: transformations in Fijian notions of the land. In E. Hirsch and M. O'Hanlon (eds), *The Anthropology of Landscape*, 163–83. Oxford: Oxford University Press.

Tuan, Y. F. 1974. Space and place: humanistic perspective. *Progress in Geography* 6: 211–52.

Veit, U. 1989. Ethnic concepts in prehistory: a case study on the relationship between cultural identity and archaeological objectivity. In S. J. Shennan (ed.), *Archaeological Approaches to Cultural Identity*, 33–56. London: Unwin Hyman.

Whittle, A. W. R. 1997. Moving on and moving around: Neolithic settlement mobility. In P. Topping (ed.), *Neolithic Landscapes*, 14–22. Oxford: Oxbow Books.

Wickstead, H. 2009. The Uber-Archaeologist: art, GIS and the male gaze revisited. *Journal of Social Archaeology* 9: 249–71.

Williams, R. 1973. *The Country and the City.* London: Paladin.

Witcher, R., D. P. Tolia-Kelly, and R. Hingley 2010. Archaeologies of landscape: excavating the materialities of Hadrian's Wall. *Journal of Material Culture* 15: 105–28.

Zimmerman, M. E. 1985. The role of spiritual discipline in learing to dwell on earth. In D. Seamon and R. Mugerauer (eds), *Dwelling, Place and Environment*, 247–56. New York: Columbia University Press.

9

MATERIALITY

Carl Knappett

What is materiality?

The materiality of the body; the materiality of the house; the materiality of landscape; the materiality of belief: everywhere archaeologists turn they encounter materiality. Yet this is a very recent development in the field, and attitudes to the term are varied. Some authors are at pains to define their understanding of materiality, while others take it as read. It is hard keeping track of the meanings of materiality when it is used in so many different archaeological contexts, not to mention in neighboring disciplines. What does seem apparent is that such varied, and often inconsistent, usage renders a review of the pros and cons of "materiality" for archaeological theory particularly timely. I shall argue here that to define materiality we need to think about it along four dimensions: material relations, social relations, vitality, and plurality. I shall also insist upon the importance of distinctive archaeological methodologies for addressing materiality in detail.

Materiality as material relations

Although publications on "materiality" have proliferated in the last couple of years, the first use of the term in anthropology can be found in 1871 in the work of E.B. Tylor (Taylor 2009: 299). However, as Taylor points out, this is not the source of the term for the recent slew of publications, which begin, rather, with Chris Gosden's 1994 book *Social Being and Time*. It is worth returning to this because of Gosden's distinction between materiality and mutuality: the former "refers to human relations with the world," while the latter "looks at human inter-relations" (Gosden 1994: 82). While this may seem unduly dichotomous, he is quick to add that the two are inseparable and mutually constitutive. What Gosden does here is identify two kinds of relations that are critical in "social being" – material relations (materiality) and social relations (mutuality). This is subsequently recognized by another archaeologist who is also an early adopter of the term "materiality." Andy Jones advocates materiality as a concept that can bridge the gap between archaeological science and archaeological theory, the former concerned primarily with material relations and the latter with social relations. Indeed, he states that:

> At this juncture, we simply need to note that at both the practical and theoretical level we are required to simultaneously consider how it is that artefacts are socially and culturally constructed, while also taking into account the physical and mechanical construction of artefacts. We do not need to study these two aspects of artefacts as separate and distinct entities. Materials science and material culture studies are therefore engaged in the same project of enquiry. (Jones 2004: 329)

The publication in the same year of the volume *Rethinking Materiality* sees still further attention devoted to this term. Some authors do take trouble to define the term, as in the introductory paper (DeMarrais et al. 2004: 2), and that by Scarre (2004: 141), but it does not seem too problematic and falls largely in line with the definition offered by Gosden. In a more recent study that also equates materiality with material relations, Nicole Boivin (2008) interprets plastering practices at the Neolithic site of Çatalhöyük by using insights drawn from her observations on the materiality of mudplaster in contemporary houses in rural Rajasthan. She views materiality as "the physicality of matter" (Boivin 2008: 129), and argues against social constructivist viewpoints. This seems to fall in line with Ingold's understanding of "materials," and earlier archaeological definitions of materiality as material relations (e.g. Gosden 1994). However, at times, Boivin (2008: 167) also states that "what is important is not just materiality, but the coming together of materiality and embodied humans engaged in particular activities." This appears to combine aspects of both material and social relations. Such an opening up from materiality as material relations to something broader that includes social relations also seems to be the approach adopted in an edited volume that is one of the first to focus on materiality (Graves-Brown 2000).

Materiality as social relations

This modified position taken by Boivin is actually more akin to what we find when we look at some recent uses of the term in socio-cultural anthropology, where materiality seems more attributable to social than to material relations. Perhaps the most prominent volume in this field is *Materiality*, the introductory chapter of which, by the volume editor Daniel Miller, offers a rich discussion of immateriality rather than a definition of materiality per se (Miller 2005). Is this because Miller considers materiality itself to be self-evident and banal, unworthy of extended discussion? If we could be sure that he views materiality in Gosden's terms, then perhaps this would be understandable. After all, in much of Miller's important work the emphasis falls more on social relations than material relations; he effectively treats materiality as a lens through which to view mutuality (or immateriality). This is a source of frustration to some, with anthropologist Tim Ingold particularly critical. Attending a conference session on materiality, indeed the session behind the above-mentioned volume *Materiality*, Ingold (2007: 2) claims that not one of the speakers "was able to say what materiality actually means, nor did any of them even mention materials or their properties." The lack of definition vexing Ingold is partly addressed in the responses to his paper by both Miller and Chris Tilley (Miller 2007; Tilley 2007). They argue that "materiality" differs from mere "materials" or "matter" in its inclusion of the social. Tilley emphasizes that he is interested in materials for their social significance, and this is where, in his opinion, the term "materiality" holds advantages over "materials."

We should be careful not to jump to the conclusion that *all* anthropological treatments of materiality are principally interested in mutuality. Webb Keane (2005), for example, with a contribution in the very same *Materiality* volume, emphasizes how materials do have their own properties that can be neither reduced to nor isolated from social relations. He expresses his perspective more directly in a subsequent publication, stating that "a fully social and historical understanding of objects demands a more robust appreciation of the relative autonomy of objects from human projects" (Keane 2006: 197). Nonetheless, this alternative view of materiality is subsumed under Ingold's critique, aimed more expansively at Miller, whose apparent subordination of materiality to mutuality is the primary source of irritation for Ingold, with material relations simply not given sufficient importance. However, Ingold's argument, that "materiality" has become more of a hindrance than a help in understanding materials, may apply to (some) anthropology, but less so to archaeology. Many archaeologists would have little problem in recognizing materiality as simply a relational perspective on materials, one that obliges us to think about their properties, qualities, or affordances. It is when the anthropological perspective starts blending or merging materiality with mutuality that a difference in perspectives appears to open up.

This merging of materiality and mutuality, or what we might also usefully call sociality, predates the regular use of the term "materiality." The other term more commonly used is "material culture," as in the sub-discipline in the Anthropology Department of University College London, where both Miller and Tilley are based, and the *Journal of Material Culture*, launched in 1996 and still edited by this UCL research group. Tilley and Miller had thus long been associated with the study of "material culture" before they began consistently using the term "materiality." Material culture, as a term, more obviously combines the material and the socio-cultural (or both materiality and mutuality, in Gosden's terms), and has been a very useful touchstone for many scholars across anthropology and archaeology (e.g. Tilley et al. 2006). This perspective can be traced back to the highly influential volume *The Social Life of Things* edited by Arjun Appadurai (1986), and arguably before this in the 1980s with the early work of Daniel Miller and Ian Hodder; this has recently been dubbed the "material-cultural turn" (Hicks 2010). In all of this work the "things" of material culture were seen as dynamic components of everyday lives able to provide unique insights on social relations.

Yet, despite the apparent focus on things, what the ensuing proliferation of "material culture studies" arguably did was to reproduce a long-standing anthropocentric bias privileging social relations without really paying attention to materiality at all (Hicks 2010; Keane 2006; Olsen 2010). Dan Hicks (2010: 69) comments on the "emergence of the strangely abstract, dematerialized quality of many material culture studies, in which things appear to disappear into spectral fields of social relations or meanings, and the complexities of materials and their change over time are not accounted for."

It is no coincidence that this critique of material culture studies comes from an archaeologist. He is, in effect, bemoaning the slippage identified above from materiality to mutuality. This is echoed by Bjørnar Olsen (2010: 34), identifying a similar malaise anticipated already by Orvar Löfgren (1997). Olsen goes so far as to identify it as a symptom of modernity generally, finding such a diagnosis a century earlier in Simmel, regretting our distance from the substance of things (Olsen 2010: 34, also 95). This critique of "immaterial" approaches to material culture finds further expression in Timothy Webmoor and Christopher Witmore (2008). They use as their starting point the edited volume *A Companion to Social Archaeology* (Meskell and Preucel 2004), in which "materiality" is given centrality; yet Lynn Meskell and Robert Preucel's conception of materiality, according to Webmoor and Witmore (1998: 55), follows the very same social constructivism seen in many earlier studies of material culture, such that humans are seen to produce materiality. This amounts to a failure to do justice to and investigate "things," which is where archaeology's strengths lie; and thus the implication is that archaeologists Meskell and Preucel have been unduly influenced by the anthropological merging of materiality with mutuality. Though there may be some truth in this critique, it is also the case that Meskell is one of the few archaeologists to develop case studies for materiality, as in an innovative volume comparing ancient Maya and Egyptian materialities (Meskell and Joyce 2003), and an edited volume, *Archaeologies of Materiality*, where she notes that scholars "have been notably remiss in producing substantive accounts of materiality for archaeological contexts" (Meskell 2005: 1).

The emergence of a more thing-centered materiality in archaeology owes a considerable debt to Actor-Network Theory, and particularly the work of Latour (Olsen 2010; Webmoor and Witmore 2008; Witmore 2007). It seems that Actor-Network Theory may also have played a key role in affecting the thinking of Miller and the move away from use of the term "material culture" to "materiality," as we see in his 2005 edited volume. This point is made by Hicks, who at the same time intimates that a similar influence might have been at play, admittedly earlier, in the important work of Alfred Gell, *Art and Agency* (Gell 1998), though only indirectly via Marilyn Strathern (Hicks 2010: 76). That Actor-Network Theory has been influential for both social constructivist and thing-centered approaches may seem rather odd, and no doubt this demands further exploration. However, I will not treat the influence of Actor-Network Theory in any more detail here as it is covered in Olsen's chapter in this volume on symmetrical archaeology.

Materiality as vitality

It appears that there is a wider move afoot in the humanities to think beyond relationality and consider the active, "brute" materiality of things that is not solely dependent on relations. As historian Frank

Trentmann (2009: 283) begins a recent article: "Things are back. After the turn to discourse and signs in the late twentieth century, there is a new fascination with the material stuff of life." Trentmann then goes on to note that history (especially eighteenth-century studies) has undergone this transformation in rather isolated fashion, and could benefit from greater openness to similar moves in other disciplines. On the one hand, he has in mind sociology and anthropology, particularly their conjoining in Actor-Network Theory by Michel Callon, John Law, and Bruno Latour. This evidently pertains to the relational component of materiality. And on the other hand, he cites in literary studies the "thing theory" of Bill Brown (2001, 2003, 2006), and others writing on the "everyday" (influenced by Merleau-Ponty and Heidegger, and de Certeau and Lefebvre). This is a rather different strand, one that is concerned less with the relational qualities of materiality, and more with the "brute" nature of thingness. One might cite in this connection Peter Schwenger (2006) on the melancholy of things: in line with Brown's thing theory, he is at pains to highlight those properties of materials that escape our efforts to define them. They are elusive.

This literary angle on the recalcitrance of things is compatible with a line taken by W. J. T. Mitchell, who hovers between literary studies and art history (Mitchell 2004, 2005). He asks "What do pictures want?," suggesting an otherness to materials that goes beyond what can be understood relationally. Indeed, it has been claimed that Mitchell and others in art history are participating in what has been dubbed variously an "iconic" or "pictorial" turn (Moxey 2008). These are perspectives in art history that have recently developed in response to the realization that for too long "meaning" has been favored over "presence" (Moxey 2008: 132). This renewed attunement to the material properties of artworks is seen, according to Keith Moxey, in the work of scholars such as Mitchell (see above), James Elkins (2008), Hans Ulrich Gumbrecht (2004), Georges Didi-Huberman (2005), and Hans Belting (2001); he also draws a tantalizing connection to Gell (1998), whose work he sees as close to Mitchell's. Though art historians may not use the term "materiality" all that frequently (but see Elkins 2008), this pictorial turn seems to share very much the same concerns.

These by no means exhaust the renewed attention to materiality. Actually, the above strands on materiality in art history and literary studies have received only very limited attention in archaeology. More archaeologists seem aware of recent work in cultural geography, with Caitlin DeSilvey (2006, 2007) using a kind of archaeological imagination to "excavate" the materiality of a Montana homestead; and

Justin Wilford (2008) exploring the materiality of homes in New Orleans post-Katrina. Both use abandonment to reveal materiality, and in this they closely resemble similar studies coming out of archaeology, such as those by Alfredo González-Ruibal (2008) and Olsen (2010). These authors take examples respectively from decaying military equipment and installations from Ethiopia, and abandoned farms and mining towns in Norway; to these one might add a study of a World War II refugee camp in Sweden (Burström 2009).

What links the above approaches to materiality, whether in history, art history, geography, or archaeology, is a desire to acknowledge the elusiveness of things: what Olsen (2010) has called trying to get at the status of "things *qua* things." It is essentially a matter of acknowledging the power of "material agency" (Knappett and Malafouris 2008), or perhaps what may be more convincingly termed "material vitality" (Bennett 2010). It is difficult to accept that one may validly speak of inorganic vitality, but Jane Bennett makes the case convincingly; and in accepting this position, one can avoid reproducing the humanocentric notion of materials that cast them as inert, stable, and ultimately entirely vulnerable to human action and conception. This perspective on materiality thus differs substantially from the social constructivist approach critiqued above (Webmoor and Witmore 2008). One might also link it to a much broader shift towards "pragmatic" approaches that critique a deeply embedded favoring of the "mental" (Baert 2005; Preucel and Mrozowski 2010; Slingerland 2008).

But this focus on things *qua* things is proving quite difficult. How can we get under their skin? We've already mentioned some of the archaeological studies using abandonment to reveal aspects of materiality, and this is actually a rather curious aspect of quite a lot of the recent attention to materiality in archaeology – it deals with the contemporary past (González-Ruibal 2008; Harrison and Schofield 2010; Olivier 2008; Olsen 2010; Shanks et al. 2004). A strength is its openness to other disciplines, such as cultural geography, which also sees such a focus emerging (e.g. DeSilvey 2006; Edensor 2005; Wilford 2008). These humanistic "poetics" do succeed in showing that, despite the indissolubility of things, and their resistance to human desire, they can reveal themselves when they are not quite themselves. Or, as Wilford (2008: 659) puts it, "to study materiality is to attempt to capture a glimpse of the thing just as it enters the world of knowledge, culture, and concepts." Archaeologists (and others) have not been sufficiently alert to the recalcitrance of things. But it is debatable how distinctively archaeological some of these approaches are, despite "things" supposedly being archaeology's strength (Webmoor and Witmore 2008). One of the few examples to explicitly apply such a perspective in an archaeological setting is Johan Normark's work on the materiality of Maya causeways (Normark 2010). His stance is consistently post-humanocentric, influenced heavily by philosophers Gilles Deleuze and Manuel DeLanda. He certainly does pursue "things *qua* things"; his work indeed draws inspiration from Olsen, while also having affinities with that of Bennett (2010).

Perhaps when materiality is theorized at arm's length, which it often is, we do not notice how different are the conceptions of it; but as soon as a closer engagement with materials is attempted, the difficulties of speaking consistently about "materialities" emerge. This is, in effect, akin to what Elkins (2008) has very pithily described for art history – materiality is relatively easy to theorize, but relatively difficult to speak about in front of individual objects. For Elkins it comes down to a problem of methodology; in art history it is phenomenology that is employed and it falls short. We can't seem to zoom in to "materials" and then zoom out to "materiality." This translation doesn't work currently. Elkins makes a telling point on the slowness of the studio: working with materials – carving, molding, painting – has a slower rhythm than working with texts. So different scales also have different tempos, rendering the transition still more problematic (this is surely part of the benefit and difficulty of experimental archaeology). This resonates, unexpectedly, with Ingold's comment that "to understand materiality, it seems, we need to get as far away from materials as possible" (Ingold 2007: 2). Although Ingold says this ironically, it is not far off the mark: materials and materiality do not occupy the same scale, spatially or temporally, which makes moving back and forth between them extremely hard.

Materiality as ensemble

So this question of scale brings us to our fourth dimension of materiality: plurality. In opening up beyond the close-up scale of materials to something broader, "materiality" hints at ensemble, at plurality. In the *Oxford English Dictionary*, materiality has lots of senses: some of them are "That which constitutes the matter or material of something"; "The quality of being composed of matter; material existence; solidity." But we also find "That which is material; (in *pl.*) material things." One of the examples used to support this definition is as follows: "1997; *Sight & Sound* Jan. 27/3: There are things in

Hitchcock that become emblems.... They are objects, portable usually, domestic and humdrum, clues, the little bit of materiality that attracts the camera." This gives the sense of a multitude of things, and hence the plurality of materiality, necessarily occupying scales beyond the immediately proximate. So "Neolithic" materiality would be the universe of materials in Neolithic communities. For example, Hodder (2011) has recently discussed the materiality of Neolithic Çatalhöyük in terms of "human–thing entanglement." One has to stand back from individual, localized materials to understand materiality. In the same vein, the materiality of the house, as understood by Wilford (2008), does not inhere in one kind of material, but in a coming together of different materials. This finds echo in the work of Ludovic Coupaye and Laurence Douny (2009: 24), who see materiality as "the ensemble of phenomenal and material properties of 'things', ensemble conceived as a form of potential or 'possibility', recognized through its physical and/or conceptual engagement."

An interesting connection here lies in Keane's notion of "bundling" (Keane 2005: 188; 2006: 200). Any quality – Keane gives the example of "red" – is invariably embodied in something in particular: Keane suggests the redness of an apple. This particular object inevitably combines other properties – in the case of the apple it is also spherical, edible, an so on. Thus various qualities are bundled together, "whose particular juxtapositions may be mere happenstance" (Keane 2006: 200). Moreover, just as Coupaye and Douny underline the potential and possibilities of things, so Keane stresses the possible futures of materiality, owing to the contingency of bundling. I believe such an outlook – recognizing the "ensemble" character of things, their bundling, across different scales – is crucial to a full understanding of materiality.

What we require are approaches that that can go beyond such recognition towards detailed empirical study. Many studies of materiality have not managed to make this move, perhaps because, as Elkins notes, the shifting of scales between materials and materiality is so problematic. However, archaeology does possess the necessary methodologies, even if not fully acknowledged as such.

Materiality, behavioral chains, and the *chaîne opératoire*

So even though materiality has been subject to mostly theoretical discussion in archaeology, this cannot be attributed just to an absence of a suitable methodology for empirical analysis. I would argue that there are at least two distinctively archaeological approaches available, though going by a single name: technology. One is firmly US-based, represented particularly in the "behavioral archaeology" of Michael Schiffer (e.g. Hollenback and Schiffer 2010; Skibo and Schiffer 2008). The focus falls on people–artifact interactions, or "behavioral chains," across the whole gamut of activities from production though to use, repair, and discard. Schiffer and colleagues have set out a number of methodological procedures and have tested them in a series of case studies. Though materiality is not a term often used or specifically defined in this literature (see Walker and Schiffer 2006), it is considered to be very close in outlook (Hollenback and Schiffer 2010: 318). A second approach with a particular methodology for studying technology is the *chaîne opératoire*. This is a method for analyzing the steps that unfold in a technological sequence, for example in the making of a pot: clay prospection and selection–paste preparation–forming–finishing–drying–firing. While some uses are descriptive and others more prescriptive (see Coupaye 2009; Knappett 2011), the method is an invaluable means of reconstructing technological choices in a way that can illuminate both their social and their technical components. It has been consistently used in ethnography and ethnoarchaeology, when techniques can be directly observed (e.g. Gosselain 2000; Lemonnier 1992; Mahias 1993), and in archaeology, where material traces of technical actions are used to reconstruct actions (e.g. in the work of Audouze, Pelegrin, Boëda, and Tixier – see references in Schlanger 1994). Arguably, its relevance to materiality has been largely overlooked because it exists within the francophone rather than anglophone tradition (Coupaye and Douny 2009; though see Jones 2004, and below). Moreover, it is an archaeological approach that is tied to anthropology in quite distinctive ways: for example, it differs from the anglophone tradition, the latter focusing on consumption.

Both of the above methodologies for studying technology can provide the zooming in and out that Elkins seeks, shuttling across the different scales of matter and materiality. Each holds its own advantages. In the life history approach of behavioral archaeology, the entire sequence of possible activities is assessed, while the *chaîne opératoire* tends to focus more specifically on production. The latter method holds some advantages over the former, though, as it integrates the moving body, the gesture, the tool, and the material. This dynamic coupling is very much the concern of a wider perspective dubbed "praxeology," developed principally by anthropologist Jean-Pierre Warnier within the setting of the French research group "Matière à Penser" (Warnier 2001, 2006, 2007). His consistent message is that we need to understand what we might here usefully call materiality as a set of sensori-motor-affective actions propped up by material culture. Although it is a very corporeal approach, he argues that the body alone (and in the same breath phenomenology) is a dead end. Praxeology thus provides the *chaîne opératoire* method with greater conceptual depth (see Coupaye 2009; Coupaye and Douny 2009; Naji and Douny 2009).

As mentioned above, the *chaîne opératoire* has been used to good effect in archaeology, revealing aspects of ancient materiality (even if the word "technology" is preferred). One might cite various examples, certainly in the francophone literature (see above), but also more than one might imagine in the anglophone world, too (e.g. Bar-Yosef and van Peer 2009; Chazan 2009; Conneller 2008; Dobres 2000; Edmonds 1990; Jones 2002, 2004; Knappett 2005a; Schlanger 1990). Indeed, Jones (2004) has sought to connect explicitly the materiality literature in archaeological theory with the *chaîne opératoire* approach and the abundant research on materials and technologies in archaeological science (see also Sillar and Tite 2000). We should not forget the impressive body of work uniting archaeological science and technology in behavioral archaeology and related approaches in the US (see Killick 2005). However, the *chaîne opératoire* approach has been more effective at drawing in bodily, sensual, and cognitive dimensions.

As the *chaîne opératoire* does concern choices, it can also be linked to cognitive approaches, as indeed we see in Nathan Schlanger's contribution to the volume *The Ancient Mind* (Renfrew and Zubrow 1994). Some of the contributions in *The Ancient Mind* fit within a Cartesian framework that sets mind apart from action, though the *chaîne opératoire*, and certainly praxeology, can work within a distributed perspective that does not differentiate so clearly between cognition, perception, and action. It is interesting that a more distributed approach did emerge in cognitive archaeology not long after this 1994 volume, with Colin Renfrew's idea of "material engagement" (2001, 2004), since developed more fully by Lambros Malafouris (2004, 2008). Although not using *chaîne opératoire*, Malafouris's approach is consistent with Warnier's praxeology, in that both consider the psychological fluidity of the bodily schema, with Malafouris thinking though ancient objects, such as Mycenaean swords, or gold signet rings, and their likely impact on bodily schemas (Malafouris 2008). A broadly similar approach at the same time saw a more explicit use of work in ecological psychology, particularly Gibson's idea of affordances (Knappett 2004, 2005b). This concept, too, fits well with praxeology, as has recently been noted in French anthropology (e.g. Coupaye and Douny 2009; Naji 2009). A distinctively archaeological approach can use affordances to understand elements of ancient "materiality" in ways that take into account the actual properties of materials and not just that relationship between human and material. When the notion of affordances is counterbalanced against the idea of constraints (see Norman 1998), one has the opportunity to access something of the specific, inorganic vitality of materials and not fall foul of the tendency to humanocentrism.

Although the focus on "technology" in many of these *chaîne opératoire* studies places us in the domain of production rather than consumption, we should note an interesting point made in the review by Myriem Naji and Laurence Douny (2009): they see a need to think about technology as *unmaking* as well as making. They have in mind both intentional acts of destruction and unintentional processes of decay and abandonment, as well as subsequent practices of recycling and repair. This does very usefully extend the scope of the *chaîne opératoire* in such a way that aligns it with those life history approaches of Schiffer and colleagues that follow things further than technological studies tend to do. One might also point to recent work on depositional practices cast in terms of materiality (Mills and Walker 2008).

One could add to this a distinctive angle on materiality that tackles "unmaking" very directly: *fragmentation* (and, more broadly, structured deposition). John Chapman has developed "fragmentation theory" as an archaeological approach to explain what he sees as deliberate patterns of breakage in some archaeological assemblages, focusing especially on the later prehistory of the Balkans (Chapman 2000; Chapman and Gaydarska 2006). In seeking to explain such patterns, he sees fragmentation as a means of creating social relations through "enchainment." Chapman's is indeed one of the very few archaeological case studies of materiality (Jones 2009: 98–9). His ideas have been developed and applied in very interesting ways in other periods too, most notably the Palaeolithic (Gamble 2007). Interestingly enough, Gamble takes the body as a starting point for material metaphor, but crucially gives means for extending beyond it (as does praxeology). Although Chapman's approach is not explicitly "cognitive," Gamble does consider these processes from a cognitive perspective, as seen in the coedited volume *Social Brain, Distributed Mind* (Dunbar et al. 2010, a volume which includes a paper by Chapman [2010]). This brings us back full circle, and allows us to imagine a position whereby ancient materialities can be studied in terms both of making and of unmaking; in terms both of the body and gesture and of the mind; and at both the micro and macro scales. Perhaps we can find ways to zoom in and zoom out between matter and materiality (if we can find ways of moving back and forth between francophone and anglophone traditions too!).

Praxeology, material engagement, and affordances all operate at the micro scale of human interactions. With the focus around individual bodies, their gestures and their micro-interactions with materials, as revealed through *chaîne opératoire* methodology, this is perhaps only natural. Yet, they do also allow us to open up to the wider scales that are essential to a fuller understanding of materiality – towards the scale of the community, the region, and beyond. Indeed, Warnier (2007) uses his praxeological approach to do just this, showing the multiple scales at which containment as a technology of power can operate. By compiling descriptions of *chaînes opératoires* across space and time, one can certainly move out to a broader scale, as Olivier Gosselain shows in his groundbreaking ethnoarchaeological work in West Africa (e.g. 2000), and even more acutely in a recent edited volume that addresses the question of how cultural dynamics work across different spatial scales (Gosselain et al. 2008a). In this the authors identify the interaction between different materialities, particularly between imported Chinese enamel wares and local pottery traditions (Gosselain et al. 2008b).

This is akin to the kind of ethnoarchaeological work, though on a smaller scale, that Bill Sillar has carried out in the Andes. He explains the similar technologies for processing grain and pottery, and even armed combat, and is able to speak of metaphors of crushing and grinding that run across society, but which are ultimately grounded in and generated from bodily gestures (Sillar 1996; note this is consistent with praxeology). One might also cite other such studies from the ancient Andes, such as Lechtman (1984) and Lau (2010); the latter achieves an understanding of materiality as "ensemble" by comparing different material technologies (ceramic, stone, textile) and how they share a similar kind of surface work.

On the subject of surfaces, another way to draw connections between materials to arrive at materiality is to consider color. This is a strategy used effectively by Jones (2004; see also Jones and MacGregor 2002). On the one hand, the physical properties contributing to the color of ancient artifacts have been the subject of much scientific study, as in the analysis of, for example, plaster or glass. On the other hand, color often has symbolic and affective properties that require us to look to the social context of artifact production and use for answers. Jones is actually pursuing a rather different agenda in some of his discussion of color: that of the divide between archaeological science and theory. His argument on this front attracts a forceful response, with the suggestion that a number of US scholars have long been incorporating the scientific and the theoretical, and by extension the material and the social, in their analysis of ancient technologies, even if not explicitly using the term "materiality" (Killick 2005).

Conclusions

One might imagine that archaeologists long ago developed robust methodologies for studying materiality; and this then being the case, that a chapter on "materiality" in a volume such as this would neither be very theoretical nor very current. Yet, curiously, this is far from the truth. Materiality is only now seeing explicit theorization, with a burst of recent interest. Moreover, this situation is not confined to archaeology: other disciplines, such as history, art history, sociology, and anthropology, also appear to be discovering materiality. What materiality actually means to different scholars, though, even within archaeology, is not very clear. It is as if mere mention of materiality is sometimes seen as enough. When, however, efforts are made to actually get up close to things and interrogate materiality through case studies, as in the handful of cases mentioned above, then some of the differences are quite abruptly exposed. Some see materiality as material relations: that is, human relations with the world. Others link it more closely to social relations or "mutuality," such that materiality becomes a relational property emergent in social interactions. Still others see materiality as a kind of vitality possessed by things independently of human action and intention. All three of these features are arguably indispensable for us to understand materiality. We might well add a fourth feature, that of plurality: things connect with other things, forming ensembles. Thus we might see materiality as emergent from dependent (material relations), codependent (social relations), independent (vital), and interdependent (plural) properties.

What next? Further theorization will surely continue. Some of the approaches that foster an "archaeological imagination" are stimulating, helping us to acknowledge the intractability of things. They also have the advantage of dialogue with other disciplines, such as cultural geography. But it seems that some of the more illuminating insights on materiality have arisen from those instances where archaeologists have tried to pursue detailed case studies. By chasing this further, and making our methodologies more explicit, such as the *chaîne opératoire*, I believe archaeologists can make a distinctive contribution to a richer understanding of the diversity of materialities across various physical and cultural contexts. Art historian James Elkins felt methodologically ill equipped to zoom in and out of scale, a necessary trick for getting at materiality. Archaeologists, however, habitually combine both long-term analysis and the microscale of archaeometry and experimental approaches; we shift spatial scales as well as tempos. As archaeologists, we are extraordinarily well placed, therefore, to study not just materials, but also materiality; we simply haven't fully realized it yet.

Acknowledgments

I wish to thank Ian Hodder and Barbara Mills for their very helpful comments on earlier drafts of this chapter.

References

Appadurai, A. (ed.) 1986. *The Social Life of Things: Commodities in Cultural Perspective*. Cambridge: Cambridge University Press.

Baert, P. 2005. *Philosophy of the Social Sciences: Towards Pragmatism*. Cambridge: Polity.

Bar-Yosef, O. and P. Van Peer 2009. The *chaîne opératoire* approach in Middle Palaeolithic technology. *Current Anthropology* 50: 103–31.

Belting, H. 2001. *Bild-Anthropologie: Entwürfe für eine Bildwissenschaft*. Munich: Wilhelm Fink.

Bennett, J. 2010. *Vibrant Matter: A Political Ecology of Things*. Durham, NC: Duke University Press.

Boivin, N. 2008. *Material Cultures, Material Minds: The Impact of Things on Human Thought, Society and Evolution*. Cambridge: Cambridge University Press.

Brown, B. 2001. Thing theory. *Critical Inquiry* 28: 1–22.

Brown, B. (ed.) 2003. *Things*. Chicago: University of Chicago Press.

Brown, B. 2006. *A Sense of Things: The Object Matter of American Literature*. Chicago: University of Chicago Press.

Burström, M. 2009. Selective remembrance: memories of a Second World War refugee camp in Sweden. *Norwegian Archaeological Review* 42: 159–72.

Chapman, J. 2000. *Fragmentation in Archaeology: People, Places and Broken Objects in the Prehistory of South Eastern Europe*. London: Routledge.

Chapman, J. 2010. Fragmenting hominins and the presencing of early Palaeolithic social worlds. In R. Dunbar, C. Gamble, and J. Gowlett (eds), *Social Brain, Distributed Mind*, 417–52. London: British Academy.

Chapman, J. and B. Gaydarska 2006. *Parts and Wholes: Fragmentation in Prehistoric Context*. Oxford: Oxbow Books.

Chazan, M. 2009. Pattern and technology: why the chaîne opératoire matters. In J.J. Shea and D. Lieberman (eds), *Transitions in Prehistory: Essays in Honor of Ofer Bar-Yosef*, 467–74. Oxford: Oxbow Books.

Conneller, C. 2008. Lithic technology and the chaîne opératoire. In J. Pollard (ed.), *Prehistoric Britain*, 160–76. Oxford: Blackwell.

Coupaye, L. 2009. Ways of enchanting: chaînes opératoires and yam cultivation in Nyamikum village, Maprik, Papua New Guinea. *Journal of Material Culture* 14: 433–58.

Coupaye, L. and L. Douny 2009. Dans la trajectoire des choses: comparaison des approches francophones et anglophones contemporaines en anthropologie des techniques. *Techniques et Culture* 52–3: 12–39.

DeMarrais, E., C. Gosden and C. Renfrew 2004. Introduction. In E. DeMarrais, C. Gosden, and C. Renfrew (eds), *Rethinking Materiality: The Engagement of Mind with the Material World*, 1–7. Cambridge: McDonald Institute for Archaeological Research.

DeSilvey, C. 2006. Observed decay: telling stories with mutable things. *Journal of Material Culture* 11: 318–38.

DeSilvey, C. 2007. Salvage memory: constellating material histories on a hardscrabble homestead. *Cultural Geographies* 14: 401–24.

Didi-Huberman, G. 2005. *Confronting Images: Questioning the Ends of a Certain History of Art*. University Park: Pennsylvania State University Press.

Dobres, M.-A. 2000. *Technology and Social Agency: Outlining a Practice Framework for Archaeology*. Oxford: Blackwell.

Dunbar, R., C. Gamble, and J. Gowlett (eds) 2010. *Social Brain, Distributed Mind*. London: British Academy.

Edensor, T. 2005. Waste matter – the debris of industrial ruins and the disordering of the material world. *Journal of Material Culture* 10: 311–32.

Edmonds, M. 1990. Description, understanding and the chaîne opératoire. *Archaeological Review from Cambridge* 9: 55–70.

Elkins, J. 2008. On some limits of materiality in art history. *31: Das Magazin des Instituts für Theorie* [Zurich] 12: 25–30.

Gamble, C. 2007. *Origins and Revolutions: Human Identity in Earliest Prehistory*. Cambridge: Cambridge University Press.

Gell, A. 1998. *Art and Agency: Towards a New Anthropological Theory*. Oxford: Clarendon Press.

González-Ruibal, A. 2008. Time to destroy: an archaeology of supermodernity. *Current Anthropology* 49: 247–79.

Gosden, C. 1994. *Social Being and Time*. Oxford: Blackwell.

Gosselain, O. 2000. Materializing identities: an African perspective. *Journal of Archaeological Method and Theory* 7: 187–217.

Gosselain, O., R. Zeebroek, and J.-M. Decroly (eds) 2008a. *Des choses, des gestes, des mots: repenser les dynamiques culturelles*. Special edition of *Techniques et Culture* 51.

Gosselain, O., R. Zeebroek, and J.-M. Decroly 2008b. Les tribulations d'une casserole chinoise au Niger. *Techniques et Culture* 51: 18–49.

Graves-Brown, P. (ed.) 2000. *Matter, Materiality and Modern Culture*. London: Routledge.

Gumbrecht, H. U. 2004. *Production of Presence: What Meaning Cannot Convey*. Stanford, CA: Stanford University Press.

Harrison, R. and J. Schofield 2010. *After Modernity: Archaeological Approaches to the Contemporary Past*. Oxford: Oxford University Press.

Hicks, D. 2010. The material-cultural turn: event and effect. In D. Hicks and M. Beaudry (eds), *The Oxford Handbook of Material Culture Studies*, 25–98. Oxford: Oxford University Press.

Hodder, I. 2011. Human–thing entanglement: towards an integrated archaeological perspective. *Journal of the Royal Anthropological Institute* (N.S.) 17: 154–77.

Hollenback, K. and M. B. Schiffer 2010. Technology and material life. In D. Hicks and M. Beaudry (eds), *The Oxford Handbook of Material Culture Studies*, 313–32. Oxford: Oxford University Press.

Ingold, T. 2007. Materials against materiality. *Archaeological Dialogues* 14: 1–16.

Jones, A. 2002. *Archaeological Theory and Scientific Practice*. Cambridge: Cambridge University Press.

Jones, A. 2004. Archaeometry and materiality: materials-based analysis in theory and practice. *Archaeometry* 46: 327–38.

Jones, A. 2009. Into the future. In B. Cunliffe, C. Gosden, and R. A. Joyce (eds), *The Oxford Handbook of Archaeology*, 89–114. Oxford: Oxford University Press.

Jones, A. and G. MacGregor (eds) 2002. *Colouring the Past: The Significance of Colour in Archaeological Research*. Oxford: Berg.

Keane, W. 2005. Signs are not the garb of meaning: on the social analysis of material things. In D. Miller (ed.), *Materiality*, 182–205. Durham, NC: Duke University Press.

Keane, W. 2006. Subjects and objects. In C. Tilley, W. Keane, S. Küchler, M. Rowlands, and P. Spyer (eds), *Handbook of Material Culture*, 197–202. London: Sage.

Killick, D. 2005. Comments IV: is there really a chasm between archaeological theory and archaeological science? *Archaeometry* 47: 185–9.

Knappett, C. 2004. The affordances of things: a post-Gibsonian perspective on the relationality of mind and matter. In E. DeMarrais, C. Gosden, and C. Renfrew (eds), *Rethinking Materiality: The Engagement of Mind with the Material World*, 43–51. Cambridge: McDonald Institute for Archaeological Research.

Knappett, C. 2005a. Pottery. In H. D. G. Maschner and C. Chippindale (eds), *Handbook of Archaeological Methods*, 673–714. Lanham, MD: AltaMira Press.

Knappett, C. 2005b. *Thinking through Material Culture: An Interdisciplinary Perspective*. Philadelphia: University of Pennsylvania Press.

Knappett, C. 2011. Networks of objects, meshworks of things. In T. Ingold (ed.), *Redrawing Anthropology: Materials, Movements, Lines*. London: Ashgate.

Knappett, C. and L. Malafouris (eds) 2008. *Material Agency: Towards a Non-Anthropocentric Approach*. New York: Springer.

Lau, G. F. 2010. The work of surfaces: object worlds and techniques of enhancement in the ancient Andes. *Journal of Material Culture* 15: 259–86.

Lechtman, H. N. 1984. Andean value systems and the development of prehistoric metallurgy. *Technology and Culture* 25: 1–36.

Lemonnier, P. 1992. *Elements for an Anthropology of Technology*. Ann Arbor: University of Michigan Press.

Löfgren, O. 1997. Scenes from a troubled marriage: Swedish ethnology and material culture studies. *Journal of Material Culture* 2: 95–113.

Mahias, M.-C. 1993. Pottery techniques in India: technical variants and social choice. In P. Lemonnier (ed.), *Technological Choices: Transformation in Material Cultures since the Neolithic*, 157–80. London: Routledge.

Malafouris, L. 2004. The cognitive basis of material engagement: where brain, body and culture conflate. In E. DeMarrais, C. Gosden, and C. Renfrew (eds), *Rethinking Materiality: The Engagement of Mind with the Material World*, 53–62. Cambridge: McDonald Institute for Archaeological Research.

Malafouris, L. 2008. Between brains, bodies and things: tectonoetic awareness and the extended self. *Philosophical Transactions of the Royal Society B* 363: 1993–2002.

Meskell, L. 2005. Introduction: object orientations. In L. Meskell (ed.), *Archaeologies of Materiality*, 1–17. Oxford: Blackwell.

Meskell, L. and R. A. Joyce 2003. *Embodied Lives: Figuring Ancient Maya and Egyptian Experience*. London: Routledge.

Meskell, L. and R. Preucel (eds) 2004. *A Companion to Social Archaeology*. Oxford: Blackwell.

Miller, D. 2005. Materiality: an introduction. In D. Miller (ed.), *Materiality*, 1–50. Durham, NC: Duke University Press.

Miller, D. 2007. Stone age or plastic age? *Archaeological Dialogues* 14: 23–7.

Mills, B.J. and W.H. Walker 2008. Introduction: memory, materiality, and depositional practice. In B.J. Mills and W.H. Walker (eds), *Memory Work: Archaeologies of Material Practices*, 3–23. Santa Fe, NM: SAR Press.

Mitchell, W.J.T. 2004. Romanticism and the life of things: fossils, totems, and images. In B. Brown (ed.), *Things*, 227–44. Chicago: University of Chicago Press.

Mitchell, W.J.T. 2005. *What Do Pictures Want? The Lives and Loves of Images*. Chicago: University of Chicago Press.

Moxey, K. 2008. Visual studies and the iconic turn. *Journal of Visual Culture* 7: 131–46.

Naji, M. 2009. Le fil de la pensée tisserande: "affordances" de la matière et des corps dans le tissage. *Techniques et Culture* 52–53: 68–89.

Naji, M. and L. Douny 2009. Editorial. *Journal of Material Culture* 14: 411–32.

Norman, D. 1998. *The Design of Everyday Things*. Cambridge, MA: MIT Press.

Normark, J. 2010. Involutions of materiality: operationalizing a neo-materialist perspective through the causeways at Ichmul and Yo'okop. *Journal of Archaeological Method and Theory* 17: 132–73.

Olivier, L. 2008. *Le sombre abîme du temps: mémoire et archéologie*. Paris: Seuil.

Olsen, B. 2010. *In Defense of Things: Archaeology and the Ontology of Objects*. Lanham, MD: AltaMira Press.

Preucel, R. and S. Mrozowski (eds) 2010. *Contemporary Archaeology in Theory: The New Pragmatism*, 2nd edition. Oxford: Wiley-Blackwell.

Renfrew, C. 2001. Symbol before concept: material engagement and the early development of society. In I. Hodder (ed.), *Archaeological Theory Today*, 1st edition, 122–40. Cambridge: Polity.

Renfrew, C. 2004. Towards a theory of material engagement. In E. DeMarrais, C. Gosden, and C. Renfrew (eds), *Rethinking Materiality: The Engagement of Mind with the Material World*, 23–31. Cambridge: McDonald Institute for Archaeological Research.

Renfrew, C. and E. Zubrow 1994. *The Ancient Mind: Elements of Cognitive Archaeology*. Cambridge: Cambridge University Press.

Scarre, C. 2004. Displaying the stones: the materiality of "megalithic" monuments. In E. DeMarrais, C. Gosden, and C. Renfrew (eds), *Rethinking Materiality: The Engagement of Mind with the Material World*, 141–52. Cambridge: McDonald Institute for Archaeological Research.

Schlanger, N. 1990. Techniques as human action – two perspectives. *Archaeological Review from Cambridge* 9: 18–26.

Schlanger, N. 1994. Mindful technology: unleashing the chaîne opératoire for an archaeology of mind. In C. Renfrew and E. Zubrow (eds), *The*

Ancient Mind: Elements of Cognitive Archaeology, 143–51. Cambridge: Cambridge University Press.

Schwenger, P. 2006. *The Tears of Things: Melancholy and Physical Objects.* Minneapolis: University of Minnesota Press.

Shanks, M., D. Platt, and W. L. Rathje 2004. The perfume of garbage: modernity and the archaeological, *Modernism/modernity* 11: 61–83.

Sillar, B. 1996. The dead and the drying: techniques for transforming people and things in the Andes. *Journal of Material Culture* 1: 259–89.

Sillar, B. and M. S. Tite 2000. The challenge of technological choices for materials science approaches in archaeology. *Archaeometry* 42: 2–20.

Skibo, J. and M. B. Schiffer 2008. *People and Things: A Behavioral Approach to Material Culture.* New York: Springer.

Slingerland, E. 2008. *What Science Offers the Humanities: Integrating Body and Culture.* Cambridge: Cambridge University Press.

Taylor, T. 2009. Materiality. In R. A. Bentley, H. D. G. Maschner, and C. Chippindale (eds), *Handbook of Archaeological Theories*, 297–320. Lanham, MD: AltaMira Press.

Tilley, C. 2007. Materiality in materials. *Archaeological Dialogues* 14: 16–20.

Tilley, C., W. Keane, S. Küchler, M. Rowlands, and P. Spyer (eds) 2006. *Handbook of Material Culture.* London: Sage.

Trentmann, F. 2009. Materiality in the future of history: things, practices, and politics. *Journal of British Studies* 48: 283–307.

Walker, W. H. and M. B. Schiffer 2006. The materiality of social power: the artifact-acquisition perspective. *Journal of Archaeological Method and Theory* 13(2): 67–88.

Warnier, J.-P. 2001. A praxeological approach to subjectivation in a material world. *Journal of Material Culture* 6: 5–24.

Warnier, J.-P. 2006. Inside and outside: surfaces and containers. In C. Tilley, W. Keane, S. Küchler, M. Rowlands, and P. Spyer (eds), *Handbook of Material Culture*, 186–95. London: Sage.

Warnier, J.-P. 2007. *The Pot-King: The Body, Material Culture and Technologies of Power.* Leiden: Brill.

Webmoor, T. and C. Witmore 2008. Things are us! A commentary on human/thing relations under the banner of a "social" archaeology. *Norwegian Archaeological Review* 41: 53–70.

Wilford, J. 2008. Out of rubble: natural disaster and the materiality of the house. *Environment and Planning D: Society and Space* 26: 647–62.

Witmore, C. 2007. Symmetrical archaeology: excerpts of a manifesto. *World Archaeology* 39: 546–62.

10

SYMMETRICAL ARCHAEOLOGY

Bjørnar Olsen

Throughout the twentieth century, anthropologists – and archaeologists – asserted with increasing conviction that the world is "culturally constituted," that the meanings of things are culturally relative, and that variations in material culture itself stem from things being imbued with this cultural difference. Grounding such claims was a widely shared conception of culture as somehow existing "prior" to or detached from matter, that cultures and peoples "already different" approach the material world in unique ways, causing the variety of material manifestations we encounter. Another expression of this ontology, equally commonly witnessed in the humanities and social sciences, is the idea of humans (subjects, individuals, actors) as at the outset pure, non-composite entities; in their original constituency they come unmixed and unequipped. In "agency theory," methodological individualism, as well as various "objectivist" social theories, the agent who constitutes such an essential component of social life is rarely supplied with more than intentions, goals, values, and a rather unspecified capacity to "act." The ever-present dichotomies between actor and structure, individual and society, leave no room for composite beings *already* mixed and entangled. It follows naturally from this doctrine that the core activity of archaeological interpretation, the "getting at people" (Gamble 2001: 73), persistently has been to reach the Indian *behind* the artifact. As observed by John Barrett (2000: 61), "[A]rchaeology seeks the individual whose actions have resulted in a material trace."

What has been called "symmetrical archaeology" grew out of increasing dissatisfaction with this dominant metaphysics. And if this approach should be stripped down to one programmatic proposition it must be that humans have always been cyborgs and that the human condition is characterized by its inextricable enmeshment with things and other non-human entities (Olsen 2003; Witmore 2007). In other words, and countering dominant tropes of embodiment and objectification, humans are not naked hominids that *enter into* relationships with things and non-humans; they rather emerge *from* such mixtures. To search for the human behind the artifact may actually be seen as a search for a pre-human condition (Serres with Latour 1995: 166). Moreover and thus allowing for a second symmetrical proposition, these non-human entities which we are immersed amidst are not passive or meaningless entities sitting in silence waiting to be embodied with socially constituted meanings. Landscapes and things possess their own unique qualities and competences which they bring to our cohabitation with them (Olsen 2010). Throughout the past the properties of soil and water, bone and stone, bronze and iron were swapped with those of humans. Thus, the claim of a symmetrical archaeology becomes very different from that of Marx (and Childe): man did not make himself!

In this chapter I shall expose in more detail some key theoretical concerns of a symmetrical archaeology. This is not an attempt to synthesize the research that has been done, which admittedly still is quite modest, but rather to explore some ontological and ethical issues and implications of such an archaeology. I shall do this by focusing on how our conception of three matters of concern – things, the past and ethics – may look different from the perspective of a symmetrical archaeology. In the final section I shall also briefly explore some interpretive consequences of this approach in relation to the study of rock art. First, however, I shall make an attempt at tracing the conceptual ancestry of this archaeology.

The genealogy of a concept

Academic teaching, debates, and discourses inevitably involve the formation, use, and criticism of concepts. Concepts conveniently structure and domesticate a world otherwise too heterogeneous and slippery by helping it look ordered, comprehensible, and approachable. Concepts, however, also act as strategic and rhetorical devices in scientific and public discourses; they confront and challenge previous concepts, emblematically proclaiming identities, differences, commitments, and new attitudes. Archaeology, of course, represents no exception to this conceptual combating. Looking back over the last fifty years, we have seen the emergence of a rich vocabulary of adjectival prefixes supposed to grasp and announce an increasing disciplinary diversity, ranging from the "new", "processual," and "analytical" to the "contextual", "feminist," and "social."

Although far from sharing the fame and influence of the mentioned approaches, "symmetrical archaeology" can be seen as a late addition to this inventory. It actually started quite innocently, even perhaps accidentally, as a proposition or suggestion that conveniently mobilized the familiar rhetoric of oppositional semantics (Olsen 2003: 88). However, it soon became "connected," started to circulate, and assembled allies (and critics) (e.g. González-Ruibal 2007; Johnson 2010; Kenderdine 2008; Olsen 2006, 2007, 2010; Perry 2009; Shanks 2007; Webmoor 2007; Witmore 2004, 2006, 2007), and thus acquired a certain strength, mass, and visibility, as exemplified also by conference sessions, websites, and by being included in this volume. The reason for this receptiveness, I guess, was that the concept and its early propositions apparently appealed to, and even named, a growing concern among a number of archaeologists with the fate of things in an interpretive environment increasingly dominated by anti-materialist theories. In other words, there was a concern with how things rarely were allowed to perform in their primary mode of being – that is, as things – but always were disguised as symbol, text, language, or whatever the prevailing intellectual fashion required (cf. Brown 2003: 82).

To a greater or lesser degree, this worry with the fate of things was a concern shared in what has become known as science (and technology) studies. Here various "principles of symmetry" had been proposed since the 1970s, starting with David Bloor's "strong program," which developed a "symmetrical" (and impartial) approach to the study of scientific knowledge (Bloor 1976). In very simple terms, symmetry here implied that we should apply the same principles of explanation when accounting for both truths and errors; neither should we discriminate among social, political, technical, and logical arguments when explaining scientific triumphs and failures. Far more relevant and directly decisive for its archaeological manifestation were the principles of symmetry proposed by Bruno Latour in his manifesto *We Have Never Been Modern* (1993). In its original French edition this work even carried the subtitle "essays in symmetrical anthropology" (Latour 1991), which for some reason never found its way to the English edition.

In this work Latour argued that modernity institutionalized a "Great Divide," two completely distinct ontological zones that became constitutive of its social and philosophical conducts. By this split, the power, interests, and politics of humans come to be placed at one pole, while knowledge about objects and the non-human was placed at the other. From this moment on, humans and non-humans were delegated to different ontological and disciplinary zones: on the one hand, those concerned with the humans-among-themselves, and, on the other, those studying the inanimate object world. This divide simultaneously produced a second divide by separating "us" (the moderns), who mastered the skill of purifying and splitting, from "them" (the others, the pre-moderns), who lacked this capacity and mixed everything together in appalling stews. Latour's cardinal point is of course that this split image of our modern existence is a grave misrepresentation. The modern condition is more than anything a meshwork of hybrid relations and translations between humans and non-humans; actually the mess has never been greater! Thus – and this is the very paradox of this trope – we have never been modern. In other words, acknowledging the "symmetry" implied by all societies being mixtures of natures–cultures, humans and non-humans, also discloses another principle of symmetry: that there is no a priori ontological distinction between the constitution of our worlds and those of the "others" (Latour 1993: 103–6).

At the outset, the use of the term "symmetrical archaeology" was clearly an allusion to Latour's "symmetrical anthropology" (Olsen 2003). It emerged from a growing concern with how things have ended up as somehow epiphenomenal or residual to the "social" and "cultural," and also with the way archaeology and material culture studies increasingly had moved away from the material qualities of things and subsumed themselves to hegemonic social–constructivist theories. It never claimed any symmetry between humans and non-humans (cf. Latour 2005: 76), or, even more absurd, that they are equal. It started out as a modest plea for paying attention to how societies consist of far more entities than those usually given precedence, not for an undifferentiated world (Witmore 2007: 547). The entities of the world are, of course, different; in fact they exhibit – between and among themselves – extremely varied forms of beings. What was claimed was that this difference should not be conceptualized in compliance with the ruling ontological regime of dualities and negativities; it is a non-oppositional or relative difference that facilitates collaboration, delegation, and exchange. In my own conception of the term, symmetrical archaeology was also an urge for realism in archaeology and material culture studies: in other words that the world, reality, is something far more independent and complex than a correlate of human cognition (Olsen 2003, 2010; cf. Bryant et al. 2011; Harman 2011).

Things and difference

The new attitude signaled by a symmetrical archaeology was founded on the premise that *things*, all those enormously varied physical entities we by effective historical conventions refer to as "material culture," are beings in the world alongside other beings such as humans, plants, and animals. All these beings are kindred, sharing certain material properties, "flesh," and membership in a dwelt-in world (cf. Merleau-Ponty 1968). They also share the capacity for making a *difference* to the world and to other beings and thus are "capable of an effect, of inflicting some kind of blow on reality" (Harman 2002: 21). However, and this is the first crucial theoretical issue to be scrutinized, what does things' difference – and thus ability to make a difference – consist of? In what way are things different from ideas and language, from text and speech?

A dominant ontological trope in modern philosophy and social theory, and especially accentuated in structuralism and poststructuralism, is that the importance and significance of entities are the products of their differences rather than some inherent qualities of the entities themselves. A central feature also of Actor-Network Theory (ANT) is likewise "that of the relationality of entities, the notion that they are produced in relations" (Law 1999: 4). ANT is even claimed to be a "semiotics of materiality" characterized by applying this "ruthlessly to all materials – not simply to those that are linguistic" (Law 1999: 4).

To be sure, things clearly attain their relative importance through their position within systems of relations and entanglements. A petrol station is utterly marginalized without roads, cars, pipelines, oil wells, petroleum plants, oil fields, and so on (Hodder 2011). The question to be asked, however, is whether things' identity and significance are appropriately grasped through such a relationalist stance. Or may something rather crucial about things' being actually be lost if the principles of semiotics (and relational theories at large) are "ruthlessly" applied to them? While a word can be replaced by any other word as long as it is consistent and different from the rest, things have intrinsic qualities that seriously restrict their exchangeability. A kayak cannot be replaced by an ax, or a burin with a hammer stone, simply because they have competences or affordances that cannot be replaced as if they were just any other "empty" signifiers. Moreover, contrary to the linguistic sign, the presence of these entities is experienced directly, through themselves; they come to us – also – in an unmediated way (Gibson 1986). In other words, despite being enrolled to serve in a network and achieve a large part of their meaning from it, a symmetrical approach asserts that "the elements of the world do retain individual integrity" (Harman 2002: 294). They are important because each of them makes a difference, not in a negative manner for the sake of the difference itself, as in Saussurian semiotics (and poststructuralism), but because of the *positive* difference they make owing to their irreplaceable uniqueness. As acknowledged by Bruno Latour (2005: 153), an actor "is exactly what is *not* substitutable."

One clarification: a symmetrical archaeology does not discard relational (or contextual) theory; quite the contrary, the insights that have emerged from such varied sources as structuralism, hermeneutics, Heideggerian phenomenology, and poststructuralism are all very valuable indeed. However, it calls attention to how the univocal and ontologized stressing of the relational has made us lose sight of the individual and irreducible qualities of things, their intrinsic power, and the way they actually *therefore* work as mediators in collective action. Things are capable of making an effect, acting on other entities, not only because they are related but also because of their essential properties. To avoid the trap of reducing things either to relation or intrinsic qualities is an important feature of a symmetrical approach.

Another and closely related point concerns things' dependency on people. In metaphysical terms, Immanuel Kant's critical philosophy ontologized this dependency by making our experience of things an a priori product of human thought. The thing-in-itself, Kant asserted, cannot be encountered face-to-face, so to speak; we can only experience it in the way it is formed by ourselves – that is, by our own thinking or reason. As explored in more detail elsewhere, Kant's philosophy, as well as an even more radical version of idealism (which grants no autonomy to the object whatsoever), has had a profound impact on theories and approaches to material culture and landscapes (Olsen 2007, 2010). According to some of these approaches, we hardly run any risk of encountering a landscape *an sich*, only landscapes constructed and made meaningful through human cognition. It follows logically that landscapes and things are of interest to us (or even exist) only insofar as they involve people.

This position is targeted by a symmetrical and realist position. By doing so we are not only interested in exposing how the "affordances" and qualities of things and non-humans affect people. We are also concerned with how they exist, act, and inflict on each other outside the human realm, and how this interaction eventually also affects human life. While there is no possibility of thinking humans outside the realms of things and natures, the opposite option is, of course, viable. However, as noted by Graham Harman (2010: 146–7),

> The real problem with subject and object is not the *gap* between them …the real problem is that human and world are taken as the two fundamental ingredients that must be found in any situation. As a result, the relation between humans and apples is assumed to be philosophically more significant than the relations between apples and trees, apples and sunlight, or apples and wind. These inanimate rapports are generally tossed aside to the natural sciences….

Archaeology is actually a field allowing for at least a partial mediation of these inanimate relations. At least since the work of the first Danish "kitchen midden committee" in the mid-nineteenth century (Klindt-Jensen 1975), archaeologists excavating and surveying have had to take into account that other agencies are involved in forming the archaeological record. Environmental and behavioral archaeology (Dincauze 2000; Schiffer 1976) has paid a lot of attention to non-human agents and the way they interact with each other. A symmetrical archaeology acknowledges this important disciplinary legacy, despite the accusations of empiricism, positivism, and even fetishism it has been subjected to (cf. Miller 1987: 110–11). Unfortunately, the latter attitude as expressed by various postprocessual archaeologies also marked a turn away from a concern with the formative powers of non-human entities in hegemonic theoretical discourses. While the advocacy of phenomenology may be seen as reintroducing a theoretical concern with landscape and the natural world (cf. Tilley 1994, 2004), the outcome was largely a reinforced conception of these entities as primarily a correlate of human experience and cognition.

In order to realize the potential of a phenomenological approach, we need to integrate how landscapes are far more than products of human experience and engagement. In other words, we need to acknowledge that the qualities and dynamics of the landscape we experience also are the products of interaction and exchange between brigades of non-human entities, such as those involved in weather and seasonal changes (cf. Ingold 2005, 2007a). A snow- and ice-covered northern landscape during winter darkness, when temperatures easily drop below minus $30°C$, is profoundly different from the geographically very same landscape during summer when the sun never sets. Owing to the interactive toil of numerous non-human actors, the entire reality of this landscape is radically transformed: its appearance, substance, sounds, smell, as well as its affordances and risks. The world is, of course, also affected by more unpredictable agents such as landslides, avalanches, floods, draught, volcano eruptions, and storms, which, despite the increasing current human impact (which actually is a human–thing impact) in what is proposed as the Anthropocene (Solli 2011), are agents acting both outside human control and in their own specific ways. In other words, for good or for bad, things and natures act on each other as well as on humans, and this needs to be taken into consideration despite the fact that these acts take place outside the realm of human intentionality. As argued by Latour (2005: 76), "[T]o be symmetric ...simply means *not* to impose a priori some spurious *asymmetry* among human intentional action and a material world of causal relations." To act is neither a human privilege, nor that of things and non-humans.

The gathering past

Modernity is often said to be characterized by its detachment from the past. Contrary to previous and "traditional" societies, where the past is supposed to have lived on in what Pierre Nora (1984) has termed "real environments of memory," the accelerated history of the modern is claimed to have left the past behind. Historicism and historical narratives likewise recall and sequence a past gone. As the narratives proceed and progress, the past is inevitably left behind. Stone ages are replaced by metal ages, medieval by modern, feudalism by capitalism, industrialization by post-industrialization. This conception of the closure and finitude of the past is, of course, related to the persistent conception of time and history as things that pass as irreversible series of discrete moments, a line of instants (cf. Lucas 2005; Olivier 2001, 2008). Less frequently talked about is that it also grounded the modern historical inquiry whereby the past became something to be recovered precisely because it is lost. The past was made *past* – the very condition for recalling and remembering it. This removal of the past, which Friedrich Nietzsche once denounced as the "illness of historicism," was made possible by a certain mode of forgetting (cf. Heidegger 1962: 388–9), a cleansing that made us blind to the past that lives on and constantly folds into, and thus forms, the present. As such it provides yet another example of the modern discrepancy between self-representation and practice.

Maybe more than any other discipline, archaeology has the potential to cure the illness of historicism. And we should start in the simplest way possible by showing how things, the material ingredients and residues of all these claimed replacements, object to the finitude and pace of history. Although aging and transforming, they stubbornly linger on. Megaliths, rock art, Roman roads and walls, medieval farms and townscapes, the myriad of used and discarded materials of the increasingly more recent past, are all gathering around us. Our own scholarly encounter with the past as archaeologist is no exception. This material past does not manifest itself as linear texts or historical sequences. As Colin Renfrew (1989: 36) rightly argued, the archaeological site is truly mixed, "consisting of a palimpsest of structures and rubbish pits, constructed and deposited at different periods." What the excavating archaeologist encounters is always a set of hybridized conditions, such as overlapping and compressed layers, superimposed structures, artifacts and debris mixed together – in short, sites that object to modernity and historicism's wished-for ideal of completeness, order, and purified time. Unfortunately, rather than actively using this material record to challenge historicism, the opted-for solutions have nearly always been to purify this entangled mess, and to reassemble the entities to conform to the expectation of linear time and narrative history. Time is not allowed to be "flattened," mixed, or hybridized, but has to be cleansed and sequenced – in short, "unlocked." Through ever more fine-grained dating methods and advanced stratigraphical and typological sequencing, prehistoric settlements and sites are cut into increasingly thinner slices of time, cleansing them from the historical conditions that grounded these presents.

The claimed rationale for this chronological (and stratigraphical) purification is that it constitutes a necessary reversal of the destructive transformational process that the archaeological record has undergone. Thus, what we have left is the distorted impression of "compressed" time; that beyond and prior to the entangled mess we excavate, there is a historical order to be restored, a pure temporal specificity. However convincing this may sound, the symmetrical archaeologist would always claim that the argument should be tested by exploring how it plays out in its own time. How would such temporal slicing work when applied to sites such as London, Rome, or Tromsø? To which age does Rome belong? How do we identify the contemporary London, the present? By excluding all entities that are more than ten, fifty, or one hundred years old? What would be left of Tromsø, in fact any site, if we applied such a rigorous chronological approach? In any case, what we would have lost is that which makes these sites what they are: the outcome of a gathering past constantly conditioning the conduct of the present.

In this sense, the palimpsestal archaeological record is providing a far more realistic and accurate image of the past than any historical narrative. Laurent Olivier (2008) has described historicism, with its unilineal conception of time, as incompatible and even antagonistic to the archaeological project. Archaeology is in essence not a form of history but more in line with memory, and thus has both the urge and potential to overcome historicism with another comprehension of time that is more true to the material we work on. The realization of this potential requires that things themselves must be emancipated from their synchronous imprisonment, the monotemporal imperative based on the seductive idea that what is rendered contemporary by the calendar necessarily belongs to the same time (Latour 1993: 73). In their own being, things are "polychronic, multi-temporal, and [reveal] a time that is gathered together, with multiple pleats" (Serres with Latour 1995: 60). Not only does this fit well with their conventional and much alluded to etymology (Old Norse, Old English *þing*/ Old High German *Thing*), meaning "gathering" or "assembly"; a less widely known and possibly older etymological root (*tenku*) discloses an even more suggestive temporal dimension: "duration," or, literally, "extended" or "stretched time" (Bjorvand and Lindeman 2000: 939ff.; Falk and Torp 1994: 903).

The past superimposes itself on the present as things, bodies, habits, and thoughts. Thus, history is not a projected stream leaving the past behind, but bends and twists in a disorderly manner, interrupting the expectations of the "have been" and the becoming. Contrary to the notion that modernity implied a radical break with the past, constituting a void that can only be filled by our willful recollections, the past proliferates more than ever in the present. In its "raw" material mode, it presses against the present, "gnaws into the future and...swells as it advances" (Bergson 1998: 4). Thus if there is a distinction between the historical "rootedness" of previous pasts and the present, it is one of degree or scale rather than of kind: in other words, we receive an increasingly greater share of the past.

An ethics extended to things

My third matter of concern is ethics. Throughout this chapter I have made the case that we are more than ever mixed with things, with our material pasts, and that these push back. As equally often repeated, the reason why – and how – they push back cannot be reduced to this entanglement itself. Things are not merely "enslaved in some wider system of differential meaning" (Harman 2002: 280), but possess their own capacities, inhabit their own compartments: in short, they have at least a partial autonomy. This conception of things both as something we are immersed amidst and as also retaining individuality and integrity is not just an issue of ontological or meta-physical concern. It also has several important and wide-ranging ethical implications that extend far beyond our disciplinary boundar-ies. However, these do not include the expected accusation of reifica-tion or *Versachlichung*: in other words, that ontologically putting humans on the same footing as non-humans inevitably fulfills the modernist and humanist horror scenario of making people into things. To the contrary, the radical ethical implication of a symmetri-cal approach is to extend humanism's attentiveness and care for people to also embrace things and non-humans. Also taking into consideration the current debate on environmental issues and the accelerated exhaustion of what the planet has to offer, such an extended ethics does not seem untimely.

Ethical issues in archaeology have frequently been raised in rela-tion to what suggestively is known as "cultural" heritage. Loss of heritage is seen as a loss of identity and self, and provides a major rationale for its protection (Brattli 2009; Rowlands 2002). Thus the major accepted imperative today for protecting and preserving things and monuments is that they are of concern to people, for their iden-tity and well-being, and/or by serving as a scientific, socio-political or economic resource (see Solli 2011 for a critical discussion). Reading through heritage conventions, rationales for stewardship of heritage, and the increasingly more abundant literature in heritage studies, it is hard to find any statement expressing any explicit concern with things in their own being (*qua* things). At best there are notions that allude to their aesthetic or historical value, which again are basically human benefits. Though a concern with things is apparent in such works as William Lipe's on conservation ethics (1974), it is nonethe-less primarily their value as an archaeological (and scarce) resource for information extraction that matters.

Without a current or prospective human concern, the ruined church, the megalith, the submerged seventeenth-century vessel, or the microblade core are considered void of value. Their significance is almost entirely rendered dependent on the significance they have for humans – local, indigenous, tourists, children, future generations, historians, archaeologists – or, in more abstract terms, for science and knowledge. Without such human attachment and utility, sites such as Stonehenge, Pyramiden, Machu Picchu, and Pompeii are hardly more than bundles of inanimate things, empty shells devoid of any need for care or ethical concern. As Laurajane Smith (2006: 3) asserts, "While places, sites, objects, and localities may exist as identifiable places of heritage... these places are not *inherently* valuable, nor do they carry a freight of innate meaning. Stonehenge, for instance, is basically a collection of rocks in a field." What makes these things and places valuable and meaningful, and thus turns them into heritage, "are the present-day cultural processes and activities that are undertaken at and around them, and of which they become a part. It is these processes that identify them as physically symbolic of particular cultural and social events, and thus give them value and meaning" (Smith 2006: 3).

This way of draining things themselves of any significance in their construction as heritage is indeed very similar to the dominant conception of landscapes and things in archaeology, anthropology, and material culture studies, as basically inert and meaningless entities (Olsen 2003, 2010). While it is indisputable that many people are concerned with what we term heritage, and that many do feel a strong attachment to certain sites and monuments, it is less evident that this attachment is just an asymmetrical product of emotive narratives and cultural habits: in other words, of a significance being imbued through human practices. It may as well be the case that "significant" sites possess conspicuous and unique qualities themselves which make them stand out as significant. Things, monuments, and natural features attract attention; they create pleasures and fears, attract and repel us. They are meaningful also in their physiognomic difference and individuality. Stonehenge is after all different from other collections of rocks in the field, and it is this inherent and exposed difference that has made it unique as heritage.

A symmetrical archaeology is grounded in the acknowledgment that things make a difference, and that their ability to affect and act on us cannot be reduced to our inescapable enmeshment with them but also is grounded in their own specific thingly qualities and relations with other things. One radical implication of this proposal is to allow for an ethics that encompasses things in their own being; that things are valuable in and of themselves. According to the dominant conception of cultural heritage, however, the things of the past are primarily of value if they are somehow put in use. Things are little but things-for-us, reduced to what Heidegger termed *Bestand*, by which only their manipulative being as "standing reserve" for us remains (Heidegger 1993; Introna 2009; cf. Olsen 2010: 82). Also in our research as analytical, interpretive, and theoretical archaeologists, things primarily serve as *means* to reach something else that is presumably more important: cultures and societies, the lives of past peoples, the Indian *behind* the artifact. To extend ethical concerns and notions of care to also embrace things is not a question about anthropomorphizing them, turning things into humans, but rather to respect their otherness and integrity (Benso 2000). It requires an attitude of knowledge, care, and respect for what things are in their own being. The dominant approach so far in material culture studies has been isomorphic, to subject things to sameness. Processes of embodiment may well have charged things with sociality and personality, but simultaneously silenced their own utterances. And if they speak, it is most likely our own voices that are heard (Andersson 2001: 30–6; Benjamin 2003: 255–6).

However, in all this we should not forget that archaeology also has another face, though one that increasingly has been shadowed and stigmatized by the humanist imperative to be "concerned with people rather than things" (Leach 1973: 768). This face of archaeology, as practiced by archaeologists, museum curators, and technicians alike, is characterized by a devotion to things. The painstaking toil of cleaning, examining, describing, drawing, photographing, conserving, and storing artifacts by technicians and curators reflects a concern with what things are in their own thingness; it expresses an attentive care for their well-being. The texture, form, size, weight, color, scars, and wrinkles of unearthed things are all meticulously accounted for, without necessarily seeing this concernful toil as a means to something else or more important. Much of this care and intimate thing knowledge has been neglected or even ridiculed in more theoretically oriented archaeology and material culture studies, where things are important only insofar as they reveal something about people (see Ingold 2007b). In this sense, the thing archaeologist, the curator, is more akin to Walter Benjamin's collector than to his theoretical counterpart. According to Benjamin, the collector's lot was the Sisyphean task of emancipating things from their use-value and commodity character, a desire to evoke a better world "in which things are freed from the drudgery of being useful" (Benjamin 2002: 39).

To extend an ethics to things clearly provokes the moral question of "bad" things. Should we extend our care to a pair of Nike shoes produced at factories using child labor? Or what about nuclear weapons, concentration camps, or run-down factories polluting our environment? Although this raises important issues to be debated, such ethical dilemmas are nonetheless not exclusive to our dealings with things or non-humans. Also among our own species the list of "bad figures" is terrifyingly endless. We can as little exclude our species from attentive care owing to the misgivings of individuals as we can use the destructive potential of some things to dismiss them a priori from any ethical concern.

Carved care

The dominant modern metaphysics has cast the material world as inert; as something to be formed and made meaningful by thoughtful human intervention. In archaeology the study of rock art provides some of the most explicit and conspicuous expressions of this metaphysics. By carving or painting, the prehistoric "artist" is turning a natural rock surface into something significant and cultural. The rock itself has mostly been regarded as devoid of any power and potential, totally dependent on this human embodiment for its so-called cultural construction. As pertinently observed by Christopher Tilley (2004: 152), "[T]he rock surfaces have been regarded as a kind of blank slate on which the carvings are inscribed and their qualities effectively ignored." However, as Tilley and others recently have shown, to carve or paint is not a unidirectional flow of action, intention, and meaning from the human actor to the rock. Rather the act itself, as well as the images and design, has often emerged through an interaction and exchange between the carver and the rock (Hauptman Wahlgren 2002; Keyser and Poetschat 2004). North Scandinavian rock carving sites provide abundant examples of how the micro-topograpy of the rock surface is incorporated into the patterns and designs (cf. Gjerde 2010; Helskog 2004; Hesjedal 1994). Cracks and lines are included in body outlines, depressions become dens in a bear scene, the curved edge of a stone constitutes the back of an elk, and so forth. Likewise, in Palaeolithic Franco-Cantabrian cave art, the interplay between figures, rock surface, cracks, and fissures is well documented, sometimes producing three-dimensional images (Clottes 2007; Hodgson 2008).

It might be that the rock features "gave life" to these images, staged and contextualized them, and thus helped them – and the rock – in *becoming* meaningful. However, from a symmetrical point of view, their "incorporation" may also reveal a different way of conceiving of the world. To create and carve was not an exclusive outcome of some human sovereign power; it involved collaboration and exchange, to release or bring forth what was already conveyed in things and landscapes and to respond to their forms and capacities (Heidegger 1993: 317–19). A crack manifesting a ready-carved leg or a sculptured head already resting in the stone were carvings *already made*, an initial figuring slumbering in the stone. To work on the rock was not to embody oneself in a substantial but inert material or to make the rocks meaningful, but to bring forth what already dwelled in them. Deep inside coastal caves in northern Norway, red rock paintings mingle on the walls with natural deposits of red iron oxide, often making the distinction between them difficult (Bjerck 1995). This suggests that to paint was to *add*, continue, or complete something already painted or carved, already meaningful. Human engagement with the world is not emerging from some "outside" position; it is grounded in a skillful and inescapable entanglement, in the sense that our being-in-the-world is in some way always familiar (Heidegger 1962: 85–8).

What, then, about the actual images? Why were these particular depictions produced and reproduced? What are their meanings? Interpretation in archaeology, material culture, and rock art studies seem nearly always driven by an urge to reach some "deeper" social or symbolic meaning: the behind. The immediate is never enough; the only interpretively legitimate role of the carvings is to serve as a window onto some cultural or cognitive realms. According to this unveiling and intellectualizing mode, a boat, an elk, or a reindeer can be claimed to represent almost everything – ancestors, rites of transitions, borders, totemic agents, supernatural powers, and so on – apart, it seems, from themselves. A boat is never a boat; a reindeer is never a reindeer; a river is always a "cosmic" river. Again, a symmetrical approach does not dismiss the images' potential symbolic significance. However, it dismisses the tendency to ignore that the depicted being itself may have been the central matter of concern. Allowing boats to be boats, elks to be elks, involves being attentive to the potential significance of their own being (Olsen 2010: 84–7, 152–4).

Modern Sámi reindeer herders have hundreds of terms that relate to reindeer. This attention is not a symbolic attention but a concernful and circumspective one. It reflects intimate knowledge and care and concern for the reindeer in its different states of being, as well as the profound significance of the reindeer to Sámi life (Demant-Hatt 1913; Turi 1987). A reindeer has value and significance in its own right, as has the herd; it should not be offended by derogatory comments or abusive attitudes but instead cared for, respected, and honored (Oskal 1995: 136–8). This concern is also manifested in the numerous carvings that reindeer herders in recent centuries meticulously have made on wood and bone while resting with the herd. Far from reflecting an attitude of domination, reducing the reindeer to resource or *Bestand*, the reindeer herder depicted what was familiar and a matter of care and concern. Thus, maybe it was "just" the world as it circumspectively appeared to the prehistoric carver through his or her own concerned engagement with it that northern rock art "is about." This was a "meaning" that in some sense was already given, and to carve was to add to, to work on, or to supplement this latent circumspective significance. In this world, the reindeer was sufficiently meaningful by just being a reindeer.

Being attentive to and respecting the integrity and otherness of things and non-humans therefore also include their right *not* to be meaningful in the dominant interpretive sense. In the latter conception, meaning has always been confused with symbolic or metaphorical meaning, never allowing the object in question to be itself. An ethics encompassing things also involves liberating things from this imperative of intellectualization, and at least to accept as a minimum requirement a position "that does not annihilate the possibility that the other be the source of its own signification" (Benso 2000: xxvii; cf. Bennett 2009: 108).

Conclusion

Symmetrical archaeology is not a unified approach, a theory, or a method. It is a concept inextricably tied to the political economy of the discipline where it acts strategically in order to promote change. It was not launched to become an entrenched approach or a new sub-disciplinary brand name but rather inserted as an attempt to initiate a transition that hopefully would make it superfluous. Moreover, despite its derivative ancestry, it is an archaeological undertaking whose legitimacy does not depend on swearing any oath of allegiance to this or that theoretical "outside." We acknowledge the profound influence of science and technology studies, Actor-Network Theory, and Latour's contributions in particular. However, as witnessed, we also allow for figures considered not too appropriate in this fashionable company, such as Henri Bergson, Martin Heidegger, and Walter Benjamin. In other words, we are confident to take our own steps to include other allies and to mix and match, which, by the way, should not be so out of line with the practices otherwise warmly recommended by our protégés. Things themselves have anyway proved too complex, unruly, and different to be intercepted by any single philosophy.

A symmetrical approach is also an urge for disciplinary confidence. What is needed today is an archaeology that doesn't look back at its own past with embarrassment and contempt but seeks to revitalize its important legacy. First and foremost, archaeology is – and has been – a concern with things, and when the object now has re-entered social and cultural discourses, archaeologists, as the most dedicated students of things, should naturally make their voices heard. Our persistent concern with things, with materials, constitutes an intellectual skill that is more than ever relevant to current debates and discourses. Moreover, owing to our concern with things, it is also appropriate that our theorizing, although in part dedicated to common phenomena and the processing of similar philosophies, should be distinguishable from other theoretical discourses. In evoking such an archaeological difference, we should learn from the object lesson taught above. In other words, we should be confident and satisfied with being archaeologists and not aspire so much to be something else (anthropologists, historians, philosophers, artists). This also involves the conceptual toil of repatriating *archaeology* from its all too common intellectual staging as a convenient but semantically obligation-free metaphor in social and cultural theory, to work for its branding as a distinct and content-filled undertaking: the discipline of things. In short, and to rephrase some of our most famous ancestors, it involves showing that archaeology is archaeology or it is nothing.

Acknowledgments

I thank Alfredo González-Ruibal, Michael Shanks, Tim Webmoor, and Chris Witmore for innumerable discussions on these and other topics from which this chapter has greatly benefitted, as well as Ian Hodder for pertinent comments on an earlier draft.

References

Andersson, D. 2001. *Tingenes taushet, tingenes tale*. Oslo: Solum forlag.

Barrett, J. 2000. A thesis on agency. In M.-A. Dobres and J. Robb (eds), *Agency in Archaeology*, 61–8. London: Routledge.

Benjamin, W. 2002. *Selected Writings, Volume 3: 1935–1938*. Cambridge, MA: Belknap Press.

Benjamin, W. 2003. *Selected Writings, Volume 4: 1938–1940*. Cambridge, MA: Belknap Press.

Bennett, J. 2009. *Vibrant Matter: A Political Economy of Things*. Durham, NC: Duke University Press.

Benso, S. 2000. *The Face of Things: A Different Side of Ethics*. Albany: State University of New York Press.

Bergson, H. 1998. *Creative Evolution*. Mineola, NY: Dover.

Bjerck, H. 1995. Malte menneskebilder i "Helvete." Betraktninger om en nyoppdaget hulemaling på Trenyken. Røst. Nordland. *Univ. Oldsaksamlings Årbok* 1993/1994: 121–51.

Bjorvand, H. and F. Lindeman. 2000. *Våre arveord: etymologisk ordbok*. Oslo: Novus Forlag.

Bloor, D. 1976. *Knowledge and Social Imagery*. Chicago: University of Chicago Press.

Brattli, T. 2009. Managing the archaeological world cultural heritage: consensus or rhetoric? *Norwegian Archaeological Review* 42: 24–39.

Brown, B. 2003. *A Sense of Things: The Object Matter of American Literature*. Chicago: University of Chicago Press.

Bryant, L., N. Srnicek, and G. Harman 2011. Towards a speculative philosophy. In L. Bryant, N. Srnicek, and G. Harman (eds), *The Speculative Turn: Continental Materialism and Realism*, 1–18. Melbourne: re-press.

Clottes, J. 2007. New discoveries at Niaux Cave in the French Pyrenees. In P. C. Reddy (ed.), *Exploring the Mind of Ancient Man: Festschrift to Robert G. Bednarik*, 281–91. New Delhi: Research India Press.

Demant-Hatt, E. 1913. *Med lapperne i højfjeldet*. Stockholm: Nordiska Bokhandelen.

Dincauze, D. 2000. *Environmental Archaeology: Principles and Practice*. Cambridge: Cambridge University Press.

Falk, H. and A. Torp. 1994. *Etymologisk ordbog over det norske og det danske sprog*. Oslo: Bjørn Ringstrøms antikvariat.

Gamble, C. 2001. *Archaeology: The Basics*. London: Routledge.

Gibson, J. 1986. *The Ecological Approach to Visual Perception*. Hillsdale, NJ: Erlbaum.

Gjerde, J. M. 2010. Rock Art and Landscapes: Studies of Stone Age Rock Art from Northern Fennoscandia. Ph.D. thesis, University of Tromsø.

González-Ruibal, A. 2007. Arqueologia simétrica: un giro teórico sin revolución paradigmática. *Complutum* 18: 283–6.

González-Ruibal, A. 2008. Time to destroy: an archaeology of supermodernity. *Current Anthropology* 49: 247–79.

Harman, G. 2002. *Tool-Being: Heidegger and the Metaphysics of Objects*. Chicago: Open Court.

Harman, G. 2010. *Towards Speculative Realism: Essays and Lectures*. Ropley, UK: Zero Books.

Harman, G. 2011. On the undermining of objects: Grant, Bruno, and radical philosophy. In L. Bryant, N. Srnicek, and G. Harman (eds), *The Speculative Turn: Continental Materialism and Realism*, 21–40. Melbourne: re-press.

Hauptman Wahlgren, K. 2002. *Bilder av betydelse: hällristningar och brons-ålderslandskap i nordöstra Östergötland*. Stockholm Studies in Archaeology 23. Gothenburg: Bricoleur.

Heidegger, M. 1962. *Being and Time*. New York: Harper and Row.

Heidegger, M. 1993. The question concerning technology. In D. Farell Krell (ed.), *Martin Heidegger: Basic Writings*, 307–42. San Francisco: HarperCollins.

Helskog, K. 2004. Landscapes in rock-art: rock-carving and ritual in the old European North. In C. Chippindale and G. Nash (eds), *The Figured Landscape of Rock-Art: Looking at Pictures in Place*, 265–88. Cambridge: Cambridge University Press.

Hesjedal, A. 1994. The hunters' rock art in northern Norway: Problems in chronology and interpretation. *Norwegian Archaeological Review* 27: 1–14.

Hodder, I. 2011. Human–thing entanglement: towards an integrated archaeological perspective. *Journal of the Royal Anthropological Institute* (N.S.) 17: 154–77.

Hodgson, D. 2008. The visual dynamics of Upper Palaeolithic cave art. *Cambridge Archaeological Journal* 18: 341–53.

Ingold, T. 2005. The eye of the storm: visual perception and the weather. *Visual Studies* 20: 97–104.

Ingold, T. 2007a. Earth, sky, wind, and weather. *Journal of the Royal Anthropological Institute* (N.S.) Special Issue: S19–S38.

Ingold, T. 2007b. Materials against materiality. *Archaeological Dialogues* 14: 1–16.

Introna, L. D. 2009. Ethics and the speaking of things. *Theory, Culture & Society* 26(4): 25–46.

Johnson, M. 2010. *Archaeological Theory: An Introduction*. Oxford: Blackwell.

Kenderdine, S. 2008. The irreducible ensemble: Place-Hampi. *The International Journal of Digital Cultural Heritage and E-Tourism (IJDCE)* 1: 139–56.

Keyser, J. and G. Poetschat 2004. The canvas as the art: landscape analysis of the rock-art panel. In C. Chippindale and G. Nash (eds), *The Figured Landscapes of Rock-Art: Looking at Pictures in Place*, 118–30. Cambridge: Cambridge University Press.

Klindt-Jensen, O. 1975. *A History of Scandinavian Archaeology*. London: Thames and Hudson.

Latour, B. 1991. *Nous n'avons jamais été modernes: essai d'anthropologie symétrique*. Paris: La Découverte.

Latour, B. 1993. *We Have Never Been Modern*. London: Harvard University Press.

Latour, B. 2005. *Reassembling the Social: An Introduction to Actor-Network-Theory*. Oxford: Oxford University Press.

Law, J. 1999. After ANT: complexity, naming and topology. In J. Law and J. Hassard (eds), *Actor Network Theory and After*, 1–14. Oxford: Blackwell.

Leach, E. 1973. Concluding address. In C. Renfrew (ed.), *The Explanation of Culture Change: Models in Prehistory*, 761–71. Pittsburgh: University of Pittsburgh Press.

Lipe, W. D. 1974. A conservation model for American archaeology. *The Kiva* 39: 213–45.

Lucas, G. 2005. *The Archaeology of Time*. London: Routledge.

Merleau-Ponty, M. 1968. *The Visible and the Invisible*. Evanston, IL: Northwestern University Press.

Miller, D. 1987. *Material Culture and Mass Consumption*. Oxford: Blackwell.

Nora, P. 1984. Entre mémoire et histoire: La problématique des lieux. In P. Nora (ed.), *Les lieux de mémoire, tome 1: La République*, xv–xlii. Paris: Gallimard.

Olivier, L. 2001. Duration, memory and the nature of the archaeological record. In H. Karlsson (ed.), *It's About Time: The Concept of Time in Archaeology*, 61–70.Gothenburg: Bricoleur Press.

Olivier, L. 2008. *Le sombre abîme du temps: mémoire et archéologie*. Paris: Seuil.

Olsen, B. 2003. Material culture after text: remembering things. *Norwegian Archaeological Review* 36: 87–104.

Olsen, B. 2006. Ting-mennesker-samfunn: introduksjon til en symmetrisk arkeologi. *Arkæologisk Forum* 14: 13–18.

Olsen, B. 2007. Keeping things at arm's length: a genealogy of asymmetry. *World Archaeology* 39: 579–88.

Olsen, B. 2010. *In Defense of Things: Archaeology and the Ontology of Objects*. Lanham, MD: AltaMira Press.

Oskal, N. 1995. Det rette, det gode og reinlykken. Ph.D. thesis, University of Tromsø.

Perry, S. 2009. Fractured media: challenging the dimensions of archaeology's typical visual modes of engagement. *Archaeologies* 5: 389–415.

Renfrew, C. 1989. Comments. *Norwegian Archaeological Review* 22: 33–41.

Rowlands, M. 2002. Heritage and cultural property. In V. Buchli (ed.), *The Material Culture Reader*, 115–33. Oxford: Berg.

Schiffer, M. 1976. *Behavioral Archaeology*. New York: Academic Press.

Serres, M. with B. Latour. 1995. *Conversation on Science, Culture and Time*. Ann Arbor: University of Michigan Press.

Shanks, M. 2007. Symmetrical archaeology. *World Archaeology* 39: 589–96.

Smith, L. 2006. *Uses of Heritage*. London: Routledge.

Solli, B. 2011. Some reflections on archaeology and heritage in the Anthropocene. *Norwegian Archaeological Review* 44: 40–88.

Tilley, C. 1994. *A Phenomenology of Landscape.* Oxford: Berg.

Tilley, C. 2004. *The Materiality of Stone: Explorations in Landscape Phenomenology.* Oxford: Berg.

Turi, J. 1987. *En bok om samernas liv.* Umeå, Sweden: Två Förläggare Bokförlag.

Webmoor, T. 2007. What about "one more turn after the social" in archaeological reasoning? Taking things seriously. *World Archaeology* 39: 563–78.

Witmore, C. 2004. Four archaeological engagements with place: mediating bodily experience through peripatetic video. *Visual Anthropology Review* 20(2): 57–72.

Witmore, C. 2006. Vision, media, noise and the percolation of time: symmetrical approaches to the mediation of the material world. *Journal of Material Culture* 11: 267–92.

Witmore, C. 2007. Symmetrical archaeology: excerpts of a manifesto. *World Archaeology* 39: 546–62.

11

THE SOCIAL LIFE OF HERITAGE

Lynn Meskell

> As the past becomes less easily reduced to a single set of meanings and
> effects, as the present is forced to orient itself amid so much history
> and so many histories, history itself emerges as both weightier and less
> deterministic than ever before.
>
> (W. Brown 2001: 5)

Social archaeology since the 1980s has been concerned with the
entwined themes of identity, experience, and politics. Archaeologists
have routinely turned their attention to issues including gender and
sexuality, embodiment, memory and materiality, and other fields of
subject making that can be uncovered from the material record. In a
sense, all of these intellectual forays could be described as projects
that broadly coalesce around the politics of location (Braidotti 1994).
While the 1980s and 1990s were predominantly characterized by
single-issue studies which often retained a narrow and privileged
focus (Meskell 2001, 2002), research in the last decade has sought
to make complex the various vectors of identity and lived experience.
Rather than simply targeting ethnicity or gender, recent archaeological work aims to embrace a wider set of social determinants in the
lives of historically situated individuals by pursuing multiple lines of
inquiry (e.g. Joyce 2004; Loren 2007; Martindale 2009; Meskell
1999; Pauketat and Alt 2005; Silliman 2010). Studying the construction of social difference and inequality in the past has necessarily
entailed being open to explorations of those configurations in the
present, and indeed our theoretical borrowings have largely been

derived from contemporary political settings. The difference lies in the precise positioning of archaeological materials: for archaeologies of the past, researchers use material culture to shed light on past identity politics; for archaeologies of the present, material culture, monuments, and sites constitute the very rallying points of identity struggles, rights to self-determination, development discourses, and so on (Byrne 2009; De Cesari 2010b; MacEachern 2010; Schmidt 2010; Segobye 2006; C. Smith and Wobst 2005; L. Smith 2004). In recognition of this intercalation, archaeologists are gradually moving to a position where informed and responsible practice is as integral to the discipline as rigorous research questions and methodologies (Colwell-Chanthaphonh and Ferguson 2008; Meskell and Pels 2005; Vitelli and Colwell-Chanthaphonh 2006).

Surveying the burgeoning scholarship within social archaeology from the last decade, the emergence of a more politically aware and ethically engaged discipline is clear. A vast new body of research directed towards both theorization and field practice is increasingly dedicated to contemporary contexts, descendant groups, heritage ethics, rights and reparations, conflict and resolution, as well as the role of memory and museums (Hodder 2003, 2009; Lilley 2000; Silliman 2008). Some might not view these developments as inherently theoretical, arguing that such work might represent a more "applied" angle to archaeological work. This is not my view. Rather, I suggest that addressing and building upon the insights of postcolonial theory, globalization, neoliberalism, rights discourse, and the moral philosophies of ethics and social justice (e.g. González-Ruibal 2006, 2009; M. Hall 2005; Lilley 2009; Scham 2009a; Silverman and Fairchild Ruggles 2008; Weiss 2007) is no less theorized than previous discussions of agency, sexuality, memory, or materiality in archaeology.

A wider framing

Archaeology's engagement with politics and its larger framing within global developments are direct outgrowths of a specific disciplinary trajectory of engagement with social theory, politics, philosophy, feminism, and indigenous scholarship (Gilchrist 1999; Hodder 1991, 1992, 2001; Joyce 2001; Layton 1994; Shanks and Tilley 1987; Watkins 2001). During the 1980s and 1990s, many archaeologists deepened their awareness and application of social theory, whereas the 1990s and 2000s were more marked by our recognition of the discipline's socio-political embedding. I would suggest that these

developments are inherently linked and that only through an attention to the inequalities of gender, class, and race could the political
inequities of present archaeological contexts be fully grasped and our
responses incorporated into our work. Positionality is key, and many
scholars with commitments to feminism or Marxism have been
equally concerned with the politics of archaeology and heritage
(Bernbeck and Pollock 2004; Joyce 2005; McGuire 2008; Patterson
2003; Pollock and Lutz 1994). Moreover, without the theoretical
insights gleaned from landscape archaeologies, studies of monuments
and place making, phenomenology and experience (Barrett 1994;
Gosden and Head 1994; Thomas 2001; Tilley 1994), coupled with
the recent inclusion of indigenous perspectives (Ferguson and Colwell-
Chanthaphonh 2006; Head 2000; Mills and Walker 2008; Preucel
2002), our accounts of heritage construction and the politics of place
would be severely attenuated.

Beginning in the 1980s, there has been a steady growth of studies
on the role of archaeology and archaeological narratives in the service
of the state (McGuire 1992; Patterson 1994; Trigger 1989). The earliest studies of nationalism focused upon nineteenth-century European
nation building (Atkinson et al. 1996; Díaz-Andreu and Champion
1996; Graves-Brown et al. 1996), followed by wider global and contemporary perspectives (Kohl and Fawcett 1995; Meskell 1998;
Rowan and Baram 2004; Ucko 1995). Questions of theory in specific
countries and the particular relationship between national concerns
and theoretical development also emerged as an important issue
(Hodder 1991; Ucko 1995). Philip Kohl (1998) provided a useful
summary documenting the development of archaeology in the nineteenth and early twentieth centuries, linking nationalism to considerations of ethnicity and identity. He outlined various cases
demonstrating the manipulation of archaeological materials. There
are obviously extreme examples such as Hitler's Germany or
Mussolini's Italy (Anthony 1995; Arnold 1990), but there are also
other national responses that are as complex yet less deterministic
in their relationships with the past (Abdi 2001; K. S. Brown 1998;
Özdoğan 1998; Scham 1998; Wynn 2008). One can argue for a whole
series of relationships between nations, regions, and individuals
and their respective pasts, and one cannot assume that conscious
"construction" and "manipulation" are the only rationales. It is
also crucial to provide socio-political linkages: the twentieth century
was rife with political restructuring and ethnic/religious upheavals
(e.g. the Balkans, the Soviet Union, Israel, India) that sparked relationships with particular historical trajectories, nostalgia and com-
memoration, and the forceful materiality of archaeological remains.

National modernities are constructed through dialogic relationships between archaeological materiality and heterogeneous narratives of the past. We might question: how has cultural heritage been deployed in quests for specific modernities, sometimes at the expense or erasure of others? How do political agendas inhere in monumentalized space?

There is great diversity in how individual nations choose to deploy the past and how that can be refracted through archaeological practice. For example, in the context of France, scholars have discussed a national archaeology rather than a nationalist one (Fleury-Ilett 1993). Here the discursive construction of archaeology is linked to wider developments such as the loss of foreign colonies, sociopolitical change, and the role of collective memory in the shaping of national culture. Identity and unity are foregrounded and monumentalized, especially since the political upheavals of May 1968 (see Demoule 1999; Dietler 1994, 1998; Schnapp 1996). European scholars have also turned their attention to the deconstruction of field practices, the place of local workers, and remnant colonial hegemonies (Fotiadis 1993; Given 1998; van Dommelen 1997, 1998). While European case studies in archaeology were once dominant, there has been a steady increase in awareness about nationalism and archaeological politics in Africa (Chirikure and Pwiti 2008; MacEachern 2007; Ndoro 2001; Reid 2002; Schmidt 2009; Schmidt and McIntosh 1996; Schmidt and Patterson 1995; Segobye 2005), Latin America (Benavides 2005; Chinchilla Mazariegos 1998; González-Ruibal 2009; Higueras 1995), the Middle East (Abdi 2001, 2008; Atakuman 2008; Bernhardsson 2006; Scham 1998, 2009b), and Asia (Byrne 1995, 2007, 2009; Fawcett 1995; Long and Sweet 2006; Miura 2005). Archaeologists are increasingly wary of strong nationalisms that may in fact mask the rights of disempowered minorities, often unacknowledged within the confines of nation. This is particularly salient in the realm of heritage, where individual and community attachments to place are often sacrificed in the abstract framing of world heritage, transacted solely by and among nation-states.

Archaeological materials have always been deeply enmeshed in politics of one sort or another. It is the very materiality of archaeology – the survival of monuments and objects, their visibility in sites and museums, their iconic value – that lends such force to the contemporary imaginary. These places and objects can be mobilized and deployed in identity struggles, whereas ethnographies and theorizing alone cannot. For so long in the shadow of our sister-discipline, this unique aspect of the archaeological project has gradually become a prime importance to disciplines like anthropology, geography, history, and cultural studies (Breglia 2006; Edensor 1998, 2005; Fontein 2005; Rojek and Urry 1997). The materiality of the past has long-term consequences in the lives of numerous generations; it can be reworked and reinterpreted, multiply claimed, appropriated, erased, or capitalized upon. Inequalities can also be reproduced in and around heritage access, control and interpretation, whether premised on sexuality, religion, ethnicity, status, or other axes of difference.

The residues of the past are often monumentalized and inescapable in daily life. Individually, the past is memory – collectively, it is history. Both are constructs entangled with identity issues. While history and memory are imagined, this does not mean that they are imaginary (Jenkins 1996: 28). According to Lowenthal (1985: 245), history and memory usually come in the guise of stories which the mind must purposefully filter; physical relics remain directly available to our senses. This existential concreteness explains their evocative appeal. Their multivalency and plasticity also result in "a diversity of icons" (Higueras 1995: 399) that are prefigured in society through their residual nature. And while archaeological remains signify materiality, identity formation is alternately fluid – the material and the immaterial in constant dialogue. Identification is always a process of articulation or suturing, rather than a subsumption (C. Hall 1996: 3): it is neither essentialist nor foundational, but, rather, strategic and positional.

Archaeologies of the modern

An archaeology of the recent past is a related stream of research that had its roots in British archaeology and material culture studies but also finds strong resonance with scholars of race, ethnicity, and colonization in the United States, Australia, and South Africa (Buchli and Lucas 2001; Byrne 2003; Casella and Fredericksen 2004; M. Hall 1992, 2001, 2006; Mullins 1999; Orser 2000; Schrire 1995). Some of the earliest work was conducted in the 1980s by Ian Hodder, Chris Tilley, and Daniel Miller on labor, alienation, choice and consumption, the academy, modern housing, and factories (Hodder 1987; Miller 1988). Victor Buchli and Gavin Lucas (2001) then took this work in a new direction, perhaps most famously in their own excavation and analysis of a council house. An archaeology of the modern might also encompass diverse subjects like the archaeology of the

Bam earthquake (Garazhian and Papoli Yazdi 2008) and the excavation of a fraternity house (Wilkie 2010) or of a colonial outpost (see Lucas 2004).

More recent work crosses over with material culture studies such as Moshenska's (2010) study of the material effects and memorialization of the London Blitz. Specifically, he examines the use of bombed churches as war memorials together with the continual recovery of unexploded bombs from beneath the city. Through these two modes of analysis he argues that public memory of the wartime bombings is fading from memory, commemorative monuments have often been elided, and these traumatic recent events increasingly risk falling from view. As significant anniversaries pass, he argues, the "London Blitz approaches the edge of living memory, and imperatives to commemorate appear with a renewed sense of urgency within memorial associations and community groups" (Moshenska 2010: 23). McAtackney (2011) offers another example by investigating wall murals in Northern Ireland, which can either facilitate communication or provide physical barriers that solidify social relations and prevent interaction. She argues that there is a need to contextualize the current and potential role of walls in the maintenance of peace and facilitating a "new" Northern Ireland. This latter contribution is typical of a new interest in reconciliation and healing in archaeology generally. Additionally, both these examples could also be said to be contributing to conflict archaeology.

Conflict archaeology, coming out of a strong British tradition, has also bridged archaeology and heritage with its own *Journal of Conflict Archaeology*. While once strictly associated with battlefield archaeology, today conflict archaeology broadly encompasses research on the complexities of conflict and its legacies through the twentieth and twenty-first centuries as well as conflict resolution through archaeological praxis (Kalshoven 2005; Rico 2007; Rowlands 1999; Saunders 2000; Scham and Yahya 2003; Tunbridge and Ashworth 1996). Good examples of the more recent and nuanced work on conflict can be seen in Burström and his colleagues' (2009) work on the Cuban Missile Crisis. Essentially a collaboration between Swedish and Cuban archaeologists, this project looks at both the tangible remains and the memories that endure from the 1962 nuclear crisis. They argue that undertaking the archaeological work, coupled with the larger heritage project, was an effective way of enabling people to remember and publicly discuss those events and their aftermath. New forms of history are made in the process, while others are unmade or dismantled. Another pertinent example would be González-

Ruibal's work (2006), focused as he is upon uncovering the archaeological traces of rampant modernity: industrial ruins, abandoned villages and towns, refugee camps, concentration camps, prisons, battlefields, totalitarian architecture, lands razed by nuclear disasters. In one study he focuses on the archaeological remains of communist Ethiopia (1974–91), the scars of war that include Soviet tanks, AK47s, barbed wire, helmets, military rations, munitions, and so on. Working in the region of Benishangul, González-Ruibal employs methods of recovery including archaeological survey and ethnographic interviews to uncover not only the scale and horror of modern conflict, but also the lasting legacies of ecological disaster, ethnic tension, and poverty.

Archaeologists increasingly need to maneuver between levels of disciplinary engagement, the lived experience of social identity and the wider political setting of archaeological praxis: both entail issues of power and difference, be it national, racial, ethnic, religious, sexual, gender, class, and so on. Archaeology has traditionally separated out studies of our "dead subjects" from the field's contemporary valences, yet the two domains emerged in tandem and are epistemically interlaced. An archaeology of the contemporary past engages us with other fields and audiences, and fulfills part of our ethical responsibility as public figures charged with the trusteeship (Bender 1998; Scham 1998) of the past.

Since politics has become so central to our work, archaeologists have grown increasingly concerned with the ethical implications of their research and, more importantly, the politics of fieldwork, and collaborations with local people, descendants, indigenous groups, and other communities of connection (e.g. M. Hall 2005; Hodder 1998; Joyce 2005; Lilley and Williams 2005; Meskell 2005a, 2005b; C. Smith 2004; Watkins 2004; Zimmerman et al. 2003). Ethics has become the subject of numerous volumes and has moved from a focus on producing codes of best practice to exploring the situated effects of the discipline from multiple competing vantage points (e.g. Brodie et al. 2001, 2006; Lynott and Wylie 2000; Meskell and Pels 2005; Messenger 1999; Renfrew 2000; Vitelli and Colwell-Chanthaphonh 2006). Importantly, these were not simply Euro-American trends but were more often driven by archaeologists based in Latin America, Australasia, Africa, and the Middle East (see Abdi 2001; Funari 2006; Ndoro 2001; Politis 2001; Scham and Yahya 2003; Shepherd 2002; C. Smith and Wobst 2005). The development of the discipline's ethical profile can be seen in journals like the *International Journal of Cultural Property* or *Archaeologies: The Journal of the World Archaeological Congress*. Moreover, organizations like the World

Archaeological Congress acknowledge the discipline's colonial history and present, and have a public mandate of social justice that seeks not only to instantiate a model of best practice, but also to go beyond in terms of reparations and enhanced livelihoods, to make a positive, felt impact for the communities within which archaeologists work. Indigenous issues and potential collaborations are slowly becoming mainstream in archaeological discussions and, while there is much that still needs redressing, I would argue that the language of restitution, repatriation, and reconciliation has gradually gained ground (see Colwell-Chanthaphonh, this volume). These are all vital disciplinary developments that have occurred at both research and organization levels and have irrevocably changed how we work.

Heritage and hybrid fieldwork

It is not simply our situated contexts that have been exposed and challenged; our methodologies have also recently been expanded and re-imagined. Given the current climate of research briefly outlined here, and the types of transnational ethical and political work undertaken, a new generation of archaeologists has pursued a broader suite of techniques and multi-sited field methods. Blurring the conventional disciplinary divides, archaeologists have increasingly conducted ethnographic work around the construction of heritage, excavated the archives, investigated media-based productions of knowledge, and worked creatively in conjunction with living communities (Meskell 2005a, 2009a). Sometimes this work is focused on the materiality of the past, but more commonly such research enjoys a strong contemporary emphasis and is concerned with unpacking the micro-politics of archaeological practice, the impacts of heritage on an international scale, and the entwined global networks of tourism, development and heritage agencies, non-governmental organizations, and so on. Additionally, there is a burgeoning literature by anthropologists on archaeological and heritage projects (Abu el-Haj 2001; Benavides 2005; Breglia 2006; Castañeda 1996; Clifford 2004; Fontein 2005; Handler 2003). Many of the old dichotomous ways of thinking have been replaced by more integrated, reflexive, and hybrid epistemologies and modes of research.

I suggest that the new millennium also brought with it a new set of concerns for archaeologists and heritage practitioners. It was no longer possible to take refuge in the past or in the comfort that the subjects of our research were dead and buried. Rather than operating within a circumscribed set of practices, archaeologists now find themselves ever broadening out to embrace the discourses and impacts of environmentalism, protectionism, and international law, or to confront the modalities of war and conflict. This expansion underlines a commitment that follows from the discipline's first forays into socio-politics during the 1980s, and stretches ever more widely into the larger, international political arenas in which we are all enmeshed. Our obligations may entail addressing the political and economic depredations of past regimes, enhancing local livelihoods, publicizing the impacts of war, or tackling head on the incursions of transnational companies and institutions. Archaeologists are increasingly being called upon to straddle these multiple scales, in large part because of the nature of our fieldwork but also, more importantly, because heritage now occupies a new position in the global movements of development, conservation, post-conflict restoration, and indigenous rights.

Studies of the archaeological present have lately evinced the local dimension, while at the same time demonstrating global relevance, including the impact of global networks and forces, and the implications of international efforts, whether aid, development, protectionism, humanitarianism, and so on. Both ends of the spectrum, local and global, have their limitations if considered in isolation and do not fully consider the "processes of self-transformation in which new cultural forms take place and where new spaces of discourse open up leading to a transformation in the social world" (Delanty 2006: 44). How the world is imagined in particular places is greatly at variance.

Archaeologists have begun to examine the ways in which local and national heritage politics are made and unmade through international discourses and regulations, how transnational bodies and organizations such as UNESCO, the World Bank, conservation and funding agencies, and even the United States' "war on terror" are curiously brought into play in local arenas (Lafrenz Samuels 2010). Balancing appeals to universalism with that of cultural diversity remains a critical tension that underlines much of the existing literature on heritage and our engagements as practitioners. These strange proximities and multiplicities are experienced in particular regions and locales in distinct ways, even though the organizational directives might aspire to a presumed universality and neutrality. More importantly, salvage politics is often united by incentives of common goods; it is promise-based, future-driven, and depends upon networks of participation, discipline, and sacrifice that discursively create desirable heritage citizens (see Hayden 2003). To adopt an Orwellian tone, interventionist policies that control the past also serve to predict future outcomes, promising sustainable development, betterment, and socio-economic uplift. What must be sublated in the present will be recouped in the future by coming generations, while international elites and the adequately resourced will be able to enjoy the spoils of heritage and conservation in the present in the form of cultural and ecological tourism and research. Such promissory strategies tend to de-privilege indigenous and minority communities, often disempowered constituencies whose land, livelihood, and legacies are threatened.

We must now take seriously the intellectual foundations and political economies of "heritage," the legal, political, and ethical strata that underlie implicit tensions over access to, preservation of, and control over the material past in a volatile present. This entails questioning the translatability of such terms and practices across a wide array of sites and locations. It requires practitioners to reveal the discursive production, consumption, and governing of other people's pasts through examination of the participants, organizations, stakeholders, beneficiaries, and victims. For some this has entailed an attention to rights, whether international human rights (Schmidt 1996, 2010; Silverman and Fairchild Ruggles 2008) or broader rights and claims (Hodder 2010; Meskell 2009b, 2010). Many emergent claims hark back to racial or ethnic exclusion or historical disenfranchisement, thus opening the space to frame heritage as contributing to human capabilities and well-being. In an ideal world, "heritage rights" would include rights of self-determination and expression, rights of access and management, rights of veto, and rights to accrued benefits, whether social, economic, spiritual, and so on. Since human rights are so often caught up in exclusions and boundaries, their discourse may not always mesh well with contested heritage sites, where archaeologists typically strive to include more constituencies, to forge inclusivity rather than exclusivity given our long temporal perspectives. Heritage rights, by their very nature, are likely to be locally and culturally understood rather than universally prescribed, though the universality of human rights has also been vigorously contested. One implication for archaeologists might be that the scale of conflict we witness today over heritage has escalated with experts like ourselves repositioning heritage as a socio-economic resource and creating the apparatus to protect, attribute, commercialize, and control sites internationally. It is our international presence, our auditing, controlling, and mastering of heritage – often externally rather than from within – that can often foster and spur on these tensions and conflicts.

These developments pertain not only to individual practitioners but also to our collaborative projects, many of which are international and strive to make a difference in our host countries. Archaeological projects are increasingly self-styled as NGOs and charities and are, in turn, supported by other NGOs. World heritage sites across the globe have a long history of entanglement with World Bank schemes, USAID funding, and other transnational adventures (Brand 2001; Lafrenz Samuels 2010; Lilley 2009; Mitchell 2000, 2002). Governments, donor agencies, and corporations have all come to see heritage and tradition as reified public *goods* that could be mobilized for the greater public *good*. But more than simply its economic instrumentality, heritage is increasingly called upon to serve as a novel vehicle for national pride, spiritual recovery and reconciliation. In the case of Palestine, De Cesari (2010a) shows how cultural heritage can be effectively interwoven with architecture, art, conservation, and urban planning in order to rescue the recent Palestinian vernacular past while constituting a meaningful strategy for consolidation and anti-colonial counter-memory. She describes this as a creative act of defiance, facilitated by NGOs like Riwaq that partner with village municipalities across the West Bank. While promoting local heritage in Palestine, they are resisting the exclusivist narration of Judeo-Christian origins, and this further connects Palestine to the wider world. My own work in South Africa documents how the rhetoric of heritage as therapy that immediately followed the 1994 democratic elections has more recently receded in the face of greater fiscal burdens and failures. The politics of therapy and social cohesion has given way to stringent neoliberalism under the ANC: rather than constituting the vehicle for empowerment and development, heritage has to pay for itself (Meskell 2009c, 2011; Meskell and Scheermeyer 2008). I suggest that cultural heritage today is always future perfect and is increasingly imagined as a vehicle for development and modernizing, as well as reconciliation and uplift. Capitalizing culture in these ways increasingly means that archaeologists have to work with and between international agencies like UNESCO, transnational projects, national governments, and indigenous groups while tackling questions as to whether cultural heritage contributes to emergent human rights, diversity and sustainability, development and capacity building, as well as human and global well-being.

Summary

At the beginning of this chapter I suggested that developments in the politics of the past since the 1980s are connected to a broader concern with issues of identity and difference in archaeology, whether race, gender, or ethnic inequalities. These developments occurred in tandem and many of the same scholars have worked across the temporal divide studying both the past in the past and the lived effects of the past in the present. Increasingly that work is blurring and producing hybrid research and writing such as Denis Byrne's *Surface Collection* (2007), where the author is not only uncovering the past and writing history but also interweaving the past's salience from a modern vantage. The combined work of Chip Colwell-Chanthaphonh and T. J. Ferguson (Colwell-Chanthaphonh and Ferguson 2004, 2008; Ferguson and Colwell-Chanthaphonh 2006) is also poised at this nexus: taking indigenous knowledge and connections seriously to critically understand past peoples, meanings, and landscapes in the US Southwest. My research in South Africa's Kruger National Park (Meskell 2011) seeks to uncover the past of that park and overturn the notion of *terra nullius* while at the same time tracking the progress of the past in post-apartheid society today. Historical understanding does not have to be jettisoned for critical cultural heritage; rather the two are enmeshed and complementary.

Albeit briefly sketched, the foregoing makes clear that the politics of the past today has moved significantly from our initial forays into the study of nationalism or colonialism (Trigger 1984). From those first important steps, archaeology has broadened its time span by examining not only the twentieth century but the archaeology of us in the here and now. Archaeologies of the recent past have grown significantly and there has been greater intersection with anthropology and material culture studies. This has led many into the arenas of conflict and post-conflict, and pushed scholars not to simply document battlefields but to consider the possibilities for heritage as therapy, reconciliation, and reparation (Scham and Yahya 2003). This also entails a more human element, collaborating with communities and developing a diverse array of field methods. We are increasingly confronted with the impacts of governments, conflicts, transnational organizations, companies, donors, and development agencies (Lafrenz Samuels 2009; MacEachern 2010) that have now also become part of our research domain. This leads us further into questions of ethics and rights, the former having a longer history of debate in the discipline, while the latter has energized the field more recently. As we move forward, we should envisage that our socio-political and interdisciplinary entanglements will only become more complex as archaeologists acknowledge their role and the role archaeological sites play in the global imaginary. As Wendy Brown observes in the opening quote, at the very moment when history and heritage are now subject to multiple explanations and interpretations, when the "foundational" nature of the past is being questioned, that same past is being called upon to do more and provide more, socially, economically, and psychically.

References

Abdi, K. 2001. Nationalism, politics, and the development of archaeology in Iran. *American Journal of Archaeology* 105: 51–76.

Abdi, K. 2008. From Pan-Arabism to Saddam Hussein's cult of personality: Ancient Mesopotamia and Iraqi national ideology. *Journal of Social Archaeology* 8: 3–36.

Abu el-Haj, N. 2001. *Facts on the Ground: Archaeological Practice and Territorial Self-Fashioning in Israeli Society*. Chicago: University of Chicago Press.

Anthony, D. 1995. Nazi and eco-feminist prehistories: counter points in Indo-European archaeology. In P. Kohl and C. Fawcett (eds), *Nationalism, Politics and the Practice of Archaeology*, 82–96. Cambridge: Cambridge University Press.

Arnold, B. 1990. The past as propaganda: totalitarian archaeology in Nazi Germany. *Antiquity* 64: 464–78.

Atakuman, Ç. 2008. Cradle or crucible: Anatolia and archaeology in the early years of the Turkish Republic (1923–1938) *Journal of Social Archaeology* 8: 214–35.

Atkinson, J. A., I. Banks, and J. O'Sullivan (eds) 1996. *Nationalism and Archaeology*. Glasgow: Cruithne.

Barrett, J. C. 1994. *Fragments from Antiquity: An Archaeology of Social Life in Britain, 2900–1200 BC*. Oxford: Blackwell.

Benavides, O. H. 2005. *Making Ecuadorian Histories*. Austin: University of Texas Press.

Bender, B. 1998. *Stonehenge: Making Space*. Oxford: Berg.

Bernbeck, R. and S. Pollock 2004. The political economy of archaeological practice and the production of heritage in the Middle East. In L. M. Meskell and R. W. Preucel (eds), *A Companion to Social Archaeology*, 335–52. Oxford: Blackwell.

Bernhardsson, M. T. 2006. *Reclaiming a Plundered Past: Archaeology and Nation Building in Modern Iraq*. Austin: University of Texas Press.

Braidotti, R. 1994. *Nomadic Subjects: Embodiment and Sexual Difference in Contemporary Feminist Theory*. New York: Columbia University Press.

Brand, L. A. 2001. Development in Wadi Rum? State bureaucracy, external funders, and civil society. *International Journal of Middle East Studies* 33: 571–90.

Breglia, L. C. (2006). *Monumental Ambivalence*. Austin: University of Texas Press.

Brodie, N., J. Doole, and C. Renfrew (eds) 2001. *Trade in Illicit Antiquities: The Destruction of the World's Archaeological Heritage*. Cambridge: McDonald Institute for Archaeological Research.

Brodie, N., M. M. Kersel, C. Luke, and K. W. Tubb 2006. *Archaeology, Cultural Heritage, and the Antiquities Trade*. Gainesville: University Press of Florida.

Brown, K. S. 1998. Contests of heritage and the politics of preservation in the Former Yugoslav Republic of Macedonia. In L. M. Meskell (ed.), *Archaeology under Fire: Nationalism, Politics and Heritage in the Eastern Mediterranean and Middle East*, 68–86. London: Routledge.

Brown, W. 2001. *Politics out of History*. Princeton: Princeton University Press.

Buchli, V. and G. Lucas (eds) 2001. *Archaeologies of the Contemporary Past*. London: Routledge.

Burström, M., T. Diez Acosta, E. González Noriega, A. Gustafsson, I. Hernández, H. Karlsson, J. M. Pajón, J. Robaina Jaramillo, and B. Westergaard 2009. Memories of a world crisis. *Journal of Social Archaeology* 9: 295–318.

Byrne, D. 1995. Buddhist *stupa* and Thai social practice. *World Archaeology* 27: 266–81.

Byrne, D. 2003. Nervous landscapes: race and space in Australia. *Journal of Social Archaeology* 3: 169–93.

Byrne, D. 2007. *Surface Collection: Archaeological Travels in Southeast Asia*. Walnut Creek, CA: AltaMira Press.

Byrne, D. 2009. Archaeology and the fortress of rationality. In L. M. Meskell (ed.), *Cosmopolitan Archaeologies*, 68–88. Durham, NC: Duke University Press.

Casella, E. C. and C. Fredericksen 2004. Legacy of the "fatal shore": the heritage and archaeology of confinement in post-colonial Australia. *Journal of Social Archaeology* 4: 99–125.

Castañeda, Q. 1996. *In the Museum of Maya Culture: Touring Chichén Itzá*. Minneapolis: University of Minnesota Press.

Chinchilla Mazariegos, O. 1998. Archaeology and nationalism in Guatemala at the time of independence. *Antiquity* 72: 376–86.

Chirikure, S. and G. Pwiti 2008. Community involvement in archaeology and cultural heritage management: an assessment from case studies in Southern Africa and elsewhere. *Current Anthropology* 49: 467–85.

Clifford, J. 2004. Looking several ways: anthropology and Native heritage in Alaska. *Current Anthropology* 45: 5–30.

Colwell-Chanthaphonh, C. and T. J. Ferguson 2004. Virtue ethics and the practice of history: Native Americans and archaeologists along the San Pedro Valley of Arizona. *Journal of Social Archaeology* 4: 5–27.

Colwell-Chanthaphonh, C. and T. J. Ferguson (eds) 2008. *Collaboration in Archaeological Practice: Engaging Descendant Communities*. Lanham, MD: AltaMira Press.

De Cesari, C. 2010a. Creative heritage: Palestinian heritage NGOs and defiant arts of government. *American Anthropologist* 112: 625–37.

De Cesari, C. 2010b. World heritage and mosaic universalism. *Journal of Social Archaeology* 10: 299–324.

Delanty, G. 2006. The cosmopolitan imagination: critical cosmopolitanism and social theory. *The British Journal of Sociology* 57: 25–47.

Demoule, J. 1999. Ethnicity, culture and identity: French archaeologists and historians. *Antiquity* 73: 190–8.

Díaz-Andreu, M. and T. Champion 1996. *Nationalism and Archaeology in Europe*. London: University College London Press.

Dietler, M. 1994. "Our ancestors the Gauls": archaeology, ethnic nationalism, and the manipulation of Celtic identity in modern Europe. *American Anthropologist* 96: 584–605.

Dietler, M. 1998. A tale of three sites: the monumentalization of Celtic Oppida and the politics of collective memory and identity. *World Archaeology* 30: 72–89.

Edensor, T. 1998. *Tourists at the Taj: Performance and Meaning at a Symbolic Site*. New York: Routledge.

Edensor, T. 2005. *Industrial Ruins: Spaces, Aesthetics and Materiality*. Oxford: Berg.

Fawcett, C. 1995. Nationalism and postwar Japanese archaeology. In P. L. Kohl and C. Fawcett (eds), *Nationalism, Politics, and the Practice of Archaeology*, 232–46. Cambridge: Cambridge University Press.

Ferguson, T. J. and C. Colwell-Chanthaphonh 2006. *History is in the Land: Multivocal Tribal Traditions in Arizona's San Pedro Valley*. Tucson: University of Arizona Press.

Fleury-Ilett, B. 1993. Identity of France: the archaeological interaction. *Journal of European Archaeology* 1: 169–80.

Fontein, J. 2005. *The Silence of Great Zimbabwe: Contested Landscapes and the Power of Heritage*. London: University College London Press.

Fotiadis, M. 1993. Regions of the imagination: archaeologists, local people, and the archaeological record in fieldwork, Greece. *Journal of European Archaeology* 1: 151–70.

Funari, P. P. A. 2004. Conquistadors, plantations, and *quilombo*: Latin America in historical archaeological context. In M. Hall and S. W. Silliman (eds), *Historical Archaeology*, 209–29. Oxford: Blackwell.

Garazhian, O. and L. Papoli Yazdi 2008. Mortuary practices in Bam after the earthquake. *Journal of Social Archaeology* 8: 94–112.

Gilchrist, R. 1999. *Gender and Archaeology: Contesting the Past*. London: Routledge.

Given, M. 1998. Inventing the Eteocypriots: imperialist archaeology and the manipulation of ethnic identity. *Journal of Mediterranean Archaeology* 11: 3–29.

González-Ruibal, A. 2006. The dream of reason: an archaeology of the failures of modernity in Ethiopia. *Journal of Social Archaeology* 6: 175–201.

González-Ruibal, A. 2009. Vernacular cosmopolitanism: an archaeological critique of universalistic reason. In L. M. Meskell (ed.), *Cosmopolitan Archaeologies*, 113–39. Durham, NC: Duke University Press.

Gosden, C. and L. Head 1994. Landscape – a usefully ambiguous concept. *Archaeology in Oceania* 29: 113–16.

Graves-Brown, P., S. Jones, and C. Gamble (eds) 1996. *Cultural Identity and Archaeology: The Construction of European Communities*. London: Routledge.

Hall, C. 1996. Histories, empires and the post-colonial moment. In I. Chambers and L. Curti (eds), *The Post-Colonial Question: Common Skies, Divided Horizons*, 65–77. London: Routledge.

Hall, M. 1992. Small things and the mobile, conflictual fusion of power, fear, and desire. In A. Yentsch and M. Beaudry (eds), *The Art and Mystery of Historical Archaeology*, 373–99. Boca Raton, FL: CRC Press.

Hall, M. 2001. Social archaeology and the theaters of memory. *Journal of Social Archaeology* 1: 50–61.

Hall, M. 2005. Situational ethics and engaged practice: the case of archaeology in Africa. In L. M. Meskell and P. Pels (eds), *Embedding Ethics: Shifting the Boundaries of the Anthropological Profession*, 169–94. Oxford: Berg.

Hall, M. 2006. Identity, memory and countermemory: the archaeology of an urban landscape. *Journal of Material Culture* 11: 189–209.

Handler, R. 2003. Cultural property and culture theory. *Journal of Social Archaeology* 3: 353–65.

Hayden, C. 2003. *When Nature Goes Public: The Making and Unmaking of Bioprospecting in Mexico*. Princeton: Princeton University Press.

Head, L. 2000. *Second Nature: The History and Implications of Australia as Aboriginal Landscape*. Syracuse, NY: Syracuse University Press.

Higueras, A. 1995. Archaeological research in Peru: its contribution to national identity and to the Peruvian public. *Journal of the Steward Anthropological Society* 23: 391–407.

Hodder, I. 1987. The contextual analysis of symbolic meanings. In I. Hodder (ed.), *The Archaeology of Contextual Meanings*, 1–10. Cambridge: Cambridge University Press.

Hodder, I. 1991. *Reading the Past*, 2nd edition. Cambridge: Cambridge University Press.

Hodder, I. 1992. *Theory and Practice in Archaeology*. London: Routledge.

Hodder, I. 1998. The past and passion and play: Çatalhöyük as a site of conflict in the construction of multiple pasts. In L. M. Meskell (ed.), *Archaeology under Fire: Nationalism, Politics and Heritage in the Eastern Mediterranean and Middle East*, 124–39. London: Routledge.

Hodder, I. 2001. *Archaeological Theory Today*, 1st edition. Cambridge: Polity.

Hodder, I. 2003. Archaeological reflexivity and the "local" voice. *Anthropological Quarterly* 76: 55–69.

Hodder, I. 2009. Mavili's voice. In L. M. Meskell (ed.), *Cosmopolitan Archaeologies*, 184–204. Durham, NC: Duke University Press.

Hodder, I. 2010. Cultural heritage rights: from ownership and descent to justice and well-being. *Anthropological Quarterly* 83: 861–82.

Jenkins, R. 1996. *Social Identity*. London: Routledge.

Joyce, R. A. 2001. *Gender and Power in Prehispanic Mesoamerica*. Austin: University of Texas Press.

Joyce, R. A. 2004. Embodied subjectivity: gender, femininity, masculinity, sexuality. In L. M. Meskell and R. W. Preucel (eds), *A Companion to Social Archaeology*, 82–95. Oxford: Blackwell.

Joyce, R. A. 2005. Solid histories for fragile nations: archaeology as cultural patrimony. In L. M. Meskell and P. Pels (eds), *Embedding Ethics*, 253–73. Oxford: Berg.

Kalshoven, F. 2005. The protection of cultural property in the event of armed conflict within the framework of international humanitarian law. *Museum International* 57: 61–70.

Kohl, P. L. 1998. Nationalism and archaeology: on the constructions of nations and the reconstructions of the remote past. *Annual Review of Anthropology* 27: 223–46.

Kohl, P. L. and C. Fawcett (eds) 1995. *Nationalism, Politics and the Practice of Archaeology*. Cambridge: Cambridge University Press.

Lafrenz Samuels, K. 2009. Trajectories of development: international heritage management of archaeology in the Middle East and North Africa. *Archaeologies* 5: 68–91.

Lafrenz Samuels, K. 2010. Mobilizing Heritage in the Maghrib: Rights, Development, and Transnational Archaeologies. Ph.D. thesis, Department of Anthropology, Stanford University.

Layton, R. (ed.) 1994. *Who Needs the Past?: Indigenous Values and Archaeology*. London: Routledge.

Lilley, I. (ed.) 2000. *Native Title and the Transformation of Archaeology in the Postcolonial World*. Sydney: University of Sydney.

Lilley, I. 2009. Strangers and brothers? Heritage, human rights, and cosmopolitan archaeology in Oceania. In L. M. Meskell (ed.), *Cosmopolitan Archaeologies*, 48–67. Durham, NC: Duke University Press.

Lilley, I. and M. Williams 2005. Archaeological and indigenous significance: a view from Australia. In C. Mathers, T. Darvill, and B. Little (eds), *Heritage of Value, Archaeology of Renown: Reshaping Archaeological Assessment and Significance*, 227–47. Gainesville: University of Florida Press.

Long, C. and J. Sweet 2006. Globalization, nationalism and World Heritage: interpreting Luang Prabang. *South East Asia Research* 14: 445–69.

Loren, D. 2007. *In Contact: Bodies and Spaces in the Sixteenth- and Seventeenth-Century Eastern Woodlands*. Walnut Creek, CA: AltaMira Press.

Lowenthal, D. 1985. *The Past is a Foreign Country*. Cambridge: Cambridge University Press.

Lucas, G. 2004. Modern disturbances: on the ambiguities of archaeology. *Modernism/modernity* 11: 109–20.

Lynott, M. J. and A. Wylie (eds) 2000. *Ethics in American Archaeology*. Washington, DC: Society for American Archaeology.

McAtackney, L. 2011. Peace maintenance and political messages: the significance of walls during and after the Northern Irish "Troubles." *Journal of Social Archaeology* 11: 77–98.

MacEachern, S. 2007. Where in Africa does Africa start? Identity, genetics and African studies from the Sahara to Darfur. *Journal of Social Archaeology* 7: 393–412.

MacEachern, S. 2010. Seeing like an oil company's CHM programme: Exxon and archaeology on the Chad Export Project. *Journal of Social Archaeology* 10: 347–66.

McGuire, R. H. 1992. Archaeology and the first Americans. *American Anthropologist* 94: 816–36.

McGuire, R. H. 2008. *Archaeology as Political Action*. Berkeley: University of California Press.

Martindale, A. 2009. Entanglement and tinkering. *Journal of Social Archaeology* 9: 59–91.

Meskell, L. M. (ed.) 1998. *Archaeology under Fire: Nationalism, Politics and Heritage in the Eastern Mediterranean and Middle East*. London: Routledge.

Meskell, L. M. 1999. *Archaeologies of Social Life: Age, Sex, Class etc. in Ancient Egypt*. Oxford: Blackwell.

Meskell, L. M. 2001. Archaeologies of identity. In I. Hodder (ed.), *Archaeological Theory Today*, 1st edition, 187–213. Cambridge: Polity.

Meskell, L. M. 2002. The intersection of identity and politics in archaeology. *Annual Review of Anthropology* 31: 279–301.

Meskell, L. M. 2005a. Archaeological ethnography: conversations around Kruger National Park. *Archaeologies: Journal of the World Archaeology Congress* 1: 83–102.

Meskell, L. M. 2005b. Recognition, restitution and the potentials of post-colonial liberalism for South African heritage. *South African Archaeological Bulletin* 60: 72–8.

Meskell, L. M. (ed.) 2009a. *Cosmopolitan Archaeologies*. Durham, NC: Duke University Press.

Meskell, L. M. 2009b. Talking of human rights: histories, heritages, and human remains. *Reviews in Anthropology* 38: 1–19.

Meskell, L. M. 2009c. The nature of culture in Kruger National Park. In L. M. Meskell (ed.), *Cosmopolitan Archaeologies*. Durham, NC: Duke University Press, 89–112.

Meskell, L. M. 2010. Human rights and heritage ethics. *Anthropological Quarterly* 83: 839–60.

Meskell, L. M. 2011. *The Nature of Heritage: The New South Africa*. Oxford: Blackwell.

Meskell, L. M. and P. Pels (eds) 2005. *Embedding Ethics*. Oxford: Berg.

Meskell, L. M. and C. Scheermeyer 2008. Heritage as therapy: set pieces from the new South Africa. *Journal of Material Culture* 13: 153–73.

Messenger, P. M. (ed.) 1999. *The Ethics of Collecting Cultural Property*. Albuquerque: University of New Mexico Press.

Miller, D. 1988. Appropriating the state on the council estate. *Man* (N.S.) 23: 353–72.

Mills, B. J. and W. H. Walker 2008. *Memory Work: Archaeologies of Material Practices*. Santa Fe: SAR Press.

Mitchell, T. 2000. Making the nation: the politics of heritage in Egypt. In N. A. Sayyad (ed.), *Global Forms/Urban Norms: On the Manufacture and Consumption of Traditions in the Built Environment*, 212–39. London: E & F Spon/Routledge.

Mitchell, T. 2002. *Rule of Experts*. Berkeley: University of California Press.

Miura, K. 2005. Conservation of a "living heritage site": a contradiction in terms? A case study of Angkor World Heritage Site. *Conservation and Management of Archaeological Sites* 1: 3–18.

Moshenska, G. 2010. Charred churches or iron harvests? *Journal of Social Archaeology* 10: 5–27.

Mullins, P. R. 1999. *Race and Affluence: An Archaeology of African America and Consumer Culture*. New York: Kluwer Academic/Plenum Publishers.

Ndoro, W. 2001. *Your Monument, Our Shrine: The Preservation of Great Zimbabwe*. Uppsala: Uppsala University.

Orser, C. E. J. (ed.) 2000. *Race and the Archaeology of Identity*. Salt Lake City: University of Utah Press.

Özdoğan, M. 1998. Ideology and archaeology in Turkey. In L. M. Meskell (ed.), *Archaeology under Fire: Nationalism, Politics and Heritage in the Eastern Mediterranean and Middle East*, 111–23. London: Routledge.

Patterson, T. C. 1994. *Toward a Social History of Archaeology in the United States*. New York: Harcourt Brace.

Patterson, T. C. 2003. *Marx's Ghost: Conversations with Archaeologists*. Oxford: Berg.

Pauketat, T. and S. Alt 2005. Agency in a postmold? Physicality and the archaeology of culture-making. *Journal of Archaeological Method and Theory* 12: 213–36.

Politis, G. 2001. On archaeological praxis, gender bias and indigenous peoples in South America. *Journal of Social Archaeology* 1: 90–107.

Pollock, S. and C. Lutz 1994. Archaeology deployed for the Gulf War. *Critique of Anthropology* 14: 263–84.

Preucel, R. W. (ed.) 2002. *Archaeologies of the Pueblo Revolt: Identity, Meaning and Renewal in the Pueblo World*. Albuquerque: University of New Mexico Press.

Reid, D. M. 2002. *Whose Pharaohs? Archaeology, Museums, And Egyptian National Identity from Napoleon to World War I*. Berkeley: University of California Press.

Renfrew, C. 2000. *Loot, Legitimacy and Ownership: The Ethical Crisis in Archaeology*. London: Duckworth.

Rico, T. 2007. Archaeology in conflict: cultural heritage, site management and sustainable development in conflict and post-conflict states in the Middle East. London, 10–12 November 2006. *Conservation and Management of Archaeological Sites* 8: 105–7.

Rojek, C. and J. Urry (eds) 1997. *Touring Cultures: Transformations of Travel and Theory*. London: Routledge.

Rowan, Y. and U. Baram (eds) 2004. *Marketing Heritage: Archaeology and the Consumption of the Past*. Walnut Creek, CA: AltaMira Press.

Rowlands, M. 1999. Remembering to forget: sublimation as sacrifice in war memorials. In A. Forty and S. Küchler (eds), *The Art of Forgetting*, 129–45. Oxford: Berg.

Saunders, N. J. 2000. Bodies of metal, shells of memory: "trench art" and the Great War recycled. *Journal of Material Culture* 5: 43–67.

Scham, S. 1998. Mediating nationalism and archaeology: a matter of trust? *American Anthropologist* 100: 301–8.

Scham, S. 2009a. Diplomacy and desired pasts. *Journal of Social Archaeology* 9: 163–99.

Scham, S. 2009b. "Time's wheel runs back": conversations with the Middle Eastern past. In L. M. Meskell (ed.), *Cosmopolitan Archaeologies*, 166–83. Durham, NC: Duke University Press.

Scham, S. and A. Yahya 2003. Heritage and reconciliation. *Journal of Social Archaeology* 3: 399–416.

Schmidt, P. R. 1996. The human right to a cultural heritage: African applications. In P. R. Schmidt and R. McIntosh (eds), *Plundering Africa's Past*, 18–28. Bloomington: University of Indiana Press.

Schmidt, P. R. (ed.) 2009. *Postcolonial Archaeologies in Africa*. Santa Fe: SAR Press.

Schmidt, P. R. 2010. Social memory and trauma in northwestern Tanzania. *Journal of Social Archaeology* 10: 255–79.

Schmidt, P. R. and R. J. McIntosh (eds) 1996. *Plundering Africa's Past*. Bloomington: Indiana University Press.

Schmidt, P. R. and T. C. Patterson (eds) 1995. *Making Alternative Histories: The Practice of Archaeology and History in Non-Western Settings*. Santa Fe: SAR Press.

Schnapp, A. 1996. French archaeology: between national identity and cultural identity. In M. Díaz-Andreu and T. Champion (eds), *Nationalism and Archaeology in Europe*, 48–67. London: University College London Press.

Schrire, C. 1995. *Digging through Darkness: Chronicles of an Archaeologist*. Charlottesville: University Press of Virginia.

Segobye, A. K. 2005. Weaving fragments of the past for a united Africa: reflections on the place of African archaeology in the development of the continent in the 21st century. *The South African Archaeological Bulletin* 60: 79–83.

Segobye, A. K. 2006. Divided commons: the political economy of Southern Africa's cultural heritage landscapes – observations of the central Kalahari game reserve, Botswana. *Archaeologies* 2: 52–72.

Shanks, M. and C. Tilley 1987. *Social Theory and Archaeology*. Cambridge: Polity.

Shepherd, N. 2002. The politics of archaeology in Africa. *Annual Review of Anthropology* 31: 189–209.

Silliman, S. (ed.) 2008. *Collaborating at the Trowel's Edge: Teaching and Learning in Indigenous Archaeology*. Tucson: University of Arizona Press and the Amerind Foundation.

Silliman, S. 2010. Indigenous traces in colonial spaces. *Journal of Social Archaeology* 10: 28–58.

Silverman, H. and D. Fairchild Ruggles (eds) 2008. *Cultural Heritage and Human Rights*. New York: Springer.

Smith, C. 2004. *Country, Kin and Culture: Survival of an Australian Aboriginal Community*. Adelaide: Wakefield Press.

Smith, C. and H. M. Wobst (eds) 2005. *Indigenous Archaeologies: Decolonizing Theory and Practice*. London: Routledge.

Smith, L. 2004. *Archaeological Theory and the Politics of Cultural Heritage*. London: Routledge.

Thomas, J. 2001. Archaeologies of place and landscape. In I. Hodder (ed.), *Archaeological Theory Today*, 1st edition, 163–86. Cambridge: Polity.

Tilley, C. 1994. *A Phenomenology of Landscape: Places, Paths and Monuments*. Oxford: Berg.

Trigger, B. G. 1984. Alternative archaeologies: nationalist, colonialist, imperialist. *Man* (N.S.) 19: 355–70.

Trigger, B. G. 1989. *A History of Archaeological Thought*. Cambridge: Cambridge University Press.

Tunbridge, J. E. and G. Ashworth 1996. *Dissonant Heritage: The Management of the Past as a Resource in Conflict*. Chichester: John Wiley and Sons.

Ucko, P. J. (ed.) 1995. *Theory in Archaeology: A World Perspective*. London: Routledge.

van Dommelen, P. 1997. Colonial constructs: colonialism and archaeology in the Mediterranean. *World Archaeology* 28: 305–23.

van Dommelen, P. 1998. Between academic doubt and political involvement. *Journal of Mediterranean Archaeology* 11: 117–21.

Vitelli, K. D. and C. Colwell-Chanthaphonh (eds) 2006. *Archaeological Ethics*. Walnut Creek, CA: AltaMira Press.

Watkins, J. 2001. *Indigenous Archaeology*. Walnut Creek, CA: AltaMira Press.

Watkins, J. 2004. Becoming American or becoming Indian? NAGPRA, Kennewick, and cultural affiliation. *Journal of Social Archaeology* 4: 60–80.

Weiss, L. M. 2007. Heritage making and political identity. *Journal of Social Archaeology* 7: 413–31.

Wilkie, L. 2010. *The Lost Boys of Zeta Psi: A Historical Archaeology of Masculinity at a University Fraternity*. Berkeley: California University Press.

Wynn, L. L. 2008. Shape shifting lizard people, Israelite slaves, and other theories of pyramid building: notes on labor, nationalism, and archaeology in Egypt. *Journal of Social Archaeology* 8: 272–95.

Zimmerman, L. J., K. D. Vitelli, J. Hollowell-Zimmer, and R. D. Maurer (eds) 2003. *Ethical Issues in Archaeology*. Walnut Creek, CA: AltaMira Press.

12

POST-COLONIAL ARCHAEOLOGY

Chris Gosden

There is a tension in archaeology between a commitment to human unity, on the one hand, and an equally strong commitment to local cultural variability and difference, on the other. An emphasis on difference can lead to a conclusion that what divides human groups is more important than what unites them, with the worst excesses of that view being found in racism, primitivism, and notions of progress. Too singular a human story means that the world and its histories are often seen only through a western intellectual lens. Difference is contained and construed within a narrow intellectual bandwidth and a recognition of truly different histories is hard to achieve.

Post-colonial archaeology resonates strongly with the possible dissonance between difference and equality or unity. Each emphasis has historical roots. Mary Louise Pratt discusses the rise of planetary consciousness as an Enlightenment phenomenon in which the notion of the world as a whole was first comprehended and a generalized view of humanity also promulgated. Today we take for granted the idea that we can discuss human history, but it sits within a broader natural history for which Linneaus and others provided frameworks for naming and classification. This global concept, now key to western liberal thought, runs up against local claims in various ways. Today there is often a tension between world archaeology and Indigenous archaeologies, between land claims, political rights, and the heritage of Indigenous people, on the one hand, and a desire to tell a global story of human colonization, settlement, and growth, on the other. The need for both a global and a local view is clear, and current concepts such as cosmopolitanism and diaspora are means to bring both together. In what follows I shall explore colonial histories, which in the recent past have unfolded on a global scale, together with local histories of land and culture. The difference between the global and the local is a question not so much of scale, but of the intellectual frameworks used to produce overall human histories and local culturally based ones. The tension between the global and the local is best seen as an intellectual and cultural one, leading us to question whether a multivocal archaeology can compound into a global appreciation of what it means to be human.

An enormous amount has changed in the field of post-colonial archaeology in the decade since I wrote the first version of this chapter. It was commonplace, and true, ten years ago to say that topics like Indigenous archaeologies were marginal and overlooked aspects of archaeology. They were seen as minor sub-fields that had little to offer the mainstream. Now a great plethora of books and articles have appeared (some referenced in the body of this chapter) as manifestations of much practical work and vibrant debate. But the state of the world has also remained static or deteriorated in many respects. Global inequalities in terms of the distribution of wealth both within and between nations have grown. War, dispossession, and the destruction of cultural heritage are all rife. Set against this, national legislation and international covenants governing land rights and cultural heritage have marginally improved, even if implementation is patchy and poor. Moreover, social networking media are starting to make a difference to Indigenous and other critical voices, as people begin to mobilize in new ways.

In this chapter I shall take post-colonial archaeology to indicate an awareness of colonial histories, in terms both of their material and economic impacts and of the forms of thought which the colonial world produced. Often explicit in the idea of post-colonial archaeology is the need to subvert and work against the various colonial heritages to create a new future. Post-colonial archaeology is political archaeology, so that, for instance, when engaging in questions of land rights, archaeologists are not disinterestedly investigating the topic, but attempting to use archaeological material and reasoning to help a group assert their claim to land. Post-colonial archaeology takes positions contrary to archaeology as science, asserting local claims and situations over global topics, trends, and conclusions. Such opposition is changing, as we shall see.

Post-colonial archaeology is by no means a single sub-field of the discipline, but a series of overlapping areas, which include Indigenous archaeologies in which Indigenous people use and change the tools of archaeology to create their own histories, and also archaeology done in pursuit of land rights claims and other court actions (Bruchac et al. 2010; Liebmann and Rizvi 2008; Lilley 2000; Nicholas 2010). Archaeologies of colonialism have often been written from a post-colonial standpoint with emancipation from colonial legacies the ultimate goal of many. Archaeology of contested or war-torn areas, such as Kosovo, Palestine, or Iraq, has to take seriously both histori-cal legacies and the political exigencies of the present, often deriving from strong, but incommensurable claims to land and cultural herit-age. In terms of its geographical spread, post-colonial archaeology is well represented in North America, South America, Australia, New Zealand, and South Africa. The archaeology of political contest is well represented in the Middle East (Boytner et al. 2010). There is surprisingly little literature from much of Africa (although South Africa is a major exception) or from South and East Asia, but this is starting to change (Matsumoto et al. 2011; Rizvi 2006).

Post-colonial studies in archaeology have taken two basic forms: the investigation of histories of colonialism from an archaeological standpoint, often driven by Native peoples in collaboration with non-Native archaeologists; and investigating the colonial histories of archaeology, physical anthropology, and social/cultural anthropology to discern hitherto unrecognized tropes of colonialism in our studies and to start to rethink the discipline along new lines which admit a greater plurality, including approaches to history within a less scien-tific idiom than has been true with processual forms. In this critical endeavour, post-colonial archaeology blends into the postprocessual critique (Hodder 2009).

Bamiyan: local action and global outrage

In February 2001, Mullah Omar, the creator and leader of the Taliban, ordered the destruction of two statues of the Buddha from the fourth and sixth centuries AD carved into cliffs in the Bamiyan valley, Afghanistan. The statues were destroyed by artillery gunfire, mines, and dynamite over the first few weeks of March. The worldwide reaction was instantaneous and hostile, as the actions were con-demned as barbarous and an assault on the common patrimony of the world. As Bernbeck (2010: 27) has argued, "The homogenous reaction to the events in Bamiyan is an indication of a strong dominant ideology in the sphere of culture, an ideology so deeply rooted in Western and Western-influenced thinking that it is no longer questionable." In order to gain some intellectual grip on why this event occurred, historical contextualization is needed. While this is not the place to explore in any depth the colonial history of Afghanistan, the state as we now know it emerged from tensions between Russia and Great Britain in the nineteenth century over spheres of influence deriving from British India, on the one hand, and Russia's push into central Asia, on the other. The Afghan state brought together a great number of different groups (Pashtuns, Tajiks, Hazaras, Uzbeks, Turkmen, etc.) who have no necessary unity, and this internal variability has continued to confront external invasions and threats of a neo-colonial kind down to the present. The Taliban emerged out of a background of prolonged violence and religious division. As Bernbeck brings out well, the Taliban's Islamist philosophy does not accord any value to objects, other than a small number with religious significance. "Western heritage ideas bestow value on objects for such reasons as age or aesthetics. ... From a Taliban point of view, the result is a vacuous praxis of worshipping things" (Bernbeck 2010: 43–4). Taliban notions of time are quite different from images used in the West. Time is primarily a moral dimension and might be seen as a series of concentric circles emanating out from the life of Muhammad, with temporal distance from this center leading to an increase in ignorance and misunderstanding. Western cultural heritage has a linear timescale behind it – increasing time depth lends value and point to artifacts as tangible products of a distant age, so that if objects are lost, a chance to connect with that past goes with them. From a Taliban point of view, certain images, particularly of the human body, are morally dangerous and their destruction is a positive, not a negative, act. The so-called universal principles underlying cultural heritage, such as those laid out in the Convention for the Protection of World Cultural and National Heritage (UNESCO 1972) and which were strengthened partly as a result of the Bamiyan case (UNESCO 2003), directly contradict the approach of the Taliban. The universal principles are seen as moral and aesthetic at base, but they of course also have economic implications given that the global heritage industry is set up to make money from buildings, landscapes, museums, monuments, and individual artifacts deemed to be heritage. Mullah Omar was not immune to such possibilities, and in 1998 had issued a decree ordering the protection of the Buddhas after attacks by the Mujahedin which "was explicitly justified in terms of potential future financial income from tourism" (Bernbeck 2010: 36). The reasons for his rapid change of heart are complex, deriving from his disillusionment with international cultural and aid agencies, as well as various stresses within the Taliban.

Two points can be adduced from this example. Firstly, current disputes, often violent, over cultural heritage derive from complex histories of colonialism and neo-colonialism, which leave a series of unresolved aftermaths. Secondly, despite the promulgation of universal principles of cultural heritage, there is considerable debate and disagreement over material things, their histories and current significances. To generalize hugely, these often take the form of a western materialism confronting religious or spiritual values of a variety of kinds. Universal values are hard to arrive at and debates over such values might be more important than a singular agreement. The strategy pursued to date by global agencies is to develop global policies and agreements commensurate with their range. A more realistic and healthy approach might be towards identifying and debating key areas of disagreement where the values inherent in heritage can be contrasted and brought to light. The fact that people disagree about heritage is an important one of which productive use should be made. Post-colonial archaeology raises key questions of what archaeologists do, why they do it, and what forms of broader engagement they need to have whilst allowing for multiple answers to these key questions.

Post-colonial archaeology is an attempt to understand and work though the complex effects of colonialism. Archaeology has borrowed and added to a broader literature on post-colonial theory, and in the previous version of this chapter I spent some space discussing the works of Said, Bhabha, and Spivak. Such a discussion is less needed now, partly because many in the area have deeply internalized such ideas. More significantly, theory has been developed through archaeological practice, creating a more obviously post-colonial *archaeology*. In what follows I will deal briefly with the theoretical basis of attempts to understand and act against the forces of colonialism, before attempting something of a survey of recent approaches. Given the range of new material appearing, I am somewhat nervous about this and my survey will be indicative, not comprehensive. Hopefully it will show the range, vibrancy, and committed nature of the field, as well as its growing contribution to archaeology more generally. The question hanging over the field is how far we are in a post-colonial world, a question that needs a historical answer.

Understanding colonialism

Colonialism has been a feature of human history for the last five thousand years, so that it is a very big claim indeed to say that we

are now in a post-colonial era. A conventional picture of colonialism
is that power emanated from a center (Uruk, Corinth, Xi'an/Chang'an,
Tenochtitlan, or London) which drew resources to that center using
economic power and military might, impoverishing its colonies in the
process. The imposition of colonies, the population of which was
partly the impoverished and dispossessed of their homeland, helped
alienate land and resources from Native groups and in extreme cases
shifted land ownership from Native to incomer populations. Elsewhere
(Gosden 2004) I have argued that colonialism was often more varied
than this top-down notion. Decentered forms occurred, with colonialism without colonies (as in the "Greek" settlements of the first-
millennium Mediterranean) being common. Negotiated forms of
interaction also existed through so-called Middle Grounds where
power relations were fluid and varied between incomers and locals,
leading to new cultural mixtures and forms. Power relations were
key in such relations, but not easily predicted or understood, and it
was certainly not always the case that the incomers were in charge.
The most violent and usurping forms of colonialism were the most
recent and historically unusual. I have labeled these *terra nullius*
forms (Gosden 2004: chapter 6), based as they were around the
deadly fiction that land was unused and unowned in places like North
America, Australia, and New Zealand prior to colonial settlement.
Terra nullius modes of colonialism saw the eventual swamping of
Native populations by incomers, mass death through introduced
diseases and war, as well as the systematic denigration of the values
of the Natives around the general concepts of the "primitive" and
the "savage." Ultimately, racist thought created fissures within ideas
of human unity, dividing the able and governing races from their
subjects mainly on the basis of skin pigmentation. It is these effects
that post-colonial archaeology is determined to counter.

Archaeology has a key role to play in understanding colonial
forms, based as they are around materials, human bodies, and land,
all of which are amenable to archaeological investigation. Archaeology
can also probe areas of colonial experience least recorded in written
records, which include the living conditions and deaths of Natives,
slaves, and the incoming colonial poor. I have argued that modes
of power that it is useful to label as colonial have existed over
five thousand years. But for only a tenth of that time, in the post-
Columbian world, have truly violent and dispossessing modes come
into being. We risk mistaking colonialism of the last five hundred
years for all forms of colonialism. This is not to say that earlier forms
were benign: they were violent and destructive. However, it is necessary to acknowledge that modern forms of violence inherent in the

creation of modern Europe and North America are historically unusual and especially devastating. The unprecedented nature of colonialism between roughly 1492 and the early 1960s does not mean that colonialism as a whole has disappeared with its cessation; we may instead have moved into a world with new, but pernicious power structures. This is the world that archaeology now exists within and which post-colonial archaeology takes seriously.

A great number of studies have been carried out over the last decade or more which have helped expose the range and variety of colonial encounters in all parts of the globe. Silliman (2011: 146) brings out the range of European invaders into the North American continent, which included the British on the east coast and in northern Canada, the French along the Mississippi and the Great Lakes, the Spanish along the borderlands from Florida through Texas to California, the Dutch in New York, and the Russians along the Pacific coast. The key change that Silliman sees in writing new colonial histories is to re-center attention and agency on Native Americans rather than seeing the European powers as dominant (Silliman 2011: 148). This requires an understanding of the longer-term histories of Native groups which set the cultural and ecological conditions into which Europeans entered. In the process of such rethinking, the categories prehistory, historical archaeology, and ethnography need to be critically reassessed as they impose a historical trajectory on the past and a set of divisions which obscure as much as they reveal. Mallios (2006) has studied exchange relations between Algonquian Indians and Jesuits at Ajacan (1570–2) and the English at Roanoke Island (1584–90) and Jamestown (1607–12), focusing on the manner in which the commodity-oriented Europeans violated the reciprocal principles of gift exchange, leading to the destruction of Ajacan and Roanoke and the near demise of Jamestown. It was the failure of Europeans to comprehend and adapt to Algonquian norms that led to the failure of their colonizing attempts. Christina Hodge's work has questioned and eroded the absolute differences between colonizer and colonized through her analysis of the New England burial ground of Waldo Farm, Dartmouth, Massachusetts, in which Wampanoag burials were indistinguishable from those from an English Quaker background. All burials lacked grave goods and unclothed bodies were wrapped in shrouds with headstone and footstone markers. Native groups converted to Christianity, but within a religious landscape that saw differences between more hierarchical Puritan forms and the egalitarianism of the Quakers (Hodge 2005: 79). The history of Wampanoag burial sees changes from interment without grave goods earlier on to some use of grave goods around the Contact period. The lack of grave goods at Waldo Farm may have been a return to earlier Native traditions of burial, within a situation in which status and gender differences might have been manifest in other arenas (Hodge 2005: 79). Against a background of massive population decline owing to disease, the excising of Native lands, and various other forms of disruption, the adoption of Christianity might well be seen not as acculturation, but as an attempt to appropriate aspects of Quaker practice so as to maintain the community's links to ancestors and to place (Hodge 2005: 80–1). In such instances, people change in order to stay the same, as Frink (2005, 2007) also found in his studies of storage and production in a Yup'ik Eskimo village in western Alaska. The adoption of novelty is not always about change as such, but is a strategy for negotiating change in a volatile and uncertain world.

The heterogeneity of colonial encounters in Africa is also brought out by recent work there, with Portuguese, Spanish, British, French, Belgian, Italian, Danish, and Dutch interventions and colonies (Schmidt and Karega-Munene 2011: 215). Recent work by Kusimba (2004, 2009a) has emphasized that the Atlantic slave trade was echoed, if more faintly, by movements of slaves across the Indian Ocean to the sub-continent. But this was a part of broader sets of movements that brought crucible steel production probably from India to East Africa in the first and second millennia AD (Kusimba 2009b).

Colonial histories of Africa are linked into those of the African diaspora, which in their post-colonial manifestations have been embedded within a series of more general struggles through the Civil Rights movement in the 1960s and 1970s down to the present. Schmidt and Karega-Munene (2011) strongly stress that for archaeologists practicing in Africa it is impossible to ignore the fact that human rights issues, the struggles against AIDS, religious tensions, and political disenfranchisement provide a real context for fieldwork and subsequent analysis. In some ways, Africa can be seen as a key node in the colonial histories of the last five hundred years, with its links to all parts of the Americas, the north Atlantic world, including Europe, and the Indian Ocean transfers of slaves, traded goods, and technologies. Parts of this mass of connections have been charted, but they have rarely been considered as a whole (Mitchell 2005).

The question of how far we are in a post-colonial world today is one of emphasis. Formal colonies have mainly disappeared. But the structures of the world now are clearly inherited from our recent colonial past, as are many of the problems experienced today. Some of the issues facing contemporary Afghanistan, discussed above, are a case in point. From this point of view, we are traveling towards a post-colonial archaeology rather than having arrived there. The critical tools provided by post-colonial archaeology hold the promise of a more emancipatory discipline. An important element in such emancipation is that archaeology is critical of its own history and its intellectual legacies.

Disciplinary histories and current debates

As good historians, we acknowledge that the histories of our discipline influence the ways we think and act as archaeologists in the present. Histories of archaeology are now definitely plural as they vary considerably across the globe, partly owing to the entanglement of all intellectual endeavors in broader colonial histories.

Areas such as East Asia have seen a complex mixture of colonial and not-quite-colonial histories which have left their own legacies. Neither China nor Japan as a whole was formally a colony (although Manchuria was briefly a colony of Japan between 1932 and 1945). Both were profoundly influenced by the expansion of European and US power, however. Mizoguchi (2011: 82) sees the Opium Wars prosecuted by the British in China in 1839 as the start of forced modernization by the West. From this point, different trajectories have unfolded, with China developing its own intellectual traditions – Mizoguchi (2011: 82) notes "China's reluctance – in stark contrast to Japan – to modernize itself by emulating Western ways outright." This has given China a unique position within the contemporary world, in which, although influenced by outside methods and techniques, it has neither deeply partaken of outside intellectual influences, nor had to strongly react to them. Japan held both Taiwan (1895–1945) and Korea (1910–45) as colonies, helping to investigate their (pre)histories in ways that tied them into Japanese mythology, especially that surrounding the imperial family (Pai 2011). *Kokutai,* which can be translated as national body, is regarded as a key Japanese concept in which the emperor was seen as the head and the people were bodily organs, held together in a state of reciprocity. This relationship dates in its origins to the Kofun period, starting in the late seventh and early eighth centuries AD, documented both by imperial chronicles and by archaeology. The imperial lineage is linked also to developments in Korea, which was tied to Japan in this period. Crucially, the preceding Jomon period was associated with the Ainu and other Native peoples in Japan, allowing them little role in the history of the state and justifying their contemporary marginal status (Mizoguchi 2011: 81). In contrast to so-called Native populations in some other parts of the world, the Ainu are still struggling to investigate the past in their own terms. And indeed mainstream Japanese archaeology may be struggling to articulate its own contemporary view: "And now, amid globalization, both the colonized and the uncolonized in East Asia still find it difficult to find our own voices in coming to terms with what we experienced" (Mizoguchi 2011: 89–90).

As so-called points of origin of civilization and key to any global story, the pasts of the Middle East and central Asia have been constructed within a specific narrative, often by westerners. Bahrani (1998) has explored how Mesopotamia has been constructed as an originary point for world history, especially western history, as the fount of civilization. But the supposedly despotic nature of the Mesopotamian polities needed freeing through the transfer of the principles of civilization to the democratic Greeks, who then passed on the torch to those further west. In the complex constructions of Mesopotamia's past, supposed ancient despotisms and those of the present were conflated. Europe's sense of itself was as a cultural form emancipated from despotic rule through an inherent openness and a set of democratic structures. Ironically, this sense that Europe had avoided or thrown off Oriental despotism led colonial regimes to feel that they were freeing their Native subjects, allowing in turn a series of despotic regimes. Archaeology and the construction of a world past from despotism to democracy has been a key element of the West's sense of itself.

A certain amount has been done to probe the histories of our disciplines, but much thought and renovation remain necessary. As Singleton (2011: 194) has written, "If decolonization means an archaeology based on non-Western precepts and assumptions, as has been proposed for anthropology as a whole…, then archaeology has a long way to go." However, as she acknowledges, the introduction of core ideas of post-colonial theory is allowing us all to start rethinking issues of race, power, slavery, and emancipation in new ways.

Slowly becoming post-colonial: ethics, cosmopolitanism, and diaspora

Not everything is rosy within post-colonial archaeology; nor should it be portrayed as such. A key moment in the last few decades was the passing of the Native American Graves Protection and Repatriation Act (generally known as NAGPRA) in 1990. The Act concerned four types of cultural items: human remains, funerary objects (associated and unassociated with human remains), sacred objects, and items of cultural patrimony. It covered many areas of most deeply felt grievance, starting with human remains taken by state institutions under a variety of circumstances and used for research which made sense to the mainstream community but appeared as desecration to Native Americans. However, the Act pertained only to Federal Government-funded institutions, meaning that many significant collections of human remains and cultural objects were outside its scope. A key issue that has arisen in the application of the Act's provisions is that of so-called "culturally unidentifiable human remains." It has been estimated that there are something like 150,000 sets of Native American human remains in federally funded institutions, of which only around 32,000 have been repatriated, leaving the vast majority where they were (Daehnke and Lonetree 2011: 251). Remains are considered unidentifiable for a number of reasons: there is insufficient evidence to link them to known groups; they seem to be linked to groups that no longer exist; or they belong to a group that self-identifies as a group, but is not federally recognized as such (Daehnke and Lonetree 2011: 250). Issues of provenance and affiliation are obviously difficult in a world which has changed a lot over the past few centuries. However, Native American groups are frustrated by the fact that they have little say in whether remains might be deemed identifiable, as it is up to the institutions to judge whether this is the case. An Act that held great promise of healing, and has indeed brought a number of positive effects, has also created considerable frustration, contributing to a feeling of powerlessness in those who were supposed to be empowered.

We should resist the urge to create too much of a dichotomy between archaeologists working in a scientific idiom and those integrating Indigenous points of view into their research. While some tensions do exist deriving from the demands of a global story as against a local one, there is also an increasing openness to the possibility of a variety of different histories. In a useful set of exchanges brought about by an article by McGhee entitled "Aboriginalism and the Problems of Indigenous Archaeology" (2008) both tensions and an acceptance of openness were evident. McGhee's central concern is with the intellectual basis of the discipline of archaeology, the methods used, and the standards of debate and proof through which evidence and its conclusions are assessed. In his reply to his critics (McGhee 2010: 241), he cites the setting up a new First Peoples' Hall in the Canadian Museum of Civilization, which occasioned debate between the curators and some Native people who felt it reasonable to say that all the Native people of the Americas originated in Asia, on the one hand, and a small Indigenous group who wanted to stress traditions indicating local *in situ* origins, on the other. In some contexts, such as Aboriginal Australia, purely local origins are emphasized, whereas others, like Maori groups in New Zealand, have traditions of migration and settlement. Explicit in McGhee's argument is that non-Western histories do not constitute a sound basis from which empirical arguments can be evaluated and chosen between: "Perhaps its proponents should be content with the fact that Indigenous archaeology is entirely a social project, and not seek an intellectual foundation that seems impossible to construct" (McGhee 2010: 243). For those sympathetic to Indigenous archaeology, it is both a social (and political) project as well as an intellectual one, as are *all* attempts to understand history. A stress on debate and openness is key for many: "An admirable goal for archaeology… is thus forming a practice of critical multivocality in which multiple perspectives and values are brought together to expand shared historical understandings" (Colwell-Chanthaphonh et al. 2010: 233).

Deeply embedded in the Western tradition is the notion of the *polis* – a democratic community, often small and intimate, deriving from shared interests, language, and a sense of place. It is too easy to critique this concept. The original Greek *poleis* were slave-based societies in which only men had the vote. In moving too quickly to critique, however, we might miss the continuing power of the consensual and rooted society. The idea of the organic society arising spontaneously as a natural outgrowth of habitual social and cultural relations in a natural setting is writ large in the case of the nation-state (Held 2003) and lies behind the anthropological idea of culture. Interestingly, some Native groups work with a similar view of an organic community which pre-existed the devastating effects of colonialism and which can be reconstituted through recuperative action working to heal the effects of colonial histories and their contemporary consequences.

Cosmopolitanism, it might be thought, can only exist as links between a series of *poleis*, but as Clifford (1994) points out when writing of diasporas, we cannot see stable isolated communities as a norm occasionally connected up by movements of people, forced or voluntary. An important idea here is that no form of community is a natural one. Instead all communal forms need to be worked at, and this work takes place within tensions of various kinds between classes, genders, and age groups. Ideas of cosmopolitanism (Meskell 2011) and diaspora (Lilley 2000) are being worked out within archaeology to get away from the straight opposition between local Indigenous groups confronting national or trans-national organizations. The

UNESCO office in Paris, which in some ways takes survey of all the world, has its own office politics and gossip, as any localized community does. Indigenous groups do not have the ability to travel or the networked communications that UNESCO takes for granted, but they are linked through large official bodies like the International Work Group for Indigenous Affairs (IWGIA) or the Inter-Agency Support Group on Indigenous Issues at the UN, or the World Archaeological Congress, as well as a mass of more informal ties within and between nations. All global forms are locally embedded and all smaller groups have a global dimension. To some degree this has always been the case.

Stressing the complicated entanglements of local and global forces is not to undermine the emotional power of community projects with their novel sets of partnerships and potentially cathartic effects (Nicholas 2010; Phillips and Allen 2010). A striking aspect of this field is the growth of collaborations between professional archaeologists (Native or not) and communities of various kinds. We do need to think about the complicated and layered nature of all our work. When a local project is discussed in a global survey of post-colonial archaeology (e.g. Armstrong-Fumero and Gutierrez 2011; Brady and Crouch 2011), it may lose some of the emotional impact for the participants, but can be seen against a background of similar work elsewhere.

Everyone feels a sense of where they come from, even though origins are not always simple or singular. The most displaced people feel most strongly their attachment to land, culture, and human connections. Post-colonial archaeology is not just about attempting to reveal, recognize, and heal the problems of the past, but it is also about trying to move towards new futures in which emotions of belonging can be strongly and proudly felt at a local level, but also effectively mobilized at more global levels to gain recognition and the resources necessary for local cultural forms to thrive. We know we are not yet post-colonial, but carry the hope that we can become so.

Acknowledgments

I would like to thank Uzma Rizvi for sending me a copy of *Handbook of Postcolonial Archaeology* (edited by Lydon and Rizvi) before it was published and to Dan Hicks and Ian Lilley for extra references and suggestions which have improved this chapter, although not removed all of its deficiencies, which are my contribution.

References

Armstrong-Fumero, F. and J.H. Gutierrez 2011. Community heritage and partnership in Xcalakdzonot, Yucatán. In J. Lydon and U. Rizvi (eds), *Handbook of Postcolonial Archaeology*, 405–11. Walnut Creek, CA: Left Coast Press.

Bahrani, Z. 1998. Conjuring Mesopotamia: imaginative geography and a world past. In L. Meskell (ed.), *Archaeology under Fire: Nationalism, Politics and Heritage in the Eastern Mediterranean and Middle East*, 159–74. London: Routledge.

Bernbeck, R. 2010. Heritage politics: learning from Mullah Omar? In R. Boytner, L. Swartz Dodd, and B. Parker (eds), *Controlling the Past, Owning the Future*, 27–54. Tucson: University of Arizona Press.

Boytner, R., L. Swartz Dodd, and B. Parker (eds) 2010. *Controlling the Past, Owning the Future*. Tucson: University of Arizona Press.

Brady, L. and J. Crouch 2011. Partnership archaeology and indigenous ancestral engagement in Torres Strait, Northeastern Australia. In J. Lydon and U. Rizvi (eds), *Handbook of Postcolonial Archaeology*, 413–27. Walnut Creek, CA: Left Coast Press.

Bruchac, M.M., S.M. Hart, and H.M. Wobst (eds) 2010. *Indigenous Archaeologies: A Reader in Decolonization*. Walnut Creek, CA: Left Coast Press.

Clifford, J. 1994. Diasporas. *Cultural Anthropology* 9: 302–38.

Colwell-Chanthaphonh, C., T.J. Ferguson, D. Lippert, R.H. McGuire, G.P. Nicholas, J.E. Watkins, and L.J. Zimmerman 2010. The premise and promise of Indigenous archaeology. *American Antiquity* 75: 228–38.

Daehnke, J. and A. Lonetree 2011. Repatriation in the United States: the current state of NAGPRA. In J. Lydon and U. Rizvi (eds), *Handbook of Postcolonial Archaeology*, 245–55. Walnut Creek, CA: Left Coast Press.

Frink, L. 2005. Gender and the hide production process in colonial western Alaska. In L. Frink and K. Weedman (eds), *Gender and Hide Production*, 128–51. Walnut Creek, CA: AltaMira Press.

Frink, L. 2007. Storage and status in precolonial and colonial coastal western Alaska. *Current Anthropology* 48: 349–74.

Gosden, C. 2004. *Archaeology and Colonialism: Cultural Contact from 5000 BC to the Present*. Cambridge: Cambridge University Press.

Held, D. (ed.) 2003. *Taming Globalization*. Cambridge: Polity.

Hodder, I. 2009. Mavili's voice. In L. Meskell (ed.), *Cosmopolitan Archaeologies*, 184–204. Durham, NC: Duke University Press.

Hodge, C. 2005. Faith and practice at an early-eighteenth-century Wampanoag burial ground: the Waldo Farm site in Dartmouth, Massachusetts. *Historical Archaeology* 39: 73–94.

Kusimba, C. 2004. Archaeology of slavery in East Africa. *African Archaeological Review* 21: 59–88.

Kusimba, C. 2009a. Practicing postcolonial archaeology in Africa from the United States. In P.R. Schmidt (ed.), *Postcolonial Archaeologies in Africa*, 57–76. Santa Fe: SAR Press.

Kusimba, C. 2009b. Landscape, economy and trade in the Afrasian littoral: archaeological evidence from eastern Africa. In S. Falconer and C. Redman (eds), *Politics and Power: Archaeological Perspectives on the Landscapes of Early States*, 163–78. Tucson: University of Arizona Press.

Liebmann, M. and U. Rizvi (eds) 2008. *Archaeology and the Postcolonial Critique*. Lanham, MD: AltaMira Press.

Lilley, I. 2000. *Native Title and the Transformation of Archaeology in the Postcolonial World*. Walnut Creek, CA: West Coast Press.

McGhee, R. 2008. Aboriginalism and the problems of Indigenous archaeology. *American Antiquity* 73: 579–607.

McGhee, R. 2010. Of strawmen, herrings and frustrated expectations. *American Antiquity* 75: 239–43.

Mallios, S. 2006. *The Deadly Politics of Giving: Exchange and Violence at Ajacan, Roanoke and Jamestown*. Tuscaloosa: University of Alabama Press.

Matsumoto, N., H. Bessho, and M. Tomii (eds) 2011. *Coexistence and Cultural Transmission in East Asia*. Walnut Creek, CA: West Coast Press.

Meskell, L. 2011. Ethnographic interventions. In J. Lydon and U. Rizvi (eds), *Handbook of Postcolonial Archaeology*, 445–57. Walnut Creek, CA: Left Coast Press.

Mitchell, P. (ed.) 2005. *African Connections: An Archaeological Perspective on Africa and the Wider World*. Walnut Creek, CA: AltaMira Press.

Mizoguchi, K. 2011. The colonial experience of the uncolonized and the colonized: the case of East Asia, mainly as seen from Japan. In J. Lydon and U. Rizvi (eds), *Handbook of Postcolonial Archaeology*, 81–91. Walnut Creek, CA: Left Coast Press.

Nicholas, G. (ed.) 2010. *Being and Becoming Indigenous Archaeologists*. Walnut Creek, CA: Left Coast Press.

Pai, H.I. 2011. Resurrecting the ruins of Japan's mythical homelands: colonial archaeological surveys in the Korean Peninsula and heritage tourism. In J. Lydon and U. Rizvi (eds), *Handbook of Postcolonial Archaeology*, 93–112. Walnut Creek, CA: Left Coast Press.

Phillips, C. and H. Allen (eds) 2010. *Bridging the Divide: Indigenous Communities and Archaeology into the Twenty-First Century*. Walnut Creek, CA: Left Coast Press.

Pratt, M.L. 1992. *Through Imperial Eyes: Travel Writing and Transculturation*. London: Routledge.

Rivzi, U. 2006. Accounting for multiple desires: decolonizing methodologies, archaeology and the public interest. *India Review* 5: 394–416.

Schmidt, P. R. and Karega-Munene 2011. An Africa-informed view of post-colonial archaeologies. In J. Lydon and U. Rizvi (eds), *Handbook of Postcolonial Archaeology*, 215–25. Walnut Creek, CA: Left Coast Press.

Silliman, S. 2011. Writing new archaeological narratives: Indigenous North America. In J. Lydon and U. Rizvi (eds), *Handbook of Postcolonial Archaeology*, 145–63. Walnut Creek, CA: Left Coast Press.

Singleton, T. 2011. Liberation and emancipation: constructing a postcolonial archaeology of the African diaspora. In J. Lydon and U. Rizvi (eds), *Handbook of Postcolonial Archaeology*, 185–98. Walnut Creek, CA: Left Coast Press.

UNESCO 1972. *Convention for the Protection of World Cultural and National Heritage*. Paris: UNESCO.

UNESCO 2003. *Declaration concerning the Intentional Destruction of Cultural Heritage*. Paris: UNESCO.

13

ARCHAEOLOGY AND INDIGENOUS COLLABORATION

Chip Colwell-Chanthaphonh

For the master's tools will never dismantle the master's house. They may allow us temporarily to beat him at his own game, but they will never enable us to bring about genuine change.

(Lorde 1984: 113)

I believe you can *only* dismantle the master's house using the master's tools. Essentially I like the shape of the house. I just think it needs some more rooms in it, maybe a couple more wings.

(Henry Louis Gates, Jr in Slaughter 1998: 32)

For as long as there have been oppressed people, there has been the question of how they should respond to their subjugation. Audre Lorde presents one view: that oppressed people must radically challenge how systems of oppression operate. Henry Louis Gates, Jr offers the reverse: that the oppressed ought to use the master's own tools against him. Lorde argues that change has to always come from outside a corrupt system; Gates argues that positive change can only be effected from within.

This question goes to the heart of archaeology for Indigenous peoples. Around the world, they have long been the subject of archaeological research without being active participants. Over the last several generations, they have come to be the focus of incalculable archaeological grants, books, articles, lectures, exhibits, TV shows, movies, and websites. Yet they have had few roles in shaping the research that explores their past – little voice in telling their story, little control over their history.

Only in recent years have Indigenous peoples begun to broadly challenge this system, gaining influence over their own heritage and actively re-employing the tools of archaeology for their own benefit. In some cases, they have developed community-driven archaeology programs. Increasingly, they have become archaeological professionals themselves. Still other Indigenous peoples have questioned whether archaeology is so unequal, so distorted that it is irredeemable, even with their participation.

In other words, these views represent archaeology's own Lorde–Gates debate, the tangled question of what to do with the master's house of archaeology. Must Indigenous peoples change archaeology as critics, from outside archaeology's practice? Or must they effect change *as* archaeologists, from within?

Evolution and revolution

Since the first imperial armadas set sail from Europe's ports more than six hundred years ago, Europeans and their descendants have been driven by a need to explain global human diversity. After the explosion of global exploration – wholly new encounters in Africa, Asia, and the Americas – Europeans began to create a hierarchical explanatory framework for humanity. This system was fundamentally based on concepts of race, religion, and technology: a view of superficial physical characteristics, and deeply infused with a perceived natural order established by God and a deceptive assessment of different civilizations' material complexity.

In the Americas, the vast diversity of nations, chiefdoms, bands, and family groups were reduced to one single race. Europe's intelligentsia eventually settled on the term "Indians" – a misnomer taken from Columbus's geographical disorientation. In time, joined by their shared experience as colonial subjects and also inculcated with the ideology of race, the vast diversity of peoples in the Americas came to think of themselves as not just Diné or Haudenosaunee but also as "Indians." Today, the terms American Indians and Native Americans – and Native peoples and Indigenous peoples, to mean people both within and outside of North America – are employed less for their racial overtones, than as a historic-ethnic category. These terms refer to the ethnic descendants of the people who were subjected to European colonial power beginning in the late 1400s.

In addition to categorizing and mapping the human species, European explorers were fascinated by the origins of people. They sought to better understand the places of the ancient past they had "discovered," and set out to systematically document, study, and claim ancient places for their own. In the United States – from the first known looting of Indian graves in 1620 by British Pilgrims to Thomas Jefferson's scientific excavation in the 1780s to Lewis Henry Morgan's theories of social evolution in the late 1800s – Native American history became interwoven with the American colonial experience, and with time it grew to be the central focus for the burgeoning field of American archaeology (Kehoe 1998).

As archaeology became a formal discipline at the turn of the last century, countries throughout the Americas established laws that identified Native American history as an anchor for national identities. These laws privileged scientific study and interpretation above all other values and interests (see Colwell-Chanthaphonh 2005). Through these laws, academic archaeologists were granted the status as the nation's stewards of the Native American past. In practice, this meant that descendant communities had no voice in shaping and no role in caring for their own heritage. It also often translated into unequal practices in which Indian history became a national public good and a resource for science.

The conversion of Indigenous peoples from mere objects to active participants in archaeology has been a slow process. At many archaeological excavations throughout the twentieth century, Native peoples worked as silent laborers, doing most of the manual work. At the same time, many Native communities objected to how archaeology disturbed sacred places and the pilfering of ancestral cemeteries (Fine-Dare 2002). In the early 1900s, Arthur C. Parker, of Seneca descent, was among the first people from an Indian nation to become a fully fledged academic archaeologist (Colwell-Chanthaphonh 2009a). But it would be decades before other Native Americans followed in his footsteps.

In the larger context of the 1960s Civil Rights movement and Pan-Indianism, the anger over archaeological appropriations began to coalesce into social action. The call to arms for this movement was Vine Deloria, Jr's 1969 manifesto *Custer Died for Your Sins*, which characterized anthropologists as narrowly self-interested. Deloria (1988: 95) concluded his scathing critique by asking, "Why should we continue to be the private zoos for anthropologists?" Indeed, many Native peoples felt that they and their ancestors should no longer be objects for experimentation and objectified as scientific specimens. Deloria himself was of two minds – one part Lorde, one part Gates – alternately advocating building "honest, sincere, and equal" relationships (Deloria 1988: 99), but also strident confrontation (Deloria 1992).

In the same period, the US government expanded the reach of scientists by empowering them to record sites in the path of development projects like dams and highways. Laws such as the National Historic Preservation Act of 1966 gave archaeologists a clear service-oriented, applied mandate of documentation and preservation for the public good (King 2008). The birth of the cultural resource management (CRM) industry eventually led scholars to develop a "public archaeology" paradigm. CRM has encouraged archaeologists to work with multiple and diverse publics (McManamon 1991).

Many Native American religious and cultural traditions instruct believers to be caretakers of the land, decreeing that caring for the water, plants, animals, and ancient sites is a spiritual duty. In this sense, it is perhaps inevitable that Native communities would seek out the modern tools of archaeology to continue their traditional roles as stewards (Two Bears 2006). In the early 1970s, as the broader CRM movement developed, tribes across the US – ranging from the Sisseton–Wahpeton Sioux Tribe to Inuit Alaskan communities – began to participate in contract archaeology projects (Stapp and Burney 2002: 50). Many tribes had already seen, for the first time, archaeology's potential utility during land claims litigation that started in the late 1940s (Royster 2008). In the mid-1970s, tribes in the American Southwest formed some of the first formal archaeology programs run by and for Native communities (Anyon et al. 2000). Today there are more than a dozen tribally run CRM companies as well as more than a hundred Tribal Historic Preservation Offices, which provide tribes with legal status to implement federal heritage laws. The benefits of these programs include economic opportunities for Native peoples to work as archaeologists in their own communities, and also the intellectual and programmatic control to ensure that archaeological projects are responsive to local interests and values.

Indigenous participation in archaeology increased further with the passage, in 1990, of the Native American Graves Protection and Repatriation Act (NAGPRA). The nucleus of this expansive federal law provides a process for human remains and certain kinds of cultural items to be returned to lineal descendants, tribes, Alaskan Natives, Native Hawaiians, and Indian groups (Mihesuah 2000). This law has significantly rearranged modern archaeology, perhaps principally by bringing Native peoples and archaeologists together, often for the first time. The resulting dialogues have led to the kind of collaborative outreach projects and exhibits that have become a hallmark of early twenty-first-century museum practices.

NAGPRA has also given Indigenous peoples a measure of power in defining how archaeological science now operates – leading to the incorporation of Indigenous views and values into archaeological work. In turn, Indigenous communities have needed to learn the language of archaeology to converse on equal terms with scholars, leading more Native students into science careers (Nicholas 2010a). Furthermore, over the last two decades, NAGPRA's intellectual and legal constructions – most notably the concept of "cultural affilia-tion," or the shared relationship between a past group and a present-day people – have swayed archaeology's language, research questions, and political engagements (Liebmann 2008).

Over the course of the 1990s, the gulf between Native Americans and archaeologists gradually narrowed – new partnerships formed, archaeology became practiced out of tribal communities, and more Native students entered anthropology programs – often under the banner of public, community-based, or participatory archaeologies (Shackel and Chambers 2004). In the last decade, scholars have increasingly framed these kinds of endeavors within the mode of col-laboration (Colwell-Chanthaphonh and Ferguson 2008; Kerber 2006; Silliman 2008). These projects aspire to foster a kind of intel-lectual synergy that provides all participants with equal power and benefits – the construction of even-handed relationships which are ethically driven and committed to a shared purpose of better under-standing the past. Full reconciliation, however, has been far from complete, as is shown by controversies such as the Ancient One/ Kennewick Man case – the struggle for control over a 9,300-year-old skeleton found in Washington state in 1996 – and the simple fact that fewer than twenty Ph.D. archaeologists, out of several thousand, today claim a Native American ethnic identity (Lippert 2008a: 121).

Although in many ways the epicenter of the Indigenous critique has been in North America, these tremors of change have been felt around the globe. The world-wide aspect of this movement is impor-tant because it provides a wealth of comparative case studies and illustrates how the theoretical ideas of Indigenous participation are being applied in multiple and myriad local contexts.

Reaching back to the 1970s, Latin American social archaeology, undergirded by Marxist thought, had advocated a critical use of archaeology to uncover the exploitation of Indigenous peoples (Patterson 1994). Today, this tradition has shifted into a call for Latin American public archaeology to move "into the real world of eco-nomic conflict and political struggle" (Funari 2001: 239). In this mode, scholars seek out meaningful engagements with Indigenous communities, and show how archaeology shapes local communities, Indigenous identities, and access to resources (Gordillo 2009; Jofré 2007; Ren 2006). These studies range from ethnographically oriented research to illuminate local perspectives – economic, religious, political – on heritage sites (Breglia 2005; Frühsorge 2007; Gnecco and Hernández 2008), to analyses that grapple with Indigenous theory and knowledge systems to interpret ancient sites and cultural landscapes (Green et al. 2003; Haber 2007a).

In Africa, many descendant communities have been alienated from their own history (Hall 1984), a fact that has prompted calls for benefits to flow to Indigenous communities and "integrating the indigenous traditional and scientific pathways to knowledge" (Ndoro 1994: 621). New research is showing how to collaboratively incorporate local perspectives in African archaeology, by establishing direct community involvement in heritage management with a focus on economic development and institution building (Moser et al. 2002; Pwiti and Chirikure 2008; Schmidt 2010).

In Australia, the battles over heritage sites such as Uluru/Ayers Rock and the reburial of human remains has made the public acutely aware of the tension between archaeologists and Aboriginal communities (Webb 1987; Whittaker 1994). Aboriginal peoples themselves have directly and openly demanded respect (Langford 1983), as there has been a growing awareness of how Australia's Aboriginal past has been appropriated to provide a deep history for the young nation (Bryne 1996). In parallel with the United States and elsewhere, collaboration situated within the post-colonial mode has emerged as a new form of ethics-driven research which incorporates Aboriginal "ways of seeing" (Lilley 2009; Roberts et al. 2005; C. Smith and Jackson 2008).

These collective efforts – linked by a common concern for the social context of archaeology, but separated by their local contexts – constitute a major paradigm shift operating on a global level. They also illustrate the challenges and areas for growth as this approach continues. For example, while, increasingly, Indigenous knowledge systems are recognized as valid in such countries as South Africa and India, there remain many questions about how alternative non-western intellectual frameworks should be balanced or integrated with scientific processes in actual practice (Green 2008). Research in Canada has inspired warnings of how collaboration may merely be used as a discourse to mask ongoing exploitation of Indigenous communities (La Salle 2010), and work in Ecuador illustrates how archaeologists continue to identify themselves as the "rightful heirs" of the past (Benavides 2009).

The latest attempt to label the importance of participation by descendant communities has produced the concept of Indigenous archaeology. This concept has dramatically changed since it was first introduced (Nicholas and Andrews 1997; C. Smith and Wobst 2005; Watkins 2000), but is now defined as an array of practices conducted by, for, and with Indigenous communities to challenge the discipline's intellectual breadth and political economy (Colwell-Chanthaphonh et al. 2010: 228). The "by, for, and with" aspect makes clear this paradigm's non-exclusive aims: it refers to Native peoples *as* archaeologists, archaeologists working *on behalf of* Native peoples, and archaeologists working *in collaboration with* Native peoples (Nicholas et al. 2008). This definition also underscores its aspiration to actively contribute to the field's intellectual growth, even as it seeks to profoundly alter the relationship of power between archaeologists and their subjects. This paradigm is now clearly seen as international, and is no way limited to the "settler societies" of North America and Oceania (Bruchac et al. 2010). Indigenous archaeology is the application of the ways descendants relate to objects, historical knowledge, ancestors, ancient places, and cultural resources (Lippert 2008b). In practice, this means connecting communities to their own heritage by equalizing power relationships and creating mutually beneficial projects. Only in recent years have projects that incorporate this paradigmatic approach been applied in specific case studies (Atalay 2007; Wilcox 2009). Although this approach is just beginning, it has the potential to extend Indigenous perspectives and participation deeply into the field's daily practices. Indigenous archaeology is showing how Indigenous peoples and their supporters can effect change from within.

Traditions and contributions

Indigenous approaches in archaeology grow out of several theoretical traditions. In the broader context of the social sciences, this paradigm's intellectual progenitor is postmodern theory. In the 1970s, philosophers began a radical critique of the modernist tradition, the European Enlightenment ideal of human progress through the scientific discovery of objective truths (Foucault 1980). Postmodern theorists explored the contingent nature of reality and focused on power relations, particularly as they are shaped by language, space, sexuality, and history. Linked to postmodern theory is post-colonial theory, which concerned itself specifically with how the last five hundred years of Euro-American colonialism have historically defined economic, political, and cultural relations (Said 1978). Both postmodernism and post-colonialism have provided the framework for Indigenous scholars to critique the anthropological method – and also offer avenues for *de*colonization, restructuring the social sciences so that they are productive resources for Indigenous communities (L. T. Smith 1999; W. A. Wilson and Yellow Bird 2005).

These ideas also influenced archaeology's own "post-" paradigm: postprocessualism. In the 1960s, the New Archaeology movement (also known as processualism) sought to formulate scientific laws, explain sociological processes, and devise probabilistic predications (Martin 1971). Postprocessualism was a reaction to this definition of archaeology's goals, instead proposing that the past must always be interpreted, and that these interpretations are inevitably partial and qualified. Scholars advocating this approach focused not on universal laws of material culture, but on the particularities of the human experience, with a particular interest in symbolism, identity, gender, and a deep concern with understanding how methods construct and bias facts (Earle and Preucel 1987). Postprocessualism is an umbrella term that covers still other types of archaeology, such as feminist and Marxist approaches, which have also informed and relate to the Indigenous critique (Conkey 2005; McGuire 2008).

The transformation of Indigenous peoples from object of study to participants in the study of their own past has contributed to archaeology's theoretical development. One major contribution is the reinsertion of oral tradition into archaeological analysis. In anthropology's early days, Native oral tradition – histories passed through the generations as unwritten narratives – was considered a vital tool for interpreting ancient sites (e.g. Cushing 1888). However, the next generation of researchers rejected the veracity of oral traditions (Lowie 1915). By the 1940s, the US court system helped re-establish the role of oral traditions as a viable source of historical data by allowing traditional knowledge to serve as evidence in land rights cases (e.g. Hart 1995). When NAGPRA became law in 1990, it included oral tradition as one of ten lines of evidence for determining cultural affiliation; in legal terms, oral tradition was suddenly on an equal footing with archaeology, and work began in earnest to understand what oral narratives could say about the past (Ferguson 2004). Much of this scholarship was able to draw from new research on oral tradition methodologies and the linking of scientific inquiry with Indigenous traditional knowledge (Cajete 1999; Vansina 1985). Nevertheless, some scholars have continued to question the role of oral tradition in archaeology (Mason 2006).

Using oral tradition as a complement to archaeology has now surpassed its legalistic purposes as a means of offering novel hypotheses and new analytical frameworks. For example, Wesley Bernardini's

(2005) research in the American Southwest used Hopi oral traditions to create hypotheses about ancient migration pathways. These hypotheses were then evaluated using sophisticated analyses of architecture, demography, rock art, and ceramic compositional study. By grounding his assumptions in the ideas of the culture he was studying, Bernardini was able to propose more informed and historically nuanced hypotheses. The result was a study that provided a respectful inquiry into the accuracy of historical processes recorded within Hopi traditional knowledge. Another example is Roger Echo-Hawk's (2000) provocative study arguing that Arikara narratives accurately document millennia of history – from the first migrants to settle the New World, to the Arikara's founding of their North Dakota homelands. Echo-Hawk shows the possibility of an "ancient American history" that harmoniously unifies oral records and the archaeological record. These examples demonstrate where oral tradition can be used outside of political or legal purposes, why archaeologists need to collaborate with Indigenous communities, and how Indigenous oral literatures rework archaeology to incorporate new propositions that explain the phenomena of history (Ferguson 2009; Whiteley 2002).

Another major contribution of Indigenous participation in archaeology has been its emphasis on multivocality. Literary theorist Mikhail Bakhtin was among the first to explore this concept, suggesting how multiple voices can come together in a single text. Examining the novels of Fyodor Dostoevsky, Bakhtin (1984: 18) described them as "constructed not as the whole of a single consciousness, absorbing other consciousnesses as objects into itself, but as a whole formed by the interaction of several consciousnesses, none of which entirely becomes an object for the other." Ideally, the goal of multivocal texts is not to create a unified narrative, but to bring together multiple perspectives to expose how each voice bares and veils different truths. In archaeology, Ian Hodder (1999) has argued that researchers have a duty to include interpretations of diverse individuals and groups, to make archaeology relevant to them but also to provide better interpretations of the past. More recently, Hodder (2008: 196) has called for a "deeper multivocality" that moves beyond mere dialogue to pursue a fully reflexive (or self-aware) methodology.

This notion of deeper multivocality can already be found in projects that are premised on a commitment to Indigenous collaboration. For example, Sonya Atalay (2008) has illustrated how the tools and worldviews of North American Ojibwe culture can inform archaeological interpretation and representation. Atalay argues that the goal is to creatively blend western and Ojibwe perspectives. The aim is not a separate-but-equal doctrine – in which two narrative streams are simply placed side-by-side – but a "comprehensive approach" that braids these narratives from a project's beginning to end (Atalay 2008: 34). As a case study, Atalay discusses an exhibition at the Ziibiwing Cultural Center of the Saginaw Chippewa Indians of Michigan, which was collaboratively constructed, bilingual (Anishinabemowin and English), and offered complex, multi-layered interpretations for objects. Another example is the San Pedro Ethnohistory Project, which used the archaeological study of a southern Arizona valley as a basis to elicit tribal histories and cultural values from four distinct Native communities (Ferguson and Colwell-Chanthaphonh 2006). The result was a project that reveals the ways in which these diverse narrative streams converge to enhance, deepen, and humanize historical understandings of changing land use patterns through time.

Other contributions to archaeological theory include a focus on the importance of place and landscape archaeology (Fowles 2010; Martinez 2006); ethnogenesis, cultural change and continuity (Ferguson 2007; Silliman 2009); how language affects archaeological interpretations (Colwell-Chanthaphonh and Ferguson 2006; Silliman 2005); and the symbolic power of the past's sacred hold (Kuwanwisiwma 2002; White Deer 1997). Through these intellectual contributions, researchers are making clear that Native peoples are not against science – only against scientific theories and practices that belittlingly dismiss their own values and viewpoints, their own rights and experiences.

The philosopher Alison Wylie (2008a, 2008b) has argued that the inclusion of Native perspectives is not anathema to archaeological science, but a necessary feature of it. In its ideal form, science is open to all views because it must always avoid the risks of intellectual insularity and entrenchment. Wylie proposes that it is precisely through collaborative engagement with descendant communities that archaeologists can critically evaluate their own knowledge systems and practices. Moreover, historical inquiry requires collecting as many sources of data as possible and avoiding an a priori privileging of one group's knowledge system. As Bruce Trigger (2008: 190) has written, "[T]he more questions that are asked and the more narratives of the past that are formulated the better. Because of that, I oppose the idea that any specific group should be accorded an exclusive right to control the interpretation of the past." Incorporating Indigenous perspectives into archaeology need not arise out of moral or political arguments; rather, it fulfills our commitments to do good science.

At the same time, these projects have acknowledged that politics and power do matter: they confront how crafting narratives of the past can impact economic relations (as in tourism, land control) and socio-political dynamics (rights and access to artifacts and sites). Hence, still another contribution of this paradigm has been its engagement with issues of intellectual property and law, nationalism and colonialism, and finding meaningful endeavors that are mutually beneficial for both scholarly and descendant communities (Dowdall and Parrish 2003; Nicholas and Bannister 2004; Preucel and Cipolla 2008). For the most part, Indigenous participation has shown that there is a fallacious divide between history and heritage – where "history" is the scholarly pursuit to explain the past and "heritage" converts historical interpretations into a political tool (Lowenthal 1996: xi). This is a false dichotomy because it presents archaeological interests as politically indifferent, the mere search for objective truth, and it treats non-archaeological interests as driven solely by politics. In fact, all history is political; all heritage is a battle for history (Gero et al. 1983; Logan and Reeves 2009). Rather than imagining a neat dichotomy between history and heritage, Indigenous projects have set out to explore how archaeology can balance its scientific interests while acknowledging its political effects in the present.

Because this balancing act can create conflicting obligations, Indigenous archaeology has advanced a dialogue on the discipline's ethical duties (Watkins 2003). For example, scholars have explored how, in the context of heritage claims, underlying the principle of stewardship is a conflict between the preservation of physical objects and the preservation of intangible culture (Colwell-Chanthaphonh 2009b; Groarke and Warrick 2006). This tension relates to how claims for the universal value of heritage as a shared resource for humanity often displaces and excludes local peoples from the cultural spaces on which they depend (Bryne 2009; Meskell 2009). To successfully mediate these conflicts – to construct sound philosophical bases for consistent and fair decisions – a commitment to ethical discourse is vital in archaeology's collaborative age (Meskell and Pels 2005).

At the beginning of active Indigenous participation in archaeology, T. J. Ferguson (1984) explained that the ethics and values of tribal archaeology programs are based on the needs of communities for cultural preservation and land management. Collaborative, community-based, and tribally run projects are often applied projects, demonstrating how archaeological theory and practice can contribute to the well-being of living Native communities (Dongoske et al. 2000). More recently, Ferguson (2003) has explained that these projects are not only more often applied, but also more anthropological than most mainstream archaeological projects. Archaeologists long simply used material culture to explain the past or human behavior, which in turn advanced scientific knowledge. Today, "reciprocal archaeology" with tribes uses material culture, traditional history, kinship, language, living culture, and religion for the purposes of furthering scientific knowledge, but also for ecotourism, education, land claims, resource management, repatriation, employment, and improving a community's social life. In this way, Indigenous archaeologies are thriving as one of the few endeavors that embraces all of anthropology's traditional sub-disciplines – ethnography, archaeology, linguistics, biology – while seeking to benefit the very communities under study.

Problems and prospects

There are at least three major potential problems with the incorporation of Indigenous views and values into archaeology, revealing the potential limits of this emerging paradigm.

First is the Indigeneity Problem – how the term "Indigenous" is itself fraught with historical baggage and conceptual inaccuracies. The very concept of "Indigenous" is an ideological construct, born out of the colonial experience. To maintain the term is in some measure to perpetuate the colonial system, since Indigenous peoples have had little role in defining what it meant to be "Indigenous" (Haber 2007b: 218). On different local, national, and international levels, the term is used strategically to serve distinct interests (Merlan 2009). Others see dilemmas in how archaeologists construct notions of the Indigenous through collaborative practices. Robert McGhee (2008), for example, has argued that Indigenous archaeology mistakenly depends on the idea of essentialized Indians – people with a timeless, immutable, blood-bound connection to their Native identity. Roger Echo-Hawk has also launched an extended critique of Indigenous archaeology, accusing Indigenous practitioners of reifying false biological categories of race (Echo-Hawk 2010; Echo-Hawk and Zimmerman 2006). Like McGhee, Echo-Hawk condemns Indigenous archaeology for propagating a counterfeit racial ideology that construes Indians as Others, made innately special and different.

No doubt the word "Indigenous" is historically complex, politically charged, and easily misunderstood. Names convey and create power. But this critique should be applied to all archaeological practices of naming: for example, the power of archaeologists to invent archaeological cultures, or to define people as "prehistoric," existing beyond history's reach (Matthews 2007). Any archaeology that seeks to categorize a group of people will face problems of categorization. Arguably, while most archaeologists today uncritically employ terms like "Clovis" or "Maya" or "Indian," it is precisely those scholars working out of the Indigenous critique who have begun to challenge and dismantle easy categories of difference (Bray 2003: 111).

The question "Who is Indigenous?" is slippery and difficult to answer directly because the category is not fixed and timeless, but relational. A cultural group might be newcomers in one period, but after a thousand years of making a place home become the "Indigenous" population. In this way, "one's 'indigenousness' is not absolute, but variable, and its characteristics are defined relative to encounters with people newer to a place" (Wobst 2010: 19). As Haber (2007b: 216) puts it, "If we are to accept the meaning of *Indigenous* as referring to the people who lived here before the colonizers arrived, a relational consideration of that term is unavoidable. ... This means that there is nothing in itself to be considered Indigenous or non-Indigenous. Instead, these are positions – sometimes quite mobile – that are embedded in networks knitted by colonial relations." The term Indigenous, in other words, defines those being categorized – and also those doing the categorizing.

The Indigeneity Problem only limits Indigenous archaeology's prospects if this paradigm centers its practice on defending racial boundaries. Instead, it must use this term as a springboard to explore how identities are always itinerant, living, born of language, land, and beliefs (Haber 2007b: 225). In the twenty-first century, the Indigenous should be about self-definition (Castañeda 2004); archaeologists must work to ensure that their terms do not diminish the sovereignty of people to determine their own identities (Paradies 2006). Furthermore, although the term of "Indigenous" emphasizes this archaeology's focus on Native peoples, its primary lens is colonialism. Indigenous archaeology's common denominator is not racial constructs, but rather the colonial context that has empowered scientists to define the "Other," control heritage resources, and interpret the past (Wobst 2010: 21). In this way, Indigenous archaeology does not serve as a racial-political gatekeeper of who is "Indigenous" (Muehlebach 2001), but works to explicate the impacts of colonialism on not just the Maya and Maasai, but also the Sami of northern Europe and Ainu of Japan (Aikio and Aikio 1994; Hirofumi 2009).

Second is the Propaganda Problem – the potential manipulation of archaeology by Indigenous people for their own narrow political ends. As Ian Hodder (2008: 199) asserts, "[P]reviously marginal groups or indigenous groups are as capable as any other group of neo-nationalism." Some consider Indigenous interventions in archaeology to be a purely political exercise. For example, a recent controversy at Mesa Verde National Park, in which the bookstore removed all books with the word "Anasazi" in the title – an offensive term to Pueblo tribes because of its Navajo etymology – could be interpreted as a political maneuver that has nothing to do with understanding history and everything to do with arbitrating heritage claims (Colwell-Chanthaphonh 2009c).

Indeed, such cases perhaps do illustrate how archaeology can be directed for political purposes. It is clear that the very ideas of "heritage" (L. Smith 2006) and "cultural property" (Carman 2005) are not ready-made things in the world, but constructed through specific socio-cultural processes. As such, they may be subject to exploitation by Indigenous communities for their own political welfare. But, again, this problem is not limited to Indigenous approaches. Studies of nationalism, for example, have demonstrated that archaeology everywhere has been employed to achieve both positive and negative political goals (e.g. Kohl et al. 2007). To accuse Indigenous archaeology of a unique political motivation while defining mainstream archaeology as apolitical ignores how politics pervades all science (Wylie 2003). Thus, the question is not about *whether* archaeology is political, but *what* those politics will be. Indigenous archaeologies, though by no means perfect, at least, are honestly grappling with what kind of politics are ethically coherent and scientifically sound.

Third is the Disagreement Problem – when archaeological and Indigenous theories collide and interpretations conflict. One might consider disagreements ranging from the body/soul debate (whether human spirits outlive their bodies or bodies are absent a soul) to the question of Native American origins (whether they migrated from Asia or people emerged from the womb of the earth).

But it is a misreading of Indigenous, collaborative, and community-based archaeologies to expect them to always resolve difference. Rather, these methods only require negotiation – that researchers respect and seriously consider these alternative views. Such disagreements are real, and at times perhaps irresolvable, but do not preclude dialogue (Zimmerman 2008). The Indigenous critique does not demand consensus, capitulation, or undue deference. The goal of this paradigm is not a *celebratory* multivocality, but a *critical* multivocality in which "[k]nowledge claims can be scrutinized and evaluated according to standards of good science (broadly defined), common sense, and critical thinking; standards such as internal coherence, consistency, explanatory power, reliability, contextual depth (match with other local evidence) and breadth (application to other situations), correspondence, and consequences" (Nicholas and Hollowell 2007: 75). Multivocality is not a lessening of a science's interpretive encumbrance, but actually represents an added burden. Many proponents of this paradigm would agree with Trigger (2008: 190) that "[m]ultivocality enhances rather than relieves the need for archaeologists to weed out erroneous assumptions and interpretations and to synthesize divergent viewpoints to produce more holistic explanations of the past."

In practice, disagreement can be beneficial because such disjunctures expose false assumptions, weak hypotheses, and historical inaccuracies. All discord may not be resolved, but science already has the built-in tools to help mediate disagreements. Scientists constantly disagree. And the process of science allows multiple hypotheses to be tested, tried, deliberated, accepted, rejected. Some old theories persist; others give way to new ideas. Most advocates of Indigenous participation are not rejecting this overarching process – only a process that instinctively dismisses traditional knowledge. Science does not require consensus, and neither does science in the Indigenous mode.

These three problems are raised to illustrate that the Indigenous paradigm is in its infancy, still in the process of imagining what it could and should be. In the end, success for this paradigm may depend less on the development of a perfect approach, and more on pushing the larger field towards new inclusive methods and theories. As George Nicholas (2010b) has recently written, the goal of Indigenous archaeology should be to transform its marginalized status into the mainstream – to incorporate community-based, ethno-critical (an analysis of difference that avoids binaries such as us/them, Western/non-Western, history/myth), and reflexive methods and modes of interpretation into all archaeological practice. When the next edition of *Archaeological Theory Today* comes out – if its proponents are successful – what we now call Indigenous archaeology might just be called good archaeology.

Conclusion

In response to the dilemma of the master's house, Sonya Atalay (2006: 295) has argued that archaeology's colonial history can be overcome – through critical reflection and multivocal methodologies – and positively contribute to the well-being of descendant communities. This process of decolonization can occur from within because "the discipline of archaeology is not inherently good or bad; it is the application and practice of the discipline that has the potential to disenfranchise and be used as a colonizing force" (Atalay 2008: 33). In this way, Indigenous archaeologies seek not to dismantle the discipline of archaeology, but to reimagine and remake contemporary archaeology. Indigenous archaeologies seek mainly to contribute to the field's development – constructing more rooms for more people, new windows for new views.

Clearly, the inclusion of more Indigenous peoples as professional archaeologists will be a central part of this process, even as we must confront the ongoing challenges that impede opening the discipline to historically disadvantaged and alienated communities (Norder 2007; C. L. Wilson 2007). But more, we must understand that simply incorporating Indigenous peoples into the field is not enough. We must change archaeology's fundamental political economy – no small task – so that multiple ways of seeing and being, diverse voices, and culturally sensitive practices can be married to the useful tools of scientific archaeology.

References

Aikio, M. and P. Aikio 1994. A chapter in the history of the colonization of Sami lands: the forced migration of Norwegian reindeer Sami to Finland in the 1800s. In R. Layton (ed.), *Conflict in the Archaeology of Living Traditions*, 116–30. London: Routledge.

Anyon, R., T. J. Ferguson, and J. R. Welch 2000. Heritage management by American Indian tribes in the Southwestern United States. In F. P. McManamon and A. Hatton (eds), *Cultural Resource Management in Contemporary Society: Perspectives on Managing and Presenting the Past*, 120–41. London: Routledge.

Atalay, S. 2006. Indigenous archaeology as decolonizing practice. *American Indian Quarterly* 30: 280–310.

Atalay, S. 2007. Global application of Indigenous archaeology: community based participatory research in Turkey. *Archaeologies* 3: 249–70.

Atalay, S. 2008. Multivocality and Indigenous archaeologies. In J. Habu, C. Fawcett, and J.M. Matsunaga (eds), *Evaluating Multiple Narratives: Beyond Nationalist, Colonialist, and Imperialist Archaeologies*, 29–44. New York: Springer.

Bakhtin, M. 1984. *Problems of Dostoevsky's Poetics*. Minneapolis: University of Minnesota Press.

Benavides, O.H. 2009. Disciplining the past, policing the present: the postcolonial landscape of Ecuadorian nostalgia. *Archaeologies* 5: 134–60.

Bernardini, W. 2005. *Hopi Oral Tradition and the Archaeology of Identity*. Tucson: University of Arizona Press.

Bray, T.L. 2003. The politics of an Indigenous archaeology. In T. Peck, E. Siegfried, and G.A. Oetelaar (eds), *Indigenous People and Archaeology: Proceedings of the 32nd Annual Chacmool Conference*, 108–13. Calgary: Archaeological Association of the University of Calgary.

Breglia, L.C. 2005. Keeping world heritage in the family: a genealogy of Maya labour at Chichén Itzá. *International Journal of Heritage Studies* 11: 385–98.

Bruchac, M.M., S.M. Hart, and H.M. Wobst (eds) 2010. *Indigenous Archaeologies: A Reader on Decolonization*. Walnut Creek, CA: Left Coast Press.

Bryne, D. 1996. Deep nation: Australia's acquisition of an Indigenous past. *Aboriginal History* 20: 82–107.

Bryne, D. 2009. Archaeology and the fortress of rationality. In L. Meskell (ed.), *Cosmopolitan Archaeologies*, 68–88. Durham, NC: Duke University Press.

Cajete, G. 1999. *Native Science: Natural Laws of Interdependence*. Santa Fe: Clear Light Books.

Carman, J. 2005. *Against Cultural Property: Archaeology, Heritage, and Ownership*. London: Duckworth.

Castañeda, Q.E. 2004. "We are not Indigenous!": an introduction to the Maya identity of Yucatan. *Journal of Latin American and Caribbean Anthropology* 9: 36–63.

Colwell-Chanthaphonh, C. 2005. The incorporation of the Native American past: cultural extermination, archaeological protection, and the Antiquities Act of 1906. *International Journal of Cultural Property* 12: 375–91.

Colwell-Chanthaphonh, C. 2009a. *Inheriting the Past: The Making of Arthur C. Parker and Indigenous Archaeology*. Tucson: University of Arizona Press.

Colwell-Chanthaphonh, C. 2009b. The archaeologist as a world citizen: on the morals of heritage preservation and destruction. In L. Meskell (ed.), *Cosmopolitan Archaeologies*, 140–65. Durham, NC: Duke University Press.

Colwell-Chanthaphonh, C. 2009c. Myth of the Anasazi: archaeological language, collaborative communities, and the contested past. *Public Archaeology* 8: 191–207.

Colwell-Chanthaphonh, C. and T.J. Ferguson 2006. Rethinking abandonment in archaeological contexts. *SAA Archaeological Record* 6: 37–41.

Colwell-Chanthaphonh, C. and T.J. Ferguson (eds) 2008. *Collaboration in Archaeological Practice: Engaging Descendant Communities*. Lanham, MD: AltaMira Press.

Colwell-Chanthaphonh, C., T.J. Ferguson, D. Lippert, R.H. McGuire, G.P. Nicholas, J.E. Watkins, and L.J. Zimmerman 2010. The premise and promise of Indigenous archaeology. *American Antiquity* 75: 228–38.

Conkey, M.W. 2005. Dwelling at the margins, action at the intersection? Feminist and Indigenous archaeologies. *Archaeologies* 1: 9–59.

Cushing, F.H. 1888. Preliminary notes on the origin, working hypothesis, and primary researches of the Hemenway Southwestern Archaeological Expedition. *Proceedings of the International Congress of the Americanists* 7: 151–94.

Deloria, V., Jr 1988. *Custer Died for Your Sins: An Indian Manifesto*. Norman: University of Oklahoma Press.

Deloria, V., Jr 1992. Indians, archaeologists, and the future. *American Antiquity* 57: 595–8.

Dongoske, K.E., M. Aldenderfer, and K. Doehner (eds) 2000. *Working Together: Native Americans and Archaeologists*. Washington, DC: Society for American Archaeology.

Dowdall, K.M. and O.O. Parrish 2003. A meaningful disturbance of the earth. *Journal of Social Archaeology* 3: 99–133.

Earle, T.K. and R.W. Preucel 1987. Processual archaeology and the radical critique. *Current Anthropology* 28: 501–38.

Echo-Hawk, R. 2000. Ancient history in the New World: integrating oral traditions and the archaeological record in deep time. *American Antiquity* 65: 267–90.

Echo-Hawk, R. 2010. *The Magic Children: Racial Identity at the End of the Age of Race*. Walnut Creek, CA: Left Coast Press.

Echo-Hawk, R. and L.J. Zimmerman 2006. Beyond racism: some opinions about racialism and American archaeology. *American Indian Quarterly* 30: 461–85.

Ferguson, T.J. 1984. Archaeological values in a tribal cultural resource management program at the Pueblo of Zuni. In E.L. Green (ed.), *Ethics and Values in Archaeology*, 224–35. New York: Free Press.

Ferguson, T.J. 2003. Anthropological archaeology conducted by tribes: traditional cultural properties and cultural affiliation. In S.D. Gillespie and

D. L. Nichols (eds), *Archaeology Is Anthropology*, 137–44. Washington, DC: American Anthropological Association.

Ferguson, T. J. 2004. Academic, legal, and political contexts of social identity and cultural affiliation research in the Southwest. In B. J. Mills (ed.), *Identity, Feasting, and the Archaeology of the Greater Southwest*, 27–41. Boulder: University Press of Colorado.

Ferguson, T. J. 2007. Zuni traditional history and cultural geography. In D. A. Gregory and D. R. Wilcox (eds), *Zuni Origins: Toward a New Synthesis of Southwestern Archaeology*, 377–403. Tucson: University of Arizona Press.

Ferguson, T. J. 2009. Improving the quality of archaeology in the United States through consultation and collaboration with Native Americans and descendant communities. In L. Sebastian and W. D. Lipe (eds), *Archaeology and Cultural Resource Management: Visions for the Future*, 169–93. Santa Fe: SAR Press.

Ferguson, T. J. and C. Colwell-Chanthaphonh 2006. *History Is in the Land: Multivocal Tribal Traditions in Arizona's San Pedro Valley*. Tucson: University of Arizona Press.

Fine-Dare, K. S. 2002. *Grave Injustice: The American Indian Repatriation Movement and NAGPRA*. Lincoln: University of Nebraska Press.

Foucault, M. 1980. *Power/Knowledge: Selected Interviews and Other Writings, 1972–1977*. New York: Pantheon.

Fowles, S. M. 2010. The Southwest school of landscape archaeology. *Annual Review of Anthropology* 39: 453–68.

Frühsorge, L. 2007. Archaeological heritage in Guatemala: Indigenous perspectives on the ruins of Iximche. *Archaeologies* 3: 39–58.

Funari, P. P. A. 2001. Public archaeology from a Latin American perspective. *Public Archaeology* 1: 239–43.

Gero, J. M., D. M. Lacy, and M. L. Blakey (eds) 1983. *The Socio-Politics of Archaeology, Research Report No. 23*. Amherst: University of Massachusetts, Department of Anthropology.

Gnecco, C. and C. Hernández 2008. History and its discontents: stone statues, Native histories, and archaeologists. *Current Anthropology* 49: 439–66.

Gordillo, G. 2009. The ruins of ruins: on the preservation and destruction of historical sites in northern Argentina. In L. Mortensen and J. Hollowell (eds), *Ethnographies and Archaeologies: Iterations of the Past*, 30–54. Gainesville: University Press of Florida.

Green, L. F. 2008. Anthropologies of knowledge and South Africa's Indigenous knowledge systems policy. *Anthropology Southern Africa* 31: 48–57.

Green, L. F., D. R. Green, and E. G. Neves 2003. Indigenous knowledge and archaeological science: the challenges of public archaeology in the Reserva Uaçá. *Journal of Social Archaeology* 3: 366–98.

Groarke, L. and G. Warrick 2006. Stewardship gone astray? Ethics and the SAA. In C. Scarre and G. F. Scarre (eds), *The Ethics of Archaeology: Philosophical Perspectives on Archaeological Practice*, 163–77. Cambridge: Cambridge University Press.

Haber, A. F. 2007a. Reframing social equality within an intercultural archaeology. *World Archaeology* 39: 281–97.

Haber, A. F. 2007b. This is not an answer to the question "who is Indigenous?" *Archaeologies* 3: 213–29.

Hall, M. 1984. The burden of tribalism: the social context of Southern African Iron Age studies. *American Antiquity* 49: 455–67.

Hart, R. E. (ed.) 1995. *Zuni and the Courts: A Struggle for Sovereign Land Rights*. Lawrence: University Press of Kansas.

Hirofumi, K. 2009. Whose archaeology? Decolonizing archaeological perspectives in Hokkaido Island. *Journal of the Graduate School of Letters* 4: 47–55.

Hodder, I. 1999. *Archaeological Process: An Introduction*. Oxford: Blackwell.

Hodder, I. 2008. Multivocality and social archaeology. In J. Habu, C. Fawcett and J. M. Matsunaga (eds), *Evaluating Multiple Narratives: Beyond Nationalist, Colonialist, and Imperialist Archaeologies*, 196–200. New York: Springer.

Jofré, D. 2007. Reconstructing the politics of Indigenous identity in Chile. *Archaeologies* 3: 16–38.

Kehoe, A. B. 1998. *The Land of Prehistory: A Critical History of American Archaeology*. London: Routledge.

Kerber, J. E. (ed.) 2006. *Cross-Cultural Collaboration: Native Peoples and Archaeology in the Northeastern United States*. Lincoln: University of Nebraska Press.

King, T. F. 2008. *Cultural Resource Laws and Practice*, 3rd edition. Walnut Creek, CA: AltaMira Press.

Kohl, P. L., M. Kozelsky, and N. Ben-Yehuda (eds) 2007. *Selective Remembrances: Archaeology in the Construction, Commemoriation, and Consecration of National Pasts*. Chicago: University of Chicago Press.

Kuwanwisiwma, L. 2002. *Hopit navotiat*, Hopi knowledge of history: Hopi presence on Black Mesa. In S. Powell and F. E. Smiley (eds), *Prehistoric Culture Change on the Colorado Plateau: Ten Thousand Years on Black Mesa*, 161–3. Tucson: University of Arizona Press.

La Salle, M. J. 2010. Community collaboration and other good intentions. *Archaeologies* 6: 401–22.

Langford, R. F. 1983. Our heritage – your playground. *Australian Archaeology* 16: 1–6.

Liebmann, M. 2008. Postcolonial cultural affiliation: essentialism, hybridity, and NAGPRA. In M. Liebmann and U. Z. Rizvi (eds), *Archaeology and the Postcolonial Critique*, 73–90. Lanham, MD: AltaMira Press.

Lilley, I. 2009. Strangers and brothers? Heritage, human rights, and cosmopolitan archaeology in Oceania. In L. Meskell (ed.), *Cosmopolitan Archaeologies*, 48–67. Durham, NC: Duke University Press.

Lippert, D. 2008a. Not the end, not the middle, but the beginning: repatriation as a transformative mechanism for archaeologists and Indigenous peoples. In C. Colwell-Chanthaphonh and T. J. Ferguson (eds), *Collaboration in Archaeological Practice: Engaging Descendant Communities*, 119–30. Lanham, MD: AltaMira Press.

Lippert, D. 2008b. The rise of Indigenous archaeology: how repatriation has transformed archaeological ethics and practice. In T. W. Killion (ed.), *Opening Archaeology: Repatriation's Impact on Contemporary Research and Practice*, 151–60. Santa Fe: SAR Press.

Logan, W. and K. Reeves (eds) 2009. *Places of Pain and Shame: Dealing with "Difficult Heritage."* London: Routledge.

Lorde, A. 1984. *Sister Outsider: Essays and Speeches*. Berkeley, CA: The Crossing Press.

Lowenthal, D. 1996. *Possessed by the Past: The Heritage Crusade and the Spoils of History*. New York: Free Press.

Lowie, R. H. 1915. Oral tradition and history. *American Anthropologist* 17: 597–9.

McGhee, R. 2008. Aboriginalism and the problems of Indigenous archaeology. *American Antiquity* 73: 579–97.

McGuire, R. H. 2008. *Archaeology as Political Action*. Berkeley: University of California Press.

McManamon, F. P. 1991. The many publics for archaeology. *American Antiquity* 56: 121–30.

Martin, P. S. 1971. The revolution in archaeology. *American Antiquity* 36: 1–8.

Martinez, D. R. 2006. Overcoming hindrances to our enduring responsibility to the ancestors: protecting traditional cultural places. *American Indian Quarterly* 30: 486–503.

Mason, R. J. 2006. *Inconstant Companions: Archaeology and North American Indian Oral Traditions*. Tuscaloosa: University of Alabama Press.

Matthews, C. N. 2007. History to prehistory: an archaeology of being Indian. *Archaeologies* 3: 271–95.

Merlan, F. 2009. Indigeneity: global and local. *Current Anthropology* 50: 303–33.

Meskell, L. 2009. The nature of culture in Kruger National Park. In L. Meskell (ed.), *Cosmopolitan Archaeologies*, 89–112. Durham, NC: Duke University Press.

Meskell, L. and P. Pels (eds) 2005. *Embedding Ethics: Shifting Boundaries of the Anthropological Profession.* Oxford: Berg.

Mihesuah, D. A. (ed.) 2000. *Repatriation Reader: Who Owns American Indian Remains?* Lincoln: University of Nebraska Press.

Moser, S., D. Glazier, J. E. Phillips, L. N. el Nemr, M. S. Mousa, R. N. Aiesh, S. Richardson, A. Conner, and M. Seymour 2002. Transforming archaeology through practice: strategies for collaborative archaeology and the community archaeology project at Quseir, Egypt. *World Archaeology* 34: 220–48.

Muehlebach, A. 2001. "Making place" at the United Nations: Indigenous cultural politics at the U. N. working group on Indigenous populations. *Cultural Anthropology* 16: 415–48.

Ndoro, W. 1994. The preservation and presentation of Great Zimbabwe. *Antiquity* 68: 616–23.

Nicholas, G. P. (ed.) 2010a. *Being and Becoming Indigenous Archaeologists.* Walnut Creek, CA: Left Coast Press.

Nicholas, G. P. 2010b. Seeking the end of Indigenous archaeology. In C. Phillips and H. Allen (eds), *Bridging the Divide: Indigenous Communities and Archaeology into the 21st Century*, 233–52. Walnut Creek, CA: Left Coast Press.

Nicholas, G. P. and T. D. Andrews 1997. Indigenous archaeology in the postmodern world. In G. P. Nicholas and T. D. Andrews (eds), *At a Crossroads: Archaeology and First Peoples in Canada*, 1–18. Burnaby: Archaeology Press, Simon Fraser University.

Nicholas, G. P. and K. P. Bannister 2004. Copyrighting the past? Emerging intellectual property rights issues in archaeology. *Current Anthropology* 45: 327–50.

Nicholas, G. P. and J. Hollowell 2007. Ethical challenges to a postcolonial archaeology: the legacy of scientific colonialism. In Y. Hamilakis and P. Duke (eds), *Archaeology and Capitalism: From Ethics to Politics*, 59–82. Walnut Creek, CA: Left Coast Press.

Nicholas, G. P., J. R. Welch, and E. Yellowhorn 2008. Collaborative encounters. In C. Colwell-Chanthaphonh and T. J. Ferguson (eds), *Collaboration in Archaeological Practice: Engaging Descendant Communities*, 273–98. Lanham, MD: AltaMira Press.

Norder, J. W. 2007. Iktomi in the land of Maymaygwayshi: understanding lived experience in the practice of archaeology among American Indians/ First Nations. *Archaeologies* 3: 230–48.

Paradies, Y. C. 2006. Beyond black and white: essentialism, hybridity, and indigeneity. *Journal of Sociology* 42: 355–67.

Patterson, T. C. 1994. Social archaeology in Latin America: an appreciation. *American Antiquity* 59: 531–7.

Preucel, R. W. and C. N. Cipolla 2008. Indigenous and postcolonial archaeologies. In M. Liebmann and U. Z. Rizvi (eds), *Archaeology and the Postcolonial Critique*, 129–40. Lanham, MD: AltaMira Press.

Pwiti, G. and S. Chirikure 2008. Community involvement in archaeology and cultural heritage management: an assessment from case studies in Southern Africa and elsewhere. *Current Anthropology* 49: 467–85.

Ren, C. A. 2006. Maya archaeology and the political and cultural identity of contemporary Maya in Guatemala. *Archaeologies* 2: 8–19.

Roberts, A., S. Hemming, T. Trevorrow, G. Trevorrow, M. Rigney, G. Rigney, L. Agius, and R. Agius 2005. *Nukun and kungun Ngarrindjeri ruwe* (look and listen to Ngarrindjeri country): an investigation of Ngarrindjeri perspectives of archaeology in relation to Native title and heritage matters. *Australian Aboriginal Studies* 1: 45–53.

Royster, J. 2008. Indian land claims. In G. A. Bailey (ed.), *Handbook of North American Indians*, 28–37. Washington, DC: Smithsonian Institution.

Said, E. W. 1978. *Orientalism*. New York: Vintage Books.

Schmidt, P. R. 2010. Social memory and trauma in northwestern Tanzania: organic, spontaneous community collaboration. *Journal of Social Archaeology* 10: 255–79.

Shackel, P. A. and E. J. Chambers (eds) 2004. *Places in Mind: Public Archaeology as Applied Anthropology*. London: Routledge.

Silliman, S. W. 2005. Culture contact or colonialism? Challenges in the archaeology of Native North America. *American Antiquity* 70: 55–74.

Silliman, S. W. 2009. Change and continuity, practice and memory: Native American persistence in colonial New England. *American Antiquity* 74: 211–30.

Silliman, S. W. (ed.) 2008. *Collaborating at the Trowel's Edge: Teaching and Learning in Indigenous Archaeology*. Tucson: University of Arizona Press.

Slaughter, J. 1998. Interview with Henry Louis Gates, Jr. *Progressive* 62: 30–2.

Smith, C. and G. Jackson 2008. The ethics of collaboration: Whose culture? Whose intellectual property? Who benefits? In C. Colwell-Chanthaphonh and T. J. Ferguson (eds), *Collaboration in Archaeological Practice: Engaging Descendant Communities*, 171–99. Lanham, MD: AltaMira Press.

Smith, C. and H. M. Wobst (eds) 2005. *Indigenous Archaeologies: Decolonizing Theory and Practice*. London: Routledge.

Smith, L. 2006. *The Uses of Heritage*. London: Routledge.

Smith, L. T. 1999. *Decolonizing Methodologies: Research and Indigenous Peoples*. London: Zed Books.

Stapp, D. C. and M. S. Burney 2002. *Tribal Cultural Resource Management: The Full Circle to Stewardship*. Walnut Creek, CA: AltaMira Press.

Trigger, B. G. 2008. "Alternative archaeologists" in historical perspective. In J. Habu, C. Fawcett, and J. M. Matsunaga (eds), *Evaluating Multiple Narratives: Beyond Nationalist, Colonialist, and Imperialist Archaeologies*, 187–95. New York: Springer.

Two Bears, D. 2006. Navajo archaeologist is not an oxymoron: a tribal archaeologist's experience. *American Indian Quarterly* 30: 381–7.

Vansina, J. 1985. *Oral Tradition as History*. Madison: University of Wisconsin Press.

Watkins, J. 2000. *Indigenous Archaeology: American Indian Values and Scientific Practice*. Walnut Creek, CA: AltaMira Press.

Watkins, J. 2003. Archaeological ethics and American Indians. In L. J. Zimmerman, K. D. Vitelli, and J. Hollowell-Zimmer (eds), *Ethical Issues in Archaeology*, 129–42. Walnut Creek, CA: AltaMira Press.

Webb, S. 1987. Reburying Australian skeletons. *Antiquity* 61: 292–6.

White Deer, G. 1997. Return of the sacred: spirituality and the scientific imperative. In N. Swidler, K. E. Dongoske, R. Anyon, and A. S. Downer (eds), *Native Americans and Archaeologists: Stepping Stones to Common Ground*, 37–43. Walnut Creek, CA: AltaMira Press.

Whiteley, P. M. 2002. Archaeology and oral tradition: the scientific importance of dialogue. *American Antiquity* 67: 405–15.

Whittaker, E. 1994. Public discourse on sacredness: the transfer of Ayers Rock to Aboriginal ownership. *American Ethnologist* 21: 310–34.

Wilcox, M. V. 2009. *The Pueblo Revolt and the Mythology of Conquest: An Indigenous Archaeology of Contact*. Berkeley: University of California Press.

Wilson, C. L. 2007. Indigenous research and archaeology: transformative practices in/with/for the Ngarrindjeri community. *Archaeologies* 3: 320–34.

Wilson, W. A. and M. Yellow Bird (eds) 2005. *For Indigenous Eyes Only: A Decolonization Handbook*. Santa Fe: SAR Press.

Wobst, H. M. 2010. Indigenous archaeologies: a worldwide perspective on human materialities and human rights. In M. M. Bruchac, S. M. Hart, and H. M. Wobst (eds), *Indigenous Archaeologies: A Reader on Decolonization*, 17–27. Walnut Creek, CA: Left Coast Press.

Wylie, A. 2003. Why standpoint matters. In R. Figueroa and S. Harding (eds), *Science and Other Cultures: Issues in Philosophies of Science and Technology*, 26–48. New York: Routledge.

Wylie, A. 2008a. The integrity of narratives: deliberative practice, pluralism, and multivocality. In J. Habu, C. Fawcett, and J. M. Matsunaga (eds), *Evaluating Multiple Narratives: Beyond Nationalist, Colonialist, and Imperialist Archaeologies*, 201–12. New York: Springer.

Wylie, A. 2008b. Legacies of collaboration: transformative criticism in archaeology. Archaeology Division Distinguished Lecture, American Anthropological Association. San Francisco, CA.

Zimmerman, L. J. 2008. Unusual or "extreme" beliefs about the past, community identity, and dealing with the fringe. In C. Colwell-Chanthaphonh and T. J. Ferguson (eds), *Collaboration in Archaeological Practice: Engaging Descendant Communities*, 55–86. Lanham, MD: AltaMira Press.

ARCHAEOLOGICAL VISUALIZATION

Early Artifact Illustration and the Birth of the Archaeological Image

Stephanie Moser

It is no surprise that archaeology – a discipline that centers on the study of material culture – relies heavily on a large suite of visual products to record, interpret, and present its findings to professional and public audiences. It is this ubiquity in the archaeologists' use of images, perhaps, that accounts for the startling degree of ignorance concerning the theoretical importance of visual representation in the discipline. Although we see visual media as invaluable to all facets of our work and we acknowledge the power they have in communicating ideas, we remain largely unaware of the highly complex ways in which they influence the production of archaeological knowledge. While the creation of visual methods for recording data and communicating ideas has been critical to the establishment of archaeology as an independent discipline, images have also been central to the construction of theories about the past. Thus, far beyond simply assuming a descriptive and communicative function, images have long been used to mount hypotheses about the scientific and cultural significance of ancient remains. This theoretical function not only stems from the capacity of images to impart messages effectively and express concepts that are difficult to articulate, but also derives from the ability of images to generate their own meanings beyond those explicitly intended by their creators.

Archaeological images assume their "independent" and powerful theoretical role through two major means. On the one hand, the visual style or aesthetics of an image can convey meaning, lending a particular understanding to the subject represented in the image. On the other, archaeological images enlist a range of pictorial conventions to highlight particular features of artifacts, sites, and ancestors, and in doing so signify what aspects of the archaeological record are considered important for understanding the past. This process of conventionalization has grown out of a long tradition of graphically depicting archaeological materials, where for over five hundred years artists and illustrators have worked alongside antiquarians and archaeologists to demarcate and define expert knowledge on antiquity through the image. The aim of this discussion is to provide some insight into the appearance of this system of visual abstraction, revealing how ancient artifacts were converted into "modern" archaeological objects through the image at a very early stage in our disciplinary history. In the first half of the seventeenth century, the naturalistic representations of artifacts produced in association with traditions of Renaissance art were transformed into conventionalized line drawings, suggesting that the creation of a "scientific" mode of representing the past was central to the emergence of archaeology as a scholarly pursuit.

Based on theories of archaeological representation, where non-academic discourses such as illustrations and museum displays are assigned an important role in the creation of knowledge and ideas about the past (e.g. Moser 2008; Smiles and Moser 2004), an argument is made here for the significance of early artifact illustration in informing thinking about archaeological classification. Initially created to record objects held in early antiquarian collections, artifact images quickly became an important means of suggesting how groups of objects were connected. This more interpretive function assumed by the images was achieved by the creation of basic visual standards or conventions, which enabled comparisons to be made between artifacts and which promoted the designation of distinctive artifact "types." The production of illustrations of this nature represent a critical stage in the creation of a distinctive epistemological device which still assumes a fundamental role in the classification and seriation of archaeological material. While the depiction of monuments and sites in the landscape was also instrumental to the articulation of an "archaeological" approach to antiquities, the emphasis here is on illustrations of portable objects because it was in the representation of these that conventions were first established to define artifacts as evidence. Artifact illustrations, in the form of clearly rendered line drawings, signified how the objects retrieved from excavations were perceived as the core data of the new science. Although the spectrum of visual products used by archaeologists has significantly expanded since these seventeenth-century beginnings,

professionals still depend on these images as a mainstay of archaeological practice.

Tracing the origins of the iconic "artifact image" requires an investigation of the illustrative practices adopted by antiquarians and
natural historians in the seventeenth century, when images of artifacts
were introduced as descriptive visual records and promptly transformed into a distinctive representational form that communicated
the "meaning" of such objects. Although initially produced to document the variety of specimens held in the antiquarian and more
encyclopedic "scientific" collections, illustrations of artifacts quickly
assumed the role of tools in the research process, serving to guide
interpretations and structure the understanding of the archaeological
record. The story of archaeological imagery presented here reveals
how the lines of the pen were first used to identify, isolate, and
demarcate what was considered meaningful about archaeological
objects. It is argued that when identifying the key developments or
"markers" in the emergence of archaeology as a discipline, such
attempts to structure knowledge through visual representation
warrant as much attention as other innovations, such as the introduction of systematic field methods and Thomsen's invention of the
"Three Age System."

Archaeological visualization as product and process

From classical times to the present, artists and illustrators have communicated ideas about the past via the visual image. Such images
have taken many forms over the centuries, from paintings on pots
and walls, to illuminations in early manuscripts, engravings in printed
books, canvases in princely collections and art galleries, drawings in
early scientific and antiquarian treatises, multimedia exhibitions in
museums, and digital creations in two and three dimensions. From
technical illustrations to more artistic renderings, all graphic representations of archaeological subjects are taken to be theory-laden in
that they go beyond mere documentation to communicating and
formulating ideas. While the earliest images that conveyed ideas
about antiquity, such as classical depictions of myths and medieval
views of "strange lands," were not produced in association with the
establishment of scholarly discourse about the past, they have been
shown to have been no less important in articulating influential ideas
about our ancestors (Moser 1998). Similarly, the engravings and
paintings of pre-civilized life produced in the Renaissance were

created long before the discipline was formally recognized as a distinct intellectual field, yet they have been shown to have established important interpretive themes in the understanding of human evolution. The significance of such investigations is that they expose the theorizing nature of the images, which on first inspection appear to innocently present the past.

That the production and history of archaeological imagery is increasingly becoming recognized as an important theoretical topic in the discipline is suggested by the emergence of archaeological visualization as a research speciality. While visualization studies in archaeology are often assumed to be concerned with the creation of virtual constructions of the past and the application of new computing techniques to generate increasingly realistic depictions of archaeological subjects, this research area has also been concerned with the theoretical implications of using digital imagery in archaeological interpretation (see, e.g., Bateman 2000; Eiteljorg 2000; Gillings 2005; Miller and Richards 1994; Zubrow 2006). Also encompassed within the remit of archaeological visualization research are the history of archaeological imagery and the role of images in disciplinary practice. The history of our graphic practices and the legacy of the various traditions of imaging demand systematic scrutiny (as opposed to cursory acknowledgment) because they underlie and continue to inform the way we interpret data. Most significantly, perhaps, an understanding of the history of archaeological imaging forces us to acknowledge that our contemporary visual practices are not necessarily "better" in meeting archaeological aims than earlier traditions, but, rather, are more varied in relation to the development of new imaging technologies. Similarly, research on the way illustrations are used in more recent archaeological research is important because it forces us to recognize the unexplored potential of imagery in our discipline (see Swogger 2000).

The term "archaeological visualization" can be seen to have two dimensions. On the one hand, it refers to the products that result from graphically representing archaeological materials, and, on the other, it refers to the process of interpretation embodied in this visual translation. In the former, a vast array of two-dimensional image types can be defined under the term "archaeological visualization," including section drawings, plans of excavation contexts and topographic sketches, artifact illustrations in the form of hand-drawn figures and digital renderings, typological diagrams, maps such as location guides and geographic information systems (GIS) images, graphs, schematic diagrams, photographs, artistic reconstructions, computer-generated models, and mixed-media creations. The list of archaeological visualization products also extends to three-dimensional images in the form of museum exhibits, interactive film and video presentations, immersive virtual reality and augmented reality environments, and 3D artifact and excavation scans. Many of these visual genres are combined in archaeological publications, used in public communication, and enlisted in the training of future generations of archaeologists. The use of such a wide range of "visuals" reveals not only how archaeologists are highly dependent on images to record, analyze, and explain the past, but also that they are increasingly exploring the potential of new computing technologies to form a key part of the research process (Chrysanthi et al. in press; Frischer and Dakouri-Hild 2008). Researchers on the AHRC Portus Project are currently exploring the way computer graphic simulations enhance archaeological interpretation, using both simple volumetric visualizations and photorealistic renderings of the Roman port and the artifacts found there to act as a focal point in analysis (see Earl et al. 2011).

The "process" of archaeological visualization refers to the agency of the products listed above and how they perform as key interpretive and explanatory tools in our discipline. While archaeological visualizations serve as a critical "gateway" through which disciplinary knowledge can be accessed by non-professionals, they also enable our own professional exploration of ideas and concepts that are difficult to identify and articulate through textual discourse. Accordingly, visualization as process is not simply about making information and ideas accessible; it concerns the delineation of archaeological knowledge in the first place. For instance, as opposed to being an easily comprehensible vehicle for presenting what has already been established, archaeological images are a "structuring agent" that guides archaeologists in their understanding of the phenomena under investigation (see below). Many levels of decision making inform the creation of archaeological images, most of which are based on the direct observation of the objects or sites represented and the adherence to conventions of illustration for rendering them. As Blum (1993: 3) has observed in her history of zoological illustration, there is a series of steps involved in the representation of a scientific subject, and this process of translating objects into pictures "seems so obvious, its conventions so central to Western picture making and to the way that people have been taught to read pictures that stating them seems tautological" (see also Davidson's [2008] arguments on palaeontological illustration). However, by highlighting particular features and characteristics of objects and sites, archaeological images function as a critical form of narration; they tell us what to look for and suggest connections that we may not have been aware of before. As Jones (2001: 338) has argued, artifact images have a "powerful effect on the way in which we subsequently engage with other archaeological artefacts." The theoretical significance of images can thus not be overemphasized as archaeological visualization concerns not merely the "presentation" of archaeological knowledge, but rather the formation of archaeological knowledge itself.

While some types of archaeological images may appear more technical and less partial than others, such as artifact illustrations compared to artistic reconstructions of ancient ancestors in their dwellings, all contain creative input. Studies in visualization are concerned with how each of the different types of archaeological images has a graphic signature of its own, where specific conventions are used to assign a particular interpretation to the material represented. For example, illustrations of stone tools, ceramics, metal, bone, and other artifacts highlight the diagnostic features that have been deemed scientifically significant by specialists. It is through the conventionalized image of such objects that assemblages of material are "converted" into meaningful archaeological data, which can then be compared and placed into classificatory schemes. The way such illustrations are laid on the printed page, collated with other plates, or represented digitally is also important, as the contexts of presentation impart ideas about the significance of the objects. Visualization research is thus concerned not only with the content of images, but with their style of rendering too, as this may also shape the definition of the subject represented.

In current archaeological practice, computer-generated images are increasingly being used to document, interpret, and present archaeological data. In some contexts, computer-generated images have superseded earlier forms of visual representation because of their ability to create photorealistic impressions of objects. There is no doubt that 3D scans of objects and the highly realistic renderings of them provide important insights into aspects of the material record not conveyed in traditional artifact images, notably object textures, colors, and the effects of illumination (e.g. Beale and Earl 2010; Happa et al. 2009; Papadopoulos and Earl in press). However, while the physically realistic qualities of these visualizations have made them appealing to archaeologists as tools for analysis, we have yet to consider the extent to which such imaging technologies might alter our perceptions of the past. For instance, human authorship is more apparent in hand-rendered illustrations, which through their use of pictorial conventions more readily expose the interpretive nature of recording archaeological objects. The naturalistic realism achieved in digital images is deceiving because it disguises the many layers of inference involved in their production: the production of 3D models, for example, is not based entirely on laser scan data as a substantial part of such models are comprised of "hand-made" geometry. Thus while virtually rendered objects are also interpretive, claims for high levels of physical realism in such images imply that we are closer to "knowing" the past than we have ever been. Like all other traditions of visualization in archaeology, however, the practice of generating images that are virtually "real" depends on its own set of conventions and shared assumptions. The relationship between hand-rendered illustration and computer-generated visualization is further complicated by the increasing availability of forms of the latter deliberately mimicking the styles of the former through non-photorealistic rendering (see Earl 2006; Frankland in press).

Of critical importance in the study of archaeological visualization is the issue of how our visual products are consumed by professional and non-professional audiences. While research has been carried out on the consumption and reception of archaeological images in the form of museum displays and temporary exhibitions (Moser 2006, in press), there are no detailed studies of how two-dimensional images have been received both within and outside the discipline (for an exception, see Frankland in press, which qualitatively examines how an audience responded to computer-generated reconstructions depicted in varying styles). In line with theories of reception articulated in the humanities, where the meaning of texts/objects is seen to be generated by the interaction of readers/viewers with them, viewing archaeological images can also be seen as a highly interactive process, whereby audiences bring their own understandings to the perception of the image and in so doing configure its meaning/s. Professional consumers or viewers of archaeological images respond to them according to familiarity with scientifically established canons of illustration, but we also respond to other elements of the images such as style and the context of presentation (e.g. association with other visuals within the publication). Reception of archaeological images by non-professional audiences is also significant because they interpret such images with a different set of referents and expectations. For example, images may be understood in terms of awareness of iconic visual elements reproduced in popular contexts. Examining how archaeological images are received in both circumstances is important in establishing the extent to which the aims of the image are met, or, as is often the case, not met. That audiences understand images in ways not initially intended is significant, suggesting that viewers assert their own interpretations just as much as the image creators do.

In addition to reception, the dissemination of archaeological images both within and outside professional contexts is a topic on the research agenda of archaeological visualization. Again, while findings have been published on the recycling and longevity of archaeological images (Moser 1998, 2001, in press), substantive research on the way such images "travel" beyond their original contexts is yet to be carried out. Beyond informing us about the preferred modes of visual communication adopted by the different specialities within the discipline, the circulation of images within archaeology reveals the extent to which particular images are rendered iconic through their use in other publications and learning contexts. The dissemination of archaeological images outside the discipline refers to the way in which certain images or elements of them are selected and re-adapted to serve completely different aims (e.g. in films, advertising, computer games). Their re-use in other contexts – particularly popular culture – can add different layers of meaning to the subject represented, often serving to create stereotypes and iconic images of ancient cultures. In this sense, the secondary use of archaeological images can alter the general perception of a subject and recast the original referent in a new light. The "travels" of archaeological images outside scholarly discourse are therefore important, as the different stages and contexts of reproduction add, enrich, and cement meaning. This concept has been investigated in a detailed study of the ornamental schema of Egyptian antiquity created by designer Owen Jones in the mid-nineteenth century (Moser in press).

Appraising the archaeological image

The role of illustration in the development of archaeology was highlighted over forty years ago by Stuart Piggott (1965). That Piggott was invited by the editors of the journal *Antiquity* to write an article on the subject of archaeological draftsmanship suggests that the archaeological community deemed the topic worthy of consideration. It is also significant that archaeologists acknowledged the importance of graphic communication before illustration became more widely recognized as an important subject of inquiry in the sciences; a fact that reveals how deeply connected archaeology and the image have always been. Before outlining the history and function of archaeological illustration, Piggott situates the tradition firmly within the field of scientific illustration, which, he argues, "translates actuality into forms and outlines in one or more colours, usually black on white, in a manner which will convey to the observers the features of the original which the illustrator wishes to present" (Piggott 1965: 165). This statement indicates that for practitioners like Piggott archaeological illustration is seen as a necessarily selective process, where the role of the illustrator is to highlight "features" or diagnostic attributes of artifacts. Accordingly, archaeological illustrations are seen to consist of an established set of symbols, and in most instances "we are so accustomed to the conventions that we tend to forget that they exist" (Piggott 1965: 165). Further observations made by Piggott reveal that contemporary visualization researchers are certainly not the first to refer to the knowledge-making capacity of illustrations. As opposed to merely complementing ideas put forward by archaeologists, Piggott describes how illustrations actually serve to *expand* the author's words.

The significance of archaeological images in creating knowledge about the past was revived as a topic of concern in archaeology in the 1990s (e.g. Gamble 1993; Gifford-Gonzalez 1993; James 1996, 1999; Molyneaux 1996; Moser 1992, 1996, 1998; Moser and Gamble 1996). This was the first phase of research on archaeological visualization as "process," which drew on scholarly traditions in the sciences that investigated the significance of visual representation in the formation of disciplines and subject knowledge. In addition to documenting aspects of the history of archaeological imagery, these archaeologists explored the nature of visual representation as a signifying practice and showed how the motifs, symbols, and formulae used in images communicated important and unstated ideas about the subjects represented. It was recognition of the significance of these findings for archaeology more widely that was the basis upon which the article on visual representation was written for the first edition of *Archaeological Theory Today* (Moser 2001). A vibrant field of scholarship on archaeological visualization has since been established, with numerous publications, conferences, research projects, and university courses testifying to its status as a disciplinary specialty (see Visualization in Archaeology Project website – *http://www. viarch.org.uk*, where publications, projects, and relevant conferences are listed).

The most significant development in archaeological visualization studies since they were initiated in the 1990s is the broadening of the research agenda beyond a focus on the content of archaeological images (what they communicate), to exploring the contexts of production, use, and reception (how they are manufactured, exploited, and consumed). The shift in interest from "content," where sources upon which images are based are identified and their authorship is examined, reflects growing awareness that the viewers of images as well as their creators generate knowledge. Furthermore, it is now more widely recognized that the meaning of an image is not discretely contained within it, but rather is formed as a result of the way viewers interact with it. The landmark work representing this "second wave" of visualization studies is Perry's (2011) detailed investigation of the way images were used in discipline building in British archaeology in the first half of the twentieth century. Here we see how the life of an image subsequent to its creation – i.e. its use – is critical in understanding the significance of archaeological visualization. In addition to articulating a detailed theory of visualization "as process," Perry shows how archaeologists skillfully deployed visual products in their training schemes and bids for institutional self-definition. Other researchers have also undertaken studies on the role of images in the professionalization of the discipline, showing how images helped to define the boundaries of the subject (e.g. Guha 2002). Additionally, studies in archaeological visualization have addressed how the development of new visual media provide opportunities to generate new kinds of interpretations of the past (e.g. van Dyke 2006) and have challenged assumptions about the traditional function of the archaeological image, offering experiments with "mixed-media" forms of imagery as a means for disciplinary self-reflection (e.g. Cochrane and Russell 2007; Perry 2009). Research in the field has also expanded to include critiques of museum displays, films, the media, and computer-generated visualizations such as computer games and virtual reality constructions (see below). Museum displays have functioned as a critical form of visualization in the representation of the past because they construct knowledge about the past through the formation of collections, their ordering and classification, and their arrangement for public presentation (e.g. Moser 2006, 2010). Films have also been shown to take an active part in constructing identities for ancient peoples through their sequencing of images, creation of sets and props, use of camera angles, color, lighting, narrative structure, sound, and music (e.g. Marwick 2010). Studies on multimedia resources, computer games, and interactive virtual reality displays have also shown how these media construct ideas about the past (e.g. Gardner 2007). The literature on digital technologies and archaeological visualization is vast and has seen a significant shift from, on the one hand, a focus on the potential of computer-generated imagery to reconstruct artifacts and sites in ever-increasing detail (e.g. Dingwall et al. 1999) to, on the other, reflections upon the role of such imagery in all stages of the interpretive process (e.g. Greengrass and Hughes 2010).

Artistic versus archaeological realism in illustration

From a theoretical viewpoint, archaeological images are important not only because they embody a uniquely archaeological "view" of material culture and sites, but also because they have undergone a complex process of encoding in order to achieve this signifying role. The birth or creation of the illustrations that are now routinely manufactured in association with archaeological investigation is an important hallmark of our self-consciousness as a profession. This is evidenced by the existence of numerous manuals on archaeological illustration, where the set of conventions that have been "purpose-built" for the work of archaeology are presented in detail (e.g. Addington 1986; Adkins and Adkins 1989; Griffiths et al. 1990; Hodgson 2001; Steiner and Allason-Jones 2005). These visual conventions are said to have been created so that the "maximum amount of information can be conveyed as economically as possible" (Adkins and Adkins 1989: 8). They also facilitate consistency in the representation of diagnostic features, which need to be compared with each other in order to assign objects a particular place in typologies and chronological sequences. In the *Guild Handbook of Scientific Illustration* it is noted that archaeological illustration differs from other types of scientific illustration because the specimens are natural materials modified by human touch, and it is these modifications that are the focus of the illustrations (Morales-Denney and Cowherd 2003: 466). Although this suggests that archaeological illustration is selective in a manner that is different to other types of scientific illustration, the underlying principles upon which archaeological illustration are based are the same. Such principles center on the identification and standardized representation of key attributes in specimens via accepted conventions. This process involves a move away from naturalist or realistic representation, which pays equal attention to all features and does not single out certain attributes at the expense of others. Illustrators have addressed this issue of realistic representation in the depiction of archaeological materials; Adkins and Adkins (1989: 9), for instance, state that "a drawing which aims at realism for a specialist audience of archaeologists is usually inappropriate and fails in its purpose." Archaeologists have also discussed how such conventions serve to designate the artifact illustration as "accurate," providing an illusion that a "realistic sense" of the object is provided (Jones 2001: 335). This is a theme that is central to, and which underlies, the early formation of a distinctive "genre" of artifact illustration as it is here that we see how the use of conventions has been critical in *defining* what is meaningful about an artifact in archaeological terms.

For at least five hundred years, archaeological objects have been depicted in images intended to impart scientific or scholarly information. While initially there was no clear style of archaeological illustration, conventions of representation were quickly established to ensure that the growing community of scholars interested in ancient remains could use such images as a research resource and study tool. Commensurate with this, images began to assume a fundamental role in facilitating an understanding of the scientific and cultural significance of antiquities. The didactic status assigned to early artifact images is reflected in the move away from the trend to produce naturalistic images of artifacts to the creation of more codified representations of them. Antiquarians, like early naturalists and scientists, enlisted these encoded images to achieve clear and effective communication with each other. With close attention paid to diagnostic attributes in the images, no distractions were offered in the form of extraneous details and ornament, enabling scholars to focus on comparable criteria.

Historians of science and art have documented how scientific illustration underwent a complex process of development as images became recognized as vital instruments in the establishment of new observational disciplines in the early modern period (see below). Although images that were produced as a result of direct observation of an original specimen may have been perceived as accurate, they were anything but straightforward visual records that were "true." As the historian of natural history David Freedberg (2002: 416) has argued, "The technologies of visual reproduction are always capable of lying. They may seem guileless and simple, and they may give the appearance of truthfulness: yet there can never be a reliable correlation between outward appearance and inner truth." Like the early natural history illustrations, the first "archaeological" images of the seventeenth century were in effect visual translations, where selected aspects of the object were enhanced or neglected and stylistic qualities provided an overall "feel" or identity for the artifact. In looking at these early images, it is possible to see how the emerging antiquarian community used them to frame their approaches towards the study of antiquity. Although these prototypes lacked a clear and rigorously applied system of conventions, they nevertheless went beyond mere description to formulating knowledge about the surviving objects from the ancient world.

Recent developments in the production of archaeological images suggest that the visual representation of archaeological materials has maintained an allegiance to core principles of scientific illustration developed in the sixteenth and seventeenth centuries. Although advances in computer technology have significantly expanded the repertoire of image types we exploit, there are prevailing continuities in our visual "toolkit" stemming from the work of early antiquarian scholars. As historians of antiquarian illustration have already shown, a serious investment was made in the image as a means of advancing scholarly pursuits in the formative years of antiquarian studies (see Michell 1982; Myrone 1999, 2007; Smiles 1994, 1999, 2007a, 2007b, in press). More specifically, images served to create archaeological "data," allowing scholars to demonstrate the significance of artifacts as indicators of cultural evolution. Antiquarians were keenly aware of this capacity, and as Smiles (in press) has argued, we must be wary of progressivist accounts that characterize antiquarian illustration as the "hesitant and faltering first steps" of archaeological illustration.

Establishing the prototype: Cassiano dal Pozzo's *Paper Museum*

As the study of classical antiquities, as opposed to literary works, became of increasing interest to humanists in the seventeenth century, the illustration of artifacts became recognized as an important means of advancing knowledge of the ancient world. Piggott (1978: 22) refers to the way in which this interest was accompanied by the creation of a system of visual representation during this time: "[I]llustration was important to the scientists to an increasing degree as they turned from ancient literary authority to a first-hand empirical study of phenomena." As humanistic study was still not separated from scientific research at this time (e.g. Pomata and Siraisi 1995), the illustration of ancient objects was linked with the visual traditions developed for portraying natural history. This association was reinforced by the fact that in addition to being illustrated in antiquarian works, archaeological objects were visually recorded in catalogues of "scientific" or encyclopedic collections, where they were typically featured together with natural history specimens (see Moser 2006: 1–32). Although these catalogues valued artifacts as one component of a wider collection of worldly curiosities, rather than presenting them in the context of a specialist interest in antiquities, the illustrations of artifacts they featured were produced in accordance with the visual traditions of representing scientific "specimens" at the time. These traditions were essentially naturalistic in that illustrators focused on creating artistically realistic images of the natural world (see, e.g., Smith 2006; Smith and Findlen 2002; Smith and Schmidt 2008). Both art historians and historians of science have documented the important ways in which artists contributed to establishing fields such as medicine (e.g. Roberts and Tomlinson 1992) and botany (e.g. Ogilvie 2006; Saunders 2009) through naturalistic representation in the sixteenth and seventeenth centuries. Archaeology followed a similar trajectory, with the antiquarian community of the seventeenth century utilizing the skills of accomplished artists to illustrate objects in their collections and to copy drawings from other collections and image archives.

Influenced by, and closely associated with, the production of catalogues of collections in the sixteenth century was the creation of a distinctive type of visual archive known as the "Paper Museum" (see Décultot 2010; Haskell 1993; Meijers 2005). These were comprehensive graphic resources, which collated original drawings of the objects/specimens held in personal collections and documented in other sources. Intended as a research resource for the growing communities of specialists interested in material culture and science, the Paper Museums formed in Europe from the mid-sixteenth century provide us with important insights into the introduction of visual conventions for representing antiquities. The most important and ambitious Paper Museum of the time was the one created by Cassiano dal Pozzo (1588–1657), an influential Italian antiquarian and scientist based in Rome. Around 1615, dal Pozzo began collecting drawings of antiquities and items of natural history, forming a vast collection of over seven thousand images designed to function as a comprehensive illustrated encyclopedia. The antiquities component constituted an invaluable and unrivalled resource for the study of the ancient world, with over four thousand images depicting architectural remains, sculptures, inscriptions, pottery, and metalwork. Although there were precedents of this type of image archive in the sixteenth century, notably that of Ulisse Aldrovandi (1522–1605), dal Pozzo's Paper Museum was the most comprehensive of its kind and clearly served as the model for the landmark publications on antiquities that were produced in the early eighteenth century, such as *L'Antiquité expliquée et représentée en figures* of 1719–24 by Bernard de Montfauçon (1655–1741), and *Recueil d'antiquités égyptiennes, étrusqes, grecques, romaines et gauloises* of 1752–7 by Comte de Caylus (1692–1765).

In addition to being highly influential in the development of the historiography of art, dal Pozzo's Paper Museum was also critical in setting "scientific" standards for the representation of antiquities. The drawings in the collection reflected how antiquarians and humanists were beginning to develop systematic approaches to classifying both cultural and natural phenomena through the means of graphic evidence, and in the case of antiquities this could be seen in the way that they were broadly grouped together in order to provide insights into the customs of antiquity, such as religious ceremonies and funerary rituals. Related to this was the attention devoted to "ordinary" objects in the dal Pozzo collection. The vast majority of images of antiquities in other graphic archives and publications focused almost exclusively on monumental, figurative, ornamental, and inscribed works, whereas the Paper Museum of dal Pozzo addressed this imbalance by including undecorated and utilitarian items of a domestic nature. The images in dal Pozzo's collection are thus very important in the history of archaeology because they reflect the rising interest in documenting the whole range of artifacts recovered from the ancient world. Indeed, and as Haskell (1993: 9) noted, a significant characteristic of the dal Pozzo collection was the way it paid "unusual attention to the usual." Bailey (1992: 3) qualifies this point, observing that although the dal Pozzo drawings are consistent with the wider trend of representing sculptural artifacts, statues, reliefs, sarcophagi, and inscriptions, the presence of small objects is "by no means negligible." While the depiction of objects with iconographic interest is linked to the development of an intellectual tradition of art history, it is in the illustrations of "small finds" that we see important attempts to create a standardized "archaeological" style for drawing artifacts. This style was different from the more aesthetic visual tradition of depicting ancient art, where attention was paid to recording the subjects represented in such works. When the range of antiquarian illustrations expanded to include the less adorned objects, a more codified style of graphic representation was created, and it was this tradition that made the possibilities of archaeology as a discipline more apparent.

The best examples of the "scientific" type of artifact images in the dal Pozzo collection are those featured in a bound album entitled *Antichità diverse*, where many small objects, including statuettes and reliefs, jewelry, amulets, weights and measures, vases, lamps and tripods, are illustrated (Vaiani in press). These images broadly correspond to subjects of antiquarian interest at the time, such as religious customs and daily life. The more specific topics of interest that they illustrate include clothing, weights and measures, masks and musical instruments, oil lamps, and drinking vessels. Of the *ca.* 500 drawings featured in the album, 150 have been drawn from originals held in personal collections and 285 have been copied from images in other compilations. These copies are testimony to the existence of other important graphic archives on antiquities, most notably the *Codex Ursinianus* from the Farnese collection in the Vatican (see Vaiani in press). The significant contribution of the *Antichità diverse* album, however, was that it featured such a large sample of domestic objects, revealing how the analysis of utilitarian items was becoming more widely recognized as an area of study within antiquarian scholarship. Prior to this, inscriptions and coins had been the focus of antiquarian scholarship and the trend was to use images of such antiquities to illustrate ideas articulated in the text. The creation of dal Pozzo's image collection signified an important shift in thinking about antiquities, where objects were seen as useful "documents" for addressing neglected topics in classical works. This shift is indicated by the fact that images of artifacts in dal Pozzo's collection were circulated and discussed in correspondence with other antiquarians such as the notable French antiquarian Nicolas Claude Fabri de Peiresc (1580–1637), with whom dal Pozzo exchanged ideas on ancient tripods (see, e.g., British Museum 1993: 233).

To facilitate communication between antiquarians on the objects held in collections, there was an attempt to introduce standards in the visual representation of certain classes of material, particularly pottery and glass vessels and domestic utensils. In Figure 14.1, for example, four glass vessels or flasks are presented together in a group. Although quite rudimentary, the illustration is important because it represents a shift from presenting isolated objects or pairs of objects to depicting groups of the same types of artifacts. Here the illustrator has assembled similar items into a typological context, attempting to show variation in a general class of object. This convention reflects how antiquarian publications were starting to feature objects of the same type in groups, an important example being the illustrations of lamps in Fortunio Liceti's *De lucernis antiquorum reconditis* of 1621. Listed in the inventory as *lagrimatori*, the vessels in the *Antichità diverse* image were thought to be for the collection of tears shed in funeral ceremonies. (They are now believed to be containers for oils, perfumes, and ointments, but there is no exact evidence for what these bottles held; they are called "*unguentaria*" by archaeologists, which is word created to imply they held unguents.) Thus, although Figure 14.1 reflects how objects were organized by subject in the first

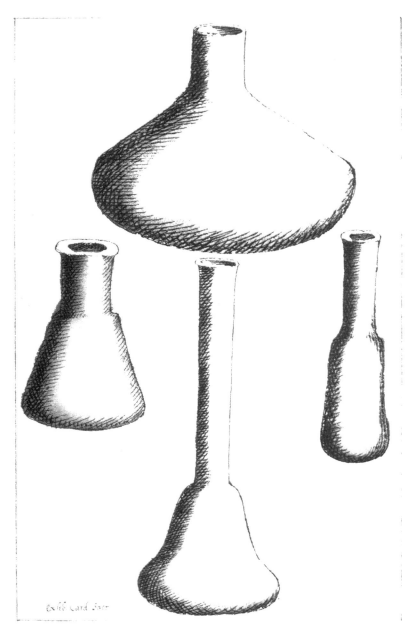

Figure 14.1. Four glass vessels from the dal Pozzo Paper Museum
Source: Antichità diverse Album no. 10205. The Royal Collection © 2011,
Her Majesty Queen Elizabeth II.

instance (in this case religious rituals), it shows how typologies were being formulated within these broader categories.

Rendered in ink with a brown wash, the drawings of vessels in Figure 14.1 are characterized by their strong simple outlines, which serve to highlight the distinctive features of the objects, namely the necks and bases. The use of hard outlines was an important technique for isolating the object from the background, emphasizing its form and shape. Cross-hatching has been used to give an idea of the volume of the objects, but beyond this there are no extra embellishments to distract from the function of the image as documentation. Another convention that is shared with the other illustrations of pottery in the collection is the distortion of the rim of the vessel so as to allow the viewer to "see inside" and also to view the detail of the rim itself. This is important because it represents the attempt to convey something of the inner structure of artifacts; it is also an illustrative device that was used well into the nineteenth century, when the modern "T" method of illustrating pottery was introduced and the section, interior, and exterior were all shown in the same illustration. Finally, two borderlines contain the image, endowing it with a sense of formality and status as a "scientific" document.

Figure 14.2 provides another grouping of vases, flasks, and jugs; however, this time the image appears to be more systematic than Figure 14.1 because the objects are arranged more formally in rows. This kind of linear arrangement encouraged the viewer to view the artifacts in sequence and indicates the intention for the plates to be consulted in a more orderly way. Presenting objects in this manner was important because it allowed antiquarians to make immediate comparisons between the objects and thus to contemplate how the items in the group might be typologically related. More significantly, this convention provided visual guidance to antiquarians, encouraging them to focus on particular features or variations in the shape or form of the objects. In this grouping of vessels, numbers are also assigned to some of the objects, revealing how the images are linked to textual description (this taking the form of an inventory that contained descriptions and a provenance for each of the objects). This convention was another indicator of the desire to make illustrations of artifacts more "informational" in nature. Finally, although, like Figure 14.1, this image is distinguished by strong outlines and cross-hatching, a significant difference is that the light source is now on the left as opposed to the right; the former becoming the standard in archaeological illustration.

A different style of representing antiquities in the *Antichità diverse* album is exhibited in Figure 14.3, which is one of a set of twelve

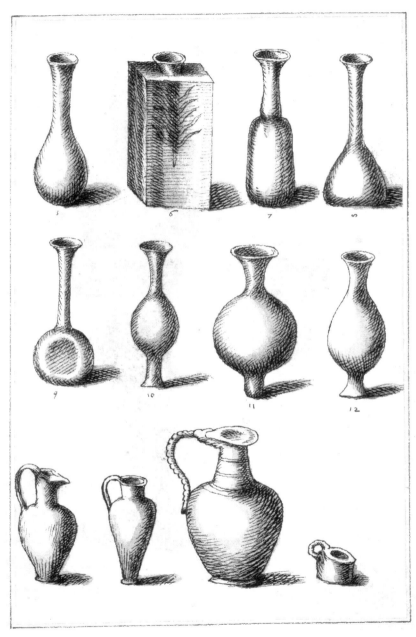

Figure 14.2. Collection of bottles from the dal Pozzo Paper Museum
Source: *Antichità diverse* Album no. 10269. The Royal Collection © 2011, Her Majesty Queen Elizabeth II.

Figure 14.3. Series of vase types from the dal Pozzo Paper Museum
Source: *Antichità diverse* Album no. RL 10294V. The Royal Collection
© 2011, Her Majesty Queen Elizabeth II.

similar images presenting collections of vase types. Copied from
plates in the *Codex Ursinianus*, these images appear to be of finer
quality than those of Figures 14.1 and 14.2, which are attributed to
the artist known as the "*Antichità Diverse Hand*." A more significant
difference is that the images attributed to the "*Codex Ursinianus
Hand*" selected certain features and omitted others from the original
drawings upon which they were based. As Vaiani (in press) notes,
archaeological details included in the earlier *Codex Ursinianus* series
of vases, namely the inscriptions on them, were omitted in the
Antichità diverse copies. While, on the one hand, this adaptation of
the "originals" can been seen as less archaeologically accurate, it was
meaningful in another sense because it led to a more conventionalized
representation of artifacts. As Claridge and Jenkins (1993: 18) note,
images such as these were not "literal" copies and they reflect how
dal Pozzo was interested not necessarily in the object itself, but rather
in the creation of sets of images grouped into classes. In the case of
these vase drawings, the concern was to identify the names of the
different types of vases and to make a clear visual statement on vase
shapes. Vaiani (in press) suggests that the criterion for the vases'
selection and their arrangement in the *Antichità diverse* series of vase
plates obeys a need for symmetry in shape and arrangement, rather
than any antiquarian requirement, and that the order of vases in the
originals from the *Codex Ursinianus* was altered owing to a concern
for regularity in the images' arrangement. Furthermore, the graphic
interpretation of the vases is said to reflect dal Pozzo's concern with
the decorative aspect of the vases' shapes, and Vaiani (in press) con-
cludes that while there is a "graphic success" of the copied images
in the *Antichità diverse* album, the success of these images in antiquarian and archaeological terms was poor. Despite this incongruity,
the set of images featuring vessel types in the *Antichità Diverse* album
can be seen as suggestive of the new kind of realism that historians
have documented in the development of seventeenth-century scientific
illustration. Whilst the omission of the inscriptions on the vases
lacked archaeological integrity in a modern sense, it nevertheless
represented a way of creating a structure for interpretation.
Furthermore, it is here that we see images being visually adapted or
translated to express what was meaningful to early antiquarians.

An interest in the organization of artifacts can also be seen in
images of other types of objects in the *Antichità diverse* album.
Figure 14.4, which features domestic utensils, including spoons,
vases, and bowls, presents the objects through a system of horizontal
arrangement in which all are oriented in the same way. This was a
convention that influenced the tendency towards a linear placement

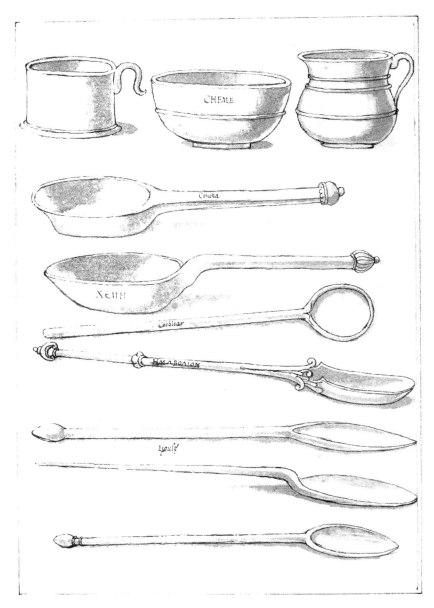

Figure 14.4. Metal utensils from the dal Pozzo Paper Museum
Source: *Antichità diverse* Album no. RL 10231. The Royal Collection
© 2011, Her Majesty Queen Elizabeth II.

of artifacts in the plates of the published works of the eighteenth century. These are simple drawings of humble objects, characterized by their clear lines and attention to diagnostic features, yet their organized arrangement on the page lends a sense of "scientific" order to the material. It appears that the artists followed unspoken rules in creating their images, yet the choices they made in representing particular elements above others effectively told the viewer what to see. As Vaiani (in press) has observed, *Antichità diverse* has an "experimental" and "miscellaneous" nature, reflecting how antiquarians were trying to establish appropriate ways to organize the material.

Another important observation concerning the dal Pozzo images and the development of "archaeological" realism in illustration is the contradictory effect of the lack of ornament in the images. On the one hand, the simplicity of the objects is made apparent by the sketched style of the drawings, yet, on the other, the selection of these objects and the decision to illustrate them in a clear, organized manner elevate them to items of significance. Indeed, it was the visual recording of so many of these seemingly inconsequential objects in this more systematic mode of presentation that ensured they became recognized as an important new class of evidence by antiquarians. The drawings also reveal how the illustrations adopted a typological nature as a result of their association with images of natural history specimens. Historians of natural history illustration have shown how modern scientific illustration emerges at the time the dal Pozzo images were being produced, when images started to become more technically precise and express greater attention to detail (e.g. Freedberg 2002; Nickelsen 2006; Ogilvie 2006). The first conventions of scientific images had been introduced prior to this in the sixteenth century, when early botanical illustrations were transformed from highly naturalistic representations into conventionalized ones. Pioneered by the early advocate of images Leonhart Fuchs (1501-66), conventionalized illustrations emphasized the typical features of specimens at the expense of individual idiosyncrasies. Strong, clear outlines were used to define the specimens and images were flattened, dispensing with perspective as conveyed by shadows and certain viewpoints. With these more simplified and less cluttered illustrations, the images went beyond description to signification. The purposefully selective nature of the drawings revealed how the illustrators surrendered their allegiance to the artistic realism of the Renaissance and committed to a new kind of realism. As Kusukawa (1997: 422) has argued, Fuchs created a "pictorial program with a very precise and explicit stipulation of the function of pictures." This program ensured that images became a key agent in communicating his theories about the medicinal power of plants. A similar process was being initiated by the early antiquarians, who were using artifact illustrations to advance their theories about the cultural practices of the ancients.

Another significant parallel between the artifact illustrations in the dal Pozzo archive and scientific illustration was the way in which visual strategies were refined to ensure that illustrations were accurate not only in appearance but also in content or substance. Recognizing that there was a conflict between producing a highly physically realistic representation of a specimen and one that conveyed its essential features or scientific "truth," the early humanists and scientists became wary of producing naturalistic types of images and begun to focus on encoding them in order to better extrapolate meaning. Ford's (1992: 2) comment that scientific illustration "can conceal a truth behind a welter of high-flown symbols" is made apparent at this very early stage in the history of scholarship, where illustrators were creating distinctive pictorial languages to advance study.

The production of archaeological images for Paper Museums such as those of dal Pozzo represented a foundational and critical phase in the establishment of the iconic "artifact image" so central to archaeological practice today. While not exhibiting all the qualities of artifact illustration we now accept as standard, these early images show what types of knowledge antiquarians were seeking to gain from the examination of ancient artifacts. Furthermore, although at this stage the images did not provide clear classificatory statements, they nevertheless represented important early attempts at ordering archaeological objects, which provided a critical basis upon which the enterprise of typology could be advanced. This brief account suggests that emergent conventions of archaeological illustration were central to communication in antiquarian studies, enabling basic comparative approaches to develop into more sophisticated categorizations of material culture. In the dal Pozzo images, we see the importance of grouping objects, presenting artifacts in rows, and using clear outlines to delineate form. The process of conventionalizing artifact images also involved the selection of diagnostic features and the stripping away of details that were thought to be superfluous or distracting. Naturalistic drawings were essentially "edited" into clear, clean line drawings with accompanying explanatory aids, resulting in a visual document that instructed the viewer on how to read the contents of the image.

In the following centuries, many important developments in the evolution of this prototype took place, revealing the extent to which antiquarians and the first archaeologists relied on this visual form to extract meanings from the material record of antiquity. Catalogues of the major encyclopedic collections published in the eighteenth century owe much to the initiatives seen in dal Pozzo's great project (e.g. Filippo Bonanni's *Musaeum Kircherianum* of 1709), but the refinement of the rudimentary set of visual conventions established by his visual archive into a clearer set of pictorial rules was systematically advanced and developed in the monumental antiquarian works of Bernard de Montfauçon (1719–24) and the Comte de Caylus (1752–7) cited above. With these publications, the artifact image became a distinctive type of illustration, reflecting a clearer sense of purpose in relation to its role in the process of archaeological classification.

Theorizing the archaeological image

At first glance, a humble artifact illustration appears to be bereft of theory. Similarly, a historical account of the emergence and development of archaeological illustration might appear to have little consequence for advancing the field of archaeological theory. However, since looking at objects is the crux of what we do, some reflection on the role of images in guiding and structuring disciplinary thought seems warranted. The central argument made here is that images were a critical factor in allowing "modern" archaeology to come into being. While illustrations of artifacts were initially produced in order to provide a visual record of the variety and types of objects known to the antiquarian community, it was not long before they went beyond having a descriptive function to assuming a critical role in the interpretation of objects. Far beyond simply constituting documentary records, illustrations provided an intellectual framework to make sense of artifacts. This expansion in the remit of the artifact image was achieved through the visual codification of illustrations, enabling early antiquarians to define and elaborate upon the relationships between classes of material more effectively. Although accuracy was a concern in illustrating artifacts, the conventions introduced in these early works represented a move towards the scientific kind of realism identified by historians of natural history. Here antiquarians recognized that the "truest" representation of an object was not necessarily dependent on a high degree of naturalism, but, rather, demanded a form of encoding in order that the image could be used as a comparable form of evidence. As we have seen in the illustrations in dal Pozzo's Paper Museum, a naturalistic form of representation was modified long before a recognized genre of archaeological illustration was established in the eighteenth century.

Visualization is essentially a process of conversion. In the case of archaeology, this act of conversion involves transforming material remains from mute, inanimate objects into archaeologically meaningful ones. Thus, the illustrator, artist, or computer designer who renders archaeological objects is not only a translator but also an active spokesperson. The role of these professionals in recording, interpreting, and presenting objects and ideas has always been vital to our discipline, and their influence on the way we approach data and the way we imagine the past cannot be overstated.

Acknowledgments

I am very grateful to the Project Officer of the Cassiano dal Pozzo Project at the Warburg Institute, Rea Alexandros, for providing access to material in the dal Pozzo collection. Eleni Vaiani kindly allowed me to see her work on the *Antichità Diverse* Album before going to press. Pim Allison, Gareth Beale, Graeme Earl, Tom Frankland, Matthew Johnson, Andy Jones, Costas Papadopoulos, Sara Perry, Rob Read, Sam Smiles, and Fraser Sturt provided useful feedback on the text. Brian Sparkes and David Woodward kindly provided help with Latin and French translations.

References

Addington, L.R. 1986. *Lithic Illustration: Drawing Flaked Stone Artifacts for Publication*. Chicago: University of Chicago Press.

Adkins, L. and R.A. Adkins 1989. *Archaeological Illustration*. Cambridge: Cambridge University Press.

Bailey, D. 1992. Small objects in the dal Pozzo-Albani drawings: first gatherings. In I.D. Jenkins (ed.), *Quaderni Puteani 2: Cassiano dal Pozzo's Paper Museum*, 3–20. Milan: Olivetti.

Bateman, J. 2000. Immediate realities: an anthropology of computer visualization in archaeology. Available: *http://intarch.ac.uk/journal/issue8/bateman_index.html* (accessed August 10, 2011).

Beale, G. and G.P. Earl 2010. The Herculaneum Amazon: sculptural polychromy, digital simulation and context. In A. Moore, G. Taylor, E. Harris, P. Girdwood, and L. Shipley (eds), *TRAC2009: Proceedings of the Nineteenth Annual Theoretical Roman Archaeology Conference*, 31–40. Oxford: Oxbow Books.

Blum, A.S. 1993. *Picturing Nature: American Nineteenth-Century Zoological Illustration*. Princeton: Princeton University Press.

British Museum (ed.) 1993. *The Paper Museum of Cassanio dal Pozzo*. Rome: Olivetti.

Caylus, A.-C.-P. Tubières, comte de 1752–7. *Recueil d'antiquités égyptiennes, étrusqes, grecques, romaines et gauloises*, 7 vols. Paris: Chez Desaint and Saillant.

Chrysanthi, A., P. F. Murrieta, and C. Papadopoulos (eds) in press. *Thinking beyond the Tool: Archaeological Computing and the Interpretive Process*. Oxford: Archaeopress.

Claridge, A. and I. Jenkins 1993. Cassiano and the tradition of drawing from the Antique. In British Museum (ed.), *The Paper Museum of Cassanio dal Pozzo*, 13–26. Rome: Olivetti.

Cochrane, A. and I. Russell 2007. Visualizing archaeologies: a manifesto. *Cambridge Archaeological Journal* 17: 3–19.

Davidson, J. P. 2008. *A History of Paleontology Illustration*. Bloomington: Indiana University Press.

Décultot, É. 2010. *Musée de papier: recueils d'Antiquités et recherches antiquaires 1650–1780*. Paris: Musée du Louvre Éditions/Gourcuff/Gradenigo.

Dingwall, L., S. Exon, V. Gaffney, S. Laflin, and M. van Leusen (eds) 1999. *Archaeology in the Age of the Internet*. Oxford: Archaeopress.

Earl, G. P. 2006. At the edges of the lens: photography, graphical constructions and cinematography. In T. L. Evans and P. Daly (eds), *Digital Archaeology*, 191–210. London: Routledge.

Earl, G. P., S. J. Keay, and G. Beale in press. Archaeological computing for recording and presentation of Roman Portus. In S. Keay and L. Paroli (eds), *Portus and Its Hinterland: Recent Archaeological Research*. Rome: Archaeological Monographs of the British School at Rome.

Eiteljorg, H., II 2000. The compelling computer image: a double-edged sword. Available: *http://intarch.ac.uk/journal/issue8/eiteljorg_index.html* (accessed August 10, 2011).

Ford, B. 1992. *A History of Scientific Illustration*. Oxford: Oxford University Press.

Frankland, T. in press. A CG artist's impression: depicting virtual reconstructions using non-photorealistic rendering techniques. In A. Chrysanthi, P. F. Murrieta, and C. Papadopoulos (eds), *Thinking Beyond the Tool: Archaeological Computing and the Interpretive Process*. Oxford: Archaeopress.

Freedberg, D. 2002. *The Eye of the Lynx: Galileo, His Friends, and the Beginnings of Modern Natural History*. Chicago: University of Chicago Press.

Frischer, B. and A. Dakouri-Hild (eds) 2008. *Beyond Illustration: 2D and 3D Digital Technologies as Tools for Discovery in Archaeology*. Oxford: Archaeopress.

Gamble, C. 1993. Figures of fun: theories about cavemen. *Archaeological Review from Cambridge* 11: 357–72.

Gardner, A. 2007. The past as playground: the ancient world in video game representation. In T. Clack and M. Brittain (eds), *Archaeology and the Media*, 255–72. Walnut Creek, CA: Left Coast Press.

Gifford-Gonzalez, D. 1993. You can hide, but you can't run: representations of women's work in illustrations of Palaeolithic life. *Visual Anthropology Review* 9: 22–41.

Gillings, M. 2005. The real, the virtually real, and the hyperreal: the role of VR in archaeology. In S. Smiles and S. Moser (eds), *Envisioning the Past: Archaeology and the Image*, 223–39. Oxford: Blackwell.

Greengrass, M. and L. Hughes (eds) 2010. *The Virtual Representation of the Past*. Aldershot: Ashgate.

Griffiths, N., A. Jenner and C. Wilson 1990. *Drawing Archaeological Finds: A Handbook*. London: Archetype Publications UCL.

Guha, S. 2002. The visual in archaeology: photographic representation of archaeological practice in British India. *Antiquity* 76: 93–100.

Happa, J., M. Mudge, K. Debattista, A. Artusi, A. Gonçalves, and A. Chalmers 2009. Illuminating the past: state of the art. *Virtual Reality* 14: 155–82.

Haskell, F. 1993. Introduction. In British Museum (ed.), *The Paper Museum of Cassiano dal Pozzo*, 1–10. Rome: Olivetti.

Hodgson, J. 2001. *Archaeological Reconstruction: Illustrating the Past*. IFA Paper No. 5. Institute of Field Archaeologists, University of Reading.

James, S. 1996. Drawing inferences; visual reconstructions in theory and practice. In B. Molyneaux (ed.), *The Cultural Life of Images: Visual Representation in Archaeology*, 122–48. London: Routledge.

James, S. 1999. Imag(in)ing the past: the politics and practicalities of recon- structions in the museum gallery. In N. Merriman (ed.), *Making Early Histories in Museums*, 117–35. Leicester: Leicester University Press.

Jones, A. 2001. Drawn from memory: the archaeology of aesthetics and aesthetics of archaeology in earlier Bronze Age Britain and the present. *World Archaeology* 33: 334–56.

Kusukawa, S. 1997. Leonhart Fuchs on the importance of pictures. *Journal of the History of Ideas* 58: 403–27.

Marwick, B. 2010. Self-image, the long view and archaeological engagement with film: an animated case study. *World Archaeology* 42: 394–404.

Meijers, D. J. 2005. The Paper Museum as a genre: the corpus of drawings in St. Petersburg within a European perspective. In R. E. Kistemaker (ed.), *The Paper Museum of the Academy of Sciences in St. Petersburg c. 1725–1760*, 19–24. Amsterdam: Royal Netherlands Academy of Arts and Sciences.

Michell, J. 1982. *Megalithomania: Artists, Antiquarians and Archaeologists at the Old Stone Monuments*. London: Thames and Hudson.

Miller, P. and J. Richards 1994. The good, the bad and the downright misleading: archaeological adoption of computer visualization. In J. Huggett and N. Ryan (eds), *CAA94 Proceedings of the 22nd CAA conference*, 19–22. Oxford: Tempus Reparatum.

Molyneaux, B. L. (ed.) 1996. *The Cultural Life of Images*. London: Routledge.

Montfauçon, B. de 1719–24. *L'Antiquité expliquée et représentée en figures*. Paris: Chez F. Delaulne, etc.

Morales-Denney, E. and J. L. Cowherd 2003. Illustrating humans and their artefacts. In E. R. S. Hodges (ed.), *The Guild Handbook of Scientific Illustration*, 461–83. Hoboken, NJ: Wiley.

Moser, S. 1992. The visual language of archaeology: a case study of the Neanderthals. *Antiquity* 66: 831–44.

Moser, S. 1996. Visual representation in archaeology: depicting the missing-link in human origins. In B. Baigrie (ed.), *Picturing Knowledge: Historical and Philosophical Problems Concerning the Use of Art in Science*, 184–214. Toronto: University of Toronto Press.

Moser, S. 1998. *Ancestral Images: The Iconography of Human Origins*. Ithaca, NY: Cornell University Press.

Moser, S. 2001. Archaeological representation: the visual conventions for constructing knowledge about the past. In I. Hodder (ed.), *Archaeological Theory Today*, 1st edition, 262–83. Cambridge: Polity.

Moser, S. 2006. *Wondrous Curiosities: Ancient Egypt at the British Museum*. Chicago: University of Chicago Press.

Moser, S. 2008. Archaeological representation: the consumption and creation of the past. In B. Cunliffe and C. Gosden (eds), *Oxford Handbook of Archaeology*, 1048–77. Oxford: Oxford University Press.

Moser, S. 2010. The devil is in the detail: museum displays and the creation of knowledge. *Museum Anthropology* 33: 22–32.

Moser, S. in press. *Designing Antiquity: Ornament, Colour and Ancient Egypt in the Designs of Owen Jones*. London: Yale University Press.

Moser, S and C. Gamble 1996. Revolutionary images: the iconic vocabulary for representing human antiquity. In B. Molyneaux (ed.), *The Cultural Life of Images*, 184–218. London: Routledge.

Myrone, M. 1999. Graphic antiquarianism in eighteenth-century Britain: the career and reputation of George Vertue (1684–1756). In M. Myrone and L. Peltz (eds), *Producing the Past: Aspects of Antiquarian Culture and Practice*, 35–54. Aldershot: Ashgate.

Myrone, M. 2007. The Society of Antiquaries and the graphic arts: George Vertue and his legacy. In S. Pearce (ed.), *Visions of Antiquity: The Society of Antiquaries of London 1707–2007*, 99–121. London: Society of Antiquaries.

Nickelsen, K. 2006. *Draughtsmen, Botanists and Nature: The Construction of Eigthteenth-Century Botanical Illustrations.* Dordrecht, The Netherlands: Springer.

Ogilvie, B.W. 2006. *The Science of Describing: Natural History in Renaissance Europe.* Chicago: University of Chicago Press.

Papadopoulos, C. and G. Earl in press. Formal three-dimensional computational analyses of archaeological spaces. In E. Paliou, U. Lieberwirth, and S. Polla (eds), *Spatial Analysis in Past Built Spaces – Workshop* (Berlin, April 1–2, 2010).

Perry, S. 2009. Fractured media: challenging the dimensions of archaeology's typical visual modes of engagement. *Archaeologies: Journal of the World Archaeological Congress* 5: 389–415.

Perry, S. 2011. The Archaeological Eye: Visualization and the Institutionalization of Academic Archaeology in Britain. Ph.D. thesis, Department of Archaeology, University of Southampton.

Piggott, S. 1965. Archaeological draughtsmanship: principles and practice. Part I: principles and retrospect. *Antiquity* 39: 165–76.

Piggott, S. 1978. *Antiquity Depicted: Aspects of Archaeological Illustration.* London: Thames and Hudson.

Pomata, G. and N.G. Siraisi (eds) 1995. *Historia: Empiricism and Erudition in Early Modern Europe.* Cambridge, MA: MIT Press.

Roberts, K.B. and J.D.W. Tomlinson 1992. *The Fabric of the Body: European Traditions of Anatomical Illustration.* Oxford: Clarendon Press.

Saunders, G. 2009. *Picturing Plants: An Analytical History of Botanical Illustration.* Chicago: University of Chicago Press.

Smiles, S. 1994. *The Image of Antiquity.* New Haven: Yale University Press.

Smiles, S. 1999. British antiquity and antiquarian illustration. In M. Myrone and L. Peltz (eds), *Producing the Past: Aspects of Antiquarian Culture and Practice*, 55–66. Aldershot: Ashgate.

Smiles, S. 2007a. Art and antiquity in the long nineteenth century. In S. Pearce (ed.), *Visions of Antiquity: The Society of Antiquaries of London, 1707–2007*, 123–45. London: Society of Antiquaries, 2007.

Smiles, S. 2007b. The art of recording. In *Making History: Antiquarians in Britain 1707–2007*, 123–40. London: Royal Academy of Arts.

Smiles, S. in press. Imaging British history: patriotism, professional arts practice, and the quest for precision. In S. Bonde and S. Houston (eds), *Re-Presenting the Past: Archaeology through Text and Image.* Oxford: Oxbow Books.

Smiles, S. and S. Moser (eds) 2004. *Envisioning the Past: Archaeology and the Image.* Oxford: Blackwell.

Smith, P.H. 2006. *The Body of the Artisan: Art and Experience in the Scientific Revolution.* Chicago: University of Chicago Press.

Smith, P. H. and P. Findlen (eds) 2002. *Merchants and Marvels: Commerce, Science, and Art in Early Modern Europe*. New York: Routledge.

Smith, P. H. and B. Schmidt (eds) 2008. *Making Knowledge in Early Modern Europe: Practices, Objects, and Texts, 1400–1800*. Chicago: University of Chicago Press.

Steiner, M. and L. Allason-Jones 2005. *Approaches to Archaeological Illustration: A Handbook*. York: Council for British Archaeology.

Swogger, J. 2000. Image and interpretation: the tyranny of representation? In I. Hodder (ed.), *Towards Reflexive Method in Archaeology: The Excavations at Çatalhöyük*, 143–52. Cambridge: McDonald Institute for Archaeological Research.

Vaiani, E. in press. *The Antichità diverse Album. The Paper Museum of Cassiano dal Pozzo*. Series A, Volume 5. London: Royal Collection Publications.

van Dyke, R. M. 2006. Seeing the past: visual media in archaeology. *American Anthropologist* 108: 370–5.

Zubrow, E. B. W. 2006. Digital archaeology: a historical context. In T. L. Evans and P. Daly (eds), *Digital Archaeology: Bridging Method and Theory*, 10–31. Abingdon: Routledge.

INDEX

Note: page numbers in italics denote figures or tables